Praise

This is the ideal book to have on hand in your home, school, or library. Though not a coffee table book as such, it functions as one in that you can keep going back to it for bite-sized pieces of real-life inspiration and important calls to action.

Ian Shanahan, Green Teacher

Our relationship with the Stone Soup Leadership Institute has benefited our students immensely. It has opened their eyes to jobs in the blue and green economies. It has helped develop ideas about students in their pathways in life. I look forward to taking the next step with the Institute to see where this leads us.

Matthew Desmarais, Principal,
BMC Durfee High School, Fall River, MA

The Stone Soup Sustainable Education Toolkit is a great way of bringing young people's stories from around the world to life. The book gives a range of useful and creative suggestions for how we might embed climate education into our lives in a human and justice focused way.

Jamie Agombar, Executive Director,
Students Organising for Sustainability

ISBN: 978-0-578-89380-8

www.stonesoupleadership.org

Table of Contents

Stone Soup, A Folktale

There was once a man who had been traveling for a long time. Having run out of food, he was weary and hungry from his journey. When he came upon a small village, he thought, "Maybe someone could share some food."

When the man knocked at the first house, he asked the woman who answered the door, "Could you spare a bit of food? I've traveled a long way and am very hungry." The woman replied, "I'm sorry, but I have nothing to give you."

So the traveler went to the next door and asked again. The answer was the same. He went from door to door and each time he was turned away. Each of the villagers had good reasons.

But then one villager said, "I have some water." "Oh, good," said the traveler. "We can make stone soup."

He then went to the center of the village and started building a small fire. From his backpack he pulled out a small pot and his magic stone and placed them in the pot. As the water started boiling, a passing villager stopped and asked him what he was doing. "I'm making stone soup," the traveler replied.

"What does it taste like?" the man asked curiously. "Well, it would be better with a few onions," the traveler admitted. "Oh, I have some onions," he replied, heading off to his home.

People from the village heard about this strange man who was making soup from a stone. They started gathering around the fire. One of the villagers offered, "I have a few carrots from last year's harvest." Someone else said, "I'll get some potatoes from my garden."

One by one, each villager brought something special to add to the pot. Pretty soon, right before their eyes there was a delicious soup—enough to feed the whole village. They all sat down together to enjoy their soup—and the miracle they'd help to create.

Anonymous,
adapted from a sixteenth-century folktale

The Cronkite Awards For Climate Education

"Ms. Larned, this is Walter Cronkite," said the distinguished voice on the phone.

Widely recognized as "the most trusted man in America," Walter Cronkite believed that journalism was a higher calling. He felt a deep sense of personal responsibility to use his platform as the anchor of CBS Nightly News to inform and educate ordinary people so they could make wise decisions about their future.

It was just before the 2000 elections, and he was very concerned about its outcome. He felt strongly that the lack of an educated constituency was threatening America's democracy. He thought that if people were uneducated about the issues, they wouldn't be prepared to vote. Instead, they would be easily influenced by fake news, and distracted by fear tactics.

When Mr. Cronkite invited me to his offices on the 57th floor of CBS headquarters in New York City, it began a life-changing journey. I was honored that he wanted to create a TV series based on my first book *Stone Soup for the World: Life-Changing Stories of Everyday Heroes.* He believed these stories could educate people about the issues of our time—and teach them by example how they too could have the courage to take a stand, even against all odds.

We did many great things together. Standing by his side, I always felt taller–and sometimes fearless. For more than a decade Mr. Cronkite served as the Stone Soup Leadership Institute's honorary chairperson. We are indebted to his leadership. Upon his passing, The Institute hosted the Cronkite Awards. His wisdom and vision of preparing youth as future leaders in their communities gave rise to this Awards Ceremony. The Award has honored those using the power of the media to create positive change in the world, including Dr. Sylvia Earle and Charlayne Hunter-Gault. Distinguished speakers have included Bob Schiefer, David McCullough, and Ted Kennedy Jr. Mr. Cronkite's family presented the Awards.

Mr. Cronkite was an ardent environmentalist. Back in 1970, he strode into the CBS broadcast center and announced his goal of featuring environmental news stories. He worked closely with his investigative team to produce a series of stories about the top environmental issues of the day. The Emmy award-winning segments came to be called *Can the World Be Saved?* By spotlighting these issues on the *CBS Evening News*, Mr. Cronkite introduced them into the national conversation with the urgency they called for. And with the same passion he had for covering the moon landing, his coverage of the inaugural Earth Day celebration rallied over 20 million Americans to launch the green movement.

It's been over fifty years since that first Earth Day – and the climate crisis is ravishing our planet every day. As severe weather issues increase in frequency and magnitude, the lack of media coverage is disconcerting. It's been estimated that merely .01% of the news is reporting on climate change. As a result, people aren't informed of the most pressing issue of our time: Climate Change.

Now, at a time when the health of our planet is being so severely challenged, we must keep Mr. Cronkite's spirit alive. He would be very proud of the young people featured in this book, who are on the frontlines of climate change and are courageously working to build a more sustainable world. Young people around the world are hungry to learn how they can adapt to climate change in their communities. Up until now, Climate Education is not being taught in our classrooms. Given the challenges facing our world, I ask myself today: "What would Walter Cronkite do?

For this Earth Week, The Institute is hosting **The Cronkite Awards for Climate Education** to honor leaders who are champions of Climate Education. Against great odds, these leaders we are honoring have passed legislation to integrate climate education at the state level. They represent a model for future collaboration; with this event we aim to build bridges between leaders across states and institutions, to push this agenda forward. The next generation deserves the best educational tools to prepare them for their future – to offset the impacts of the climate crisis. We need universal climate education now to help build a more just, equitable, and sustainable future for all.

At the event we will launch the **Stone Soup Climate Education Curriculum** including this book. We want to make it easier for educators to take the lead in educating all of us. To help spread the word about the urgency of the climate crisis and the innovative solutions in this book that will inspire their students to pursue sustainable career pathways. We hope that these stories inspire everyone —teachers and students, parents, grandparents, along with our leaders from business, government and education --to join them, follow their lead, so together we can meet this urgent challenge.

In 2002, at The Institute's Celebration of Heroes in New York City, Walter Cronkite urged everyone to pledge to build a more peaceful and sustainable world. Since then, the dangers to our planet, and to our democracy have grown more urgent. At the Cronkite Awards for Climate Education we will invite everyone to sign this Pledge.

Our Call-to-Action Pledge with Walter Cronkite

We accept Walter Cronkite's challenge for a new kind of engaged activism,
to be a force for positive change in the world.

We will join with the Global Hero Award recipients and carry on the legacy of
Mahatma Gandhi, Eleanor Roosevelt, Cesar Chavez and Dr. Martin Luther King Jr.
to improve the conditions of our neighborhoods, our countries and the world
through individual action and working with others.

Together, we will forge new directions for the global economy,
bridge the gap between the haves and have nots
and strive to build a more peaceful, sustainable world.

INTRODUCTIONS

Overview

The Stone Soup Leadership Institute is pleased to present educators with the Stone Soup Climate Education Curriculum with the book, ***Stone Soup for a Sustainable World: Life-Changing Stories of Young Heroes.*** The book features real-life stories of features 100 stories of climate education champions, green inventors & entrepreneurs, environmental justice changemakers, pioneers & trailblazers from 38 countries and 32 U.S. cities who are building a more just, equitable and sustainable future.

The Stone Soup Climate Education Curriculum is a dynamic, solutions-oriented set of lesson plans and classroom activities that make these stories come alive!

The Stone Soup Climate Education Curriculum is a diverse, inclusive, and extensive STEM and solutions-oriented set of individualized lesson plans for each story. It offers multifaceted activities to help you incorporate the principles of sustainability and climate education into your Language Arts and STEM courses. Each lesson plan also includes practical information about sustainable career pathways, to help guide students toward the millions of blue and green jobs that are emerging in the transition to a sustainable economy, and that will help rebuild the planet.

The Stone Soup Leadership Institute is committed to a future in which sustainability is at the heart of our economies. Unfortunately, too few students today are obtaining the STEM education they'll need to navigate that new reality, or even a basic understanding of how important sustainability and climate issues are for their future. However, as the news reveals every day, the rebuilding of our world in a sustainable way—one that provides opportunities for everyone, but not at the cost of future generations, or of the planet—is urgent.

The Stone Soup Climate Education Curriculum is a dynamic pedagogical tool designed to help teachers hone their students' skills in STEM and ELA. It is aligned with Next Generation Science Standards (NGSS) state standards as well the Green New Deal and President Biden's Plan for Climate Change and Environmental Justice. It will help prepare your students for the transition to a sustainable economy.

Our goal is to inspire your students to understand the importance of climate issues and explore the world of sustainability.

About the Lesson Plans

We designed the lesson plans to be user-friendly. They provide educators with clear and easy-to-follow guidelines to help them organize their own lessons, while complying with their state's Department of Education requirements. We have taken great care to create lesson plans that are aligned with state standards and that have clear and well-defined assessment methods, both formative and summative. Every assessment is designed with a specific academic goal in mind, and the standards are included along with each lesson plan to make it easier for teachers to plan their classes and design their assessments.

- **Values**: We've identified the values each person embodied as they pursued their goals.
- **Language Arts.** This section is designed to help students develop their critical thinking, reading comprehension, and verbal and written communication skills.
- **STEM Activities.** This section is interactive, engaging, and project-based. It is designed to motivate students to use technology, creativity, and innovation to actively participate in problem solving.
- **Sustainability Innovations.** This section features people and organizations around the world who are tackling similar issues. It directs your students to a wide range of resources so they can continue their exploration with independent projects and science fairs.
- **Sustainable Career Pathways.** This section grounds sustainability practices in the real world. We want students to understand that just as the sustainability problems we are facing are real, so are the solutions to them. In this section we offer students real-world examples of careers in sustainability that they can explore to become part of those solutions.

Why Standards?

We have designed our lesson plans around state-specific standards to ensure that teachers are able to seamlessly include the lessons in their curriculum, and that students are receiving the best possible training in skills that will ensure their academic success. By aligning our lesson plans with state standards, we ensure that all students have the opportunity to develop the same skills, regardless of their ethnic background or socioeconomic status. Basing our lesson plans on state-specific standards guarantees that students will develop the skills their state expects them to learn; helps them to achieve academic success; and sets them up to succeed in their future professional lives. **The Stone Soup Climate Education Curriculum is aligned with the following state standards:**

The Next Generation Science Standards (NGSS) The NGSS is the national standard, and is becoming a global standard. We model our lesson plans using NGSS, since these standards take into account scientific innovation, and are designed to improve American students' ability to compete internationally towards scientific disciplines and careers. Twenty states use NGSS standards: Arkansas, California, Connecticut, Delaware, Hawaii, Illinois, Iowa, Kansas, Kentucky, Maryland, Michigan, Nevada, New Hampshire, New Jersey, New Mexico, Oregon, Rhode Island, Vermont, Washington and the District of Columbia (DC), These states represent over 35 percent of US students.

English Learning (ELA)

- Massachusetts Department of Education State Standards
- California Department of Education State Standards

Professional Development Educator Module focuses on how to use climate education as a means to keep students engaged, as they develop the skills they need to succeed in their academic lives.

Our Team: We are proud to have an exceptionally strong team comprised of academics, educators, researchers, and youth leaders from a diversity of cultures. We have used a collaborative learning process to develop this companion curriculum. The diverse cultural, professional, and educational backgrounds of our team ensures that we represent diverse points of view, and that each of the lesson plans has a rich, engaging, and global perspective.

Praise from Young Heroes for the Curriculum

Wow! This is amazing! If you made similarly robust curriculum for all 100 entries... I'm wildly impressed!!!!

Anna Lappé, Small Planet Institute, CA

Stories can and do change the world. Youth are the secret ingredient- full of drive and passion. Combining the two was a masterstroke by the Stone Soup Leadership Institute. And now their lesson plans have arrived to raise the next generation of storytellers.

Elliot Connor, Human Nature Projects, Australia

This lesson plan is fantastic and such a great way to get kids involved in storytelling and the youth climate movement.

Slater Jewell-Kemper, Youth Unstoppable, Canada

It is amazing to see our story as a lesson ! We are honored to be part of the Stone Soup Leadership Institute. By learning from others I hope that the youth of today can make a better tomorrow. We must act now to save our world.

Niven & Tiara Ganegama, Youth Force Sri Lanka

I'm honored to participate in the Stone Soup Leadership Institute's great work and am very grateful for everyone who's helped along the way. Really proud to be a part of this project.

Nainoa Thompson, Polynesian Voyaging Society, Hawaii

It is not only important to learn the reasons why system change is necessary, but the means we have to make it possible. Art is one of the most powerful means for this.

Alejandro Martinez, Juventud Por El Clima, Spain

The lesson plan is wonderful! I am so excited about what my story and the ninety-nine other stories in the book will be able to teach young people.

Salvador Gomez-Colon, Light and Hope for Puerto Rico

For humanity to live sustainably on this planet, we must learn how to create and operate sustainable enterprises. I hope that this curriculum, and the example of my grandfather Ray C. Anderson, can inspire a new generation of future business leaders to reimagine our economic status quo.

John A Lanier, Ray C Anderson Foundation, Atlanta, GA

Thank you so much for sharing this. It has been so amazing to work with the stone soup family. I look forward to joining such interactive classes.

Shreya KC, NYCA, Nepal

We are so honored to be part of this great Stone Soup project and hope to inspire many others who are seeking to be changemakers. We can all help protect the planet and all its inhabitants.

Asha & Jia Kirkpatrick, Petitiongirls.com, London

I like to think that having an impact on someone's life can make a difference, the course of life changed this way and I do wish that telling my story to youth can have that impact. I might not be the one who leads a revolutionary change but my voice could inspire others to do it

Azza Faiad, Egypt

We believe in leading by example, to motivate others to take responsibility for the safe and proper handling and disposal of their personal rubbish - "in the bin, and NOT on the ground". No one is too young to learn this, and the younger the better. It is the young who will shape the future, and building a caring generation is so important.

Lilly Platt, Lilly's Plastic Pickup, Netherlands

It's important for people to understand the lessons of the past and know the elders on whose shoulders we stand today. My story is just one piece of bridging the past and present, and I'm grateful to be included in this project.

Carmen Perez-Jordan, The Gathering for Justice

I've known I wanted to work on climate since a high school teacher convinced me that addressing climate change could make the world more awesome. I hope this curriculum and my story helps kids to imagine themselves as problem solvers working to make a better world for all.

Ana Sophia Mifsud, RMI, New York/Colorado

I'm so excited to see my work as a tool to inspire more youth towards creating a better future. I'm honoured to be a part of the Stone Soup Leadership Institute.

Aadya Joshi, The Right Green, India

It is my pleasure to be a part of this wonderful work , I am proud that my story is part of the education curriculum, I thank all the people behind this project and what we see today is really the fruit of a great effort I was absolutely amazed at the way the story was included so that it was ready to be part of an educational course.

Alaa Salah, Sudan

In our world, more than ever before, young people need something to give them a sense of possibility, open up their strengths and gifts, and inspire them to do whatever they can, to be of service to their communities and our shared world. The Stone Soup curriculum is aiming for just that. I hope it will guide us towards new paths of imagination and creativity and show us how to find meaningful ways forward, together.

Sainath Manikandan, UAE

We all gathered 'round to read the curriculum last night and everyone was blown away.

Bethany Yarrow

I am very grateful and honored to be a part of the Stone Soup Leadership Institute. I strongly believe that together we can create a wave of change. Let's H.E.L.P (Heal the environment, love the planet)

Shilpa Jain, YES!

Praise from Educators, Principals and Superintendents

These stories provide invaluable resources to significantly enhance our program, transform instructional practices, offer initiatives that personalize learning and provide extended learning opportunities for all students in the Environmental Science program.

Principal, California High School

This has benefited our students immensely. It's opened their eyes to jobs in the blue and green economies. It's helped them develop ideas about careers they can explore for pathways for life.

Principal, Massachusetts High School

This provides our students with a remarkable learning experience in leadership development, sustainability and civic engagement.

Superintendent, Massachusetts High School

We're eager to have many more students experience the powerful result of these STEM-Sustainability tools and leadership training.

Principal, Hawaii High School

Media Reviews

One of the most important books a children's library or environmental leader can pass onto future generations. Stone Soup for a Sustainable World provides a tool kit of inspiration and a message of how making a difference is important and shows the steps to actually achieve these goals.

Midwest Book Review

Stone Soup for a Sustainable World includes the realities of the climate change crisis of 100 young people from different continents. They are intelligent, resourceful, and committed to doing whatever it takes to wake people up to the climate crisis.

Climate News Earth Day Recommended Reading List

Independent

Welcome Message from Trevor Tanaka

Sustainability Coordinator

Young people are concerned about climate change – and climate anxiety affects many of us. We see how climate change is affecting our communities and to people around the world. We want to get involved but we aren't sure what will really make the difference. We recycle, we are conscious buyers, we avoid single-use plastics. We join marches with millions of others. We sign petitions. We want to do more.

However, up until now climate education hasn't been taught in our schools. So we struggle to learn how we can take effective action.

As a 16-year-old student at Konawaena High School on the Big Island of Hawaii, I had a passion for the beauty of the natural world, and was dedicated to protecting it, but I wasn't learning about it in school. The Stone Soup Leadership Institute gave me the unique opportunity to help create what has become the Stone Soup Climate Education Curriculum. With its 100 inspiring stories from 38 countries, it gives young people the tools and the inspiration we need to turn our dreams into action. It is a gift to students everywhere.

Working with The Institute's team, we were able to get a resolution passed by both the House and the Senate of the State of Hawaii that amended the state's Board of Education policy to include sustainable education in all public schools. It was a life-changing experience. My passion fueled my drive to overcome challenges–like my fear of public speaking–so all students could learn how they can be more environmentally conscious and how to care for our planet. For the last ten years, I've worked with the Institute to develop and test online education tools for teachers to help guide their students in learning about climate change and discovering solutions to the challenges we face.

I'm honored to be one of the 100 young heroes featured in the book ***Stone Soup for a Sustainable World: Life-Changing Stories of Young Heroes***. Along with the Institute's other youth leaders who are featured in the book like Josue Cruz, Kassandra Castillo, Taynara Goncalves, and Chris Aring, we have shared our stories and planted seeds with young people in diverse communities. It has been an honor to work alongside them to shine the light on sustainable solutions in countries around the world.

We believe it is important for students to be able to understand both the problems we are facing today, and how they can play an integral role in solving them. The Climate Education Curriculum provides educators and others who work with young people with a set of dynamic resources and activities that bring these stories about climate change and sustainability solutions to life. It is designed to help bridge the gap between traditional classroom materials and the global environmental issues we are facing today. They are aligned with the UN Sustainable Development Goals, NGSS (Next Gen STEM Standards), and state standards.

The 100 lesson plans—one for each story in the book – include Language Arts and STEM activities, Sustainability Innovations, and information about Sustainable Career Pathways. They serve as windows into a whole world of sustainable solutions that students can learn about to face today's challenges and become engaged in hands-on activities with real-world effects. It is our hope that the Stone Soup Climate Education Curriculum will help students ignite their passion, unlock their potential, and pursue their dreams of creating a more just, equitable, and sustainable world.

A Note to Educators

The book ***Stone Soup for a Sustainable World: Life-Changing Stories of Young Heroes*** features the real-life stories of 100 stories of climate education champions, green inventors & entrepreneurs, environmental justice changemakers, pioneers & trailblazers from 38 countries who are building a more just, equitable and sustainable future. These young global leaders will inspire your students to open their minds, expand their horizons, and increase their understanding and appreciation of both the rich cultural diversity of the global community and the fascinating world of science. It will also make them aware of the urgent challenges facing people in these countries from climate change. We invite your students to become actively involved in practical, real-world sustainability actions taking place around the world, as well as in their own communities. Thank you for all your good work as you prepare our youth for the future. We hope you find the ***Stone Soup Climate Education Curriculum*** helpful. We'd love to hear about your experiences as you bring them into your classroom.

TODAY! RIGHT NOW!

The ***Stone Soup Climate Education Curriculum*** has 100 lesson plans to help you bring the stories in this book to life for your students. Each of the lesson plans is designed by experts in curriculum development, to help you organize your classes around the stories in the book with concrete suggestions while meeting state standards.

- ***Values:*** Highlights values shown by the person in the story to inspire your students to live a values-based lives.
- ***Language Arts:*** Creative ideas for how to incorporate sustainability into your English & Language Arts classes.
- ***STEM Activities:*** Expand student experience with engaging, hands-on project-based learning projects.
- ***Sustainability Innovations:*** Links to rich resources where students can deepen their appreciation for solutions.
- ***YouTube: Safe for Kids:*** The Institute's Education Channel features hundreds of videos to enrich your lessons.
- ***Multifaceted Social Media Campaign.*** Each week we showcase one of the 100 stories

from each book with a week-long series of posts that bring them to life -- drawing on Story-a-Week; a Hero Report video. We feature an Honor Roll and Call to Action to invite people to support their efforts. We feature these posts on Facebook, Instagram, Twitter, and LinkedIn.

- ***SustainWDN™*** - The Institute's cutting-edge sustainable workforce development platform is an online ecosystem that connects youth to STEM & workforce development opportunities that lead to internships, apprenticeships, certificates and good-paying renewable energy jobs.
- ***Sustainable Career Pathways:*** Guide your students toward exciting sustainability-oriented jobs as they pursue how they can find their place in the world of work, while helping to rebuild the planet.
- ***Sustainable Career Video Series:*** sustainability practitioners in renewable energy, marine biology, environmental education, wastewater management share their journey and inspire students to pursue these careers.
- ***Sustainable Career Mentor Initiative:*** A disruptive model designed to match students with sustainability practitioners who can mentor them for the millions of emerging sustainability-oriented jobs.

A Note for Principals

At the Stone Soup Leadership Institute, we know that principals are striving to provide their students with the best education that they can, with limited resources. Imagine what the 10 million new jobs in emerging green energy industries could mean for your students. These jobs represent the opportunity for them to have meaningful careers, while helping to rebuild our planet. As a principal you have the extraordinary opportunity to help your students, your community and our world, by taking the first steps toward that world.

Up until now, Climate Education is not being taught in our schools. At a time when we need more STEM education to help students prepare for the transition to this sustainable economy, implementing STEM curricula in schools can be a challenge. Schools are facing not only instructional challenges when it comes to implementing successful, multidisciplinary STEM curricula; they are also facing administrative challenges: budgetary constraints and a lack of appropriate teacher training.

At the Institute, we consider our partnership with schools to be crucial to our mission. We are partnering with school administrators across the country to facilitate the implementation of sustainability and STEM curricula in their schools. We are committed to providing dynamic resources for educators to increase their students' appreciation for STEM, with a special focus on climate education and sustainability solutions.

The transition to a sustainable economy
is the most challenging issue of the 21st century.
Innovation is the key to building a more sustainable world.

About the Stone Soup Leadership Institute

For over 20 years, the Institute has been a leader in developing dynamic educational tools, trainings, and resources that expand young people's appreciation for STEM, climate education and sustainable solutions. We pride ourselves on creating educational programs that bring sustainability issues to life and STEM activities into the classroom, to help prepare multicultural youth for a wide range of STEM-related career pathways. We have designed an engaging, comprehensive, and solutions-oriented program that prepares students for the environmental, economic, and social issues we face today.

Our team of seasoned educators created the ***Stone Soup Climate Education Curriculum*** as a Companion Curriculum for the book, ***Stone Soup for a Sustainable World: Life-Changing Stories of Young Heroes***. It is ideally suited for high school educators and students to help teachers meet the requirements of state standards. And since we strive for diversity, our curriculum has a multicultural approach to help educators ensure their students' academic success and become leaders of a more just, equitable, and sustainable world. The curriculum adheres to the Next Generation Science Standards, a set of standards focused on helping students develop a coherent and scientifically-based view of the world and convert their ideas into tangible, real-life projects. These standards focus on Physical and Life Sciences, Earth and Space Science, and Engineering; they have been adopted by 20 states in U.S.

For Guidance Counselors

The transition to a sustainable economy is the most challenging issue facing us. Imagine what the 10 million new jobs in the sustainable economy could mean for your students, your community and for our country.

It's a whole new world!

Young people are concerned about the planet and want to help. As a guidance counselor, you could be the one to expand your students' awareness of how they can navigate this whole new world. Just imagine...your students could be the next engineers who invent new products to clean up the planet. Imagine if your students could be inspired by, learn from and be mentored by those pioneers of the sustainable economy.

Today's companies are increasingly hiring young adults who are ready for these green careers. These jobs represent the opportunity for students to find meaningful careers, while helping to rebuild our planet. For over 25 years, the Institute has been a leader in developing dynamic educational tools, trainings, and leadership and workforce development initiatives that empower students to help build a more sustainable world.

The ***Stone Soup Climate Education Curriculum*** features practical tools that assist career counselors to guide students toward the green jobs that will pay good wages while rebuilding the planet. It offers students real-world examples of careers in sustainability that they can explore.

The ***Sustainable Career Pathways Section*** features over 200 green jobs in different industries including: renewable energy, regenerative agriculture, marine life, water management, as well as eco-entrepreneurs and education. From scientists and engineers; to marine biologists and wildlife veterinarians, and environmental conservationists.

Professional Development Training Module

- ***SustainWDN™*** - The Institute's cutting-edge sustainable workforce development platform is an online ecosystem that connects youth to STEM & sustainable workforce development opportunities that lead to mentors, internships, apprenticeships, certificates and good-paying renewable energy jobs. It offers guidance counselors tools that will enable students to explore dynamic sustainable career pathways and different types of post-secondary education. ***SustainWDN™*** serves as an economic planning tool that allows guidance counselors the opportunity to meet the needs of all students.

- ***Sustainable Career Pathways:*** Guide your students toward exciting sustainability-oriented jobs as they pursue how they can find their place in the world of work, while helping to rebuild the planet.
- ***Sustainable Career Video Series:*** sustainability practitioners in renewable energy, marine biology, environmental education, wastewater management share their journey and inspire students to pursue these careers.
- ***Sustainable Career Mentor Initiative:*** A disruptive model designed to match students with sustainability practitioners who can mentor them for the millions of emerging sustainability-oriented jobs.

CURRICULUM SECTIONS

Curriculum Sections

English Language Arts (ELA)

English Language Arts (ELA) is all about using language proficiently to communicate ideas. For students, proficiency in language is a fundamental educational component plays a key role in creating a successful future – and a very important foundation for lifelong learning.

The lesson plans in this section are designed to help students think more critically about the information they receive. The activities combine classroom discussions and presentations, with writing assignments to deepen the lessons learned through reading the stories in Stone Soup for a Sustainable World. These engaging, hands-on activities are designed to strengthen students' speaking, listening, reading, writing, and digital media skills, while inspiring their curiosity, encouraging them to ask difficult yet important questions, fostering collaboration, and showing them how they can apply what they see, hear, and learn to their own lives. More importantly, it encourages students to turn their learning into actions. We want students to do something with what they're learning - to make a difference! These activities can be the spark that lights the fire.

STEM Activities

Imagine your students creating something groundbreaking that can change the world for the better. Like Sainath Manikandan, one of the young heroes featured in Stone Soup for a Sustainable World, who used what he had learned in robotics classes to invent a robot that collects trash from water sources. He went on to win multiple prizes, awards, and international recognition. More importantly, his invention is going to contribute to cleaning up ouroceans. Not bad for a 12-year-old!

Real-world, hands-on learning is vitally important in preparing students for today's competitive modern workforce; and science, technology, engineering and math (STEM) skills are in high demand. Regardless of what career path students choose to take, STEM education cultivates critical thinking. As an educator, you hold the key to unlocking the talents of the next generation of problem-solvers and change-makers. Adding hands-on, project-based learning activities to your curriculum will provide your students with a valuable perspective on how technology can help solve the problems we are facing, and give them the self-confidence they need to take part in creating those solutions. This Sustainable Education Toolkit will provide you with the tools, resources, and ideas you need to ignite their curiosity and inspire them to enjoy learning—and finding ways to do something about these problems!

There are more than 300 STEM activities in these lesson plans: that they offer a hands-on approach to solving real-world problems using math, engineering, and computer science concepts and skills. Each lesson plan features at least three STEM-related activities inspired by one of the stories in Stone Soup for a Sustainable World. These activities will empower your students to take charge of their own learning and learn from one another as well as from you. It will also help them develop key skills: how to think creatively, and how to collaborate and communicate with others to solve complex problems. Through these activities, students will learn how working together strengthens us; how a variety of approaches and perspectives can inspire new and better ideas; and how we can use what we've learned to better our world.

Sustainability Innovations

What is sustainability? The dictionary defines sustainability as "using a resource so that the resource is not depleted or permanently damaged." Taking it one step further, the United National Sustainable Development Goals (UNSDG) say sustainability is "meeting our needs without compromising the ability of future generations to meet their needs." Unfortunately, we have created a consumer-based culture that is focused on creating a constant supply of products and consumer expectations and demands, without considering whether we have adequate resources to meet those expectations and demands. Now, as a global community, we must come together to create a more sustainable world by changing or eliminating many of the products we are accustomed to, and stop making choices that are harming ourselves and the Earth.

Technological innovation has developed fracking, gold and diamond mining, unethical manufacturing practices in a variety of industries, and has created and a great many products that are causing direct harm to the earth. It is long past time to make a change. This section features "sustainable innovations" that are aiming to offset some of the harmful things we have done to our environment and begin to repair the damage. The innovations featured here will introduce your students to some of the products, apps, ideas, and new developments that are focused on solving sustainability-related issues, or are creating alternatives to harmful current practices that society has normalized. We hope that learning about these innovations will inspire you and your students to see some of the ways that technology can help to make our lives and communities both healthier and more sustainable.

Sustainable Career Pathways

Sometimes the right word, the right kind of encouragement, the right lesson from a trusted teacher or guidance counselor can set the course for a student's entire life path. This section features more than 200 green jobs across ten sectors including water, energy, agriculture, business, and education. The jobs range from engineers and scientists to teachers and environmental mental health counselors, from community organizers, eco-entrepreneurs, and green business managers to policy advisors, wildlife veterinarians, and conservationists--among many others.

This section offers students interesting ideas and inspiration for possible future career paths, with links to websites that offer additional information on how to explore, prepare for, and/or pursue those paths. Class discussions about these careers can be used as a prompt to further investigation into these fields. Most importantly, the many exciting careers featured here can expand their understanding of the myriad of green jobs that are available, and increase the chance that they will choose green jobs and help to build a sustainable future. They might even come up with some innovative ideas of their own, for new green jobs that haven't been created yet!

The transition to a sustainable economy is the most challenging issue of the 21st century. Imagine what the 10 million new jobs in the blue/green economy could mean for our young people and for our country.

UN SUSTAINABLE DEVELOPMENT GOALS: STORIES MATCHED

UN Sustainable Development Goals: Stories Matched

1. **No Poverty**

- Kerry Kennedy (Ripples of Hope) – Washington DC (+SDG 16)
- Vanessa Nakate (Rise Up Africa!) – Uganda (+ SDG 13)

2. **Zero Hunger**

- Anna Lappé (Tackling the Root Causes of Hunger) – Berkeley, CA

3. **Good Health and Well-Being**

- Hillary Peterson (Healthier Skin with True Botanicals) – Mill Valley, CA (+ SDG 9)
- Lara Nuer (Learning as Leadership: Humanizing Business) – San Fransisco, CA & Paris (+ SDG 16)
- Shilpa Jain (Walking between Worlds) –Berkely, California (+ SDG 16)
- Gitanjali Rao (Invent Something to Help Others) – Colorado (+ SDG 9)
- Taynara Goncalves (A Multicultural Leader) – Martha's Vineyard Youth Leadership Initiative
- Niven & Tiara Ganegama (Youthforce Carries on Dr. Ari's Legacy) – Sri Lanka (+ SDG 16)

4. **Quality Education**

- Chris Aring (Be the Change) – Martha's Vineyard (+ SDG 9)
- Scott Warren (A Call to Civic Action) – Providence, RI
- Destiny Hodges (Generation Green) – Washington DC (+ SDG 13)
- Josue Cruz (How Can I Help?) – Puerto Rico (+ SDG 16)

- Iqbal Badruddin (Awareness Campaigns) – Pakistan (+ SDG 13)
- Mohamad Al Jounde (Building Community for Climate Refugees) – Syria/Sweden

5. Gender Equality

- Adenike Oladosu (Eco-Feminist for Climate Action) – Nigeria (+ SDG 13
- Hafsat Abiola (Empowering Women to Lead) – Nigeria

6. Clean Water and Sanitation

- Gary White (A Life of Service: Water.org) – Kansas City, Missouri
- Autumn Peltier (Water Walker) - Canada
- Benita Davis (The Land of Many Waters) - Guyana

7. Affordable and Clean Energy

- Ana Sophia Mifsud (Applied Hope: Building Resilitent Communities) – New York City
- Henk Rogers (A Sustainable Legacy of Blue Innovation) – Hawaii
- Illai Kenney (Sustainability for Black Communities) – Washington DC (+ SDG 12)
- Salvador Gabriel (Light and Hope for Puerto Rico)- Puerto Rico (+ SDG 9)
- Ed Begley (Sustainable Business, Sustainable Living) – Los Angeles, California (+ SDG 11)

8. Decent Work and Economic Growth

- Cesar Chavez (Carrying on His Grandfather's Legacy) – California (+ SDG 10)

9. Industry, Innovation and Infrastructure

- Alex Perkins (Engineering Solutions to Climate Change Problems) – Nantucket/Vermont (+ SDG 7)
- David Dietz (Creating Mission-Driven Companies) – USA
- Perry Raso (Farming the Ocean) – Rhode Island, USA (+ SDG 12 and 11)
- Vincent Kimura (Sustainable Farming for Our Future) – Hawaii (+ SDG 11)
- Nainoa Thompson (Navigating by the Stars) – Hawaii (+ SDG 11)
- Azza Faiad (Turning Waste into Fuel) – Egypt (Also SDG 7)
- Fergus Moore (Rise and Grind: Minimizing Food Waste) – Scotland (+ SDG 11)
- François van den Abeele (Sea2See Eyewear: Sustainable Products with a Conscience) – Barcelona, Spain
- Sainath Manikandan (Robots for Fighting Plastic Pollution) – United Arab Emirates (+ SDG 14)

10. Reduced Inequalities

- Evon Peter (An Indigenous Leader) – Alaska (+ SDG 16)
- U.S Congressman John Lewis (Good Trouble) – Atlanta (Also SDG 16)

- Carmen Perez (Raising our voices for change) – New York (+ SDG 16)
- Sam Jacobs (Creating a New Social Contact) – New York (+ SDG 17)

11. Sustainable Cities and Communities

- David Dietz (Creating Mission-Driven Companies) – California (+ SDG 8)
- Gary Hirshberg (Service is just what you do) – New Hampshire (+ SDG 8 and 12)
- Feliza Fenty (Nature's Little Secrets) – Virgin Gorda Youth Leadership Initiative (+ SDG 12)
- Trevor Tanaka (What Does Sustainability Mean to You?) – Sustainable Hawaii Youth Leadership Initiative (+ SDG 4, 9)
- John Lanier (For Tomorrow's Child; An Environmental Epiphany) – Atlanta, Georgia (+ SDG 8 & 9)

12. Responsible Consumption and Production

- Elliot Hoffman (Building a Sustainable Business Ecosystem) – San Francisco, California (+ SDG 11)
- Jasper Ralph (We Can Do Better) – Martha's Vineyard (+ SDG4)
- Kassandra Castillo Cruz (From Recycling to Resale: Rebag) – Vieques, Puerto Rico (+ SDG 11)
- Asha & Jia Kirkpatrick (A Petition Changes Food Industry) – London (+SDG 15)
- Lilly Platt (Caring for the Circle of Life) – The Netherlands (+ SDG 14)

13. Climate Action

- Alec Loorz (iMatter) – Olympia, Washington
- Iris Zhan (Climate Movements in a Digital World) – Maryland
- Jamie Margolin (All Hands on Deck: This is Zero Hour) – Seattle, Washington
- Jett Zhang (Digital Toolkits for Inclusive Climate Justice Movements) – Florida (+ SDG 17)
- Kevin J. Patel (We Are the Leaders of Today) – Los Angeles, California (+ SDG 3)
- Parker Liautaud (To the Ends of the Earth…and Bank) – California
- Valentina Ossa (The Children Will Lead the Way) – New York
- Xiye Bastida (Indigenous Leader Invites Youth to Share Their Gifts) – Mexico/ New York City (+ SDG 17)
- Jerome Foster III (Changemaking from the Nation's Capital) – DC, New York City (+ SDG 16)
- Alyssa Lee (Divestment for a Sustainable Future) – Massachusetts (+ SDG 17)
- Alejandro Martinez (The Art of Saving the Planet) – Spain

- Arshak Makichyan (Standing Alone, Together) – Russia (+ SDG 16)
- David Wicker (Saavy Social Media Influencer Strikes for our Future) – Italy
- Jean Hinchliffe (Hope Springs from the Land Down Under) – Australia
- Shreya K.C. (Acting Locally & In Solidary with Others) – Nepal
- Linus Dolder (We Will Rock This) – Switzerland
- Mitzi Jonelle Tan (Fighting Alongside the Most Vulnerable Among Us) – Philippines (+ SDG 10 & 16)
- Nicki Becker (Jovenes Por El Clima) – Argentina
- Slater Jewell-Kemker (Youth Unstoppable) – Canada (+ SDG 9)

14. Life Below Water

- Perry Raso (Farming the Ocean) – Rhode Island
- Nainoa Thompson(Navigating by the Stars: The Polynesian Voyaging Society) - Hawaii
- Daniela Fernandez (Never Apologize for Dreaming Too Big) – San Francisco, California
- Angelique Pouponneau (A Voice for Youth & Oceans) - Seychelles
- Cruz Erdmann (Seeing the Ocean in a New Way) – New Zealand (+ SDG 4)
- Joel Enrique Peña Panichine (Hope from the Ends of the Earth) – Chile

15. Life On Land

- Julia Butterfly Hill (Luna) – California
- Aadya Joshi (Planting the Right Kind of Green) – Mumbai, India (+ SDG 4)
- Elliot Connor (Human Nature Products) – Australia (+SDG 17)
- Felix Finkbeiner (Plant-for-the-Planet) – Germany
- Lesein Mutunkei (One Goal at a Time) – Kenya (+ SDG 17)
- Vihaan Agarwal (Turning Trash into Trees) – India (+ SDG 12)
- Jessa Garibay (Traveling with a Purpose)- The Philippines (+SDG 11)

16. Peace, Justice, and Strong Institutions

- Betsabe Reyna (A Voice for the Voiceless) – New Jersey
- Samantha Smith (Like Kids Everywhere) – Maine, USA (+ SDG 17)
- Alaa Salah (Thirsty for Change) - Sudan
- Arun Gandhi (We Must Be the Change We Want to See in the World) – South Africa
- Lucia Ixchiu (An Indigenous Rebel with a Cause) – Guatemala
- Maria Ressa (Speaking Truth to Power) – Philippines (+SDG 13)
- Sami Awad (Planting the Seeds for Peace) – Palestine
- Srdja Popovic (A Blueprint for Climate Revolution) – Serbia

- Jill Bhowmik (The Peace Corps in Malawi) – San Diego, California (+ SDG 4)
- Leila and Maison (A Citizen of the World) – Burundi/Belgium (+ SDG 3)
- Severn Suzuki (The Girl who Silenced the World for 5 Minutes) – British Columbia, Canada (+SDG 13 & 10)

17. Partnership for the Goals

- Jonah Wittkamper (A Future Forged in Radical Inclusion) – New York City (+ SDG 13)
- Demi Weitz (An Opportunity to Give Back – via Zoom!!) – Los Angeles, California (+ SDG 16)
- Joshua (Generation Waking Up)- Berkely, California (+ SDG 16)
- John R. Seydel (Captain Planet: A Philanthropic Environmental Leader) – Atlanta, Georgia
- Michelle Dilhara (From Invisible to Visible) – Sri Lanka (+SDG 13 & 4)
- James Ellsmoor (Connecting Islands Virtually for Climate Action) (+ SDG 9)

LESSON PLANS

Stone Soup for a Sustainable World: Table of Contents

I

WAKE UP

Climate Change Trailblazers

Thanks to Greta Thunberg and the youth leaders featured in this book who are charging us into the future. They challenge us to do everything we can, precisely because there is hope. They've shown us the way forward. Now it's time for us to come together as one and step up to the challenge.

Ed Begley Jr.

All Hands On Deck: This Is Zero Hour

Jamie Margolin, Zero Hour
Seattle

Call to Action

Join Zero Hour to demand climate action now! thisiszerohour.org
Buy Jamie's book: www.youthto-powerbook.com
Follow Jamie on Twitter: @jamie_margolin

Values

- Initiative
- Ambition
- Determination
- Courage
- Leadership

Lessons Learned

It's better to take action than to complain about the inaction of others.

The climate crisis is not just one isolated issue: there are multiple and overlapping problems related to climate change.

Ensuring climate justice for future generations is an enormous task: it will take well-organized collective action.

Jamie Margolin is a youth climate justice activist inspiring the world to take action on behalf of the planet.

In the wake of Hurricane Maria, the Canadian wildfires, and other environmental disasters, Jamie decided that enough was enough: if political leaders weren't going to take the climate crisis seriously, then she would. And so, at age 15, she cofounded the Zero Hour Organization. Zero Hour is a youth-led movement that aims to get young people involved in the conversation around climate and environmental justice. Zero Hour provides training, resources, and support systems for those who want to make an impact in the fight against climate change. On July 21, 2018, the inaugural Youth Climate March took place in Washington D.C. With this first-of-its-kind event, Jamie changed the game for the youth climate movement, inspiring activists from around the world, including Greta Thunberg.

Jamie went on to organize the first Youth Climate Summit, a three-day climate justice event in Miami. All in all, the summit trained more than 350 youth, as well as older allies, in climate justice activism and organizing. In 2018, at the age of 16, Jamie was named one of People Magazine's 25 Women Changing the World.

Language Arts

Jamie mentions the word "intersectional." Create a 15-20-second Tik Tok video explaining this concept, and how it applies to climate change. Then create a series of at least four Tik-Tok videos designed to bring awareness to the way climate change affects various areas of society. On a separate sheet of paper, explain your choices: Why did you choose the issues you chose? Why did you decide to present the information the way you did?

Create a fake Instagram profile[1] for an (imaginary) organiza-

tion that is dedicated to spreading awareness about the interconnectedness of social justice issues and climate change. In a separate document, explain your choices: why you chose to use the images you used, and why you think Instagram would be a good platform to create awareness of this particular issue. Then submit your template to a Zero Hour Chapter[2] near you, explaining why you are interested in this issue, and how you plan to create awareness of it.

Thinking about Jamie's experience with the Seattle legislator who dismissed her for being "too young," create a script for a fake conversation with this person: How would you convince them to listen to you? Knowing that their main focus is economic, what kind of argument would you present to them in order to get their attention? The script must be at least three pages long.

STEM Activities

Climate change is a broad topic to address, under the umbrella of sustainability. Identify one species or part of an ecosystem that is drastically affected by climate change, and explain the consequences of losing this organism as part of our ecosystem.

- Example: One of the organisms that is most commonly affected by climate change is coral. Coral reefs serve as a coastline's natural protection against storms and erosion, and they are being drastically affected by climate change.

In addition to the effects of climate change on our local ecosystems, it has adverse effects on our coastlines as well. Find aerial photographs[3] and articles about coastal erosion in the U.S. over the past 100 years. Explain how coastal erosion has affected humans and wildlife in these areas.

Now that you are an emerging expert in climate change, create an outline for a climate campaign that you would like to hold at your school. Describe the three most prevalent issues you would like to address, and for each of them, propose an actionable solution that you and your peers can take within your community.

Sustainability Innovations

Jamie has shown that identifying communities that are unable to speak for themselves is just as important as taking action. After researching and understanding Intersectional Environmentalism[4], identify three such communities and write an article that shares their stories. Explain the importance of Intersectional Environmentalism and how it pertains to these communities.

In addition to Zero Hour's individual efforts, #Vote4OurFuture[5] is a joint campaign between Zero Hour and the National Children's Campaign that aims to galvanize Americans to fight for future generations. Identify a political issue that is not being adequately addressed in your community and write a letter to Jamie about why this should be at the forefront of the joint campaign.

Hurricane Maria is just one of many natural disasters with long-lasting effects in the U.S. Write a letter to a Zero Hour Chapter[6] near you detailing a natural disaster that has affected you personally, or people that you care about, and explaining why you would like to get involved in Zero Hour's efforts.

Sustainability Career Pathways

Climate Justice Organizer. Engaging one's community around important environmental and social challenges (and how they interconnect) is an important career path in community service. There are many programs to learn organizing, from online courses (such as this one[7]), to one-year environmental organizing field schools like Green Corps[8].

Environmental Lobbyist. When Jamie was 15, she was already talking with a Republican legislator about climate change. Asking elected officials for change is an essential part of campaigning (especially when supported by grassroots organizing). Some make a full-time career lobbying (though few are able to do so, admittedly, for environmental or social change). Want to be a lobbyist? Start here[9].

Democracy Advocate. In this video[10], Jamie mentions that she was the youngest delegate at the 2020 Democratic Convention. Engaging in the democratic process--not just as a voter but as an organizer, campaign volunteer or staffer, or in party politics, is another important pathway of change. Here's a good introduction to how to get involved in politics[11].

Elected Official. Along with getting people engaging with their government, it's important that they have good candidates to vote for. Might you want to run for elected office? One typically starts by running for a local office, or working for an elected official to learn the ropes. But there are many paths you can take. Listen to this NPR story to get a better sense of the process of running for office[12].

---

1 https://mediamodifier.com/mockup/instagram-highlights-mockup-generator/8109
2 http://thisiszerohour.org/chapters/
3 https://climate.nasa.gov/images-of-change?id=723#723-drought-shrinks-chiles-el-yeso-reservoir
4 https://www.intersectionalenvironmentalist.com/
5 https://nationalchildrenscampaign.org/news/press-releases/virtual-vote4ourfuture-campaign-launched-on-july-23rd/
6 http://thisiszerohour.org/chapters/
7 https://www.coursera.org/learn/community-organizing
8 https://greencorps.org/
9 https://www.princetonreview.com/careers/88/lobbyist#:~:text=There%20are%20no%20licensing%20or,future%20lobbyists%20in%20good%20stead.
10 https://www.youtube.com/watch?v=R6imDtM_eQo
11 https://www.nytimes.com/guides/year-of-living-better/how-to-participate-in-government
12 https://www.npr.org/2019/10/15/770332855/how-to-run-for-office

An Inconvenient Youth

Alec Loorz, iMatter
Olympia, Washington

Call to Action

Visit the Climate Reality Project
climaterealityproject.org

Values

- Dedication
- Commitment
- Creativity
- Communication
- Environmentalism

Lessons Learned

Let your passion be your inspiration and your guide.

Reach out to those you admire, make your voice be heard, and let your passion shine through your words.

Make connections with people through the things you are both passionate about.

After watching Al Gore's documentary film, An Inconvenient Truth, Alec Loorz was inspired to mobilize other young people to learn about the climate crisis. He was the youngest person to attend Al Gore's Climate Reality training. First, he founded Kids vs. Global Warming, and then iMatter. In 2011, Alec was represented by Our Children's Trust when he led the legal battle against the U.S. government, claiming that they haven't done their part in preventing the global climate crisis.

Alec has received numerous awards from environmental groups, including the Young Environmental Hero award, the Ventura County Global Warming Activist Award, and the International Eco-Hero Award. He has acted in an advisory capacity for various climate advocacy groups, including Inconvenient Youth, the Alliance for Climate Education, and The Future We Want. He is now pursuing his passion for film and photography, using these media to help preserve and protect the beauty of nature.

Language Arts

Write a letter to your favorite climate change activist. Explain to them how they have inspired you, and how you plan to aid their cause. After you finish your letter, save it as a PDF and post a copy on social media.

Create your own "Inconvenient Truth": create a short film (between 15 and 25 minutes), in which you use data, interviews, etc. to explain the current state of climate change in the world, what is being done to help curb it, and what else needs to be done.

Write a research essay on Alec's iMatter lawsuit. How and where did the idea start, and where does it stand now? Then, create a short presentation (no more than 10 slides) to explain the lawsuit and its significance to your peers.

STEM Activities

Alec wanted to do more than just write letters and stage protests, so he decided to go out and experience other ways of being involved with climate justice, such as visiting organic sustainable farms. Conduct a mini research project on technological advances throughout agricultural history, and their impact on sustainability. How can agricultural technology contribute to fighting the effects of climate change? Have students work in teams to design a type of technology (tools, app, etc.) that would help farms be more sustainable.

Are there relationships between solar energy, global energy transfer processes, climate, and biomes? What evidence suggests that our climate may be changing more rapidly than living species can adapt to? Is human activity causing climate change? How can we reduce our impact on the biosphere and on our global climate, while still meeting human needs?

Every year, land is destroyed by mining processes. In this activity[1], students will learn about the resource extraction process, how minerals are used in our daily lives, and the impact it has on the environment. Then, in groups, students will think of ways to reduce the adverse effects mining has on the environment.

Sustainability Innovations

As a teenager, Alec realized that students were not engaged in sustainability issues at an adequate level, so he took matters into his own hands. Today, students have many more options of sustainable programs to become involved with, such as Ecorise[2]. EcoRise is an online platform that helps students tackle real world challenges in their schools and communities while highlighting sustainability issues. Check out EcoRise to see their innovative projects and the impact they are having.

When it comes to sustainability, kids often want to be involved, but don't know where to start. In this podcast on UNGA Guide Virtual[3], Julia Zimmerman and Olyindamola Adegboye address Sustainable Development Goal (SDG) micro-projects, and how their inclusion of young people's environmental advocacy and projects could make the world a different place. What SDG micro-projects could you implement in your community?

One of Alec's greatest accomplishments stems from the development of iMatter Youth. Visit imatteryouth.org[4] and identify projects that you would like to participate in.

Sustainability Career Pathways

Storyteller. Telling stories is a powerful way to mobilize people, as An Inconvenient Truth so clearly demonstrates. Stories can inspire, inform, and encourage others to take action, as Alec learned in his own efforts to tell his story. Becoming a journalist (including for your school paper), blogger, novelist, filmmaker, or other type of communicator can channel your storytelling skills to make a difference in the world. Learn more and receive training in climate communications at the Climate Reality Project[5].

Carbon Mitigation Specialist. Humanity will need work collectively to create a carbon-restorative economy by 2050 (meaning actually pulling more co2 out of the air than we are putting in) if we are to slow down and reverse the adverse effects of climate change. To do this, a whole new sector of carbon mitigation will crop up in the years to come: through afforestation and forest management, effective landscaping, restorative agriculture, energy efficiency, renewables, even painting roofs white to reflect sunlight into space--all sectors that will offer an abundance of jobs). But to be most effective, these actions will need to be coordinated. Perhaps that's a job for you? One group, The Carbon Trust[6], demonstrates the integrated approach specialists can provide in this complex process.

Park Ranger. Alec was dismayed by the efforts to reduce the size of Bears Ears National Monument. Parks are a key place where the public learns about nature--including what's native and non-native to their area. Park rangers are both educators and leading protectors of the world's parklands. This is a career opportunity for those who want to educate and care for forests and parks. Learn more about being a park ranger here[7].

1 https://uasmat.edmethods.com/wp-content/uploads/2016/06/Lesson-plan-Impact-of-mining-on-the-environment.pdf
2 https://www.ecorise.org/
3 https://ungaguide.com/event/innovative-solutions-youth-activism-changing-the-game-with-sdg-micro-projects/
4 https://www.imatteryouth.org/
5 https://www.climaterealityproject.org/training
6 https://www.carbontrust.com/who-we-are/purpose
7 https://www.parkrangeredu.org/

Caring For The Circle Of Life

Lilly Platt, Lilly's Plastic Pick Up
The Netherlands

Call to Action

Join with Lilly to Recycle, Renew, Reuse, Refuse, and Refill. Refuse to use plastic. Pick up trash. Follow Lilly : Instagram: @lillys_plastic_pickup & Twitter: @lillyspickup

Values

- Enthusiastic
- Compassion
- Energy
- Confident
- Environmental Leader

Lessons Learned

Lilly turned her dismay at learning how damaging and harmful plastic waste is into action: what issue or issues do you care about? Can you think of some possible solutions to these problems?

When Lilly started out, she was working alone, but now people all over the world are following her and helping her to make a difference. There is strength in collective action!

Lilly was only six when she decided to do something about plastic pollution: no one is too young to make change.

Children should have the courage to speak up about the wrongs they see in our world: and adults should listen to them!

When Lilly Platt was six years old, she took a walk with her grandfather one day and was horrified to count 91 pieces of trash in just a 20-minute walk. She was even more upset when she learned that the plastic trash that ends up in the ocean not only pollutes the water but also kills marine animals. She set out on a mission to fight plastic pollution and protect the ocean that has led to her becoming one of the youngest, most well-known environmentalists in the world.

"My hope is that people will finally realize that we should never take our planet for granted," Lilly says. "Our planet is one in a billion, billion trillion. That's a one followed by 33 zeros! People really need to know that our planet is sacred, and we need to take care of it. Who's with me?"

Language Arts

In order to make Lilly's story accessible to young children, rewrite her story as a children's book. Use pictures, rhymes, anything you think will make the story more appealing to a younger child, and will make them want to become conservationists.

Write a short scene between Lilly and her grandfather. Have Lilly ask her grandfather why people pollute; show how his explanation is so powerful that it inspires her to get involved in fighting pollution at only six years old.

How would you inspire someone younger than you to become involved in Lilly's cause? Write a one-page list of things you would say to this person, what examples you would use, etc.

STEM Activities

Lilly says that our planet is "one in a billion, billion, trillion." NASA's Jet Propulsion Laboratory actually puts the odds of an Earth-like planet in a given solar system similar to our sun at around 2 percent, but Lilly has the right idea. The problem isn't that our planet is so rare, it's that space is unimaginably vast. The nearest possible Earth-like exoplanet (Alpha Centauri) is 4.2 light years away, which means it would take about 4.2 years to get there if you were travelling at the speed of light. It's about 40,208,000,000,000 kilometers (km) away! The current speed record for a space-travelling vessel is 6,100 km/hour, set by the brave astronauts on the Apollo 10 mission. Assuming you had unlimited life support and fuel, how many years would it take to reach Alpha Centauri if you were going as fast as Apollo 10?

The Great Pacific Garbage Patch is a collection of plastic debris in the Pacific Ocean that's about twice the size of Texas. Learn how plastics break down into smaller particles (microplastics and nanoplastics), and how they affect marine life, the food chain, and our own health. Explore an existing scientific or social solution that can help solve this problem (e.g. plastic-eating enzymes[1], community based initiatives[2], biodegradable plastics[3], recycling programs). Then create a visual presentation of your findings to share with your class.

Lilly's family takes broken electronics that they find on their cleanups to be repaired at "repair cafes." In the United States, the "Right to Repair" is a hot topic being debated at all levels of government. Profit-oriented technology companies don't want you to be able to fix your devices by yourself (or at a third-party company) because they don't make any additional money from the repair. Find an electronic device in your home or school that seems fragile, then do research online about how you could fix it yourself instead of replacing it in the event of accidental damage. Next, research what the effects of throwing that device into the trash would be. (In other words, find out what materials it is made of, and research how they break down). Present your research to the class, or prepare a science fair exhibit.

Sustainability Innovations

Lilly's focus on recycling, and her consistent effort to reduce the use of plastic is just one example of an individual taking on a larger issue for the health and safety of our planet. In addition to Lilly's efforts, the companies and organizations listed below are targeting similar issues:

- **Clear Blue Sea**[4] focuses on reducing the use of plastic, and pollution of the world's oceans.
- **Algalita**[5] is addressing the problem of plastic reduction by having conversations about the damaging effects of plastic for individuals, businesses, the community, and our environment.

After learning about some of these organizations, select a type of plastic product—for example, a water bottle or a plastic bag. Then find out what type of plastic it is made of (polyethylene, polypropylene, etc.), and the properties that make it useful (shelf life, reactivity, melting point, etc.). Find a non-plastic alternative that could serve as a replacement for that product, that would work for both producers and consumers.

Sustainability Career Pathways

We have spent the last 50 years creating a world that relies on plastic at every level of the economy. We will need to find alternatives—both in the form of behavior and cultural changes, as well as alternative kinds of packaging.

Social Scientist (Psychologist, Sociologist, Anthropologist). Understanding how people behave at the individual, societal, and cultural levels is essential in changing behaviors. Corporations often use the services of these experts to more effectively market their products to new demographics. This expertise can also be used to move us toward consuming less, and consuming differently as well. Explore these fields here[6].

Biochemist or Biotechnologist Designing. Alternatives to plastic has already begun, especially by exploring the materials nature has evolved over millions of years (a new field called biomimicry[7]). Would you like to design alternatives to plastic? If so, becoming a biochemist[8] or a biotechnologist[9] may be the right career choice for you.

Industrial Designer. In addition to designing and creating new materials, we need to find ways to turn them into effective and economical products. Would you like to help design products that use less plastic, or that are designed in such a way that the plastic can be reused or recycled? Explore industrial design here[10].

Eco-entrepreneur. With billions of tons of plastic in circulation, in landfills, and in the ocean, we need to find ways to recycle that stock into new materials while also making communities healthier and more sustainable. Plastic can be made into a variety of different products. For example, Bureo[11] is a US skateboard company that works with fishing communities in South America to collect ruined fishnets and melt them down into skateboards. What ways can you think of to profitably convert plastic waste into new products?

1 https://www.theguardian.com/environment/2020/sep/28/new-super-enzyme-eats-plastic-bottles-six-times-faster
2 https://www.afrik21.africa/en/ghana-an-initiative-for-community-plastic-waste-recovery/
3 https://www.explainthatstuff.com/bioplastics.html
4 https://www.clearbluesea.org/
5 https://algalita.org/
6 https://www.bestcolleges.com/careers/humanities-and-social-sciences/social-science/
7 https://biomimicry.org/what-is-biomimicry/
8 https://www.environmentalscience.org/career/biochemist
9 https://www.prospects.ac.uk/job-profiles/biotechnologist
10 https://www.thebalancecareers.com/engineering-job-titles-2061493
11 https://www.goethe.de/ins/cz/prj/fup/en13860350.htm

Climate Movements in a Digital World

Iris Zhan, Fridays For Future Digital
Maryland

Call to Action

Learn how to take digital climate action to the next level with Iris at Fridays for Future Digital(FFFD): fffdigital.carrd.co

Values

- Curious
- Courageous
- Initiative
- Preserverance
- Leadership

Lessons Learned

When you see what needs to be done, if no one else is doing it, find a way to begin to make it happen.

Iris is shy, so they found a way to use their skills and talents to make a contribution. You can do the same!

Iris found their place working in digital media platforms. Think about what your skills are, and what you like to do. Then find a way to use them to help protect our planet, and make the way for a better future.

Iris Zhan first learned about the climate crisis in the third grade. "When our teacher told us about climate change, it really took a toll on me," they say.

They went to school the next day ready to learn more about what could be done. But their class was already on to another subject. "We were presented with our dire situation, and that was the end of our climate education," they say. But that wasn't going to stop Iris from making an impact. First they educated themself on the topic; later they went on to found HoCo Climate Action, and Fridays For Future Digital (FFFD). "Everybody can play a part," they say. "And it takes all kinds of people...It doesn't matter who you are or what you look like. If you can light the fire in somebody, that person will live an inspired life because of you."

Language Arts

Working in small groups, create a 16-week week-by-week outline of what an ideal Climate Change curriculum should look like (choose between four and eight issues to teach in the class). After you have completed your outline, choose one of the topics you selected, and write a lesson plan for the rest of the class. Your lesson should include the information you will present to the class through lectures, videos, discussion, etc.); several class activities; and one way to measure what students have learned (for example, a short quiz).

In your opinion, what is the most pressing climate issue in your region? Write a five-paragraph essay explaining what this issue is, who is affected by it, and how they are affected. Draw on at least two secondary sources, and document these sources in MLA format[1].

How did Iris's story impact you personally? How would you collaborate with their organization? Create a 2 to 4-minute video explaining how their story affected you, how you would like to contribute to FFFD, and why it is important for young people to be involved in environmental organizations.

STEM Activities

Iris found their passion and was able to transform their introverted nature, and criticism from their peers, into positives. Design a short story/animation about climate change that can enhance your peers' knowledge base and their motivation to create sustainable change. Develop an animated character that best displays your personal attributes and explain how animated characters can help to create a positive impact on others.

Create a 5-7 question survey via Google forms about climate change that is designed to identify what you already know about climate change. Then, based on the responses you receive from your peers and family, create a virtual presentation to share with them that will help educate them in areas that they might not be as knowledgeable in. You can include information about organizations targeting aspects of the issue, as well the history and projected future of climate change.

Iris maximized their impact among their peers by cofounding Fridays for Future Digital (FFFD) in order to expand digital climate protests. Due to the global pandemic, the country has shifted to digitally focused learning and working. Research the negative and positive impacts that the shift to virtual media has had on climate action. Create a presentation to share with your peers how society can maintain some of the positive changes, and decrease or eliminate the negative ones.

Describe your ethnic background. Then choose one thread of your ethnic heritage, and research the sustainability-focused challenges that people in your family's (or ancestors') country of origin have faced or are currently facing. Share this with your class and create a project that displays the ethnic diversity of your class and explains how countries around the world are helping to positively impact climate change.

Sustainability Innovations

Today there are many online tools that can help you reach more people.

- **350 Campaigns**[2] is an open platform available to anyone who would like to start their own campaign to impact our climate crisis.
- **Patagonia**[3] is one of the most impactful companies that is addressing climate change. They currently have a teen-focused climate crisis campaign that you can get involved in.

Sunrise Movement[4] is one of the major climate change projects that Iris participates in. Identify one aspect of the Sunrise movement that you would like to introduce to your peers.

Sustainability Career Pathways

Climatologist (Climate Scientist). Iris studied our climate challenges in depth in order to understand them. Climate scientists devote their careers to better understanding the scope, causes, and effects of the climate crisis—and communicating them to others. Want to become a climate scientist? Here is an introduction to the field[5].

Climate Educator. Currently few schools require climate change as part of the curriculum. But there are efforts to change that in many states: New Jersey is the first state to require climate education[6]. Teachers will have both the opportunity and the expectation to teach their students about climate change from K-12, to help better prepare them for the future they're inheriting. There are many opportunities to be a climate educator: certainly in schools, but also in museums and parks, or organizations like Alliance for Climate Education[7].

Web Manager. Because Iris is an introvert, they were most comfortable becoming an online activist/organizer. At the heart of every organization and social movement is a website. Website design and management is a field that involves making websites easy to navigate and engaging, and it offers boundless employment opportunities. If you are interested in a career in maintaining websites, read more about the specifics here[8], and a day in the life of a web manager here[9].

Social Media Manager. Building a movement online now requires the effective use of social media. Many organizations hire a full-time social media manager to manage their 'brand' across a variety of platforms. Good writing, social media, and general communication skills are essential. You can learn more about social media management in this introduction[10]. And here are 9 key skills you'll need to thrive in this field[11].

1 https://www.easybib.com/guides/citation-guides/mla-format/
2 https://campaigns.350.org/
3 https://www.patagonia.com/climate-goals/
4 https://www.sunrisemovement.org/?ms=SunriseMovement
5 https://www.environmentalscience.org/career/climatologist
6 https://www.globalcitizen.org/en/content/nj-introduces-climate-change-curriculum-schools/
7 https://acespace.org/about-us/
8 https://www.zippia.com/web-manager-jobs/
9 https://www.careerprofiles.com/job-seeker-advice-tips/one-day-in-the-life-of-a-web-content-manager/
10 https://www.mediabistro.com/climb-the-ladder/skills-expertise/what-does-a-social-media-manager-do/
11 https://sproutsocial.com/insights/social-media-skills/

Hopes from the Ends of the Earth

Joel Peña, Chiloé Protegido
Santiago, Chile

☀ Call to Action

Protect our oceans and find ways to help sustain marine life. Follow Joel on Twitter at: @joelpanichine

☀ Values

- Leadership
- Internationalism
- Solidarity
- Community Building
- Environmentalism

☀ Lessons Learned

Wherever you are, look for inspiration in the nature that surrounds you.

Be a teacher, and a helper: show people what areas of their lives and the environment could be improved, and find ways to help them to improve them.

When the challenge seems enormous, organize, recruit, and include the rest of your community. Then tackle the problem together.

For Joel Peña, it was an intimate encounter with one marine animal that made him want to become a climate activist.

The son of a family of seafarers, Joel grew up spending summers along the coasts of Chile with his grandfather, fishing. One day, finding himself within an arm's reach of a dolphin, he was inspired to dedicate himself to preserving his country's unique biodiversity.

After joining the Chilean branch of the Fridays for Future movement, Joel founded an NGO to support his own community. Called Chiloe Protegido, the organization aims to bring awareness to the unique biodiversity of the Chiloe islands in Patagonia, through a number of creative techniques such as beach clean-ups, animal tracking, and conservation training for young people.

☀ Language Arts

Working in groups, create a presentation about five animal species that can only be found on Chiloe Island. What are these species like? What makes them unique? What is their role in the environment? Why are they endangered? What is being done, or what can be done to preserve them?

Write a research essay on biodiversity in Patagonia. Start by defining what biodiversity is, and why it is important; then write about Patagonia and what makes the species that thrive in this region unique.

After watching your peers' presentations and using the information you learned in your research, create a series of six TikTok videos in which you educate people about the importance of these species (choose your favorite six); the need to preserve them; and how people can get involved in preservation efforts.

STEM Activities

In this lesson plan from Teach Engineering.org[1], students learn how dolphins use echolocation to locate prey, escape predators, and navigate their environment (for example, how they avoid gillnets set by commercial fishing vessels).

Comprising 71 percent of Earth's area, water serves as a fundamental resource for both humans and wildlife. Oil spills inflict damage upon wildlife, destroy ecosystems, and toxify drinking water. In this activity from Marineland[2], students examine how oil interacts with water, and build their own marine ecosystem and explore methods for cleaning up oil spills. Background information[3].

This lesson plan from the National Marine Sanctuaries[4] introduces students to the National Marine Sanctuary System (NMSS). Students explore the digital resources of NMSS to learn how national marine sanctuary sites are designated, and why they are important to protect and preserve the ocean. Then they conduct independent or small group research on specific national marine sanctuaries using 360° videos, photos, and print resources. Finally, they use the information they have collected to compare and contrast the four different sites and create a slideshow presentation.

Mission Blue[5] seeks to raise public awareness and inspire action to protect marine areas around the world called Hope Spots[6]. What makes an area a Hope Spot? Are there any Hope Spots located in or near Chile? What makes it a Hope Spot? What is the closest Hope Spot to you? Why is it a designated Hope Spot? Is it a formal marine protected area? Are there any marine areas near you that you think should be a Hope Spot? If so, you can nominate it to become a Hope Spot by following the directions provided here[7].

Sustainability Innovations

Joel is one of many Chileans who are actively involved with climate change issues. This article[8] highlights 10 different sustainability innovations in Chile, including bee colony systems and systems for food storage among many others.

In 2014, the Organization for Economic Cooperation and Development (OECD) created an analysis, Chile's Pathway to Green Growth: Measuring Progress at a Local Level[9], to assess progress toward sustainable goals in Chile. What are some of the highlights of their goals, and how have they changed in the past seven years?

Joel had the rare opportunity to participate in COP25 in Madrid thanks to his work with Fridays for Future. Chile[10] had originally been scheduled to host COP25, but they had to cancel due to civil unrest, so Spain hosted instead. After reading about this situation, how do you think climate change and social change affect one another?

Sustainability Career Pathways

Marine Biologist. Marine biologists study creatures, and their ecosystems, in oceans around the world--from the charismatic and highly intelligent dolphins to the far humbler creatures that make up the base of the food chain. Learn more about the career of marine biologist here[11].

Oceanographer. An oceanographer is a scientist who studies the ocean, and helps to protect, conserve, and restore marine environments. Oceanographers can study the life, chemicals, fluid dynamics and physics, and even the geology of the oceans' floors. Check out this field and its many variations here[12].

Community Environmental Educator. Many communities offer environmental educational opportunities to their residents through local governments, parks, museums, and even neighborhood associations. Do you love teaching? Working with volunteers? Organizing community events? This could be the career for you. Explore the field of community environmental education here[13].

1 https://www.teachengineering.org/lessons/view/duk_bycatchunit_musc_less2

2 https://marineland.net/wp-content/uploads/2020/03/Whats-in-the-Water-Lesson-Plan.pdf

3 https://marineland.net/wp-content/uploads/2020/03/Whats-In-the-Water-Background-Builder-Web-Edit.pdf

4 https://nmssanctuaries.blob.core.windows.net/sanctuaries-prod/media/docs/20200606-system-lesson.pdf

5 https://mission-blue.org/

6 https://mission-blue.org/hope-spots/

7 https://mission-blue.org/hope-spot-nomination-guidelines/

8 https://marcachile.cl/en/innovation-entrepreneurship/10-green-innovations-made-by-chileans-the-chilean-captain-planets/

9 https://www.oecd.org/cfe/leed/Green_growth_Chile_Final2014.pdf

10 https://www.climatechangenews.com/2019/10/30/chile-pulls-hosting-cop25-climate-talks/

11 https://www.thebalancecareers.com/marine-biologist-125619

12 https://www.environmentalscience.org/career/oceanographer

13 https://naaee.org/eepro/blog/community-environmental-education

Hope Springs From The Land Down Under

Jean Hinchliffe, School Strike 4 Climate Australia

⁂ Call to Action

Support School Strike 4 Climate in Australia www.schoolstrike4climate.com

Follow Jean on Twitter @jean_hinchliffe

Values

- Leadership
- Commitment
- Determination
- Environmentalism

Lessons Learned

True warriors for justice will tackle injustice wherever they find it.

Make sure your voice is heard, even if it means defying conventional wisdom and those in power.

The only tool to achieve real change is education. A real education is the product of passion and commitment; so be passionate and committed!

Jean Hinchliffe is a 15-year-old climate change activist leading the youth movement in Australia on many fronts.

She first made an impact at age 13, when working with the Vote Yes campaign, which won the fight for marriage equality in Australia. She is also a vocal supporter of the #StopAdani movement, which aims to stop the construction of the largest coal mine in the country. In 2018, Jean organized the national School Strike 4 Climate, to bring awareness to our current climate emergency. On March 15, 2019, the movement had more than 300,000 students and adults participating across Australia.

Language Arts

Write a research essay on Australia's ecosystems and climate change: What makes Australian ecosystems unique? How has climate change affected Australia? What can be done to reverse the damage?

After reading Jean's story, highlight the main ideas in the story. Select two of these main ideas and develop them in a series of TikTok videos, in which you explore how these ideas may affect your community.

Write a blog post in which you respond to an imaginary politician who believes that young women should only worry about academics and not get involved in activism. What would you say to this person to change his mind and make him see that young women have as much a right to their opinions as everyone else, and the same responsibility to express them?

☀ STEM Activities

In this activity from CoolAustralia.org[1], students explore the positive and negative impacts of climate change on biodiversity. Working in groups, they investigate the impacts on five animals – the Yellow-Footed Rock-Wallaby, the Giant Gippsland Earthworm, the Common Clownfish, the Southern Corroboree Frog, and Regent Honeyeaters.

In this activity, students will visit Mt. Resilience[2] – an augmented reality experience that allows students to explore and analyze a town that's been designed around climate change and disaster preparedness. The app[3] works on both phones and tablets.

Research and explore bushfires in Australia. What causes bushfires? What impact do they have on the community and the environment? Design an interactive map[4] that highlights some of Australia's most dangerous bushfires. Examples of interactive resources you can use include small 3D images, flaps, questions, multimedia resources, and animation.

☀ Sustainability Innovations

How can you get involved in Schools Strike 4 Climate[5]? Review their website and their Instagram account. How can you assist Jean's campaign from the U.S.?

In addition to Schools Strike 4 Climate, there is a separate website, #StopAdani[6], that highlights five ways that everyone can get involved to stop the Adani coal mine. How can you assist this cause?

In order to reach Australia's Sustainable Development Goals (SDGs), public awareness of the issues is necessary, and organizations must find ways to collaborate. Act on Climate[7] highlights the NGOs in Australia that share the core values of sustainability and adaptation to climate change. How could Schools Strike 4 Climate partner with one of these NGOs? Working together, what could they do to achieve progress toward these goals?

☀ Sustainability Career Pathways

Actor. At 15, Jean has already starred in a TV show (The Unlisted). While it's a difficult profession to enter, actors can use the projects they participate in and their celebrity to encourage others to live more sustainably. Want to become an actor? Start here[8].

Firefighter. Climate change is going to increase the profusion of fires in the years to come. Thus the world will need more firefighters--both urban firefighters, and those who specialize in protecting forests and wilderness areas. Here's an introduction to the field[9], and a 10-step list on how to follow this path[10].

Ecological Restoration. One of the best ways to limit the local effects of climate change is to heal local ecosystems whether wetlands, lakes, forests, or others. The field of ecological restoration[11] focuses on this area, with restoration ecologists, field technicians, and others working together to "rewild" degraded areas. Learn more about opportunities in this field here[12].

1 https://www.coolaustralia.org/activity/climate-change-and-biodiversity-in-australia/

2 https://www.abc.net.au/cm/lb/12802478/data/mt-resilience-ar-app-%25E2%2580%2593-teacher-resource-%28pdf%29-data.pdf

3 https://www.mtresilience.com

4 https://www.schools.aidr.org.au/media/4647/00_lessonplan_bushfires_231017.pdf

5 https://www.schoolstrike4climate.com/

6 https://www.stopadani.com/

7 https://www.aoc.org.au/australia-ngos

8 https://www.careersinfilm.com/actor/

9 https://collegegrad.com/careers/firefighters

10 https://www.firerescue1.com/career-1/articles/becoming-a-firefighter-10-must-do-things-wmOqMRqBfrm8Jflg/

11 https://www.ser-rrc.org/what-is-ecological-restoration/

12 https://www.ser-rrc.org/what-is-ecological-restoration/

Luna

Julia Butterfly Hill
California

☀ Call to Action

Learn more about the forests in your area, and find out what steps are being taken to protect them. Join together with other activists to educate your fellow citizens about the importance of our forests, and find ways to help sustain them! www.circleoflife.org

☀ Values

- Courage
- Commitment
- Tenacity
- Patience
- Determination
- Environmentalism

☀ Lessons Learned

Changing your perspective can help you discover the beauty of the world around you.

Respect the Earth and other living beings; they have been here longer than we have, so we should treat them like our honored elders.

Stand up for what you believe in, even if it means standing alone.

In 1997, Julia "Butterfly" Hill climbed up an ancient redwood tree named "Luna" in Northern California. Like many of the trees around it, Luna was scheduled to be cut down. Julia climbed the tree to protest its being cut down, and went on to live in the tree for more than two years. She had to brave the cold and the heat, the wind and the rain, and the sound of chainsaws cutting trees down all around her. Thanks to her sacrifice and dedication, Julia managed what seemed impossible: to save this ancient redwood tree, and also educate millions of people about the dangers of deforestation. Through her courage and tenacity, she became a famous environmental activist.

☀ Language Arts

Create a series of short videos for TikTok or YouTube, in which you answer the following questions: What are redwood trees? Where do they grow? How old are the redwood forests in the U.S.? At what rate are they being cut down? Are there any efforts being made to replant the trees that have been cut down? How long would it take a redwood forest to recover from the kind of deforestation described in the story? What can be done to prevent the destruction of these forests?

Using illustrations (either your own, or images you find on the internet), rewrite Julia and Luna's story as a children's book, telling it from Luna's perspective.

Aside from killing trees, what other environmental problems are caused by deforestation? Create a 10-minute video in which you explain how the practices of the logging industry cause environmental damage that goes well beyond the cutting down of trees.

Read the following articles about the health benefits of forests: Bathing in the Wisdom of Forests – The Esperanza Project[1] and Forest Bathing is an Evidence-Based Wellness Practice[2]. Highlight the main ideas in each article. Then, based on those ideas, write an essay explaining why it is good for kids to spend time in treehouses, wooded areas, and playing in trees.

Create a collection of images (it can be drawings or photographs, either your own, or ones you find on the internet) in which you explore what it would be like to live in a treehouse: what you would need to pack to be comfortable, types of food and clothing you would bring, etc.

STEM Activities

Using this curriculum on California redwoods[3], students will explore the causes and impacts of climate change as it affects redwood trees.

Research and evaluate different conservation techniques being used around the world to preserve forests and trees, taking into account economic, social, and environmental cost-benefit ratios.

Research and learn about the kinds of trees found in your area. Which of the trees are native to the area, and which are not? What benefits (or problems) do these trees bring to the local ecosystem? How does climate change impact these trees? What are some of the ways we can reduce the effects of climate change on them?

Sustainability Innovations

In addition to Julia's forest-planting efforts, Calforests[4] and similar organizations focus on legislative and regulatory changes to ensure the safety of California forests.

Save the Redwoods[5] is an organization that highlights different types of redwood trees, and the threats they face. Review the land and restoration projects that Save the Redwoods and their partners are focusing on.

As technology and society progress, what are some innovations that can assist reforestation and tree-saving projects? One Tree Planted[6] highlights 10 innovative breakthroughs to help with reforestation. Research one of the 10 breakthroughs and the latest advancements that have improved this innovation.

Sustainability Career Pathways

Environmental Educator. As Julia notes, "We are of this Earth and from this Earth[7]." Teaching students about our connection with the planet, through environmental studies, outdoor education, and embedding sustainability in all academic subjects is essential in helping future generations understand the environmental challenges we face--and their possible solutions. Learn more about this field here[8].

Forest Ecologist. Recently we've come to learn how much trees communicate with and support each other--even across species[9]. But there is so much more to learn about forest ecosystems. Do you want to study forests? Learn more about the field of forest ecology here[10].

Park Ranger. If you love trees, but don't necessarily want to live in one for two years like Julia did, becoming a park ranger could be for you! Park rangers are both educators and leading protectors of the world's parklands. This is a career opportunity for those who want to educate and care for forests and parks. Learn more about being a park ranger here[11].

1 https://www.esperanzaproject.com/2021/ecotourism/bathing-in-the-wisdom-of-forests/

2 https://health.uconn.edu/student-wellness/physical-wellness/evidence-based-wellness/

3 https://drive.google.com/drive/folders/1J6jB_CoGVnawHbcdZI7bBH_BPsN1Gwbt

4 https://calforests.org/

5 https://www.savetheredwoods.org/what-we-do/our-work/partner/conservation-organizations/

6 https://onetreeplanted.org/blogs/stories/breakthroughs-for-forests

7 https://www.youtube.com/watch?v=cZ-ZUOR2Oy0

8 https://www.environmentalscience.org/career/environmental-educator

9 https://www.npr.org/sections/health-shots/2021/05/04/993430007/trees-talk-to-each-other-mother-tree-ecologist-hears-lessons-for-people-too

10 https://bestaccreditedcolleges.org/articles/become-a-forest-ecologist-education-and-career-roadmap.html

11 https://www.parkrangeredu.org/

Plant-For-The-Plant

Felix Finkbeiner, Plant-For-The-Planet
Germany

Call to Action

Help save the world, one tree at a time. Download the Plant-for-the-Planet app and share your stories! Follow Felix's advice: Stop talking. Start planting! Follow Felix on Twitter @FelixFinkbeiner and www.plant-for-the- planet.org

Values

- Determination
- Internationalism
- Leadership
- Optimism
- Environmentalism

Lessons Learned

No matter how young or old we are, we can always learn from each other.

In helping the planet heal, we help ourselves grow.

Dream big and you will achieve great things!

When Felix was five years old, he got a present: it was a stuffed polar bear, almost as big as himself.
Four years later, when he prepared a presentation about the climate crisis for his classmates, he realized that his beloved polar bears were in danger. He came up with a simple but effective solution for the problem: planting trees. He started working on this project with just his classmates, but soon other schools joined in. That was the beginning of Plant-for-the- Planet, an organization that today has over 75,000 members and has planted more than 14 billion trees. But Felix has more ambitious plans: he wants to plant one trillion (that is, one thousand billion) trees all over the world. "Planting trees is the easiest thing we can do to alleviate the climate crisis, and everyone can contribute," he says.

Language Arts

Choose one species that is currently endangered due to climate change. Write and deliver a three-minute speech to your class about this species: why it is endangered, what efforts are being made to preserve it, and how people can get involved in conservation issues to help this particular species. After you are done presenting, give your classmates a copy of your speech.

After everyone in your class has delivered their speeches, break up into groups of three or four people. Select three of the speeches that were given (not yours or anyone else's in the group). Discuss among yourselves how the speech affected you, if it changed your opinion on this matter (and why or why not), and what were the most effective strategies the speaker used in the speech. Write down your answers as a group and then discuss them with the class.

Working with your group, create a 20-minute lesson about the importance of reforestation in one area of the world

(each group will be assigned a different area). Your lesson must include handouts, an oral presentation, a video, and a short quiz to be administered at the end. You will teach your lesson to your class and grade their quizzes at the end. After you grade their quizzes, write a one-paragraph reflection essay about which parts of your presentation seemed to work better than others, and how you can hone your education skills in the future.

Germany has been one of the world's pioneers in sustainable living. How and when did this shift begin? How has it changed the country? Using a poster board, create a timeline of the sustainability movement in Germany over the past 50 years.

STEM Activities

In this activity from NASA.gov[1], students use satellite data to study changes in temperature and snow-ice coverage in the South Beaufort Sea, Alaska. They will then correlate the data with the United States Geological Survey(USGS) ground tracking of polar bears and relate their findings to global change, sea ice changes, and polar bear migration and survival.

Using this lesson guide from Calacademy.org[2], students will learn about and model the carbon cycle, and explore ways in which human actions play a role in this cycle.

In this lesson plan from Cumberland River Impact[3], students will measure their carbon footprints using online tools. Then they explore how much carbon dioxide is stored in a tree and calculate how many trees they would need to plant to cover their own personal carbon footprint.

A nuclear power phase-out is the discontinuation of usage of nuclear power for energy production. Since the March 2011 Fukushima nuclear disaster, Germany has permanently shut down eight of its 17 reactors and plans to complete the nuclear phase-out by 2030. What alternative energy sources is Germany using to replace nuclear energy? Are they sustainable and environmentally friendly? If not, what are some other sustainable sources they could use?

Sustainability Innovations

In addition to the work of Plant-for-the-Planet, there are many apps that are focused on tree planting:

- **Forest App:** This app is a productivity app that plants trees while you focus on other tasks. If you turn on your phone, your tree dies, and you have to start over. As you plant trees, you gain credits towards planting trees in real life. Take a look at the Forest App [4]and the description of its new features.

- **Ant Forest App:** This China-based app allows users to gain points based on making eco- friendly decisions like bringing plastic bags into stores or paying bills online. These activities allow the points to be converted into virtual trees representing trees planted. Result: over 120 million trees planted from users. This article[5] highlights the Ant Forest app and how it is making positive changes to our carbon footprint.

View the global map on Plant-for-the-Planet[6], and identify the restoration program closest to your location. How can you donate to or otherwise assist this project?

Research the tree planting projects that The Nature Conservancy[7] is leading in Brazil and the U.S. How do they differ, and what can students do to participate?

☀ Sustainability Career Pathways

Tree Planter. It may not be the most lucrative career path, but tree planters get to spend their days outdoors; travel; and do something good for the Earth--planting trees! Here is a look at what a day in the life of a tree planter[8] is like, and here is a look at qualifications, expected earnings, and an opportunity[9] to apply to plant trees (for Canadians).

Agroforester. Although forests are increasingly being cut down and replaced with unsustainable forest plantations of lumber or palm oil, the field of agroforestry[10] is rapidly developing. Agroforestry is the sustainable farming of forest crops--from coffee and cocoa to maple syrup and mushrooms. Want to learn more about this field? Visit here[11].

App Designer. Increasingly, people aren't just exploring the world through the internet, but also through numerous smartphone apps. This is another potential way to use technology to help educate and encourage more sustainable living[12], designing anything from a tree planting counter or a carbon calculator to apps that help you borrow or buy used instead of new stuff .Want to get into app design? Here's a good starting point[13].

---

1 https://mynasadata.larc.nasa.gov/sites/default/files/2018-12/March%20of%20the%20Polar%20Bears-%20Global%20Change%20Sea%20Ice%20and%20Wildlife%20Migration.pdf

2 https://www.calacademy.org/educators/lesson-plans/carbon-cycle-role-play

3 https://docs.google.com/document/d/1q1YcuulxR3npQTum4QSL1WD0cQN2y6bGXp36QiR1eNQ/edit

4 https://www.forestapp.cc/

5 https://www.ecowatch.com/tree-planting-app-china-ant-forest-2646446781.html

6 https://www1.plant-for-the-planet.org/

7 https://www.nature.org/en-us/get-involved/how-to-help/plant-a-billion/south-america/

8 https://onetreeplanted.org/blogs/stories/tree-planters-video

9 https://www.agreforestation.ca/tree-planting.html

10 https://newcropsorganics.ces.ncsu.edu/herb/medicinal-herbs-and-non-timber-forest-products/forest-farming-in-north-america/

11 https://www.environmentalscience.org/career/agroforester

12 https://www.cnet.com/news/10-apps-that-help-you-be-more-sustainable-in-every-area-of-life/

13 https://learnappmaking.com/how-to-make-an-app/

Savvy Social Media Influencer Strikes for Our Future

David Wicker, Fridays For Future Italy
Italy

Call to Action

Follow David:
Twitter: @davidwicker_hf
Facebook: @dhf.wicker
instagram: @davidwickerhf
Fridays for Future's website:
www.fridaysforfutureitalia.it/

Values

- Dedication
- Commitment
- Creativity
- Communication
- Environmentalism

Lessons Learned

Keep fighting for what you believe in. If you're tired, rest, and go back to the fight refreshed.

Climate change affects everyone, which is why we need everyone's input to tackle it. Listen to each other, regardless of age.

Fighting climate change needs to be a global effort. The only way to win the fight is by uniting and leaving politics aside.

David Wicker is an environmental activist fighting against climate change on the European front.
At age 14, he became an organizer with the Fridays for Future (FFF) movement, and currently leads the activist group's efforts in Turin, Italy. Fridays For Future is a school strike movement that is asking governments around the world to place the climate change issue as their top priority – particularly as it relates to respecting the Paris treaty and the UN's Intergovernmental Panel on Climate Change. David, along with thousands of other students in, was motivated by the likes of Greta Thunberg, Luisa Neubauer, and Vanessa Nakate to join in this movement.

As a talented computer programmer, David is working on innovative ways to streamline messaging and communications. By integrating people onto more responsive and younger community-based platforms, he hopes to expand the reach of FFF's message around the globe.

Language Arts

Create a presentation about northern Italy in which you show the impact climate change has had on the region. How has climate change affected the economy, the culture, the health of the population, and the ecosystem of northern Italy?

One of the challenges northern Italy is facing because of climate change is a decrease in the availability of drinking water. This is a problem that is likely to threaten the whole world in the future. Design a series of digital posters in which you describe the issue of drinking water, the dangers that arise from not having enough, and some possible solutions to the problem.

In your opinion, what is the best way to teach young people about climate change? Italy was the first country in the world to make Climate Change education mandatory in schools, but there has been trouble implementing it because of budgetary issues. Working in groups, create a syllabus for an imaginary required course on climate change for people in the same grade as you, and a viable way to implement this program in your city (be sure to say how it could be paid for). Then, individually, have each person write a short essay explaining your choices.

Based on the previous activity, break up into groups and prepare a debate between students in which you discuss the pros and cons of implementing this (imaginary required) class, and the pros and cons of the proposed methods of obtaining funds to implement it.

STEM Activities

In this activity from Safewater.org[1], research and evaluate five different water treatment processes, and identify the effectiveness, practicality, and applicability of each one. Then examine other methods that influence water quality and treatment methods, including education, funding, policy, and rights.

Using this set of activities and resources from PBS[2] , learn about the impacts of drought through news videos of communities that are facing serious water shortages; analyze drought data and models from NOAA; and research and evaluate potential solutions to the problem of water shortages.

Design an application (web, desktop, or mobile-based) that can help combat climate change, such as an app that collects some type of data, facilitates communication, or shares knowledge of different types of climate change-related issues. As an extension activity, take your design and build it!

Sustainability Innovations

David has had the unique opportunity to begin his sustainability journey at a young age after witnessing climate change and its effects on his community. The students from Fridays for Future Italy have a similar opportunity to make an impact based on the changes they see in their community. Review Fridays for Future Italia[3] and compare their events and campaigns to Fridays for Future USA. How can these two movements collaborate and learn from each other's actions?

In addition to young activists, organizations such as Sustainable Development Foundation Italy are vital to the success of addressing climate change. Fondazione Per Lo Sviluppo Sostenible[4] has made continuous strides toward a more sustainable future by participating in activities addressing campaigns, politics, a circular economy, and green infrastructure.

Climate organizations and activists have been at the forefront of the climate change movement, but it will take the efforts of both government and companies to continue to make these changes a reality. Carbon Sink[5] is a consultancy company that focuses on sustainability strategies and compensation for CO2 emissions in Italy.

Slow Food[6], which was founded in Italy, is an exciting sustainable agriculture innovation, focused on preventing the disappearance of local food cultures and traditions, counteracting the rise of "fast living," and combating people's dwindling interest in the quality of the food they eat. It's now in 1600 communities, and is working to ensure that everyone has access to good, clean, and fair food.

Sustainability Career Pathways

Social Media Manager. Building a movement online now requires the effective use of social media. Many organizations hire a full-time social media manager to manage their "brand" across a variety of platforms. Good writing, social media, and communication skills are essential. If you're interested in learning more about social media management, check out this introduction[7]. Here are key skills you'll need to thrive in this field[8].

Assisting the Elderly. As David notes, older people are more susceptible to the effects of climate change, as well as other societal challenges. There are many ways one can help the elderly live healthy, sustainable lives. Here is an introduction to working with the elderly[9], from nursing and social work to continuing education, and even ways to help them to join in the climate fight[10].

Translator. In this video[11], you can see David translating for three global climate activists. Translating is both an asset in global movements, and a good way to make a living. This is a skill that can be used in international governance, conferences, publishing, medicine, activism, refugee centers, and in many other contexts. If you love languages and want to learn about becoming a translator, read this seven-step guide[12].

1 https://www.safewater.org/

2 https://www.pbslearningmedia.org/collection/climate-change-impacts-and-solutions/

3 https://fridaysforfutureitalia.it/portavoce/

4 https://www.fondazionesvilupposostenibile.org/english/

5 https://www.carbonsink.it/en/news/the-made-green-in-italy-brand

6 https://www.slowfood.com/

7 https://www.mediabistro.com/climb-the-ladder/skills-expertise/what-does-a-social-media-manager-do/

8 https://sproutsocial.com/insights/social-media-skills/

9 https://www.publicservicedegrees.org/careers/working-with-the-elderly/

10 https://www.eldersclimateaction.org/

11 https://www.youtube.com/watch?v=ZAkHXEODD7c

12 https://www.fluentu.com/blog/how-to-become-a-translator/

A Petition Changes the Food Industry

Asha & Jia Kirkpatrick, petitiongirls.com
London, UK

Call to Action

When you go to the supermarket the next time, check the ingredients list on the products in your shopping cart. If they include palm oil, try to find alternatives. If you can't, it's okay: the most important step is the first one— becoming aware of the problem. You can also follow Harv, the friendly orangutan on Twitter:@ Harv49905493

Values

- Determined
- Persistent
- Courageous
- Leaders
- Environmentalists

Lessons Learned

Learning about the ingredients used in the products we consume is important.

As Asha says, if you think something is wrong, you can change it: but you have to put the effort into it.

When you become aware of a problem, it is important to learn about it and try to come up with solutions.

Asha (12) and her sister Jia (10) love orangutans.

So they were shocked to learn that their favorite cereal was made with palm oil--after all, the production of palm oil means that large swaths of rainforest, the orangutans' natural habitat, are being cut down every year. They started an online petition and intense lobbying effort to force a global company to change its business practices. With more than 800,000 signatures, their initiative was a spectacular success--and the sisters already have plans to continue their efforts to help save our rainforests.

Language Arts

Read Asha and Jia's original petition. Then make a bullet-point list of the strategies they used to encourage people to sign their petition. Which of these strategies would you use to write your own petition, and why?

Write a letter trying to persuade a company to switch from using palm oil to a more sustainable alternative. How would you combine these three rhetorical approaches—ethos, pathos and logos (ethics, feelings, and logic)—to maximize the persuasiveness of your letter?

Write the script for a PSA (public service announcement) aimed at raising awareness on the issue of palm oil and the environmental devastation that is associated with it.

Create a video of your PSA. Work as a team to research the statistics, find or create cool graphics, record a voiceover using your script, and edit the video. Share it with your friends, school, community, social media.

Standards are essential in improving food production--whether regarding products that use palm oil, or

the many other commodities we rely on. Researchers and environmentall organizations have publicized the limits to current standards. Review this Greenpeace report and this Monga bay article[1] and write an essay on how you would go about making palm oil standards stronger.

STEM Activities

Palm oil has become a staple ingredient in many products that we consume on a daily basis. When the Green Century Balance Fund filed a shareholder resolution against Starbucks over concerns about their use of non-sustainable palm oil, they switched to buying 100 percent of their palm oil from certified sustainable sources.

- **Research one food company** that still uses palm oil that is not sustainably sourced; then write a letter to the company detailing the harmful effects of palm oil, and offering sustainable alternatives.

Palm oil production accounted for approximately 8 percent of the world's deforestation from 1990-2008. In addition to the displacement of orangutans, deforestation has numerous other harmful effects, including the displacement of other species, and an increase in carbon emissions.

- **Compile a list of other species that are being endangered**, or lost, as a result of deforestation.
- **Research the increased amount of carbon emissions** caused by palm oil deforestation. Compare these effects to the effects of sustainable palm oil production. Resource: Palm Oil: The Carbon Cost of Deforestation[2].

Conventional palm oil production is an example of monoculture farming, where only one crop is grown in a given area at a time. Monoculture farming has been shown to decrease biodiversity and expedite the spread of diseases.

- **As a class, research and brainstorm the different types of sustainable farming techniques** (for example, permaculture, polyculture, crop rotation, and hydroponics/aquaponics).
- **Working in small groups, have students incorporate one sustainable farming technique into a plan to redesign a monocultural palm oil farm.** To be sustainable, the farm must maintain good public health; improve quality of life; be profitable; promote biodiversity; and responsibly manage natural resources. Then have students present their design to the rest of the class.

Sustainability Innovations

Many organizations have made it their goal to reduce the use of and adjust the production process of palm oil:

- **Roundtable on Sustainable Palm Oil (RSPO)[3]** - This NGO connects stakeholders from the seven sectors of the palm oil industry to develop standards for palm oil.
- **Palm Oil Innovation Group[4]** - This group helps to connect individuals who are building on the RSPO standards in order to improve responsible palm oil production practices, and share stories about company/individual success.

RSPO has made progress toward expanding their network of companies to become RSPO-certified, but there are many products that still need to receive certification. L'Occitane en Provence[5], a French company, received their RSPO certification in 2011 and is striving to support sustainable farmers/initiatives. Here is some information on their sustainable sourcing:

- **Research two companies** that are RSPO-certified whose products you use, or would consider using.

Sustainability Career Pathways

Corporate Sustainability Officer. As Asha and Jia demonstrated, companies tend to prioritize growth, even at the expense of the environment (and thus society's long-term well-being as well as their own). Corporate cultures are slow to change, but change has started. Many companies now have a corporate sustainability officer to help drive change from within. This career path offers the opportunity to improve the environmental effects of the world's most influential businesses. Want to learn how? Read here[6] and here[7].

Forest Ecologist. Forests are deeply threatened by climate change--from invasive pests killing countless trees to dry conditions that are causing more and more catastrophic fires. Better understanding forests, and how trees can adapt to these changes will be essential to protecting the "lungs of the land." As a forest ecologist[8] you can help!

Agroforester. While forests are often cut down and replaced with forest plantations to grow trees for lumber or palm oil, the field of agroforestry[9]—the sustainable farming of forest crops, from coffee and cocoa to maple syrup and mushrooms—is rapidly developing. You can learn more about this field here[10].

Sustainable Agriculture. More young people are being drawn to careers in farming, as groups like The Greenhorns[11] reveal. If you're interested in being a farmer, this introduction to the field of sustainable agriculture[12] is a good place to start.

Want to help make the food system more sustainable, but not sure how specifically you want to contribute? Here's a great essay[13] that explores the many ways that you can help make the food system more sustainable through careers in agriculture, communications, advocacy, law, and public health.

1 https://news.mongabay.com/2018/07/rspo-fails-to-deliver-on-environmental-and-social-sustainability-study-finds/

2 https://www.sciencedaily.com/releases/2018/06/180619123018.htm

3 https://www.rspo.org/about

4 http://poig.org/further-resources/rspo-and-poig/

5 https://www.loccitane.com/en-us/pages?fdid=sustainable-sourcing

6 https://www.careerexplorer.com/careers/sustainability-officer/

7 https://impakter.com/choosing-the-harder-path-the-journey-towards-a-job-in-corporate-sustainability/

8 https://bestaccreditedcolleges.org/articles/become-a-forest-ecologist-education-and-career-roadmap.html

9 https://newcropsorganics.ces.ncsu.edu/herb/medicinal-herbs-and-non-timber-forest-products/forest-farming-in-north-america/

10 https://www.environmentalscience.org/career/agroforester

11 https://greenhorns.org/

12 https://greencollarblog.org/sustainable-agriculture-jobs/

13 https://foodprint.org/blog/get-to-work-jobs-in-food-sustainability/

Standing Alone, Together

Arshak Makichyan, Fridays For Future Russia
Russia

Call to Action

Support Arshak by using the hashtag #LetRussiaStrikeForClimate on social media platforms. Join with Arshak and those organizing climate action strikes on the Fridays for Future website: www.fridaysforfuture.org

Values

- Determination
- Collaboration
- Leadership
- Optimism
- Inspiration

Lessons Learned

One single voice can shatter the silence imposed by a government. Be courageous, and speak truth to power.

Bravery inspires. Be an inspiration to your peers.

Civil disobedience is our right; educate yourself about this right, and don't be afraid to use it.

In pursuit of a broader collaborative effort to raise awareness about the global impacts of climate change, Arshak Makichyan, 24, has had to learn how to go it alone.

In Russia, where he grew up, protests of more than one person are considered an illegal gathering, unless approved by the state. Undeterred, Arshak, a music student in Moscow, began to protest every week in Pushkin Square. His solo protest soon turned into a much larger movement, and his activism has inspired other young people in cities and towns across Russia to join him.

Other climate activists, like Greta Thunberg, have taken note of his message and supported Arshak in his quest to get the world's fourth-biggest carbon emitter to do more to protect the climate.

Language Arts

Create a video in which you explain the difference between legitimate protest (for example, exercising your right to free speech and freedom of assembly), and criminal activities (things like looting, aggression against other people, etc.). Focus not only on the differences between the two, but the dangers of conflating the two (both for individuals and for society as a whole).

Do you think governments should legislate against the right to protest? Write an argumentative essay in which you explain your position on this matter. Back it up with data from external research sources.

What is the current situation of protest and free speech in the United States? Write a series of 10-12 tweets designed to bring attention to the challenges facing Americans who want to express unpopular opinions; the legal protections they have (or the ones they need); and how people can help support them.

Having a free press and access to news through social media and the internet are privileges that are not present in all countries of the world. Unfortunately, sometimes dishonest organizations take advantage of those privileges to plant false information for political and/or financial gain. Read the following guidelines to help spot fake news[1]. Then read this article[2] about fake news being used to manipulate Latino voters in the 2020 U.S. election. After reading both articles, write a short reflection paper on the effect that misinformation masked as news can have in a society, and propose 5 suggestions for how to fight it.

How do you think the international community can help climate activists who are being oppressed in other countries? Conduct research on this issue, and then create an informational presentation in which you explain to your peers how they can get involved. End with a concrete call to action in which you suggest a safe and effective way to get involved with this cause.

STEM Activities

Read this article about environmental activism in Russia[3], and the barriers that environmental activists there are facing. Create a chart that depicts issues that are unique to people in Russia and ways such issues could be addressed if they were to become a challenge in the U.S.

Arshak is not just a climate activist, he is also a music student. Music, and sound in general, is produced when something vibrates and causes the air molecules to also vibrate, initiating a chain of soundwave vibrations that move through the air and into your ear. Besides making music, sound is also used for measuring distances. Learn about the properties, sources, and applications of three types of sound waves; how engineers use ultrasound waves in medical sonography devices and ocean sonar equipment; and how ultrasonic sensors are engineered. Activity link[4].

STEM Career[5] is one virtual resource that Arshak and others can utilize to engage students in Russia about the vital importance of sustainability.

Sustainability Innovations

Russia is limited in its sustainable efforts. However, the Russian Social Ecological Union[6] was one of the first sustainability-focused NGOs in Russia. Founded in 1992, RSEU is targeting major ecological issues, with a focus on climate change, energy efficiency, and nuclear threats.

Russia is a very dangerous place to protest, but Arshak made the decision that ignoring climate change was even more dangerous. Global Climate Strike[7] is a website hosted by 350.org that allows individuals to get involved and collaborate to address global climate issues. Find out how your support and collaboration could help Arshak and other protesters in Russia.

Sustainability Career Pathways

Musician. Music, like other forms of art, offers a powerful way to draw attention to environmental causes. Listen to the temperatures rising in this powerful "A Song of Our Warming Planet,[8]" for cello. Or read this article[9] about many musicians—from Paul McCartney and Sheryl Crowe to Grimes and Lil Dickey—who are using their celebrity to draw attention to climate change. If you have a musical gift, you too can use it to draw attention to our sustainability crisis, and to call for solutions.

Human Rights Lawyer. Lawyers can help activists avoid, or at least navigate their way through difficult court systems. They can also help fight human rights abuses wherever they occur in the world. While this is not an easy path, this article offers an introduction on how to become a human rights lawyer and what you can do with such training[10]. Note: Knowing more than one language is a plus for this path.

Foreign Correspondent. With the climate changing, and with youth demanding action and political change all over the world, it seems like the news cycle is accelerating. Only with journalists accurately covering the stories can people learn about these important events. Journalists play a key role in drawing attention to political activism, disasters, and many other things that people need to know about. Do you want to report the news in other parts of the world? Perhaps international journalism is the career path for you. Learn more about being a foreign correspondent here[11].

Geographer. Russia is going to suffer significant effects due to a warming climate, from melting permafrost to forest fires. Geographers can help explore what these effects will be, and figure out how to mitigate their impacts on the Russian people and wildlife. Want to learn about how to become a geographer? Here is an introduction[12]. And here are resources for exploring the field[13].

Climate Activist. Now and in the years to come, there will be a growing need for individuals who are dedicated to building political commitment to stabilizing Earth's climate. This is an activity you can be involved in now. Organize a Friday climate strike[14] at your town hall, or pressure your school to divest from fossil fuel stocks and/or invest in renewable energy. As Arshak has demonstrated, it only takes one person to start a movement. The best way to enter this field and make a difference is to get active now! And for ideas about future career opportunities, visit Idealist.org[15] to explore thousands of activist jobs, internships, and volunteer opportunities.

---

1 https://www.factcheck.org/2016/11/how-to-spot-fake-news/
2 https://abcnews.go.com/Politics/latino-voters-misinformation-targets-election-2020/story?id=74189342
3 https://www.csis.org/analysis/environmental-activism-russia-strategies-and-prospects
4 https://www.teachengineering.org/activities/view/nyu_soundwaves_activity1
5 http://stemcareer.com/
6 https://rusecounion.ru/index.php?q=eng
7 https://fridaysforfuture.org/
8 https://www.youtube.com/watch?v=5t08CLczdK4
9 https://www.newscientist.com/article/2206461-the-musicians-helping-make-climate-change-a-cultural-movement/
10 https://www.humanrightscareers.com/magazine/how-to-become-a-human-rights-lawyer/
11 https://www.masterclass.com/articles/how-to-become-a-foreign-correspondent#how-to-become-a-foreign-correspondent
12 https://collegegrad.com/careers/geographers
13 https://www.gale.com/geography
14 https://fridaysforfuture.org/
15 https://www.idealist.org/en/

The Art Of Saving The Planet

Alejandro Martinez, Juventud Por El Clima
Spain

Alejandro Martinez is leading the Spanish branch of the Fridays for Future student climate mobilization movement.

Called Juventud x Clima, these young climate activists have a challenging task ahead of them: Spain — known for the rich colors and natural beauty that have inspired artists over the centuries — could become two-thirds desert in the coming decades because of climate change. Alejandro, an artist and designer, wants to make sure that the climate movement takes into account the importance of preserving his country's natural beauty in its fight to correct the errors of past generations.

Language Arts

Create a series of cartoon strips (or an animated short[1]) about a climate issue that is threatening your own community. Focus on the threat it presents to the environment and the people; what might be lost if it is left unchecked; and what can be done to stop it.

Write a compare and contrast essay in which you juxtapose the environmental destruction inflicted on your region of the world, with that being inflicted on Spain. Are there any similarities? What are the differences? What is to be lost, in both cases, if nothing is done? Use images, graphics, and photographs to help support your position.

Using the information you researched for your essay, create a series of tweets that raise awareness about the environmental threats in your area; explain the result of not addressing them; and present a call to action for that lets people know what they can do, or which organization they can join, to help.

Call to Action

Join Alejandro in calling for Climate Action Now! Follow #FridaysForFuture Espana on Twitter: @JuventudXClima and bring #FridaysForFuture to your community: fridaysforfuture.org

Values

- Creativity
- Solidarity
- Internationalism
- Leadership
- Environmentalism

Lessons Learned

If you want to change the world, find what you love, then work to protect it.

If you want to unite people for a cause, focus on the things they love in common; then together, build a plan to fight for them.

Let what you love guide you toward lofty goals.

STEM Activities

Scientists have estimated that by 2050, two-thirds of Spain could be covered by deserts. Scientists can make such predictions using climate models. This lesson[2] will help students understand how such models are constructed, how they can be used to make predictions, and how they can help us understand the effects of our changing climate.

Alejandro loves art, but he also liked science as a kid, especially topics like biodiversity. Biodiversity refers to the variety of organisms that are present in a given ecosystem; it can be measured many different ways, including by measuring genetic variation as well as species and ecosystems variation, within an area. This module[3] defines biodiversity and allows students to look at it from all three aspects. Students will also learn about threats to biodiversity from invasive species, habitat destruction, climate change, and genetically modified organisms.

In this lesson plan from Trop ICSU[4], students discuss the importance of increasing renewable sources of energy such as wind power by applying differentiating functions to compare the rates of increase in wind energy production in several different countries (from given datasets).

Sustainability Innovations

What is eco-innovation? This question is answered by the Eco-Innovation Action Plan, which highlights 20+ different European countries and their current sustainability efforts. Eco-Innovation Spain assesses the Eco-Innovation outputs, activities, inputs, and socioeconomic and resource efficiency outcomes. See where Spain ranks on the 2019 Eco-Innovation Scoreboard here: Eco-Innovation Spain[5].

When assessing the ambitious climate energy goals based on the COP21 framework, European companies must form partnerships and devise solutions to meet their goals. The Be Smart Project EU[6] has focused on the increased use of Building-Integrated Photovoltaics (BIPV) as a driving force to help to meet these goals in urban areas and cities.

In addition to technological advancements directly targeting CO2 emissions and climate change, advancements in the food industry have become a major contributor to reaching Spain's sustainability goals. Food and Wines from Spain[7] highlights sustainable products, projects, and plans by companies in the food and beverage industry. What are the sustainable impacts in the field of art and animation? How could that field adopt strategies similar to those in the food and beverage industry?

Sustainability Career Pathways

Animator. If you have ever watched Spirited Away, Wall-E, or even the computer-graphic-heavy Avatar, you know that animated movies can play a huge role in inspiring connection to the Earth, and sustainable behaviors. If you love to draw, this is certainly a field in which you could help paint a (moving) picture of a sustainable future. Want to learn more? Start with this great overview of becoming an animator[8].

Artist. Both visual and performing artists use their talents to draw attention to social and environmental challenges. Sometimes they do this directly through their works of art and sometimes through the platform their fame offers. If you are driven to be an artist, don't forget about the opportunity this can offer in drawing attention and resources to causes you care about. Here is an article about six visual artists who are using their talent to draw attention to the environmental challenges we are facing[9]. How could you use your artistic talents to do the same?

Sustainable Tourism Industry. Like so many places around the world, Spain has an inherent beauty--one that can inspire visitors to become champions of sustainability in their own countries. Tourism can be unsustainable (if it includes global travel), but it can also help inspire deeper connection to the Earth and to other cultures. Today there is a growing sustainable tourism sector, one that embeds environmental knowledge in tours, makes hotels greener, encourages more local experiences, and so on. There are many ways to be part of this industry, from tour operator to travel guide, from hotelier to turning part of your home into an AirBnB and offering green tours of your town. If this is a path for you, read these 10 tips on how to make a career in sustainable tourism[10].

1 https://www.moovly.com/blog/make-your-own-cartoon-video-for-free

2 https://www.climatechangeeducationexchange.org/home/climate-change-lesson-plans

3 https://cosm.georgiasouthern.edu/mbi/biodiversity-a-teaching-module-for-a-high-school-classroom/

4 https://tropicsu.org/lesson-plan-polynomial-and-logistic-diffn-wind-energy-data/

5 https://ec.europa.eu/environment/ecoap/spain_en

6 https://www.besmartproject.eu/mission

7 https://www.foodswinesfromspain.com/spanishfoodwine/global/foodtech-from-spain/foodtech-detail/articles/articles-detail/sustainable-products-projects-spanish-food-beverage-companies.html?id=FEX2020867665&l=CWB2020867668

8 https://www.thebalancecareers.com/animator-career-information-525982

9 https://mymodernmet.com/environmental-art/

10 https://sustainability-leaders.com/ten-tips-sustainable-tourism-career/

Thirsty For Change

Alaa Salah
Sudan

☀ Call to Action

Learn how you can support Sudanese women and children in their fight for a more just society, and a better life for all. Follow Alaa on Instagram: @alaa_salah39

☀ Values

- Courage
- Commitment
- Social Justice
- Equality
- Environmentalism

☀ Lessons Learned

The fight for justice doesn't end when a tyrant falls. Instead, that's when it truly begins.

Education is a precious privilege. Always remember there are people out there willing to risk their lives to obtain it. What will you do to help them?

There are many challenges that stand between dreams and reality; let hope be the fuel that propels you toward your goals.

Known internationally as the "Woman in White," or Sudan's "Lady Liberty," Alaa Salah rose to fame as one of the activists who helped to topple the corrupt regime of Omar al-Bashir.

The photo of her standing on the hood of a car amidst a group of peaceful protesters became a viral symbol of the grassroots fight for freedom in Sudan. Even after the al-Bashir regime fell, Alaa has made it her mission to create a better country for future generations. Her goal is to ensure that all Sudanese are able to access an education. This includes educating future generations about climate change, which is threatening to disrupt the traditional farming patterns of communities in Sudan, and lead to increasing instability.

☀ Language Arts

Working in groups, you will create a poster in which you examine Alaa's mission, her accomplishments, and her influence in Sudanese politics, specifically the plight of women in Sudan, and her fight for women's rights. After creating your poster, conduct a Gallery Walk[1] with your peers.

Read Alaa's statement before the U.N.[2] Pull out the main ideas and write a brief explanatory essay on the major topics she addressed, and their importance for Sudan, Africa, and the world.

What is the story of Darfur? How did climate change contribute to the genocide that happened in this region? Create a presentation in which you explore how climate change has caused or contributed to war and genocide in this region that was once part of the "Bread Basket of Africa."

Who was Omar al-Bashir? What was life like for women in Sudan during his regime? How did his actions (or lack of action) worsen conditions for the Sudanese people, especially women? After finding the answers to these questions, write a narrative from the point of view of a young Sudanese woman from Darfur, in which you have her explain these issues to an audience unfamiliar with Sudan and its people.

STEM Activities

In this lesson plan from Trop ICSU[3], students will learn about river systems, and the features that determine their significance for the regions they flow through. The Nile is one of the longest rivers in the world; it flows through 11 countries in northeastern Africa. Students will explore the Nile's role in providing food and water security, and in influencing the economy of Sudan -- and the impact climate change is having on the river.

In this activity from PBS[4], students will be introduced to the factors that contribute to desertification, and will explore some of the solutions that have been implemented in Africa. The lesson includes an in-depth analysis of NASA data related to rainfall and desertification; an investigation of vulnerability to desertification, and population density; and a student-led microclimate investigation.

Sudan's vulnerability to climate change is shown by the fact that food security is mainly determined by rainfall. Examine this dataset of rainfall data in Sudan from 1901-2015[5]. What is the average trend in rainfall over that period of time? Is the amount of rainfall increasing, decreasing, or constant? What inferences can you make from this data, about likely future precipitation trends in Sudan? How does climate change affect average rainfall?

Sustainability Innovations

As a part of the United Nations voluntary national review, five key messages have been highlighted as the basis for reaching Sudan's sustainable development goals (SDGs). Learn about organizations[6] that are addressing Sudan's SDGs. How can each of these organizations expand their outreach?

As a part of the United Nations Environment Programme, Sudan launched its first-ever State of Environment and Outlook Report[7]. What needs are highlighted in this report? How do Alaa's goals correspond with the needs of Sudan as depicted in the report?

The CTC Group[8] is a privately owned group of companies in Sudan that focus on leading private sector businesses with diversified goals. They currently have 17 partnerships to assist Sudan in reaching its SDGs, and to highlight future technologies to help reduce the carbon footprint in their business processes.

Sustainability Career Pathways

Architectural Engineer. Alaa studied architectural engineering[9], which is a multidisciplinary approach to planning, designing, building, and operating buildings in ways that factor in energy use, environmental considerations, and sustainability. If you like to think about how to design sustainable buildings, you might want to consider a career in architectural engineering. Learn more here[10].

Permaculturalist. Agriculture can be extremely hard on the land in a variety of ways, including by expanding desertification. On the other hand, it can also be restorative. Permaculture[11] agricultural practices can produce higher yields, employ more farmers, heal the land, and not harm people or animals. Today there are hundreds of opportunities for training in permaculture, which can be applied on large farms, small farmsteads, in back yards, urban or school gardens, or anywhere you might raise plants. Learn more at freepermaculture.com[12], which has an online introduction to permaculture, and a database of permaculture jobs and volunteer opportunities.

Environmental Security Expert. Just as climate change and desertification can cause conflict over shrinking resources, conflict can in turn inflict ecological damage. The new field of environmental security[13] works to reduce environmental conflicts, and prevent environmental damage caused by conflict. Jobs are available in governments, with the United Nations, or with institutions like the World Bank, and in think tanks like the Woodrow Wilson Center's Environmental Change and Security Program[14], which offers internships[15] in the field.

1 https://www.youtube.com/watch?v=Shk9Liavzqk

2 https://www.womenpeacesecurity.org/resource/statement-unsc-wps-open-debate-october-2019/

3 https://tropicsu.org/

4 https://mass.pbslearningmedia.org/resource/249a2eb4-0461-4361-b81e-3e071d40e37c/farming-the-desert-science-lesson-plan/

5 https://tradingeconomics.com/sudan/precipitation

6 https://sustainabledevelopment.un.org/memberstates/sudan

7 https://www.unep.org/resources/report/sudan-first-state-environment-outlook-report-2020

8 https://ctcgroupltd.com/sustainability

9 https://en.wikipedia.org/wiki/Architectural_engineering

10 https://www.ae.psu.edu/academics/what-is-architectural-engineering.aspx

11 https://en.wikipedia.org/wiki/Permaculture

12 https://www.freepermaculture.com/

13 https://en.wikipedia.org/wiki/Environmental_security

14 https://www.wilsoncenter.org/program/environmental-change-and-security-program

15 https://www.wilsoncenter.org/opportunity/internships-the-environmental-change-and-security-program

To the Ends of the Earth...and Back

Parker Liautaud, Arctic Expeditions
California

Parker Liautaud is an Arctic explorer and environmental campaigner. By the time he was17, he had already made three expeditions to the Arctic.

In 2010 he and Arctic explorer and environmental campaigner Doug Stoup made a well-publicized attempt to reach the geographic North Pole: it was Parker's goal to be the youngest person to ever set foot there. However, the weather conditions did not allow them to achieve their goal, and they had to abort the mission. Parker was deeply disappointed. But he didn't give up: and in 2013, he and Doug embarked on The Willis Resilience Expedition, a scientific and exploratory expedition aimed at reaching the South Pole to study climate change. On this expedition, they set a record for making the fastest human-powered trek from the coast of Antarctica to the South Pole, and in the process, Parker became the youngest man in history to complete the journey to the South Pole. Now, as a policy advisor to the White House Office of Science and Technology Policy, he is helping to address the challenges of climate change. Parker has been recognized by Time Magazine's 30 under 30. He has spoken at and been interviewed by such prestigious outlets as the World Economic Forum, TEDx, the United Nations Foundation, The Wall Street Journal, and the Clinton Global Initiative.

Call to Action

Learn more about Parker's advocacy work as an environmental campaigner at One Young World. www.oneyoungworld.com

Values

- Courage
- Curiosity
- Perseverance
- Determination
- Environmentalism

Lessons Learned

Let your passion guide you, and remember that setbacks can be opportunities to become stronger.

When feeling overwhelmed by the task ahead, remember Ernest Shackleton's words: "Difficulties are just things to overcome."

When you see problems that need to be addressed, rather than waiting for someone else to intervene, think about what you could do to begin to solve them.

When you face frustrating circumstances in your personal life, try to think about how you could become involved in something larger than yourself.

Language Arts

Write a research paper about the meaning of a 3-degree C increase in the temperature in Antarctica: What are the consequences of this increase? What is causing it? What can be done to stop it, or even reverse it?

Write a short story about what it would be like to be in an Arctic, or Antarctic, expedition at your age: How would you feel about it? What would you be excited about? What would your expectations be?

Working in groups of 3-5, create an informational campaign about the current situation in Antarctica. Your campaign must include videos, pictures, and written material (including two blog posts) about the situation at the South Pole.

STEM Activities

The following lesson plans are from the National Museum of Natural History[1].

This lesson plan on glaciers[2] introduces students to the carbon cycle, the greenhouse effect, the impact of glacial melting on sea level rise, and feedback mechanisms. Students explore the issues and impacts of climate change associated with melting glaciers in polar regions by modeling the carbon cycle.

In this lesson plan on teleconnections[3], students analyze data to study how events and conditions in one location can affect the climate/weather in a distant location, especially the polar regions. Students use a spreadsheet to analyze historical data and determine El Nino and La Nina events based on their graphs.

In this lesson on Arctic plants[4], students analyze the ability of these plants to absorb different wavelengths of light, and describe how this affects animals living in different biomes. Students analyze photos taken through various filters, and explore spectral data taken by satellites.

How much have glaciers melted in the last 50 years? Calculate the average rate of ice loss. Has the average rate of loss increased, decreased, or stayed the same over the years? Assuming the current trend continues, how long will it take for the world's glaciers to disappear? How do glacial lakes contribute to increased flooding in areas like Germany, the Alps, and the Third Pole? Sources: Bloomberg article[5], ABC News article[6].

Sustainability Innovations

Climate change is drastically affecting the globe, but the Arctic, in particular, is being dramatically affected. This National Snow and Ice Data Center article[7] highlights climate change, and maps the thermal effects in the Arctic. Why has the temperature increase in the Arctic doubled compared to the rest of the globe over the past 30 years?

In addition to the direct effect on glaciers and the environment, other ecosystems are also disproportionately affected by the drastic effects of climate change in the Arctic. This World Wildlife Fund article[8] addresses the effects on those ecosystems, and explains how either positive or negative changes would further affect these ecosystems.

Watch this video[9] of Parker explaining his journey from exploring the South Pole to serving as a policy advisor for natural resources at the White House Office of Science and Technology Policy. What is a policy advisor? How can Parker assist in the fight against climate change?

Sustainability Career Pathways

Policy Advisor. Policy advisors research and analyze policies in various fields, and help make recommendations for policymakers, government agencies, schools, businesses, think tanks, and so on. Do you love research and analysis? Learn more about being a policy advisor here[10].

Explorer. There are parts of the world still to explore--from Antarctica to the bottom of the ocean -- and many scientific discoveries still to be made. One can be a geographic explorer, a scientific explorer, an archaeological explorer, or even an explorer who explores new destinations and writes about them for travel agencies and magazines. Learn more about being an explorer here[11].

Climatologist (Climate Scientist). Climate scientists devote their careers to better understanding the scope, causes, and effects of the climate crisis--and communicating these to others. Want to become a climate scientist? Here is an introduction to the field[12].

Actuary. Because of climate change, insurance is a rapidly changing business. It is also an industry that is helping to shape the climate discussion. Actuaries help calculate the risks and payouts for insurance policies. Curious? Check out this article on being an actuary, and five other interesting jobs in the insurance industry[13].

1 https://www.amnh.org/

2 https://www.amnh.org/learn-teach/curriculum-collections/polar-climate-change-lesson-plans/why-are-the-glaciers-melting

3 https://www.amnh.org/learn-teach/curriculum-collections/polar-climate-change-lesson-plans/teleconnections

4 https://www.amnh.org/learn-teach/curriculum-collections/polar-climate-change-lesson-plans/is-it-getting-greener

5 https://www.bloomberg.com/news/articles/2021-04-28/glaciers-are-melting-more-rapidly-risking-floods-and-droughts

6 https://abcnews.go.com/International/risk-flooding-melted-glaciers-increase-climate-warms-study/story?id=77505422

7 https://nsidc.org/cryosphere/arctic-meteorology/climate_change.html

8 https://www.worldwildlife.org/pages/six-ways-loss-of-arctic-ice-impacts-everyone

9 https://www.youtube.com/watch?v=i1YzSt1uVys

10 https://www.zippia.com/policy-advisor-jobs/

11 https://careertrend.com/list-6317181-types-explorer-jobs.html

12 https://www.environmentalscience.org/career/climatologist

13 https://americasprofessor.com/general/6-profitable-and-interesting-jobs-in-the-insurance-industry/

Turning Trash into Trees

Vihaan & Nav Agarwal, One Step Greener
India

Call to Action

Segregate your trash. Produce less trash in the first place. Buy fewer packaged products. Learn more about Vihaan's and Nav's work at www.onestepgreener.org.

Values

- Innovative
- Inspiring
- Environmentalist
- Dedicated
- Community Service
- Compassion

Lessons Learned

You are never too young to do something to improve the world around you.

You can be a source of inspiration for others, regardless of your age.

Don't be afraid to ask questions, experiment, and innovate. That is how great ideas are born!

When Vihaan Agarwal read about a fire at a large landfill in Delhi, he learned that trash was causing almost 20 percent of the city's air pollution.

He decided to do something about it; and together with his younger brother Nav, he started One Step Greener, an organization that collects and separates trash, and recycles it. Then they use the money they earn from picking up and selling waste from more than 700 households in Delhi to plant urban forests, to further improve air quality.

"When you do something that actually creates a difference, everyone will want to do something that is as inspiring as the things you do," Vihaan says. He adds, "What you're doing might not make a difference directly, but the domino effect it creates will create huge change-- even something as small as planting a tree in your backyard."

Language Arts

Find out what the greatest environmental issue is in your community. Then write a cause-and-effect essay in which you discuss the link between that particular environmental issue and public health problems in your area.

Write a children's story about Vihaan and Nav's "trash experiment," and include illustrations. Focus on these two questions: What did the brothers learn? How did this inspire them to found One Step Greener?

Write a short story in which you explain what air pollution is; but write it from the perspective of one of the old trees in Vihaan's neighbourhood who has now been joined by newly planted trees. How does the old tree feel about the newcomers?

STEM Activities

Create a chart that displays the amount of waste produced and recycled materials in the United States, and nine other countries of your choice. Compare the results and the population sizes of each country. Then try to explain what you think the causes of the differences from country to country might be.

Explain the difference between the benefits of recycling e-waste versus the benefits of recycling traditional materials. Which one do you think is most common? Why are recycling problems different in some countries?

- **Example:** China, India, and the U.S. are three of the leaders in e-waste. Why is this, and what should be done about it?

Create a Venn diagram that compares and contrasts the culture and lifestyles in India and in the United States. Focus on CO2 emissions; trees planted per square mile; amount of electronic waste recycled per capita; and overall recycling rates over the past 5 years. Conduct research to see if your assumptions in the previous activities were correct or not. Then explain why projects like Vihaan's and Nav's are essential to both India and the United States.

Sustainability Innovations

One Step Greener[1] has expanded their separation of trash to include composting, e-waste, and tree planting. They have expanded from simply targeting the resulting trash to also assessing and identifying environmental laws in India than need to shift their focus to recycling.

In addition to the original goals of One Step Greener, the expansion to composting and dealing with e-waste is important. Many people understand the importance of recycling, but they do not always associate it with electronics. The EPA - International E-waste Management Network[2] has helped officials from around the world be able to collaborate and together address the threats that e-waste poses to our environment.

The Nature Conservancy[3] is one organization that has had a great influence on all aspects of sustainability. In addition to their commitment to recycling waste and planting trees, they have more than 100 marine conservation projects, and they operate in more than 70 countries, helping individuals like Vihaan and Nav who are striving to bring about positive change.

The Netherlands is one of the world's leaders in e-waste recycling. The Journal of Engineering[4] posted this article highlighting the importance of recycling e-waste, and the amount of harmful materials that have been recycled in the Netherlands.

The concept of a circular economy is an economic system in which economic growth is redefined, with a focus on creating products that have positive, society-wide benefits. Fairphone[5] is a sustainable smartphone designed for long life that can be completely dismantled and recreated with recyclable parts. Would you like to help design goods that last a long time, and that at the end of their usefulness can be fed, with zero waste, into the next generation of products? Learn more about the circular economy and get inspired here[6].

Sustainability Career Pathways

Local Recycling Coordinator. Most states, like Connecticut[7], require every town to have a recycling coordinator to help residents and businesses get their recyclable waste recycled. Many corporations also have dedicated recycling managers, and recycling plants need many employees to manage their operations. If you want to help ensure that waste is turned into new products instead of just becoming garbage, the field of recycling may be for you. If you are interested in the field of recycling, read here[8].

Extended Producer Responsibility Manager. More countries are requiring corporations to be responsible for the goods they produce, from creation to disposal, including how products are packaged. This means that there are many new jobs being created; in government, to oversee Extended Producer Responsibility (EPR); in companies, to manage the packaging, recycling, and disposal of goods; and in nonprofit organizations, to help companies effectively manage environmental requirements. EPR is a growing expectation for increasing number of products, including electronic products, and even mattresses-- thus it is a future career path with much potential. If you want to learn more, start with this overview[9].

Designer in the Circular Economy. Recognizing that waste represents a significant cost to companies as well as to the planet, a whole new generation of designers is creating products that can be fully dismantled--reusing long-lived parts, recycling worn parts, and enabling repair and replace services for goods that do not have the toxic disposability (and planned obsolescence) often designed into these goods. For example, while most phones can't be easily recycled or repaired, and are designed to have a lifespan of only a few years.

---

1 https://www.onestepgreener.org/

2 https://www.epa.gov/international-cooperation/where-epa-works-around-world

3 https://www.nature.org/en-us/get-involved/how-to-help/plant-a-billion/

4 https://www.researchgate.net/publication/318804805_The_Circular_Economy_of_E-Waste_in_the_Netherlands_Optimizing_Material_Recycling_and_Energy_Recovery

5 https://www.fairphone.com/en/

6 https://ellenmacarthurfoundation.org/topics/circular-economy-introduction/overview

7 https://portal.ct.gov/DEEP/Reduce-Reuse-Recycle/Local-Municipal-Recycling-Coordinators

8 https://bestaccreditedcolleges.org/articles/recycling-coordinator-job-description-duties-salary.html

9 https://en.wikipedia.org/wiki/Extended_producer_responsibility

Traveling with a Purpose

Jessa Garibay-Yayen, Center for Sustainability PH
Philippines

☀ Call to Action

Empower local people to protect their lands.
Know your rights. Get it on paper!

☀ Values

- Community Service
- Commitment
- Cooperation
- Solidarity
- Environmentalism

☀ Lessons Learned

The best way to create a positive impact in the world is to work with other people who share that goal. Go out into the world and find them!

It is important to allow younger generations to become involved in conservation. They bring not only passion and energy, but new ideas and skills to the fight for the Earth.

If you want to protect the environment, look no further than your backyard. Preserve and protect the place you live, and you will make an impact in the world.

As a teenager, every year at the start of the rainy season, Jessa would wake up at 4 a.m. to celebrate the Feast of the Forest.

"It's a massive community event," she says. "We're all hauled in gigantic garbage trucks and taken up to the mountains to plant trees." When she was 21, she went to the United States to work with EarthCorps, where she met youth environmental leaders from other countries. Then she returned home to create the Centre for Sustainability PH in the Philippines (CSPH), a women-led youth environmental conservation NGO. "We believe the best way to ensure the sustainability of our island is by legally protecting our natural resources," Jessa says.
She works with local people to help them understand how their lands are being ravaged by illegal logging, mining, monocropping, and poaching. Now 29, the heart of Jessa's work is focused on conserving the forests. "We want to conserve as much forest as possible in the next 10 years," she says. "If we as youth all act together, support each other, and help each other rise up, the impact we can have is unimaginable."

☀ Language Arts

What is a metaphor? What is the meaning of Jessa's "Avocado Moment"? Write an explanatory essay in which you explain what a metaphor is, and how Jessa's metaphor works in terms of referring to learning about the world.

How has unsustainable tourism affected the Philippines, specifically the Palawan region? Working in groups of 3-5 students, create a presentation in which you explain what unsustainable tourism is, and how it has adversely affected this region of the world.

Look at the list of sustainable career pathways below and reorganize them by personal preference (from the one

you're most interested in to the one you find the least attractive). Then create a series of three short videos (one for each career), in which you motivate young people to become involved in these careers. Your video must explain what the career consists of, where they can train for it, and why they should consider it.

STEM Activities

Research the forests of the Philippines. What has caused the forests to decrease in area to just 3 percent of what they used to be? How are forests tied to the economy of the Philippines? Explore and analyze some of the solutions that are being used to manage the remaining forests. Are they effective? What other sustainable practices can be implemented to help protect the forests?

Imagine that you are in charge of 1,200 acres of forested land that will be harvested in the next year. Develop a brief management plan based on the following: cutting practice, regeneration, timber value, habitat, and resource protection.

Create an interactive graph that illustrates the decrease of forest land in the Philippines over time. Source: Global Forest Watch[1].

Sustainability Innovations

As the cofounder of the Centre for Sustainability PH[2], Jessica has shed light on the importance of forestation and habitat maintenance in the Philippines. What are the flagship projects for this center, and how are they evolving?

In this Rappler article[3], the situation of forests in the Philippines is addressed, based on the effects of government policy and regional climate change. How has the combination of governmental decisions and climate issues affected various regions in the Philippines?

Deforestation and climate change don't only impact the people; they also affect wildlife in the area. The Department of Environment and Natural Resources and USAID launched a five-year wildlife program (2016-2021) that targeted the wildlife trade and degradation of animal sanctuaries in the area. What has resulted from this program? What more could be done to protect animals in the Philippines?

Sustainability Career Pathways

Sustainable Tourism Industry. Tourism can help inspire a deeper connection to the Earth and to other cultures. The growing sustainable tourism sector embeds environmental knowledge in tours, makes hotels greener, encourages more local experiences, and so on. There are many ways to be part of this industry, from tour operator, to travel guide, from hotelier, to turning part of your home into an AirBnB and offering green tours of your town. If this is a path for you, read these 10 tips on how to make a career in sustainable tourism[4].

Conservationist. Do you want to help preserve and protect wildlife habitats, and their many rare and awe-inspiring wildlife inhabitants? Conservationists play many different roles: as advocates, liaisons with government and affected communities, managers, fundraisers, and so much more. This witty essay looks at the 12 different types of conservationist[5] you could be. And this article gives a more thorough introduction to the field[6].

Lobbyist. As Jessa discovered, one of the best ways to protect nature is with the law. Lobbying elected officials for change is an essential part of social change (especially when supported by grassroots organizing). Some make a full-time career lobbying; others lobby as part of larger campaigns. Want to be a lobbyist? Start here[7].

Endnotes

1https://gfw.global/3qYLkVD

2 https://centreforsustainabilityph.org/what-we-do

3 https://www.rappler.com/environment/hectares-land-philippines-forested/

4 https://sustainability-leaders.com/ten-tips-sustainable-tourism-career/

5 http://www.jamesborrell.com/the-12-types-of-conservation-career-and-how-to-choose-which-one-is-for-you/

6 https://www.thebalancecareers.com/conservationist-526002

7 https://www.princetonreview.com/careers/88/lobbyist#:~:text=There%20are%20no%20licensing%20or,future%20lobbyists%20in%20good%20stead.

We Are The Leaders Of Today

Kevin J. Patel, One Up Action
California

Call to Action

Make yourself heard about climate initiatives in your hometown. Join the discussion about what is being done on the issues that directly affect you. Get the support you need from One Up Action: oneupaction.org.

Values

- Pioneer
- Committed
- Citizen Leader
- Environmentalist
- Solidarity

Lessons Learned

Health issues and climate issues are intertwined.

Many affluent communities are not as affected by the climate crisis as marginalized communities are.

In the face of adversity, people need to step up.

When Kevin was in sixth grade, suddenly his heart started acting crazy.

He was rushed to the hospital, where he learned that he had heart palpitations caused by smog and air pollution. His health crisis inspired him to become an environmental activist. First, he started an environmental club in his school. Later he started One Up Action, an organization that supports young climate activists from marginalized communities.

"I wanted to create an organization that can give funds to young changemakers and help them by providing them with connections and opportunities," he says. He also created a Youth Climate Commission that is advising the Los Angeles County administration on climate initiatives. "Young people are very, very smart," Kevin says. "We are not only the leaders of tomorrow. We are the leaders of today."

Language Arts

Drawing on Kevin's experience, research how pollution (air, water, or soil) can affect young people. Then, with the information you have found, create a series of posters to use in an information campaign. In a separate essay, explain why you chose the images and words you chose, and which type of social media you would use for your information campaign.

Create a series of 4-6 TikTok videos that explains the concept of environmental justice through the use of concrete examples.

Write a speech aimed at local political leaders in which you explain and make the case for supporting the UN's 17 Sustainable Development Goals.

Write a Facebook post inviting people to actively partici-

pate in Kevin's organization, One Up Action. Explain not only what the group does, but why it is important, and how it can benefit society as a whole.

STEM Activities

Like most highly motivated students, Kevin's ability to organize and unite people began when he organized the environmental club at his school. Find out what clubs are offered at your school. Then design the structure for a club that addresses a sustainable issue that is not being currently addressed by the clubs at your school. Select a teacher or member of your community to be the advisor for your club.

Kevin often refers to marginalized communities and issues that he and others face living in Los Angeles. Compare the carbon footprint of LA to that of the town that you live in, and two other major cities. Display this data on a graph and explain how it is related to climate change.

Write a note, or create a presentation to send to the 25 members of the Youth Climate Commission in LA about an issue that you would like to assist in solving.

Monitor the air quality in your community, and identify some of the factors that may be contributing to the deterioration of air quality.

Sustainability Innovations

Kevin's organization, One Up Action[1] , enables anyone to start their own youth climate commission by completing the forms available on their website. Kevin belongs to the only West Coast-based Youth Climate Commission Chapter in the United States. What is holding you back from joining him in this cause?

There are many organizations striving to create a more sustainable future for the people of Los Angeles. California Green Works[2] and Communities for a Better Environment[3] are two leaders in aiding communities of color and improving the sustainable footprint of Urban LA Communities.

In addition to progressive efforts like One Up Action, organizations like Tree People[4] have been working on making Los Angeles greener for 45 years. Tree People strives to educate people about the importance of trees, and how they affect greenhouse gas, water management, and making the city's air more breathable.

Sustainability Career Pathways

Climate Activist. When asked what role young people should play in solving the climate crisis, Kevin responded, "We should all be activists." Climate activism is a career path listed time and again in these lesson plans; that's because without climate activism we cannot stop the climate crisis. Interested in becoming a climate activist? You can get active locally right now. Join your school environmental group, or a nearby chapter of Fridays for the Future, Extinction Rebellion, the Sunrise Movement, or Kevin's group, One Up Action. If there are no chapters in your community, you can start your own. As you develop your activist skills, many full-time activism opportunities will open to you.

Environmental Protection Agency (EPA). National and state governments play an essential role in regulating and enforcing environmentally sustainable behavior. Working for the EPA or for your local environmental department can be a rewarding and useful career path. The EPA employs 15,000 people around the United States, and needs people with a variety of skills, from communications to computer programming. Want to learn more? Visit here[5]. Other agencies, from the Department of Agriculture and the Department of Energy to the Bureau of Land Management also offer many opportunities to help protect the environment and make a difference in your community.

Environmental and Public Health Advocate or Practitioner. The quality of the environment has a direct effect on human health--from air and water quality and exposure to toxins to the amount of green space present in communities. You could become an advocate for environmental health[6] or public health; or, by becoming a doctor, nurse, or medical professional, you can draw attention to the links between environmental and human well- being. Here is an introduction to the field of environmental health[7].

Greengrocer. Like Kevin, about 23 million Americans[8] live in "food deserts," neighborhoods that have little or no access to fresh food and produce. But there are ongoing efforts to build grocery stores, natural food stores, and farmers markets in inner cities, helping to remedy the poor health and nutrition suffered by residents of these communities. Are you interested in starting a farmers market, or becoming a manager of a sustainable grocery store? This is a career that can really help your community. Here's a nice overview of what it's like to manage a grocery store[9]. Want to start a farmers market? Here's a great introduction from the USDA[10], and a longer guide from the Texas Department of Agriculture[11].

1 https://oneupaction.org/ycc-final/
2 https://californiagreenworks.org/
3 http://www.cbecal.org/
4 https://www.treepeople.org/about/what-we-do
5 https://www.epa.gov/careers/why-work-epa
6 https://www.healthypeople.gov/2020/topics-objectives/topic/environmental-health
7 https://www.apha.org/topics-and-issues/environmental-health
8 https://www.ncbi.nlm.nih.gov/pmc/articles/PMC7299236/
9 https://thegrocerystoreguy.com/what-does-a-grocery-store-manager-do/
10 https://sfyl.ifas.ufl.edu/agriculture/starting-a-farmers-market/
11 https://farmersmarketcoalition.org/wp-content/uploads/2017/03/FarmersMarketGuide-online_version_lo-res.pdf

An Inconvenient Youth

Linus Dolder, Fridays For Future Germany
Switzerland / Germany

Call to Action

Don't be afraid to speak up. You won't be alone: you will find people who are willing to stand with you in the fight against climate change. www.fridaysforfuture.org.
You can follow Linus on Twitter & Instagram @linusdolder

Values

- Commitment
- Energy
- Collaboration
- Leadership
- Environmentalism

Lessons Learned

Raise your voice to protect your own future, and the future of the planet.

Anger can be used as an engine for change. Use it carefully and wisely.

If you want to promote change, start with an open dialogue about the key issues. In other words, listen as well as speak.

Keep fighting for what you believe in. Don't give up!

Linus Dolder has been an environmentalist from an early age -- he used to organize bake sales with his friends to raise money for environmental organizations.

But he soon realized that wasn't enough. So when the Fridays for Future movement started, he decided to organize a strike in his hometown, and to his surprise he and his friends gathered a crowd of 800 people. "We all felt so empowered, because we just put tons of effort in," Linus said. "We got them to come here, we got them to raise their voices. It felt so great!" Soon, he started to organize even bigger events, and he joined the international movement of climate strikers. "With good campaigning and smart strategic moves, we're actually able to change some things," Linus said. "I doubt there's anything at the moment that makes me happier."

Language Arts

Using Linus's example of Switzerland, do you think the wealthier countries, who are the biggest polluters, should take a greater share of the responsibility for preventing or dealing with climate change? Write an argumentative essay agreeing or disagreeing with this position. Support your opinion using secondary sources.

What makes a campaign successful? What do you need to consider when designing one? Choose an environmental issue you'd like to be involved with. Then, after researching the topic, create a video that explains how to build a successful campaign to promote change in environmental issues, and show your video to your peers.

After watching everyone's videos in class, conduct a Round Table discussion[1] in which you talk about how to better engage the people in your community in the cause of fighting global warming.

STEM Activities

Is there evidence that climate change has arrived in your "backyard"? Identify something in your community that has been impacted by climate change (for example, heat waves, floods, drought, desertification, fewer birds and other species, etc.). Then research the possible causes of these changes. Design a project that your community can participate in to help mitigate the effects. Then create a presentation based on your findings and solutions.

In this activity from Carleton College[2], students build skills and gain experience in analyzing and interpreting real geologic data on the Grinnell Glacier in Glacier National Park, to estimate when the glacier will be completely melted. For more recent data on the Grinnell Glacier, students can use Google Earth imagery, USGS repeat photographs[3], or images from the Glaciers of the American West[4].

This lesson plan from TropICSU[5] teaches students about the geomorphic characteristics of mountains, different types of mountains, and major mountain systems of the world. What factors determine mountain climates, and how do they affect the surrounding regional climates? Given these factors, how can climate change impact mountain climates, and in turn, regional climates?

Sustainability Innovations

Innovations like the Solar-Powered Mountainous Farm[6] in the Swiss Alps are vital for making progress and learning how to take advantage of our natural resources. How is this farm contributing to dealing with the effects of climate change? How could the principles they are developing be applied elsewhere?

As global warming continues, organizations like CIPRA[7] are critical in order to preserve the Alpine region. Review CIPRA's projects and learn how they are educate individuals about the challenges in the Alpine region.

What are the key aspects of environmental protection in Switzerland? This article[8] addresses this topic and explains how innovation is essential to environmental sustainability in Switzerland.

Sustainability Career Pathways

Glaciologist. Do you love ice and mountains? Why not study glaciers? Glaciologists do research on glaciers, explore, and often teach. Get to know the job here[9] and the field of glaciology here[10].

Sustainable Baker. Germany encourages youths to follow their passions and even provides apprenticeship tracks[11] to study everything from engineering to baking. Baking is a valuable career path and entrepreneurial bakers are forging ways to make this field more sustainable. Read more about sustainable bakeries, here[12] and here[13], and how to become a baker here[14].

International Governance Advocate. The United Nations Environment Programme[15] is playing a critical role in creating a more sustainable, more equitable future. UNEP has jobs and internships available here[16]. Other UN agencies, like the UN Development Programme[17], also are worth checking out.

Digital Organizer. Much movement-building occurs online now, through email, social media, and other communication tools. Becoming an expert in these areas helps build and sustain global movements like Fridays for Future. Learn some useful tactics here[18], and explore job opportunities at Climatebase.org[19].

1 https://www.youtube.com/watch?v=KvhPDg6EH7U&t=134s

2 https://serc.carleton.edu/quantskills/activities/glacial_retreat.html

3 https://www.usgs.gov/centers/norock/science/grinnell-glacier-mount-gould-1938-1981-1998-2015?qt-

4 http://glaciers.geos.pdx.edu/

5 https://climatescienceteaching.org/lesson/mountains/overview

6 https://www.euronews.com/green/2021/05/14/extraordinary-views-from-the-world-s-first-mountainous-solar-farm

7 https://www.cipra.org/en

8 https://houseofswitzerland.org/swissstories/environment/key-aspects-environmental-protection-switzerland

9 https://www.careermatch.com/job-prep/career-insights/profiles/glaciologist/

10 https://en.wikipedia.org/wiki/Glaciology

11 https://en.wikipedia.org/wiki/Apprenticeship_in_Germany

12 https://www.ordermentum.com/blog/5-ideas-to-make-your-bakery-greener-and-more-sustainable

13 https://www.bakingbusiness.com/articles/33390-six-bakeries-making-sustainability-a-priority

14 https://www.allculinaryschools.com/baking-pastry/pastry-chef-interview/

15 https://www.unep.org/

16 https://www.unep.org/work-with-us

17 https://www.undp.org/careers

18 https://www.brightest.io/resources

19 https://climatebase.org/

Youth Unstoppable

Slater Jewell-Kemker, Youth Unstoppable
Canada

Call to Action

VOTE. If you're too young to vote, make sure the people around you are educated. It will take all of us, but we can adapt to climate change if we work together.
Follow Slater's work at www.youthunstoppable.com, @slaterfilms & linktr.ee/YouthUnstoppable

Values

- Perseverance
- Commitment
- Dedication
- Communication
- Environmentalism

Lessons Learned

Listen to people's stories and be inspired by them. And tell your story to inspire others.

Persevere. Even if everything seems lost, persevere.

Be unstoppable!

Slater has been a director since an early age: she shot her first movie when she was just six years old.
So when she joined the youth movement to fight climate change, she did so with a camera in her hand. Fifteen years later, she has produced a documentary about her time as an activist and the people around her: Youth Unstoppable.

Language Arts

Working in a group of 3-5 people, create a script, and then film a short movie (between 7 and 10 minutes) in which you discuss how climate change has affected your region of the country and what can be done to address the problem.

Conduct an interview with a member of your community or school who is interested in environmental issues. The interview must consist of 10-15 questions that address their interest in environmental causes; why they got interested in these causes; which organizations they are active in; and what their level of involvement is. Write down the results of your interview in a magazine format. Or submit it for publication in your school or local newspaper.

Write a research essay on the Paris agreement. What is it about? Why is it important? Which countries signed it? What are the consequences of the U.S. withdrawing from it? And from rejoining it?

STEM Activities

Using this dataset from the Environmental Protection Agency[1], graph the level of carbon emissions from the U.S since 1990. What years recorded the highest levels? What year recorded the lowest? What is the overall trend? Are carbon emissions increasing or decreasing since 1990? What about over the last five years?

After reading this article on lighting design[2], and this one on how lighting works on a film set[3], first explore, and then demonstrate how lighting design in theaters and movie production could be made more sustainable.

Optical engineers need to understand how light rays work in order to design and make cameras. In this activity from TeachEngineering.org[4], students construct their own pinhole cameras to observe the behavior of light. How does light travel? How does the size of the pinhole affect the brightness of the image? How does the size of the pinhole affect the sharpness of the image? How could you improve the camera?

Sustainability Innovations

Documentaries are often the best source of information about sustainability for young people. Review this article[5] highlighting 16 of the best environmental films. David Attenborough's newest film, A Life on Our Planet, is one of the films listed. How is the subject matter of Slater's film different from David Attenborough's? Why are they equally important?

In addition to producing the film Youth Unstoppable[6], Slater has created an impact distribution campaign to help engage kids in becoming part of the solution.

Review the Green Production Guide[7]. Why is it important to not only highlight the importance of sustainability in films, but also to implement sustainable strategies on the set?

Sustainability Career Pathways

Documentary Filmmaker. Film is a powerful tool for drawing attention to an issue and sparking change. Do you want to become a filmmaker? If so, here are some tips for you[8]. And here are some tips about how to actually make a living doing it.[9]

Storyteller: Telling stories inspires, informs, and encourages others to take action. Becoming a journalist (including for your school paper), blogger, novelist, podcaster, filmmaker, or some other kind of communicator can allow you to channel your storytelling skills to make a difference in the world. Learn more about storytelling here.[10]

Climate Activist. Visit Idealist.org[11] to explore hundreds of job openings in the climate movement, from climate law interns and campaign organizers, to consultants, and city climate specialists.

1 https://www.epa.gov/ghgemissions/sources-greenhouse-gas-emissions

2 https://www.buildinggreen.com/feature/lighting-design-health-and-sustainability-guide-architects

3 https://www.ibc.org/trends/green-production-how-to-be-sustainable-on-set/3883.article

4 https://www.teachengineering.org/activities/view/cub_soundandlight_lesson8_activity1

5 https://earth.org/best-environmental-films/

6 https://www.youthunstoppable.com/campaign

7 https://www.greenproductionguide.com/about-us/

8 https://www.masterclass.com/articles/ken-burns-shares-tips-for-becoming-a-documentarian#ken-burnss-7-tips-for-becoming-a-documentarian

9 https://www.desktop-documentaries.com/how-to-make-a-full-time-living-as-a-documentary-filmmaker.html

10 https://storynet.org/how-to-become-a-storyteller/

11 https://www.idealist.org/en/jobs?q=climate&searchMode=true&sort=relevance

II

RESPECT

Environmental Justice Changemakers

It's great to meet so many multicultural young people in this book who are environmental justice changemakers. They show us how we can be compassionate and courageous as we dialogue about this critical issue and do the work to create a more equitable, just and sustainable world.

Danny Glover

An Indigenous Leader

Evon Peter, Tanan Ch'at'oh
Alaska

☀ Call to Action

Support Gwich'in language revitalization: www.tananchatoh.com
Follow Evon on Twitter: @evonpeter
Visit www.nativemovement.org

☀ Values

- Community
- Respect
- Leadership
- Sustainability
- Environmentalism

☀ Lessons Learned

Respect for Indigenous peoples and their communities is key to sustainability.

If you want to make a difference, find where your true passion lies, and follow that path. Go back to your roots. They are the true source of your strength.

Learn to redefine the meaning of success by focusing on your skills and your own individual wisdom and decide how you can use them to help your community.

Evon Peter grew up in a village nearly 100 miles above the Arctic Circle.
Despite being surrounded by natural beauty, Evon faced challenges early in his life. His mother moved him to Fairbanks so he could have a better education, but when he was 14 the school counselor told him and other native boys they were more likely to end up dead, or in jail, by the time they were 25 than they were to graduate. Evon dropped out of high school, but later graduated from the University of Alaska. While in college, he became active in student government, organizing and co-leading a native student organization. This led to his lifelong quest to improve life for native peoples. Today he works with issues related to trauma and integrating Indigenous cultural practices with behavioral health interventions. His major goals are preventing suicide, which is at epidemic proportions in native communities, and preserving native Alaskan languages. He is also concerned about the effects of climate change: "It's impacting the health and well-being of our people," he says.

☀ Language Arts

Evon talks about the quality of his education in public school and his mother's education in boarding school. Conduct a Socratic Seminar in which you and your classmates discuss how education has been used as a tool for oppression in Indigenous communities, and how we can change that and use it as a tool for healing, growth, justice, equality, and multiculturalism.

How have climate change and pollution affected native communities in Alaska? Create a group presentation about this topic. Focus on the economic, cultural, social, and health consequences for these communities.

After watching Evon's video Indigenous Wisdom and Healing with Evon Peter[1], answer the following questions: How do Evon's definitions of success and wealth differ from our traditional definition? Do you agree with him that we should look at success and wealth from his point of view? Why is he opposed to Indigenous communities accepting contracts from the energy industry or the military? Do you think he is right? Why or why not? Discuss your answers with the rest of the class. After the discussion, write a brief paragraph in which you explain how this discussion has changed, or affected, your point of view on these issues.

Research boarding schools for Indigenous peoples. What was their purpose? Working in groups of 3-5 people, create a presentation in which you discuss colonialism: What it is? In what ways did the American government try to colonize Indigenous communities? What were some of the consequences of these attempts (both for the Indigenous populations and for the U.S.)? What can be done to heal the wounds these attempts have caused? After the presentations, conduct a Round Table[2] discussion on these subjects with your peers. Ask yourselves what you can do as a group, or individually, to help right past wrongs?

STEM Activities

In this media-rich lesson from PBS[3], explore the ways in which Alaska natives understand and relate to the world. Then complete a science fair project that demonstrates how traditional knowledge can be applied to a scientific topic. The lesson ends with a classroom science fair, during which projects are evaluated on both their cultural and scientific content.

In this lesson plan on permafrost[4], students will learn about permafrost and coastal erosion, and subsistence living, and will develop an understanding of how Alaska Native peoples rely on permafrost, and are being affected by changes to it.

Research the Arctic National Wildlife Refuge (ANWR) and brainstorm why it is protected. Why is this area important to the Gwich'in? What resources does it provide that they rely on? Why is it important to their history and culture? In what ways are the Gwich'in being negatively affected by climate change?

Sustainability Innovations

Evon expanded his work by assessing oppressive systemic power structures as a member of Native Movement[5]. Today, Native Movement thrives by allowing members to shape their own leadership models through an Indigenous worldwide view. How could such a view affect someone's place-based knowledge and sense of community?

When addressing climate change, organizations of all sizes assess the impact that Indigenous people have on the land. The UN[6] has identified the challenges and opportunities for Indigenous peoples in sustainability; in particular, in using traditional knowledge to solve climate issues.

In this Yale School of the Environment article[7], native tribes and their ability to lead the movement against climate change is addressed. Their deeply rooted ties to tradition and the Earth allow native tribes to better prepare for preserving sustainable practices for future generations.

Sustainability Career Pathways

Environmental Mental Health Counselor. As environmental conditions worsen, more people will suffer mental health challenges due to the effects of climate change, and fears about the looming sustainability crisis[8]. This is another reason to consider the field of psychology, mental health counseling, or even ecotherapy[9] (which uses nature to help heal psychological trauma). Here is a brief introduction to the field[10]. If you want to gain some experience now, the Samaritan Helpline--which offers free counseling for those suffering from depression, loneliness, and suicidal thoughts—also offers free training to those who commit to volunteer for the helpline for nine months[11].

Indigenous Educator. Educational opportunities are valued highly in Indigenous communities, and yet they may be less available. Have you considered teaching Indigenous students--especially in ways that value and respect the culture and history of these peoples[12]? The Indigenous Educators Corps helps to place teachers in Indigenous communities. Learn more here[13].

University Administrator. It's not only professors who work at universities. Administrators (an average of 500 per university) maintain everything from admissions and financial aid to budgeting, housing, diversity coordination, and sustainability planning; they help keep these centers of education running smoothly. If a career in university administration sounds interesting to you, learn more here[14].

1 https://www.youtube.com/watch?v=pDeL209qVro
2 https://www.youtube.com/watch?v=KvhPDg6EH7U
3 https://mass.pbslearningmedia.org/resource/ean08.sci.ess.earthsys.lpnativeways/alaska-native-ways-of-knowing/
4 https://www.alaska.edu/k12reach/pdf-lessons/mshs-lessons/permafrost_thaw_teacher_guide_HS.pdf
5 https://www.nativemovement.org/leadership-development
6 https://www.un.org/development/desa/dspd/2021/04/indigenous-peoples-sustainability/
7 https://e360.yale.edu/features/how-native-tribes-are-taking-the-lead-on-planning-for-climate-change
8 https://www.latimes.com/politics/story/2020-12-27/for-young-californians-climate-change-is-a-mental-health-crisis-too
9 https://www.goodtherapy.org/learn-about-therapy/types/econature-therapy
10 https://onlinecounselingprograms.com/become-a-counselor/counseling-careers/mental-health-counselor/
11 https://samaritanshope.org/get-involved/volunteer-on-the-helpline/
12 https://en.wikipedia.org/wiki/Indigenous_education
13 https://www.nacainspiredschoolsnetwork.org/nisn-americorps-opportunities
14 https://www.princetonreview.com/careers/40/college-administrator

An Indigenous Rebel with a Cause

Lucia Ixchiu, Festivales Solidarios
Guatemala

☀ Call to Action

Join with others in your community to fight for a cleaner, safer, sustainable environment. Inspire others to join you through the use of art & music. Support Festivales Solidarios: @festivalesgt on Twitter

☀ Values

- Solidarity
- Justice
- Equality
- Leadership
- Environmentalism

☀ Lessons Learned

Our choices define us.

Creativity, education, and passion are essential for success in all endeavors in life.

Let what you love the most inspire you to fight for change.

Lucia Xchiu's first act of activism came early: when she was four years old she became the first girl to ever take karate lessons in her Indigenous community. When she was older, she founded Festivales Solidarios — a music and art gathering that seeks to protect land defenders and free political prisoners in Guatemala. A lawyer, journalist, activist, and artist, Lucia doesn't fit into the boxes typically drawn around Indigenous women. Her mission is to support her community through nonviolent activism and awareness building around issues like human rights and climate change.

☀ Language Arts

Write a research essay about the plight of Indigenous peoples in Guatemala: What are their living conditions like? How is their culture, economy, standard of living, and access to basic services being affected by politics? What is being done to help them?

Working in groups of 2-4 people, create a presentation about how the effects of climate change have increased the importance of Lucia's work and that of others who are protecting land defenders among the Indigenous peoples of Guatemala.

Working in groups of 3-5, create an information campaign about Human Rights violations against Indigenous populations in Guatemala. Your campaign must include a 5-minute video, 6-8 Instagram posts, one Facebook post (at least 500 words long), and a series of 10-12 Twitter messages.

STEM Activities

Using the dataset links below and a spreadsheet (or a graphing calculator, or graphing by hand), construct a line graph of Guatemalan men and women (horizontal axis) and the percentage of people below the poverty level (vertical axis). Then on the same graph, plot the percentages of Indigenous people who are below the poverty level. Label the graphs "Total number of people" and "Indigenous people." What can you say about these variables? Resources: Dataset from the World Bank[1], data from MacroTrends[2], Borgen Project[3].

Guatemala's Maya Biosphere Reserve was established in 1990 to protect the rainforest from accelerating levels of deforestation, illegal logging, and forest fires. Individuals known as land and environmental protectors are also on the front lines of protecting the earth's land, but oftentimes they are killed. Create a graph or chart highlighting the total number of land defenders who have been killed since 2002. What percentage of those killed were from Guatemala? What is the average rate of growth or decline in the total number of people killed since 2002? Is the average rate of those killed in Guatemala higher or lower than the total? After reading this article[4], who or what do you think is perpetuating these killings (industries? governments? or others?).

- **Sources: Land and Environmental Defenders: Annual Report Archive from Global Witness[5]**
- **Using this resource on literacy rates of various groups in Guatemala[6], what is the average rate of growth or decline in literacy rates among women between 1960 and 2020?** Write an equation to calculate the average. Calculate the instantaneous rate of change for the years 1960, 1980, 2000, and 2020 using the derivative. Has the average rate of change increased or decreased over the years?

Sustainability Innovations

Lucia has built Festivale Solidarios - Medium[7] as a way to highlight issues occurring in Guatemala City and its surrounding areas. Many of the articles address the protection of land defenders and explain why it's extremely important in Guatemala City.

Review this circular economy project[8] in Guatemala City. How did the establishment of AbonOrganiCo assist the community in their transition towards sustainability?

How has Guatemala adjusted to the challenges of the COVID-19 pandemic? This article[9] highlights how Indigenous people were affected by the pandemic.

Sustainability Career Pathways

Defender of Environmental and Indigenous Rights Activists. Indigenous peoples are often bold defenders of the Earth, and are thus often subject to threat or violence. Supporting them in their quest to protect and heal the land can be a valuable way to help. Groups like the Center for International Environmental Law (CIEL) undertake efforts to protect environmental activists. Learn about CIEL's work here[10].

Musician. Music, like other forms of art, is a powerful way to draw attention to environmental causes, as this article[11] demonstrates. It's not easy to become a professional musician, but it is possible: this article explains how[12].

Green Architect. Architects, by their very work of designing buildings, can play a huge role in creating a more sustainable future. For example, designing energy efficient, passive solar, healthy buildings means that less energy will be used in heating and cooling. Interested in designing buildings? Learn how to be an architect here[13].

Martial Arts Instructor. There are few sports more sustainable than martial arts, where one needs little to no equipment, not even shoes! While martial arts are not as popular as they once were, there are more than 20,000 martial arts schools in the United States. Want to be an instructor? First find a school[14] and become a master; then look for an instructor job, or start your own dojo[15].

1 https://databank.worldbank.org/data/download/poverty/987B9C90-CB9F-4D93-AE8C-750588BF00QA/SM2020/Global_POVEQ_GTM.pdf

2 https://www.macrotrends.net/countries/GTM/guatemala/poverty-rate

3 https://borgenproject.org/indigenous-poverty/#:~:text=Indigenous%20groups%20make%20up%20more,35%25%20suffering%20from%20food%20insecurity.

4 https://www.sierraclub.org/sierra/last-year-was-deadliest-for-environmental-activists-defenders

5 https://www.globalwitness.org/en/campaigns/environmental-activists/land-and-environmental-defenders-annual-report-archive/

6 https://knoema.com/atlas/Guatemala/topics/Education/Literacy/Adult-literacy-rate#:~:text=Guatemala%20%2D%20Adult%20(15%2B)%20literacy%20rate&text=Adult%20literacy%20rate%20of%20Guatemala,average%20annual%20rate%20of%206.21%25.

7 https://festivalessolidarios.medium.com/

8 https://www.researchgate.net/publication/335566914_Reflections_on_Service_Learning_for_a_Circular_Economy_Project_in_a_Guatemalan_Neighborhood_Central_America

9 https://news.un.org/en/story/2020/08/1070862

10 https://www.ciel.org/issue/defending-the-defenders/

11 https://www.newscientist.com/article/2206461-the-musicians-helping-make-climate-change-a-cultural-movement/

12 https://www.academiccourses.com/article/how-to-become-a-professional-musician/

13 https://www.environmentalscience.org/career/architect

14 https://dojos.info/

15 https://globalmartialarts.university/2021/05/19/what-are-the-requirements-to-becoming-a-martial-arts-instructor/

A Blueprint for Climate Revolution

Srdja Popovic, Otpor!, CANVAS
Serbia

☆ Call to Action

Learn how you can build a movement or support those transitioning to democracy: canvasopedia.org
Follow CANVAS:
Twitter @CANVASNVS
Facebook: @PeoplePowerCANVAS

☆ Values

- Committed
- Imaginative
- Courage
- Creative
- Environmentalist

☆ Lessons Learned

Activism works. Get involved. Use your voice. Bring your ideas. Change the world!

Violence breeds violence, so refuse to participate in that cycle. If you have a cause to fight for, use your intelligence and your compassion, not your fists, or weapons.

Pacifism is the ultimate act of defiance against a tyrant. Nonviolence is the one weapon that can bring an end to tyranny.

Identifying the root of a problem is the first step in solving it. The second step is proposing a way to solve it.

Renegade rocker turned nonviolent activist, Srdja Popovic wrote the handbook for nonviolent resistance—a text that's now taught around the world, from the halls of Harvard to the frontlines of Extinction Rebellion's global environmental movement.

In his twenties, Srdja founded Otpor! a Serbian resistance movement that helped to overthrow the dictator Slobodan Milošević. Srdja later went on to found the Center for Applied Nonviolent Action and Strategies (CANVAS), which has supported and built nonviolent resistance movements around the world. Now, he says, the next frontier of the global resistance struggle is a common one: climate change.

☆ Language Arts

Who was Slobodan Milosevic? Write a research paper about the War in the Balkans and explain why Srdja's choice of using nonviolence to fight Milosevic is so impressive.

Who are the most influential activists you know of who have achieved significant change using nonviolence? Make a list of at least 10, then choose six of them. Create a Tik Tok video for each activist you have chosen that focuses on how they used nonviolence to effect significant change in their countries, or in the world.

Read the article Countdown: Top 10 Civil Resistance Stories of 2020, Looking Forward. Choose one of the conflicts mentioned in the article, and research it thoroughly: its origins, the government's position, the opposition's position, what possible solutions there are, and the current status of the conflict. With the information you have gathered, create a 10-15-slide Power Point presentation explaining the conflict to your peers.

Watch Srdja's Ted Talk on How to Topple a Dictator[1]. Some of the tactics he and his friends used to topple Milosevic were guerrilla theater, humor, and satire[2]. Choose one issue in the world that you would like to change and write a guerrilla theater-style script aimed at achieving change.

STEM Activities

War and conflict can have devastating impacts on the environment, including the destruction of habitats, and pollution. Lead bullets in shrapnel shells, rifles, and machine gun cartridges, a major source of pollution of water and soil; can cause damage not only to people, but to the environment as well. Have students research the effects of lead on various parts of the human body (the nervous, circulatory, digestive systems, etc.), individually or in groups. (If they are working in groups, each group should choose a different body system.) Then students will create posters or 3-D models to present their findings; they should include information on symptoms, physiology, long-term effects—and prevention!

Between 1946 and 1958, the United States set off 23 separate nuclear explosions near the Bikini Atoll, about halfway between Papua New Guinea and Hawaii, to test the impacts of nuclear weapons on naval ships. Each of these explosions raised the surface temperature of the sea to 55,000 degrees Celsius (the sun's surface temperature is 5,500 degrees Celsius). In this activity[3], students will learn how an increase in ocean temperature can lead to coral bleaching.

Students will analyze and develop mitigation plans for the global CO2 emissions that will be necessary to forestall global climate change by reviewing various models for mitigation strategies. Guiding question: "What would it take to reduce carbon dioxide emissions on a global scale such that atmospheric concentration reaches a stable level of 350 ppm, and the global average temperature change stays below 2 degrees Celsius in 50 years?"

- Activity Link[4]

Sustainability Innovations

Srdja was able to collaborate with other individuals his age to address the issues caused by the dictatorship in Serbia. This Ted Talk[5] highlights his approach and the things that transpired during this effort.

Srdja was able to accomplish monumental feats in Serbia, but not all countries are dealing with the same issues. The United States Institute of Peace highlights strategies and situations to deal with various issues of oppression globally.

As society has developed, the use of technology has advanced the push toward reducing oppression. This article[6] features some of the ways activists have used technology to fight oppression. One of the main highlights of the article is the information about the Digital Citizen Fund[7], a 501(c)3 nonprofit based in Afghanistan that helps women in developing countries gain access to technology for collaboration.

Sustainability Career Pathways

Nonviolent Civil Disobedience Trainer. CANVAS isn't the only organization providing training in non-violence. There are organizations doing this around the world. Typically, one learns these skills as part of their experience in activism. But one can also learn how to train others. Here is a list of trainings and organizations[8] to explore--whether to be trained yourself, or perhaps one day, to become a trainer. Want to learn more about one group's effort, check out the Fellowship for Reconciliation[9].

Conflict Mediator. There are a growing number of career opportunities in the field of conflict resolution: mediators, arbitrators, consensus-builders. Mediators help parties resolve conflict--whether two individuals, organizations, or communities--and whether the conflict concerns financial issues, territorial disputes, or environmental concerns. Want to learn more about this field? Visit here[10]. Are you interested in a career in conflict resolution? Read this step-by-step guide[11].

Social Psychologist. People, being social by nature, sometimes experience the dark sides of social interaction--whether it is dictatorship at the state level, or bullying at the individual level. Social psychologists study and help address key social issues like bullying, crime, community health problems, and so on. Do you want to become a psychologist? Here is an overview[12], including how to become one and what you can use these skills for.

Political Scientist or Social Movements Expert. Some years ago, Erica Chenoweth found that nonviolent revolutions have been far more successful than violent revolutions over the course of history. Scholars of political science, social movements, and revolution contribute significantly to the power of movements. Read more about Chenoweth's findings here[13] and consider becoming a political scientist[14].

Documentary Filmmaker. PBS's Bringing Down a Dictator[15] is a powerful documentary: like so many others, it reveals the power of documentary to help change history and mobilize people. Perhaps you want to become a filmmaker? Here are some tips about how to become a filmmaker[16] by none other than Ken Burns. And here you will find tips on how to actually making a living doing it[17].

---

1 https://www.ted.com/talks/srdja_popovic_how_to_topple_a_dictator?language=en

2 https://study.com/academy/lesson/guerrilla-theatre-definition-examples.html

3 https://www.dropbox.com/s/wlz6vlw5lc6altq/Coral%20Bleaching%20in%20Caribbean.pdf?dl=0

4 https://www.clarkson.edu/stem/project-based-climate-modules/mitigation

5 https://www.ted.com/speakers/srdja_popovic

6 https://www.fastcompany.com/3066519/watch-these-activists-explain-how-technology-helped-them-fight-oppressive-governments

7 https://www.digitalcitizenfund.org/about

8 http://nonviolencetraininghub.org/events/categories/

9 https://forusa.org/what-we-do/educate/leadership-training/

10 https://careersinpsychology.org/conflict-resolution-careers/

11 https://www.indeed.com/career-advice/finding-a-job/how-to-become-a-mediator

12 https://careersinpsychology.org/becoming-a-social-psychologist/

13 https://www.hks.harvard.edu/faculty-research/policy-topics/advocacy-social-movements/paths-resistance-erica-chenoweths-research

14 https://www.truity.com/career-profile/political-scientist

15 https://en.wikipedia.org/wiki/Bringing_Down_a_Dictator

16 https://www.masterclass.com/articles/ken-burns-shares-tips-for-becoming-a-documentarian#ken-burnss-7-tips-for-

17 https://www.desktop-documentaries.com/how-to-make-a-full-time-living-as-a-documentary-filmmaker.html

Changemaking from the Nation's Capital

Jerome Foster II, OneMillionOfUs, Washington DC

Jerome Foster grew up near our nation's capital.

I always understood what BLM (Black Lives Matter), women's rights, and other mainstream social justice movements were about," he says. "But I never realized that these had anything to do with climate change. And when I did, I decided to do something about it."

In 2017 he founded The Climate Reporter, a collection of writing by international youth about climate change, global warming, environmental justice, and other sustainability issues around the world. This environmental news site now receives roughly 600,000 views a month. In 2019, Jerome also organized the DC chapter of the worldwide youth movement, School Strikes for Climate. To show her support for the Global Climate Strikes, Greta Thunberg traveled for the very first time by sailboat from Europe to New York, and then went on to Washington D.C. to join with Jerome in increasing media attention to the issue.

Language Arts

Choose an environmental issue you feel passionate about. Using the app "Fakebook"[1], create a fake profile for an organization that would deal with the issue you have chosen. The profile must have at least three images in addition to the profile and background pictures. You must also create a "favorites" list, and at least five posts for the organization. In a separate document, explain why you made the choices you made in terms of images and posts.

Make a list of 10 strategies you would use to create a successful social media campaign including creating profiles on several different social media platforms (Facebook, Instagram, Twitter, Tik-Tok, Snapchat, etc.). Explain which platforms you would use and why.

Create a Tik-Tok video aimed at creating awareness of the link between the climate change and social justice

Call to Action

Get informed on the latest global news on climate & sustainability at Jerome's online hub, The Climate Reporter - medium.com/the-climate-reporter.

Values

- Innovative
- Committed
- Collaborative
- Leader
- Environmentalist

Lessons Learned

When you find an issue that interests you, read everything you can about it.

It is important to understand that social and environmental issues are often interconnected.

When you see a problem, you can be part of the solution.

Social media can help raise awareness of how various social and environmental issues are interrelated, by promoting communication between people of different cultures and backgrounds.

movements. Then write a five-paragraph essay explaining why you chose those particular issues, and how they are connected.warm summers.

STEM Activities

Jerome started a company that uses VR technology to bring virtual experiences to students in the classroom. VR headsets are used to "translate" a 2D image from a phone into a 3D environment; but this technology is often expensive. Google offers an affordable option with their Google Cardboard. Depending on available resources, obtain Google Cardboard kits ($20-$25) and have students think of ways to improve the design of this basic VR headset. For example, how could they be made more comfortable to wear, or easier to hold for a longer period of time? Or how could a head strap be added? Alternatively, students can build their own cardboard headset by downloading the Google Cardboard design specifications[2] and obtaining some lenses like these[3]. Have students test and evaluate their improved headsets by following the engineering process.

OneMillionOfUs is a nonprofit organization founded by Jerome to promote and encourage youth voting. However, for many young people, the Electoral College system in U.S. elections is confusing. This activity will show students how proportional reasoning can be used to show how some election methods work better than others. To model different election systems, students will hold a class election to establish the best candy, with the winning candy shared with the class at the end. Select three or four different types of candies, but do not identify them until after the first round of voting. Then have students evaluate the fairness and efficiency of each voting method. Are there problems with any of them? How could they be improved?

- **The first round will model the direct popular vote, in which each person gets one vote, and each vote is weighted equally.** Students will submit their favorite candy in a secret ballot and the winner will be the candy with the most votes.
- **The second round will model representative voting, in which one representative is chosen to vote on behalf of a group. Announce the candies that the class will be voting on.** Then arrange the students in groups of different sizes, and have each group select one person to represent them. Each representative will then vote for their favorite candy without consulting the rest of the group.
- **The third round of elections will model a modified version of the electoral college.** Using the same groups as in the last round, have each elector consult with the other members of the group and establish the group's favorite candy. Any ties should be dealt with within the group. The elector will then vote for the group's choice, and the candy with the most electoral votes wins.
- **Suppose that the total number of votes equals the number of students in the class: ask students how the votes should be distributed among the groups.** Now suppose that 100 votes must be received: how would they distribute the votes then? Students should explain their solutions using proportional reasoning.

Jerome runs a blog called The Climate Reporter[4] to spread awareness about climate issues. Have students pick an issue they are passionate about, or interested in, and build a simple static website using HTML. The site should include text, images, and links. Students can take these HTML and CSS tutorials on Codecademy to learn the basics of HTML[5] and CSS[6]. For an optional challenge, students can follow this tutorial[7] on deploying their website to the internet using GitHub.

Sustainability Innovations

Jerome's inner motivation has led him to work toward engaging and enabling youth to understand the current state of the world and how we can make positive, sustainable changes for a better future. Research one policy or law that is addressing sustainability in the U.S. and create a blog post that you would send to The Climate Reporter to raise awareness on this issue. See examples.[8]

Through the work of his company, his blog, and his nonprofit organization Jerome has found a way to connect young people for the purpose of reaching common goals.

- Identify one issue facing the students in your community/school and design a school club to connect students with similar viewpoints. Create three goals that you would like to accomplish, and research one organization/company in the community where your "club" would like to volunteer.

Sustainability Career Pathways

Digital Entrepreneur. The internet is a vast frontier that offers countless opportunities for innovation. Every day people are creating new apps, games, media platforms, and tools to connect; and are raising funds, or educating others through blogs and online courses. All of these can help inform people about how to live more sustainably. Would you like to be a digital entrepreneur? Here's an article introducing the field of digital entrepreneurship.[9]

Environmental Journalist. Jerome created his own Medium channel, The Climate Reporter. But many people who love to write, including about the climate and environmental issues, make their careers as full-time journalists. Some are freelancers, pitching stories to a variety of outlets. Others work full time for a news outlet. To learn more about this career, read here[10]. The Society of Environmental Journalists[11] is a valuable resource that offers job boards, mentoring, annual conferences, and listservs for environmental journalists.

Organizer. Engaging one's community around important environmental and social challenges, as well as in getting out the vote and strengthening democracy, is an important career path, and a valuable community service. There are many programs for learning organizing skills and strategies, from online courses (such as this one[12]), to one-year environmental organizing field schools like Green Corps.[13]

Elected Official. Along with getting people to vote, it's important that they have good candidates to vote for. Perhaps you should run for elected office? One typically starts by running for a local office, or working for an elected official to learn the ropes. But there are many paths. Listen to this NPR story to get a better sense of the process[14] of running for office.

1 https://www.classtools.net/FB/home-page
2 https://arvr.google.com/cardboard/
3 https://www.amazon.com/Biconvex-Pop-Tech-Bi-convex-Diameter-Cardboard/dp/B012HYF4A2/ref=sr_1_6?dchild=1&keywords=google+cardboard+lenses&qid=1608519175&s-r=8-6&tag=sciencebuddie-20
4 https://medium.com/the-climate-reporter
5 https://www.codecademy.com/learn/learn-html
6 https://www.codecademy.com/learn/learn-css
7 https://www.khanacademy.org/computing/computer-programming/html-css/web-development-tools/a/hosting-your-website-on-github
8 https://thesustainabilityalliance.us/environmental-sustainability/
9 https://copyblogger.com/digital-entrepreneur/
10 https://www.openschoolofjournalism.com/specializations/environmental-journalism
11 https://www.sej.org/
12 https://www.coursera.org/learn/community-organizing
13 https://greencorps.org/
14 https://www.npr.org/2019/10/15/770332855/how-to-run-for-office

Divestment for a Sustainable Future

Alyssa Lee, DivestEd
Olympia, Washington

Call to Action

To get involved with one of the many educational institutes, nonprofit organizations, and community programs taking on fossil fuel consumption through divestment campaigns, please visit divested.betterfutureproject.org.

Values

- Determination
- Cooperation
- Leadership
- Social Justice
- Environmentalism

Lessons Learned

You are the one who decides how to live your life. Make wise decisions that take the future and well-being of the planet into consideration.

Be resilient, be brave, be creative, and be fierce!

Looking at problems from a different perspective can help you find innovative solutions.

A successful community is built on the wisdom of multiple generations. Strength comes from diversity.

During her first year at UCLA, Alyssa Lee became obsessed with the problem of plastic pollution.

"What really got me on the case was a speech by Van Jones called "Plastic Pollution is a Social Justice Issue." That was the first time I ever heard the term environmental justice. And it was the first time I heard environmental issues related to issues of class and race." The more she came to understand the destructive actions of powerful institutions, the bigger the issues she began to focus on. "And what bigger issue does the environmental community face than fossil fuels?" So she started the Fossil Free UCLA divestment campaign.

Alyssa's divestment movement targeted universities, aiming to prompt them to remove their investments from fossil fuel companies. She went on to her work supporting youth activists with the Better Future Project, Divest Ed, and the Future Coalition.

Language Arts

Research the most common practices for disposing of plastic waste in the U.S. Create a presentation in which you focus on "Sacrifice Zones." Explain what they are, where they are located, the environmental impact of this practice, the consequences for public health in regions where they are present, and which populations are most affected by their existence. End your presentation with a call to action: What can be done to eliminate this practice, or at least minimize it?

Write an argumentative essay in which you argue for divesting from fossil fuels. Support your argument with facts (based on research). You should also address at least one counterargument.

After watching this tutorial[1], create an animated presentation in which you explain the divestiture movement: its origins, its importance in the climate change movement, its current state, and its goals for the future.

Using the platform of your choice, create a petition to make sustainability education available to the public in your area. Focus not only on the dangers created by the lack of education, but on the benefits that this type of education can bring to your community.

STEM Activities

Select a college or university that you are interested in attending and find out whether they invest in or profit from fossil fuel companies. Based on your findings, how are their investments contributing to environmental damage and/or impacting human health? What would be the effects if they decided to stop investing in fossil fuels? What are some alternatives they could turn to?

Research the general processes of plastic production, use, and disposal, and identify one way that it negatively affects humans (toxins in seafood, water pollution, toxins in commercial packaging, etc.). Design a solution to help mitigate this issue.

Using this activity guide[2], research and test several different microplastics filtering methods on commercial products brought from home, and design an experiment to identify the impact of microplastics on human health.

Record the purchases you make over the course of a week. Assess the ecological impact of your purchases, or look at the companies you bought from and assess their ecological footprint. What is the total ecological impact of your purchases?

Sustainability Innovations

There are hundreds of fossil fuel divestment campaigns targeted at universities, pension funds, and other organizations. Go Fossil Free[3] is a project of 350.org that serves as a host to start a local campaign or participate in current fossil fuel divestment campaigns. There are currently 667 campaigns in the U.S., 230 in Europe, and several others across the globe.

As the director of Divest Ed[4], Alyssa assisted in focusing the efforts of fossil fuel divestment campaigns and creating increased collaboration between colleges. What other types of divestments are occurring based on climate change and moral issues?

Private prison reform has also become a recent focus of many activists and community leaders. Families for Freedom[5] is an organization that addresses the correlation between undignified immigration and the for-profit prison industry. Research the private prison industry: highlight areas of strength and areas that need improvement.

Sustainability Career Pathways

Green Investor. With billions of dollars being invested, where that money goes shapes the future of business. Do we invest in oil companies or renewable energy companies? In downtown real estate or suburban malls? Working with a socially responsible investment firm, or with a university, city, or foundation as an asset manager, can be a great way to help develop the sustainable business sector. Here is a brief introduction[6] to the many jobs in the field.

Divestment Campaigner. Around the world, students and activists are pushing for divesting from fossil fuels. There are also many focused on ensuring that major banks and international financial institutions like the World Bank are investing money in ways that help people and the planet. Through organizations like DivestEd[7] and the Bank Information Center[8] there are ways to make a living fighting this important fight.

Renewable Energy Advocate. Renewable energy is a rapidly growing field: it will make up an ever-larger percentage of the world's energy mix in decades to come. Becoming part of a renewable energy company--as a manager, salesperson[9], or support staff--is a way you can help with this transition. Or, by joining one of the many nonprofit organizations that are promoting or lobbying for the transition to renewable energy, you can help draw attention and investments to this worthy cause.

1 https://www.youtube.com/watch?v=DoyE48W3RUY

2 https://www.teachengineering.org/lessons/view/uok-2116-plastisphere-microplastics-pollution-wastewater-treatment

3 https://campaigns.gofossilfree.org/?_ga=2.246024774.372712381.1619415086-897762842.1619415085

4 https://divested.betterfutureproject.org/forms/user_sessions/new

5 https://familiesforfreedom.org/

6 http://finanzasostenibile.it/wp-content/uploads/2017/04/13-04-2017_FBicciato_ProfessioniSRI_SdR.pdf

7 https://divested.betterfutureproject.org/forms/user_sessions/new

8 https://bankinformationcenter.org/

9 https://www.greentechmedia.com/articles/read/cleantech-careers-solar-sales-at-a-residential-installer

Fighting Alongside the Most Vulnerable Among Us

Mitzi Jonelle Tan, Youth Advocates for Climate Action PH, Philippines

Call to Action

Get involved with Mitzi's chapter at yacap.org. If you're not from the Philippines, connect with the global youth climate movement at FridaysforFuture.org.

Values

- Courage
- Committed
- Leader
- Environmentalism
- Solidarity
- Creative

Lessons Learned

When Mitzi learned directly from the Lumad people about how they were being threatened, harassed, and even killed, she knew she had to do something to help them. We all need to listen to the people who are protecting our environment, and find ways to help them.

Mitzi has formed a bridge between the people living on the land that is being destroyed, and worldwide organizations that are working to fight the effects of climate change. This kind of collaboration is essential in order to solve the global problems we're facing.

It is important to shine a light on, and listen to the people who are impacted the most by climate change. They can't do it alone, and the protection of the earth protects us all.

In 2017, Mitzi Jonelle Tan went with her college's student council on an integration project with the Lumad indigenous people, where one of the leaders told her about how his people were being displaced, harassed, and even killed just for protecting their lands and the environment from extractive mining companies. "The simplicity of how he said something so tragic, in passing, about his way of life… I realized that individual lifestyle change is not enough when peoples' lives are at stake. It's on us to do more." So Mitzi founded Youth Advocates for Climate Action Philippines (YACAP) in partnership with Fridays For Future, to help change the conditions for Most Affected People and Areas (MAPA) in the Philippines. She focuses much of her time fighting for Indigenous defenders of the environment. "They are the ones who really keep me going on this journey," she says. "What I do is easy."

Language Arts

As climate change becomes more prevalent, more and more people will join the ranks of "vulnerable populations." Write a list of no more than six steps that people in the developed world could use to help vulnerable populations fight back. Support your suggestions with at least one source for each suggestion that you have consulted in your research. (Several of your suggestions may be supported by the same source.) After you have your list and your sources, create an annotated bibliography of the sources. The bibliography must include citations (MLA format); a brief summary of the source; and why you found it relevant.

Choose any of YACAP's points of unity[1] and write a research paper on what it means; what it would entail to act on this particular principle; and what would be the best ways to get involved. Based on your research, create your own points of unity to apply to your country.

Erosion is one of the biggest issues for populations that live near the coast. The Philippines is incredibly vulnerable to this type of environmental damage because it is made up mostly of islands. Conduct an online search about the damage erosion has caused to the Philippines; then create a photographic or video diary of the damage, showing how it has affected the lives of the people.

STEM Activities

Mitzi is a very well-rounded sustainability activist. She participated in the Youth Advocate for Climate Action Philippines Global Climate Strike in 2019. Create a list of the pros and cons of a climate strike. Follow up with a written summary explaining why it's important not only to participate, but to also understand the reasons why you are participating.

As Mitzi has shown, the Philippines is one of the world's most susceptible countries to natural disasters. Research one sustainability issue that citizens in the Philippines are facing. Identify an organization that helps to combat this issue; if there isn't one, explain why the development of such an organization is important.

Compare and contrast the effect of climate events in the Philippines to those in your local community. If there is a difference, explain why it is important to acknowledge these differences and assist communities that do not have the supplies to adequately combat these events.

Sustainability Innovations

Care[2] **and Team Rubicon USA**[3] are two of the major players assisting the Philippines in disasters like Typhoon Haiyan. How could Mitzi partner with these organizations to increase preparation for, as well as post-disaster relief?

In addition to organizations that assist with disaster relief, Global Giving includes a group called the International Disaster Volunteers[4]**;** they are currently working on 386 projects in the Philippines alone. Identify one of these projects and convince your teacher that you and your classmates should support this project.

Sustainability Career Pathways

Environmental and Climate Activist. While Mitzi hopes the job of climate activist will one day no longer be necessary, that time will be many decades from now. In the meantime, monumental effort is needed to slow down the building of fossil fuel infrastructure and the extraction and burning of coal, gas, and oil; and to more quickly shift to greener sources of energy. You can become an activist right now: organize a Friday climate strike[5] at your town hall, or pressure your school to divest from fossil fuel stocks and/or invest in renewable energy. Visit Idealist.org[6] to explore activist jobs, internships, and volunteer opportunities available near you.

Defender of Environmental and Indigenous Rights Activists. As Mitzi's story reveals, Indigenous peoples are often bold defenders of the earth, and are thus often subject to threat or violence. Supporting them in their quest to protect and heal the land can be a valuable way to help. Groups like the Center for International Environmental Law undertake efforts to protect environmental activists. Learn about CIEL's work here[7].

Sustainable Land Management. Mitzi calls the foresters, farmers, and fishers "defenders of nature." Have you considered a career caring for the land in sustainable farming[8], sustainable aquaculture[9], or agroforestry[10]?

Coastal Zone Manager. 45 percent of the world's people live on coasts. With climate change bringing about sea level rise, there will be a significant need for individuals to help manage development and coastal protection, which includes everything from habitat conservation and restoration to building coastline defenses. For a look at the broad field of coastal management visit here[11].

Disaster Management Specialist. The Philippines is one of the countries most vulnerable to the effects of the climate crisis. But between flooding, fires, droughts, and other climate effects, every community needs to be prepared for and able to respond to disasters, including the management and allocation of limited resources. Does this field sound interesting to you? Learn more here[12].

1 https://yacap.org/about/
2 https://www.care.org/our-work/where-we-work/philippines/
3 https://teamrubiconusa.org/
4 https://www.globalgiving.org/donate/3243/international-disaster-volunteers-idv/
5 https://fridaysforfuture.org/
6 https://www.idealist.org/en/
7 https://www.ciel.org/issue/defending-the-defenders/
8 http://greencollarblog.org/sustainable-agriculture-jobs/
9 https://www.discoveryeducation.com/
10 https://www.environmentalscience.org/career/agroforester
11 https://coast.noaa.gov/
12 https://www.environmentalscience.org/career/disaster-management-specialist

Get Into Good Trouble!

U.S. Representative John Lewis
Atlanta

Call to Action

VOTE! Racial inequality continues to this day, and, sadly, racism is all around us. We each have a responsibility to change this: to inform ourselves, and to speak up. Go out and get into good trouble! Watch the movie Good Trouble. Be inspired!

Values

- Courage
- Dedication
- Commitment
- Justice
- Community Service

Lessons Learned

There is only one appropriate response to injustice: Do something about it!

Exercise your right to vote, and fight to strengthen our democracy. It is the most powerful tool we have against tyranny.

When facing unjust laws, do what John Lewis encouraged us to do: get into "good trouble."

U.S. Congressman John Lewis urged people to get into what he called "good trouble, necessary trouble."
As a child in Alabama, he experienced racism and segregation. When he was just 15 years old he heard Dr. Martin Luther King Jr. speak on the radio, and it inspired him to join the Civil Rights movement. But when it was time for him to go to college, he was not allowed to enroll in the school he wanted to attend, because it was for whites only. He was a founding member of SNCC (Student Nonviolent Coordinating Committee), and he became one of the youngest leaders of the Civil Rights movement. He dedicated his life to fighting for equality and justice. Many times he put himself in personal danger in order to fight for fundamental rights for his people, including for many years as a U.S. Representative from the state of Georgia. The John Lewis Voting Rights Act is named in honor of his lifelong dedicated championship of voting rights.

Language Arts

What was the Civil Rights movement in America? What was John Lewis's role in it? Create a 5–10-minute video in which you explain his lifelong involvement in and contributions to the movement.

Write a research essay explaining the link between civil rights and climate change, and how Congressman Lewis used his experience fighting for civil rights to fight for climate justice for his constituents.

Based on Congressman Lewis's story, what does getting into "good trouble, necessary trouble" mean? Why was he an advocate of this type of trouble? Can you think of any situations nowadays that would warrant the need to get in "good trouble"? Used the attached handout to conduct a Pinwheel Discussion[1] on these topics.

Watch this [clip of John Lewis's historic speech][2] as a young man, in 1963, in the March on Washington. After watching it, write a short description of his mannerisms, tone of voice, diction, and other details of the delivery of his speech. How did these things affect his speech, and its effectiveness? In your opinion, what was the most important thing he did in that clip in order to make the greatest possible impact on his audience, and to get his ideas across?

STEM Activities

In this lesson plan on redistricting[3], define the practice of congressional redistricting, and analyze why it takes place. Then reflect on the practice of gerrymandering. Explore why it's so controversial, and learn about efforts to reform the redistricting process. Finally, practice redistricting a state, using an online simulation game.

In this lesson plan on algebraic variables and expressions[4], explore various variables related to literacy, with a focus on differences in literacy rates by race. Then, explore the variables that you think are important in order to propose an action that you might take as a class to impact literacy rates in your local community.

Working in groups, figure out the hourly wage necessary for a family in Chicago to afford housing, by looking at real data about hourly wages and the cost for renting a home each month[5]. Then, using linear equations and graphs, show the challenges that families in Chicago face. The goal is to use mathematics to decide whether or not you think these six families in Chicago are being paid fair wages. Links to resources[6] are provided to adapt the task for other cities.

Using this lesson plan on data analysis[7], examine demographic data about your school, and critically consider what story that data tells by interpreting and explaining the data through various types of graphs; determining and constructing appropriate graphs to display data; and describing the story that is being told by a graph and explaining why it is important.

Sustainability Innovations

Congressman John Lewis had the unique opportunity to experience working with Dr. Martin Luther King Jr., and the election of the first Black president in the United States. Review The Civil Rights Movement[8] and compare activism in the 1960s to current activism in the U.S. How have things changed? What can we learn from individuals like Congressman John Lewis to achieve progress in our future?

The John Lewis Voting rights Act, which still needs to be passed by the Senate, is one part of a greater movement to create efficacy on the ballots, and a proper representation of the American people. In 2021, further advancements were proposed through H.R.1 - For the People Act of 2021[9]. H.R. 1 states, "To expand Americans' access to the ballot box, reduce the influence of big money in politics, strengthen ethics rules for public servants, and implement other anti-corruption measures for the purpose of fortifying our democracy, and for other purposes." Review H.R.1, and highlight one aspect of the House bill that has resulted from the work of Congressman John Lewis and others over the years.

How can activists gain support from the government to reach their goals? In this USAID article[10], partnerships between NGOs and their government partners are discussed.

Sustainability Career Pathways

Nonviolence Trainer. Nonviolence is not only recognized as an effective protest strategy but is increasingly sought after as a more effective means of crisis prevention. Hospitals, nursing homes, prisons, and schools are all starting to recognize the value of nonviolent de-escalation of conflict. Would you like to become an expert in nonviolence and train others to use these skills as well? Here's one example of nonviolent crisis intervention training to explore: The Crisis Prevention Institute[11].

Elected Official. Along with getting people to engage with their elected representatives, it's important that they have good candidates to vote for. Perhaps you should run for elected office! One typically starts by running for local office, or working for an elected official to better learn the ropes. But there are many paths. Listen to this NPR story[12] to get a better sense of the process of running for office.

Human Rights Lawyer. When rights aren't protected, lawyers can help activists avoid, or at least navigate, difficult court systems--either in one's own country or in others. One can also help fight human rights abuses wherever they occur. While this is not an easy path, this article[13] offers an introduction on how to become a human rights lawyer, and what you can do with such training.

1 https://www.socialstudies.org/sites/default/files/pinwheel_discussion_instructions_types_of_questions.pdf
2 https://www.youtube.com/watch?app=desktop&v=Xy8Nf2UIwVI
3 https://www.clevelandmetroschools.org/Page/13183
4 https://francesharper.com/lesson-plans/algebra/variables-variable-expressions-literacy-issues/
5 https://francesharper.com/linear-equations-and-graphs-fair-living-wages/
6 https://francesharper.com/linear-equations-and-graphs-fair-living-wages/
7 https://francesharper.com/lesson-plans/other-math-topics/data-analysis-school-demographics/
8 https://www.history.com/topics/black-history/civil-rights-movement
9 https://www.congress.gov/bill/117th-congress/house-bill/1/text
10 https://www.usaid.gov/partnership-opportunities/ngo
11 https://www.crisisprevention.com/
12 https://www.npr.org/2019/10/15/770332855/how-to-run-for-office
13 https://www.humanrightscareers.com/magazine/how-to-become-a-human-rights-lawyer/

Generation Green

Destiny Hodges, Generation Green
Washington D.C

Call to Action

Understand that climate change issues are multifaceted: social, economic, and generational. Help us search for holistic solutions! Learn more about Destiny's ventures: www.gen- green.org.

Values

- Solidarity
- Collaboration
- Communication
- Respect
- Environmentalism

Lessons Learned

Use your voice to speak for those who have been neglected, or whose voices may not be being heard.

Climate change affects more than the planet's temperatures: it affects people's health, their standard of living, and their future.

To engage a community and achieve change, build deep and meaningful relationships with people.

Destiny Hodges always wanted to become a journalist. She joined her middle school's broadcasting class, and became a news editor in high school.

She even started her school's newspaper Out of the Blue. She knows how important it is to have one's story told. That is why, when she learned about climate change, she was shocked to see that reporting on climate change left out one of the most important parts: the stories of the communities most affected by the climate change; for the most part, people of color. Destiny has made it her mission to change that. With her NGO Generation Green, she is building networks between activists, and amplifying the voices of young black environmental activists around the world.

Language Arts

Write a newspaper article[1] about the air quality in your community: Are there any factories or businesses that are polluting the air around you? What are the biggest pollutants in your area? What are the consequences in terms of the health of your community? What does your community's situation have in common with Destiny's situation? Why do you think that is?

Working in groups of 5-7 people, create an Editable Newspaper Template[2] using Google Docs. Use it to create a newspaper page featuring the articles you wrote in the previous activity.

Present your newspaper page to the rest of your class. After the presentations are done, organize a class discussion in which you compare and contrast the information you and your classmates found with the information presented in your local newspaper. Write a short essay detailing your findings. Get it published in your school or local newspaper.

STEM Activities

Using a weather app or website, monitor the UV index in your community and compare that to another community of your choice that is a significant distance away. Choose a type of graph or chart to display the results. What is the average UV index in your community? What is the average UV index of the other community?

In this lesson plan from TeachEngineering.org[3], students explore the concepts of air pollution, air quality, and climate change. First they use M&M® candies to create pie graphs that express their understanding of the composition of air. Next, they watch and conduct simple experiments to develop an understanding of the properties of air. Finally, they develop awareness and understanding of the daily air quality using the online Air Quality Index (AQI).

What does climate change look like in your community? How do you see its effects in your everyday life? What depictions of climate change have you seen in the media? What new ways can you imagine to depict climate change? Use technology and online tools to create a different way to communicate the impacts of climate change in your community.

Sustainability Innovations

Assess the work of Generation Green[4]. How can students collaborate to highlight the work of these young leaders and shed light on these issues with others as well?

In addition to her work with Generation Green, Destiny Hodges is one of the team members of Hip Hop Caucus. Hip Hop Caucus[5] helps to connect the hip hop community with the civic process in order to create change. Do you think that hip hop and political agendas have been mutually exclusive in their approach to engaging the community? How could collaboration between these two entities, and similar collaborations, serve to create a better world?

Destiny's greatest strength is her ability to engage people and shed light on issues that others may not be properly addressing. In this World War Zero Article[6], Leah Thomas describes how climate justice is social justice. Compare the work of Leah and Destiny. What are some of your takeaways? How would you address our intersectional problems?

Sustainability Career Pathways

Environmental Journalist. Journalism is a powerful tool for drawing attention to and encouraging reform. Environmental journalists focus on sustainability, climate, toxic substances, and environmental justice. Learn more about this career here[7]. Another valuable resource is the Society of Environmental Journalists[8], which offers job boards, mentoring, annual conferences, and listservs for environmental journalists.

Sustainability Director at a University or School. Colleges, universities, and even some high schools are hiring sustainability directors, who coordinate sustainability initiatives throughout different departments--from maintenance and transportation, to energy use, and even classroom curricula. Learn more about this job—which is heavy on management, leadership, and coordination--here[9].

Environmental Justice Advocate. Environmental justice[10] grapples with improving the air and water quality of urban areas and other affected communities. Check out jobs at thousands of small community organizations, national organizations[11], and government agencies like the EPA[12] and its environmental justice efforts.

1 https://www.youtube.com/watch?v=T6C8N-lRd4o

2 https://www.youtube.com/watch?v=P0sAnr2GaY8

3 https://www.teachengineering.org/lessons/view/cub_air_lesson01

4 https://www.gen-green.org/howwework

5 https://hiphopcaucus.org/team/destiny-hodges/

6 https://worldwarzero.com/magazine/2020/07/climate-justice-is-social-justice/

7 https://therevelator.org/environmental-journalism/

8 https://www.sej.org/

9 https://www.studyinternational.com/news/jobs-of-the-future-how-do-i-become-a-sustainability-manager/

10 https://en.wikipedia.org/wiki/Environmental_justice

11 https://www.onepercentfortheplanet.org/stories/nonprofits-fighting-for-social-environmental-justice

12 https://www.epa.gov/environmentaljustice/environmental-justice-your-community

Indigenous Leader Invites Youth to Share Their Gifts

Xiye Bastida, Re-Earth Initiative, Fridays for Future NYC, New York

Call to Action

Learn more about Re-Earth Initiative: www.reearthin.org

Values

- Solidarity
- Leadership
- Commitment
- Compassion
- Environmentalism

Lessons Learned

We must look to our ancestors to learn how to respect and take care of our home: the Earth.

Balance is the key to a sustainable future. Strive for balance in your life. Teach the importance of a balanced life to those around you.

Just as the darkness of the world can't extinguish the light of one candle, the wall of silence of our institutions can't silence a group of voices fighting for change. Be vocal. Speak up. Keep going! You will be heard.

Climate change issues are human rights issues.

In 2015, Xiye Bastida's hometown of San Pedro Tultepec in Mexico was hit with massive floods after a prolonged period of drought.

"At the time, I didn't understand climate change and its role in these increasingly volatile weather emergencies. I never even considered that there were people and businesses who didn't care about Mother Earth the same way my family and I do." But what happened in her hometown made Xiye realize that the climate crisis was here, and was affecting frontline communities. She set her sights on fighting climate change on behalf of the most vulnerable among us. In March of 2019, she rallied 300,000 students to strike for climate with Fridays For Future NYC. She has gone on to work with TED, the People's Climate Movement, Re- Earth Initiative, and other organizations that are helping to mitigate the climate crisis.

Language Arts

Watch Xiye's Ted Talk[1]. Write your own letter to a family member of your choice, in which you express and explain your position on climate change, which issues are the most pressing, and how and why you plan to "leave everything better than you found it."

What are human rights[2]? How do human rights and climate change intersect? Working in groups of 3-5 people, create a presentation (15-20 slides) in which you analyze how the environmental destruction being caused by climate change is violating human rights. Be sure to mention which rights are being violated, and which specific climate change issue is causing the violation.

Make a list of 4-6 unconventional abilities or skills that you think can be useful in the fight against climate change. Create a series of TikTok videos in which you explain how each of these abilities can be put to work in service of the planet. Create one video for each skill.

Xiye's organization, ReEarth Initiative, participated in the Escazu agreement. Create a video explaining what this agreement is, why it is so important, and how people can get involved in supporting it.

STEM Activities

Xiye's hometown in Mexico experienced drought and flooding, one of the side effects of climate change. Select one type of extreme weather (flooding, hurricanes, wildfire, frost, heat waves, etc). and research how climate change can affect the intensity or frequency of these events. How would it affect different parts of society (health, agriculture, infrastructure, etc.) and how would it affect natural ecosystems? What are some ways to reduce/mitigate these effects?

Seeing the effects of climate change in her own hometown inspired Xiye to join the fight against climate change. Use online tools and resources to research and track the changes in temperature and weather patterns over time in your community. Does the data reveal the effects of climate change in your area? If so, what are some things that yourcommunity can do to mitigate these effects? How could these figures be improved?

Young people around the world are realizing that climate change is not a future event; it is happening now. And they are leading the fight against climate change. Many of them have been inspired through personal experience and education to take on this challenge. In this module[3], students are introduced to the science of climate change, and can explore the various impacts it is having in the world right now. Students are then challenged to think of ways to join the fight, through raising public awareness via social media, staging protests in their community, writing letters to politicians and/or companies, etc.

Sustainability Innovations

One of Xiye's greatest accomplishments is her participation in the Re-Earth Initiative. Re- Earth began in 2020 after Earth Day in response to global digital protests and the motivation of youth. Learn how you can get involved with the Re-Earth Initiative[4].

In addition to Fridays for Future, it is important for motivated young people to transform their drive for sustainability into careers. This article addresses Digital Sustainability and Entrepreneurship[5] and explains how digital innovations can help tackle the climate change battle.

One of the main issues youth are facing is their lack of knowledge in how to participate in sustainable movements and innovations. However, online platforms are developing ways to educate students on these topics. Coursera is currently offering a five-week course on Sustainable Digital Innovation[6], highlighting the business opportunities and strategies that the future offers.

Sustainability Career Pathways

Indigenous Studies Scholar. So much knowledge--of the land, of a sustainable way of life, of living through a world-changing societal crisis[7] --exists in the experience of Indigenous peoples. Learning from and sharing this knowledge could be a powerful and valuable career path. If this is a path for you (as it is for Xiye's parents), you can start your explorations of this career at the Native American and Indigenous Studies Association[8] , or at the Center for World Indigenous Studies[9].

Social Entrepreneur. Like so many of the other young people featured in this book, Xiye identified a societal challenge and created an organization to help solve it. A social entrepreneur is much like a business entrepreneur, but creates something to solve a societal problem, through a nonprofit organization, business, or other initiative. Interested in becoming a social entrepreneur? Start here[10].

Nonprofit Manager. Sometimes it's better to not start a new organization, but rather to plug into an effective existing organization. But few in the field have any formal management training, which is an ongoing problem in this sector. There are programs to train managers for nonprofit organizations specifically. While many of these are masters' levels programs (such as these leading programs[11]), there are informal and undergraduate opportunities to learn essential management skills as well. And if you're really serious about this path,here's a 500+ page introduction to the field[12].

1 https://www.youtube.com/watch?v=KWkIgCnUWvY
2 https://www.un.org/en/about-us/universal-declaration-of-human-rights
3 https://ourclimateourfuture.org/videos/
4 https://care.org/our-work/where-we-work/philippines/
5 https://journals.sagepub.com/doi/full/10.1177/1042258719899425
6 https://www.coursera.org/learn/sustainable-digital-innovation
7 http://earthed.info/wp-content/uploads/2017/08/SOW17_chap4_IndigenousEd.pdf
8 https://www.naisa.org/
9 https://www.cwis.org/
10 becoming a social entrepreneur? Start here
11 https://www.usnews.com/best-graduate-schools/top-public-affairs-schools/nonprofit-management-rankings
12 https://www.amazon.com/exec/obidos/ASIN/1119585457/stansociinn09-20

Jóvenes Por El Clima

Nicki Becker. Jóvenes por el Clima Argentina

☀ Call to Action

To learn more about Jovenes por el Clima (Youth For Climate) Argentina: www.jovenesporelclima.com Instagram @jovenesporelclimarg Twitter @jovenesclimarg. Follow Nicki on Instagram: @nicki-becker or Twitter @nickibeckerok

☀ Values

- Commitment
- Dedication
- Industriousness
- Leadership
- Environmentalism

☀ Lessons Learned

Asking questions, seeking answers, and sharing information are the first steps toward global change. Get started today!

Information can be a weapon. Learn to use it to fight for change.

Everything is interconnected. Once people understand this, they become much more open to change.

Growing up, Nicki Becker was aware of environmental issues, especially since there was mega- mining going on in Argentina that was having a devastating effect on the land and the people.

But until she was in her teens, she didn't know much about climate change. One day, she learned how young people in Europe were calling for the first international Fridays for Future strikes. That made her want to learn more, and the more she learned how pressing the climate crisis was, the more she couldn't understand why no one in her country was talking about it. So she formed Youth for Climate Argentina (YFCA). In 2019, YFCA organized huge rallies across Argentina— and their call for climate action was successful. The government listened to their demands and declared the country in a state of climate emergency. It was the first country in Latin America to do so, and it set the stage for wide-sweeping reforms in the region.

☀ Language Arts

How long has the concept of climate change been known to the world? Create a 10-minute presentation following the time-line of the climate change phenomenon throughout the world (from its discovery until today). Focus on your particular region in terms of education on the issue, government response, and the conse-quences of this response. Share your presentation with your peers.

One of Nicki's objectives was to prompt the Argentinian government to create laws aimed at curbing the damage mining operations were causing the environment. Choose one country in South America where mining is a prevalent issue, and write a research paper focusing on the environmental, social, and economic damage caused by mining operations in the country you have chosen.

In Nicki's words, "Hope is a great motivator." When looking at the challenges created by climate change throughout the world, it is very easy to lose hope. Create a three-minute video in which you list all the reasons we have to be hopeful in the fight against climate change. You may talk about one particular activist or initiative, or you may choose to make a Top-Ten-style list

What was the COP26 Summit in Scotland, and why is it important? Create a presentation in which you explain to your peers what the summit was for, its mission statement, and why it is important. Afterwards, check out this link: https://www.mockcop.org/treaty/[1] and create a video explaining what these 18 policies are and why they are important for the future of our planet.

STEM Activities

What is mega mining? Which South American countries have large mega mining projects, and how is it affecting them? Choose three such countries to research.

- **Calculate the percentage of land mass that is being destroyed in the mega mining process.** Compare mining vs. mega-mining projects, and explain the differences between them.

What is the effect of climate change/CO2 emissions in Argentina? What is the net effect of CO2 in the deforestation process, and what actions occur throughout the mega-mining process?

Nicki believes that without social justice, especially for women, there can be no climate justice. Research the ways that climate change affects women. Include statistical figures, taking into account location, income, and source of representation in politics, etc. Create graphs based on the data and perform a statistical analysis (median, mean, standard deviation, etc.) on the data set. What is one conclusion you can draw from these results?

Sustainability Innovations

The Asociación de Cooperativas Argentinas (ACA) uses digital agriculture to grow food more efficiently and sustainably. This system uses machine learning, geospatial data analysis, and cloud computing to give farmers real-time advice. In this Forbes article[2], the work of ACA, and the positive effects it has had on farming in Argentina, is explained.

In addition to dealing with mega-mining, Argentinian land laws have made life increasingly difficult for small farmers. Leasing to profit-oriented properties companies who do not value long-term sustainability has increased the prioritization of short-term profits. Dialogo Chino[3] highlights this issue, and many others that shed light on the sustainable issues and projects in Argentina.

Like many countries, Argentina is a part of the Organization for Economic Cooperation and Development (OECD). These documents outline policies, frameworks, and various innovations in Argentina.

- **Agriculture Policies in Argentina**[4]
- **Green Growth and Eco-Innovation**[5]

Sustainability Career Pathways

Human Rights. Fighting for human rights isn't just for activists. Within this sector, there are educators, social media experts, programmers, lawyers, campaigners, and fundraisers. Here is an introduction to all the ways you can help advance human rights[6], and a list of five exciting human rights careers[7] to explore.

Government Employee. As Nicki notes, "There is no climate justice without justice for women and social justice." There are many government agencies, like the Equal Employment Opportunities Commission[8] in the U.S., that employ staff to investigate and enforce equal employment laws. Other agencies help promote development, and support minorities and small businesses. Working for the government offers many opportunities to help support social change across many sectors. Want to learn more? Start with this pro and con list of working for the government[9].

Legislative Aid. As Nicki notes, changing the law is a key way to create a sustainable future. Elected officials drive new policies and introduce new bills. Working with them as legislative aides can be an important way to help push for and craft environmental legislation. Does this sound like the path for you? Explore this introduction to the field[10].

---

1 https://www.mockcop.org/treaty/

2 https://www.forbes.com/sites/sap/2019/10/22/argentina-grows-a-more-sustainable-and-efficient-agricultural-sector-with-machine-learning-and-geospatial-technology/?sh=79d02b9663bc

3 https://dialogochino.net/en/agriculture/39089-argentinas-land-laws-stifle-sustainable-agriculture-soy/

4 https://www.oecd.org/officialdocuments/publicdisplaydocumentpdf/?cote=TAD/CA(2018)9/FINAL&docLanguage=En

5 https://www.oecd.org/innovation/inno/greengrowthandeco-innovation.htm

6 https://www.humanrightscareers.com/careers/

7 https://www.humanrightscareers.com/magazine/5-exciting-human-rights-career-paths/

8 https://www.eeoc.gov/

9 https://www.thebalancecareers.com/the-pros-and-cons-of-a-government-job-1669764

10 https://www.thebalancecareers.com/government-job-profile-congressional-staffer-1669626

Raising our Voices for Change

Carmen Perez, The Gathering For Justice, Oxnard, California / New York

Call to Action

Raise your voice for change! Join Carmen in the fight for justice. Follow her on Twitter & Instagram: @msladyjustice1 & learn about the Gathering for Justice: gatheringforjustice.org

Values

- Compassion
- Dedication
- Solidarity
- Reconciliation
- Commitment
- Diligence
- Leadership

Lessons Learned

You can rise above personal tragedy to become a better person, and change your life.

Learning from our mentors and heroes can help us find the way to bring their wisdom into the challenges we face today and find solutions to create a sustainable future.

By working together in solidarity we can achieve much more.

One of the founders of the Women's March, Carmen Perez, rose to national fame in 2017.

But her path to get there was not without challenges—and she learned many lessons along the way. These lessons came as much from her forebears—leaders like Nane Alejandrez, the founder of Barrios Unidos, and Harry Belafonte, a civil rights activist and singer who started The Gathering for Justice—as well as from her basketball coaches Pat Bell and Terrel Harrison, her professor Aida Hurtado, and from her own family, and her personal history of loss and forgiveness. Through these struggles, she realized the importance of looking at injustice from many perspectives,including an environmental one.

Language Arts

Write 15 questions you would like to ask Carmen about her life, her activism, and the incidents that prompted her to become involved in it. Why did you choose those questions? (Write your answer out in a full paragraph).

Farm workers in California have an extensive history of activism. Perhaps the best-known activists in this movement are Cesar Chavez and Dolores Huerta. Write a research paper about them, explaining how their work helped pave the way for younger generations to get involved in the issues affecting farm workers.

Create a five-minute video explaining the adverse effects of using pesticides on crops, not just on consumers, but on the people harvesting the food and living near the fields. What are the most common adverse effects of being exposed to these chemicals? What types of regulation need to be in place to ensure that people are not being hurt by these chemicals?

One of the biggest issues for farm workers is the lack of access to Personal Protective Equipment (PPE). The Covid-19 pandemic has only made the problem more serious. Write an essay about the threat to public health that farm workers face on a daily basis because of the lack of PPE.

STEM Activities

Although Carmen does not directly address mental health issues, her story is centered around her resilience, and her ability to deal with tragedy in her life and transform emotional suffering into a positive outcome. Create a mock mental health workshop to which you could invite a counselor to speak to your peers about the importance of mental health, creating an environment in which students can speak about their experiences.

Carmen has faced many difficult times, but in that regard, she is not unlike many young adults. Design a group activity that allows students to talk about national or personal events that have affected them, and have made them want to change something in their lives or communities.

- **Example:** Scene from Freedom Writers. Have all of the students stand in a line, and step forward or backward if the statement spoken applies to them.

Two of the greatest problems facing our country today are climate change/non-sustainable practices, and racism/injustice. Explain how these two problems are connected, and suggest ways that both problems could be solved simultaneously.

Sustainability Innovations

In addition to helping people in prisons turn their lives around, there are hundreds of wrongfully imprisoned individuals in the U.S. The Innocence Project[1] is one of many organizations working to exonerate wrongfully imprisoned individuals based on DNA testing and reform.

- **Examples -** *Just Mercy* (Movie) and *The Innocence Files* (Netflix TV Show)

The National Alliance on Mental Health[2] and the American Health Association[3] are two organizations that prioritize mental health, and create an open environment that welcomes everyone to speak about and understand the importance of mental health.

Barrios Unidos[4] is an organization founded by Nane Alejandrez with the mission of promoting multicultural social justice, nonviolence, and economic equity through cultural healing, civic leadership, and youth and community development.

Sustainability Career Pathways

Criminal Justice Reformer. The criminal justice system needs reform: there is a desperate need to shift the emphasis away from long prison sentences to rehabilitation, reconciliation and healing. This will require the help of dedicated individuals--from holistic defense attorneys and progressive prosecutors, to prison educators and society reentry specialists. For an introduction to the many opportunities in this field, read this American Bar Association article[5].

Restorative Justice Advocate. Restorative justice shifts the focus away from punishment, to repairing the harm done to the victim and the community. This reframing of justice is in its infancy; it will require passionate organizers and communicators to change peoples' understanding of these issues. Organizations like the Centre for Justice & Reconciliation are a good place to start; they offer advice on how you can create local efforts to support restorative justice[6]. Also, here is a listing of jobs and organizations focused on justice and peace[7].

Spiritual Leader. Ministers, rabbis, imams, and other spiritual leaders have played a key role in social reform for centuries. If you are a religious person, you might want to consider becoming a leader in the spiritual community of your faith, and use this position to help heal your community, and to address issues of environmental injustice, xenophobia, misogyny, prison reform, and climate change. Ministers are required to get both a bachelor's degree, and a divinity degree, but there are other spiritual callings (and jobs in religious NGOs) that require less schooling. For more on this calling, read here[8].

Diversity & Inclusion (D&I) Officer. More corporations are recognizing the opportunity and responsibility to maintain diverse workforces, and to ensure that all workers feel included in the company culture. There are now a variety of D&I jobs at many large companies, from VPs of D&I, to diversity managers, to D&I trainers. For an introduction to this field[9] and opportunities[10], read these articles.

---

1 https://innocenceproject.org/

2 https://innocenceproject.org/

3 https://www.aha.org/mental-health-awareness-month

4 https://barriosunidos.net/

5 https://www.americanbar.org/careercenter/blog/new-opportunities-in-criminal-justice-reform/

6 https://restorativejustice.org/resources/

7 https://justiceandpeace.georgetown.edu/resources/careers/

8 https://www.learnhowtobecome.org/minister/

9 https://www.aihr.com/blog/diversity-and-inclusion-jobs/

10 https://www.shrm.org/membership/communities/chapters/pages/studentarticleconsideranhrcareerindi0620.aspx

Rise Up For Africa!

Vanessa Nakate, The Rise Up Movement, Fridays For Future Uganda, Uganda

☀ Call to Action

Join Vanessa & other youth climate activists around the world in fighting for climate action now.
Follow on Twitter: @vanessa_vash @RiseupMovement1 & listen to the "Why Climate Activism?" podcast

☀ Values

- Tenacious
- Integrity
- Resourceful
- Self-Confident
- Self-Respect

☀ Lessons Learned

Representation from all countries and regions—and recognition of those who are doing the work—is important, especially when it comes to fighting the effects of climate change.

Vanessa turned a personally hurtful and disrespectful incident into an opportunity to use her voice to speak up for millions for African people. We all must stand up for each other.

Standing up for what you believe in all can blossom - like for Vanessa, into a national movement.

When Vanessa Nakate was cropped out of a photo with Greta Thunberg and other white climate change activists, she said, "You didn't just erase a photo. You erased a continent. But I am stronger than ever.".

With these words, Vanessa made an important point about the global fight against climate change: representation — of all colors, creeds, and continents — is critical. For years, Vanessa has felt that African countries have been left out of the picture when it comes to climate change activism. Her goal is to change the narrative.

At Davos, online, and in her home country of Uganda, she has made it her mission to shine a light on African activists who are making a difference. After months of solo protests in front of Uganda's parliament, she founded the Rise Up Africa Movement with Fridays for Future International. Vanessa is not waiting to make her voice heard: she's lifting it up now.

☀ Language Arts

Using Vanessa's life story for inspiration, write a fable that deals with reaching her specific goals. Choose another climate change activist, and write a poem about their cause. Choose a third, and write down ten questions you'd like to ask them.

Write a five-paragraph research essay explaining the major threats the African continent is facing because of climate change.

Create a graphic novel-style narrative of Vanessa's story.

STEM Activities

Following Vanessa's example, organize a climate strike in your school. This will take much planning: you will have to mobilize other students to engage and co-lead; promote your event; organize the logistics of the strike (e.g., timing and location); and coordinate the artistic elements of producing signs, street theatre, and presentations. If your numbers are small in the beginning, don't be discouraged: as Vanessa has shown us, even a strike of just one person can grow into a large movement.

Write a proposal for your school to convert to more efficient lighting, or to install solar panels on your school's rooftop. Calculate how much energy these changes would save or generate. How much would the initial investment be? How quickly would the investment pay for itself and start saving money for the school? Bonus: Calculate how much CO2 would be saved (factoring in the initial ecological costs of lighting or solar panels).

Sustainability Innovations

Many organizations in Africa have made it their mission to attack climate change and improve sustainability efforts throughout the continent. Here are some organizations that are making positive changes:

Climate Change Institute Uganda[1]: This institute was founded in 2017 to target the issue of climate change by tackling policy changes; reducing fossil fuel usage; and proper waste management.

African Wildlife Foundation[2]: This foundation has focused its efforts on climate-smart agriculture, access to secure water resources, protecting forests, and many other important issues.

Advocates Coalition for Development and Environment[3]: ACODE is a public policy research and advocacy think tank based in Uganda. Their projects include enabling policy conditions for the inclusion of a green economy, gender-responsive budgeting, and supporting business opportunities for rural women.

Sustainability Career Pathways

Climate Activist. Now, and in the years to come, there will be a growing need for individuals dedicated to building the political commitment to stabilize Earth's climate. This is an activity you can join in with now. Organize a Friday climate strike[4] at your town hall; or pressure your school to divest from fossil fuel stocks, or invest in renewable energy. As Vanessa has shown, it only takes one person to start a movement. The best way to enter this field and make a difference is to get active now! Visit Idealist.org[5] to explore thousands of jobs, internships, and volunteer opportunities for activists.

Community Organizer. Engaging one's community around important environmental and social challenges is an important career path and community service. There are many programs that teach how to organize, from online courses such as this one[6], to one-year environmental organizing field schools like Green Corps[7].

Storyteller. Storytelling is powerful. Stories inspire, inform, and mobilize others to take action. Vanessa's initiative, 1 Million Activist Stories[8], is one effort to chronicle and share the stories of activists who are working to make a difference. Becoming a journalist (including in your school paper), blogger, novelist, or other type of communicator can be a way for you to channel your storytelling skills into making a difference in the world.

National and International Governance. The United Nations and national governments are playing (or at least should be playing) a key role in negotiating and mapping out the pathway to a zero-carbon future. Perhaps your career lies in helping to negotiate climate commitments? Or creating ways to incentivize our transition to a sustainable future? Explore this booklet on international relations-focused government jobs in the United States[9] or this introduction to working at the United Nations[10].

1 https://www.climateinstituteug.org/#:~:text=Climate%20Change%20Institute%20Uganda%20is,on%20climate%20change%20in%20Uganda
2 https://www.awf.org/land-protection/climate-change
3 https://www.acode-u.org/green-economy
4 https://fridaysforfuture.org/
5 https://www.idealist.org/
6 https://www.coursera.org/learn/community-organizing
7 https://greencorps.org/
8 https://www.riseupmovementafrica.org/
9 https://successworks.wisc.edu/wp-content/uploads/sites/39/2017/06/Making-Global-Impact.pdf
10 https://careers.un.org/lbw/Home.aspxf

Sustainability for Black Communities

Illai Kenney, HBCU Green Fund, Atlanta

Call to Action

Support Illai's work to create an equitable, environmental infrastructure, with green endowments for Historically Black Colleges & Universities. hbcugreenfund.org

Values

- Committed
- Determined
- Self-Confident
- Leader
- Social Justice
- Environmentalist

Lessons Learned

Illai's family gave her the gift of a passion for activism, and the strength of character to pursue change.

Our choices play a large role in creating the world we live in. Making responsible choices is the way to create a better world.

People of all ages, backgrounds, and ethnicities can contribute to make the world a better, more sustainable place. A good leader sees this, and finds ways to inspire and encourage everyone to play their part.

If you want to pursue a goal, you must first educate yourself. Accurate, relevant information will allow you to make better choices, and these choices will empower you.

From her mother's work in sustainability issues, even as a child Illai Kenney understood that marginalized communities like hers are very often the communities most negatively impacted by issues like global warming and climate change.

And as a kid, she felt it was unfair that she didn't have a say in the matter. "We are the ones who are going to be most impacted by the decisions being made. But what recourse do we have? We can't vote. We can't lobby. It was a daunting realization to come to," she says. That the planet, and her right to a healthy, sustainable future, could be ruined because of the decisions of a generation disconnected from her own, was disempowering. So, in 2003, at the age of 12, she decided to form the nonprofit Georgia Kids Against Pollution.

This journey toward a more sustainable world culminated with the founding of the HBCU Green Fund – a fund that supports projects that reduce energy and water usage at Historically Black Colleges and Universities.

Language Arts

Write an essay about why poor communities of color are more affected by climate change than wealthier ones. How does economic status and race affect someone's access to basic needs, such as clean water, clean air, and quality food? In your opinion, what can be done to correct this problem?

Write the script of an imaginary conversation between a young environmental activist and members of the board of directors of an energy corporation (natural gas, nuclear energy, coal power, or oil). During the conversation the activist tries to convince the executives to adopt more environmentally friendly practices. As you write your script, ask yourself: How could the activist convince them? What should he or she focus on? How can young people make their voices heard, and be taken seriously, in a corporate setting?

A big part of Illai's activism was inspired by her mother and grandmother. Write a narrative essay in which you reflect on a member of your family, a teacher, or a friend whose presence in your life has inspired you to fight for a goal that would benefit not only you but those around you.

STEM Activities

Compare the asthma rates of states with a history of lower air quality to those in states with higher air quality, and construct a bar graph comparing the data. Calculate the center (median, mean) and spread (interquartile range, standard deviation) of two or more different data sets.

- **Air Quality Tracker**[1]
- **CDC Asthma Data**[2]

Invisible air pollutants make the air dangerous for people to breathe, causing respiratory illnesses such as asthma. Some engineers make it their specialty to design vehicles, machines, and manufacturing plants that emit as few pollutants as possible. In this activity[3], students will learn about the major types of air pollutants and how they affect our health; conduct a simple invisible air pollutant test; explain how pollutants from the air can affect water and plant growth; and describe how engineers are addressing the problem of invisible air pollution.

Have students brainstorm a list of uses of water in the school or at home, and design a data collection plan to find how much water is being used. Then, using a spreadsheet with the collected data, have them create graphs to show the results. Ask them to research scientific resources that estimate the amount of water used for different activities (showering, drinking from water fountains, etc.), and compare these estimates with the data they have collected. Then have them research water-flow control devices and estimate the total investment needed to install these devices in the school or at home; and the total water savings (in both gallons and costs) that could be realized by using them in one year.

- **Using the water usage data collected,** ask students to identify and carry out relevant calculations to support the development of a water conservation plan for their school or home (e.g., average amount of water used per student/person, and by the entire school/household over a certain time period).
- **Compare the students' water usage data** to water usage in island nations like the Seychelles.

Sustainability Innovations

Illai and Felicia have become models for their community through their voices, and their projects, which are making a difference for everyone. In addition to environmental goals, sustainability is concerned with eliminating racism, and empowering all. YWCA Los Angeles[4] is one of the leading organizations in Southern California that is targeting the elimination of racism, and the empowerment of women. They operate empowerment centers throughout the city to help with the development of their programs, which address issues of child development, sexual assault, and domestic violence, among many others.

Illai is one of many strong Black women who are taking charge of creating a better future. For example, Jacqueline Patterson, the director of the NAACP's Environmental Climate and Justice Program, has helped to shed a light on the disproportionate issues facing Black females. She founded the NAACP's Power to the People[5] campaign, targeting the high energy costs for Black Americans, and the disproportionate exposure to coal plants of African American children.

Illai founded Georgia Kids Against Pollution at a young age; many other students today have the same passion for activism. Hannah Testa is an environmental activist who at a young age founded Hannah4Change[6], which is focused on addressing the plastic pollution crisis in the U.S.

Sustainability Career Pathways

Sustainability Director at a university or school. Most colleges and universities, and even some high schools, now have a sustainability director, who helps to coordinate sustainability activities throughout the different departments--from maintenance and transportation to energy production, and even classroom curricula. They also often serve as liaison to the city or town the university is in, helping to address surrounding environmental issues and ensuring that the university is a good environmental steward. Does this job--heavy on management, leadership, and coordination--sound good to you? Learn more here[7] .

Corporate Sustainability Officer. Companies tend to prioritize growth, even at the expense of the environment—and thus their own long-term well-being, as well as society's. Unfortunately, corporate cultures are slow to change. But change has started. Many companies now have a corporate sustainability officer to help drive change from within. This is an opportunity to improve the environmental effects of the world's most influential entities. Want to learn how? Read here[8]. Or read a personal account here[9].

Green Fund Manager. With billions of dollars being invested in companies, where that money goes shapes the future of business. Do we invest in oil companies, or renewable energy companies? In downtown real estate, or in suburban malls? Working with a socially responsible investment firm, or with a university or foundation as an asset manager can be a great way to help develop the sustainable business sector. Here is a brief introduction to the many jobs in the field[10].

1 https://www.epa.gov/outdoor-air-quality-data/air-data-daily-air-quality-tracker
2 https://www.cdc.gov/asthma/nhis/default.htm
3 https://www.teachengineering.org/activities/view/cub_air_lesson03_activity1
4 https://ywcagla.org/advocacy/
5 https://www.greenamerica.org/climate-change-100-reasons-hope/power-people-fueling-revolution-energy-justice
6 https://www.hannah4change.org/
7 https://www.studyinternational.com/news/jobs-of-the-future-how-do-i-become-a-sustainability-manager/
8 https://www.careerexplorer.com/careers/sustainability-officer/
9 https://impakter.com/choosing-the-harder-path-the-journey-towards-a-job-in-corporate-sustainability/
10 http://finanzasostenibile.it/wp-content/uploads/2017/04/13-04-2017_FBicciato_ProfessioniSRI_SdR.pdf

Water Walker

Autumn Peltier, Chief Water Commissioner, Anishinabek Nation, Canada

☀ Call to Action

Respect water. Take a stand for the water rights of Indigenous peoples. Follow Autumn on Instagram and share her posts: @autumn.peltier.

☀ Values

- Courage
- Commitment
- Dedication
- Respect
- Legacy

☀ Lessons Learned

Stand up for what you know is right. Raise your voice and speak the truth, even to very powerful people.

It's not enough to believe in what's right: we are all called to do something about it—to walk the walk.

We can do more in our homes and at the local level, through awareness campaigns: inspiring people to bring about change.

The grandniece of Josephine Mandamin--an Anishinaabe First Nations elder who started the Water Walk movement—Autumn Peltier has activism in her blood. Still in her teens, she has been a powerful voice for Indigenous people everywhere, calling on world leaders to protect precious water resources that are threatened by drilling for oil pipelines and climate change. She has especially held her own government in Canada accountable, and famously told Prime Minister Justin Trudeau that she was "very unhappy" with the choices he had made regarding First Nations lands. She continues to talk the talk and walk the walk every day for water rights around the world.

☀ Language Arts

Research the fight of Indigenous people for water rights in your country. With the information you have gathered, write a short story for children that helps to explain the importance of clean and safe water for everyone.

Using public domain images, create a series of posters (no less than six) inviting people to participate in water conservation activities. The posters must have both images and text. Explain your choices (why you chose the images and the words you chose).

Write a letter to your local government highlighting the importance of clean, safe water in your area, and the adverse effects of not having access to it.

STEM Activities

Research and evaluate one current project/development that negatively affects Indigenous lands, and explain why you disapprove of the project; then offer alternative solutions.

Compare the price of and access to clean water in Indigenous communities to that in suburban areas. Create a graph to display the differences between these communities.

Identify one long-term drinking water advisory that is currently in effect that should be remedied; explain why addressing this particular advisory is a priority[1].

Sustainability Innovations

Evaluate the various aspects of water efficiency. Create a flow chart that details the problems, and shows the steps that can be taken to solve them[2].

Access to fresh water and sanitation is a challenge, particularly in slums. Here is an article describing three different strategies for providing sanitation in slums[3]. Assess the pros and cons of each. Then work as a group to think of other strategies that could work.

Access to water is a fundamental human right. Yet often water is treated as a commodity to be sold--sometimes at unaffordable prices. Explore the conflict between community water rights and the commodification of water. Watch The Story of Water[4], then research and write about one of the case studies mentioned in the video.

Sustainability Career Pathways

Do you want to dedicate your career to bringing fresh water to people? Here is a good article[5] to describe the dozens of careers you could choose to do just that. And here are a few examples:

Water Rights Activist. Nearly a billion of the earth's people lack access to clean water; it will take concerted action to hold governments accountable for providing this essential right to people. As activists, we can put pressure on governments to build the infrastructure needed and protect the sources of water for communities, and on companies to ensure they don't pollute the waters. Interested in learning more? Read this review of water activism[6] and visit groups like Clean Water Action[7] to learn about their work.

Environmental Lawyer. In many countries, clean water is protected by law. Lawyers can help to enforce these laws, and can sue to stop violations of these laws, as groups like Earthjustice[8] do. Here is a brief overview of what an environmental lawyer is[9], how to become one[10] , and a guide to careers in Environmental Law[11].

Water and Sanitation Engineer. Would you rather help actually get the water to the people, than fight for their right to have it? Water and sanitation engineers help plan and build the water systems and piping needed to deliver fresh water to communities, and take away sewage. Here is an introduction to this essential field[12].

Water and Wastewater Managers. Water and sanitation systems need trained operators to maintain them. Technicians, managers, and plant operators are all essential for the smooth delivery of water and the removal of waste. These essential jobs are in demand all around the world. Learn more here[13].

1 https://www.sac-isc.gc.ca/eng/1506514143353/1533317130660
2 https://www.allianceforwaterefficiency.org/impact/research-priorities
3 https://www.good.is/articles/the-silicon-valley-of-shit-nairobi-is-ground-zero-for-sanitation-innovation
4 https://www.youtube.com/watch?v=04jTleV0gK0&feature=emb_logo
5 https://www.learnhowtobecome.org/make-a-difference-careers/clean-water/
6 https://www.bloomberg.com/news/articles/2016-12-30/the-year-in-water-activism
7 https://www.cleanwateraction.org/about/who-we-are
8 https://earthjustice.org/healthy-communities/clean-water
9 https://www.environmentalscience.org/career/environmental-lawyer
10 https://www.sierraclub.org/sierra/cool-schools-2017/how-be-environmental-lawyer
11 https://hls.harvard.edu/content/uploads/2008/07/full-working-draft.pdf
12 https://www.careerexplorer.com/careers/water-engineer/
13 https://www.environmentalscience.org/career/wastewater-treatment-operator

III

INSPIRE!

Education Champions

It's been a delight to have met many of the young people featured in this book. They are inspiring spokespersons and courageous champions of caring for our animal friends and the planet. Let their numbers grow!

DR. JANE GOODALL

A Call To Civic Action

Scott Warren, Generation Citizen
Rhode Island

Call to Action

Learn more about Scott's work helping to educate young people in basic civics at generationcitizen.org. Check out his book, Generation Citizen: The Power of Youth in Our Politics

Values

- Civic-Minded
- Citizen
- Leader
- Committed
- Determined
- Informed

Lessons Learned

We need to have an action-oriented approach in order to bring young people into politics.

It is important to engage young people through working on issues they care about.

Young people hold a great amount of power. It's important to channel and direct it in positive ways.

Scott Warren is an emerging leader in the youth civics and voting rights movements.
The organization he cofounded, Generation Citizen, works to ensure that every student in the US receives an effective civics education, which provides them with the knowledge and skills necessary to participate in our democracy as active citizens. Scott is also a leading voting rights advocate, fighting to lower the voting age across the country to 16. Scott is the author of a book about his nonprofit work and advocacy, called Generation Citizen: The Power of Youth in Our Politics. His work has been featured in US News and World Report, Time Magazine, the New York Daily News, The Hill, the Christian Science Monitor, the New York Post, the Baltimore Sun, and Education Week, among others.

Language Arts

Do you agree with Scott that the voting age should be lowered to 16 years old? Why or why not? Write an argumentative essay (no less than 1,000 words), supporting your opinion. You must use at least two secondary sources to support your opinion.

- How would you motivate your friends and family to register to vote? Find out where your polling place is and design an invitation to send to people to motivate them to go and register.

Build a Jeopardy game[1] designed to educate young people on civics, the concept of democracy, and the importance of voting. You can use the template found here.

Create an Escape Room game. If you need ideas, here is a good article[2] to get you started. Use basic civics concepts as your clues, and make sure you increase the level of difficulty as you go. The "escape room" must have at least three rooms, and a minimum of five clues per room.

STEM Activities

Lowering the voting age across the country is just one battle that voting advocates face. In addition to voting eligibility, it is important that voters understand their rights and the liberties extended to them. What are your voting rights? How does the way votes are tallied in the U.S. compare to the voting process in other countries?

What percentage of the US population is currently being either partially or fully impeded from voting? Consider the situation for resident aliens, prisoners and former prisoners, and citizens of cities like the District of Columbia, and territories like Puerto Rico. Assess the size of these populations and calculate the total number of citizens that are being disenfranchised. Is it larger or smaller than the number of 16 and 17-year-olds that could be added to voter rolls if the voting age were lowered? Use statistical analysis (mean, medium, spread, etc) to analyze the data.

In addition to advocating for voting rights, students need to understand the policies they are voting for or against when they become eligible to vote. Research one policy that was voted on during the past election and explain why it is important to you, and how your vote would matter as a part of the election process.

Generation Citizen seeks to bring civics education back into the classroom in order to teach and inspire youth to participate in politics. Games can be an engaging way to motivate students to learn more about civics. Visit iCivics and select a few different games to play. Then, to test your own civics knowledge, take the U.S. Civics test[3] that's given to applicants seeking to become U.S. citizens.

Sustainability Innovations

Scott has done amazing work as a part of the voting rights movement. Campus Vote[4] and many other great organizations have made it part of their mission to tackle barriers for young voters and help them gain access to the polls. Identify one organization in your community that focuses on advocating for youth voting rights that you would like to collaborate with or volunteer at.

Create a flyer about the importance of youth voting and prepare a pitch to your school principal on why the flyers should be distributed throughout the school and supported by the student body government.

Sustainability Career Pathways

Civics Educator. Too few students today graduate with a strong understanding of how government works, and how it can work to make their countries and the world a better place. As Scott's efforts show, an engaged civics education program can do more than just inform; it can also inspire action. Want to be a civics teacher? Explore Generation Citizen's teacher-led civics education model[5]. Also, seek out a trusted teacher who could help bring civics education to your school, if you don't already have it.

Nonprofit Manager. Many people work for nonprofit organizations; some, like Scott, even create new nonprofits. But very few have any formal management training, which is an ongoing problem in this sector. There are programs to train managers for nonprofit organizations specifically. While many of these are masters' level programs (such as these leading programs[6]), there are also informal and undergraduate opportunities to learn essential management skills. If you're really serious about this path, here's a 500+ page introduction to the field[7].

International Governance. The United Nations and its agencies, for example the UN Environment Programme, play a critical role in creating a more sustainable, more equitable future. Perhaps your career lies in working for the United Nations[8]? Or in working for one of the many nongovernmental organizations working to address the numerous challenges in international governance?

1 https://jeopardylabs.com./

2 https://teachingideas.ca/2020/05/17/escape-room-2/

3 https://www.uscis.gov/sites/default/files/document/crc/M_1778.pdf

4 https://www.campusvoteproject.org/youth-voting-rights

5 https://www.nea.org/advocating-for-change/new-from-nea/forgotten-purpose-civics-education-public-schools

6 https://www.usnews.com/best-graduate-schools/top-public-affairs-schools/nonprofit-management-rankings

7 https://www.amazon.com/exec/obidos/ASIN/1119585457/stansociinn09-20

8 https://careers.un.org/lbw/Home.aspx

Acting Locally & In Solidarity With Others

Shreya KC, Nepalese Youth For Climate Action Nepal

Call to Action

Invite your friends to join you in organizing a clean-up campaign in your community! Visit NYCA: www.nyca.net.np
Follow Shreya on Twitter @KCShreya1 & read her blog https://kcshreya.wordpress.com/

Values

- Committed
- Enthusiastic
- Determined
- Responsible
- Leadership

Lessons Learned

When you first learn about the terrible effects of climate change, decide to dig down and educate yourself on the issues.

Even though climate change is a global problem, if we act locally and in solidarity with others in our communities, we can make meaningful change.

The climate crisis is real: we all need to recognize our responsibility, and acknowledge our power to do something about it.

Nepal is a country that is being hit especially hard by the effects of climate change.
So when Shreya accidentally ended up taking a class in environmental science, she was immediately interested in the subject. She started to work with a Nepalese youth organization and organized many events and campaigns. She even got to represent Nepal at the COP25 conference in Madrid. For Shreya, one thing is clear: today's youth have to accept their responsibility and assume the power they have to change the future of our planet for the better.

Language Arts

Write an essay (at least five paragraphs) explaining why you should be allowed to attend the UN's Youth Conference on Climate Change in your region. Explain not only on what you would learn at the conference, but also on what you can contribute to it.

The biggest challenge a country like Nepal has when it comes to educating their people in global issues is its remoteness, and the people's lack of access to technology. However, most people nowadays have access to a cell phone. Select a part of the world where people have little access to traditional means of information sharing, and create an Instagram or Tik Tok campaign designed to educate people in that part of the world about the effect climate change is having on their region.

Write a short speech (no more than five minutes long) about the importance of educating people about climate change in your part of the world, and explaining what people can do to mitigate the adverse effects it has in your home country.

Write a research essay about what the life of a Nepalese teenager is like, and explain how climate change has affected his or her life.

STEM Activities

Shreya's greatest gift is not only her motivation to work for a sustainable future, but also her pride in her community. Research one sustainability goal that you would like your state or county to target in 2021. Create a diagram explaining this issue and what needs to be done to address it.

Shreya began her journey by organizing a trash pickup in her community. Research and share one alternative material or product that helps to reduce trash pollution

- **Example:** Stasher bags[1] are 100% silicone food-grade reusable bags that are a great alternative to plastic bags or other non-sustainable storage options.

Nepal is famous as the location of Mt. Everest, the world's tallest mountain, and a world heritage site that 100,000 people visit each year. Since the mountain was first scaled in 1953, thousands of people have climbed Everest and have left garbage strewn up its face. Nepal is working to solve this problem, including requiring climbers to each bring down with them 8 kilograms of garbage, or forfeit a $4,000 deposit. Read about these efforts[2], then brainstorm other strategies to both prevent more garbage from being left behind, and ways to get rid of this trashy legacy of the past 70 years.

Sustainability Innovations

Shreya enhanced her knowledge of sustainability and nurtured her internal drive at the 6th National Youth Conference on Climate Change. Identify a climate change conference you would like to participate in, and write a letter to a prospective sponsor explaining why participating in this conference is important.

After her experience at the conference, Shreya's focus shifted to her involvement with the Nepalese Youth for Climate Action Network (NYCA). The Climate Action Network (CAN)[3] has numerous working groups and connects individuals globally. Identify one CAN working group that addresses issues that students might like to pursue a career in.

Sustainability Career Pathways

Environmental Educator. It was Shreya's exposure to environmental issues in college that led her to become a leading climate activist. The role of teachers in informing and energizing students cannot be overstated. Yet a surprising number of schools lack educators who are versed in sustainability and environmental issues. Educators who either directly or indirectly incorporate sustainability into their lessons, or focus on environmental issues, are essential in helping future generations understand the environmental challenges we face--and their possible solutions. Learn more about the field here[4].

Environmental Organizer. By mobilizing her community, Shreya was able to start a transformation: making one street prettier, its residents prouder, and local businesses more responsible. Engaging one's community around important environmental and social challenges is an important career path and community service. There are many programs that teach how to organize, from online courses (such as this one[5]), to one-year environmental organizing field schools like Green Corps[6].

International Governance. The United Nations and its agencies, for example the UN Environment Programme, play a critical role in creating a more sustainable, more equitable future. Perhaps your career lies in working for the United Nations[7]? Or in working for one of the many nongovernmental organizations working to improve the challenging issues of international governance?

International Development. As countries develop, many grapple not just with governance issues but with sustainability challenges as well. There is a vast field of careers in international development, some of which focus on "sustainable development." Here is a large database of international development jobs[8]. The Peace Corps sends young Americans to foreign countries for two-year assignments as development ambassadors. If you're from the U.S., explore working with The Peace Corps[9], or find an equivalent program in your country.

1 https://www.stasherbag.com/collections/the-stasher-ecosystem
2 https://www.nationalgeographic.org/article/trash-and-overcrowding-top-world/
3 https://climatenetwork.org/our-work/can-working-groups/
4 https://www.environmentalscience.org/career/environmental-educator
5 https://www.coursera.org/learn/community-organizing
6 https://greencorps.org/
7 https://careers.un.org/lbw/Home.aspx
8 https://www.devnetjobs.org/
9 https://www.peacecorps.gov/

A Voice For Youth & Ocean

Angelique Pouponnea, SYAH
Seychelles

Call to Action

Learn more about best practices in the Blue Economy: seyccat.org
Learn about Angelique's work with young people here: syah- seychelles. weebly.com

Values

- Committed
- Dedicated
- Responsible
- Innovation
- Environmentalist
- Leader

Lessons Learned

Many of the answers for living a sustainable life can be found in community involvement.

Economic growth should not come at the price of the destruction of the Earth. We need to work together to find ways to grow sustainably.

Change is best achieved when communities come together to fight for it.

When Angelique returned home to the Seychelles after studying abroad, she almost didn't recognize her beloved island home.

Where once there had been a footpath along a marsh, now there was a fancy new hotel—and mountains of plastic trash. Together with an organization she founded, Angelique managed to make plastic pollution a decisive political issue for an upcoming election—and the beginning of the end for single-use plastic bags in the Seychelles.

Language Arts

Write a script for a telephone outreach campaign in which you invite people in your community to advocate for change. Which environmental issue would you choose to tackle, and why? How would you persuade people to join you? Focus on the arguments you would present, and the possible counterarguments that others might challenge you with.

Create a series of no less than six before-and-after posters that explain the damage that is being done to coastlines because of real estate development. Then, in a separate poster, offer three possible sustainable alternatives. Use both images and text. On a separate sheet of paper, explain your choices.

Using the example of the Seychelles, write an essay in which you explain the dangers of uncontrolled industrial or other growth in coastal areas. How does the growth affect the people living in these places? How does it affect the wildlife? What are the consequences of the destruction caused by indiscriminate growth along vulnerable coastlines?

Angelique's experiences when she returned to her home from London must have been incredibly upsetting. Drawing on her story for inspiration, write a short children's story about a young person who has to deal with the destruction of his or her home, and who turns that heartbreak into inspiration to bring about positive change. (You may use pictures to complement your writing if you like.)

STEM Activities

Calculate the amount of waste, and the amount of recycling that has been collected in the Seychelles this year. Compare these numbers to the volume of waste in the Seychelles over the past 20 years. Describe how you think assistance from individuals like Angelique could have impacted the Seychelles throughout its history.

The Ocean Conservancy[1] releases annual reports on trash collected from the oceans around the world. Have students review these reports and create a graph of one of the aspects of data presented over time - such as the number of volunteers per country, the amount of trash collected by weight or by location, or the top 10 items collected. Then use this graph to create an equation that models the average rate of growth or decline. Depending on the data selected, if the growth (or decline) continues at the same rate, predict what the Ocean Conservancy's 2050 report on that data will look like.

Assess the Small Island Developing States Youth Aims-Hub (SIYAH), and the projects they are working on. Identify 2-3 projects that you consider to be the most important for creating change and the momentum needed to reach their sustainability goals.

First research SIYAH and the Seychelles. Then imagine being in Angelique's shoes, as CEO of the Seychelles' Conservation and Climate Adaptation Trust Fund. Create a list of 8-10 issues the Seychelles and other similar islands are facing, and create a proposed distribution of funds, indicating the percentage that you would allocate for each issue, and explaining why.

Angelique was devastated to see that the quiet, beautiful marsh she had known as a child, once filled with life, now littered with plastic waste. Plastics are made of polypropylene, which takes a very long time to break down. Scientists and engineers are looking for ways to develop biodegradable alternatives to these plastics. In this experiment[2], students will create polymer materials made from renewable, nontoxic components, and will evaluate their biodegradability, and compare them to PET or PLA plastics brought from home.

One of the ways we can reduce plastic pollution is by not using plastic in the first place! Challenge students to redesign a new type of packaging—for example, for candy, body wash/lotion, or take-out food–using sustainable and environmentally friendly materials. Students can create a 3d model, drawing, or package label to illustrate their improved packaging. Hold a design fair where students can share their ideas for better packaging with each other. For inspiration, have them read this article: Genius Solid Shampoos Use No Plastic Packaging By Leaving Out Water[3].

Take students on a field trip to a local beach, waterway, or park to safely collect debris. Have them record their findings using a shared Google sheet; or have them contribute their data to a global database using apps like the Marine Debris Tracker[4] or Clean Swell[5]. Then have them analyze and interpret their data, and use it to recommend strategies for reducing debris in their local community.

Sustainability Innovations

The Seychelles Sustainable Tourism Foundation[6] is a leading foundation whose goal is to combine the work of the public and private sectors, along with NGOs, to build the Seychelles as a model for sustainable tourism. This is of vital importance to the Seychelles, since they have seen tourism double between 2009-2018--and along with this growth in tourism, increased negative effects on the environment.

Many people view plastic straws and other traditional uses of plastic as the main threats to island communities. However, as reported in this article in the Christian Science Monitor[7] - Seychelles, the Aldabra Clean-up Project also collected 60,000 discarded flip flops and abandoned fishing gear.

When visiting island communities, it is important to follow their travel guidelines, and be respect their travel tips. For example, the Seychelles has a list of Sustainable Travel Tips[8] that can assist in the drastic reduction of carbon emissions, the maintenance of ecological stability, and the reduction of waste.

Sustainability Career Pathways

Blue Economy Business Incubator Manager. The blue economy is in its early development--with new technologies being rapidly developed. Many universities, port cities, and even island nations are encouraging investment in the blue economy. But even when the money is available, as Angelique notes, sometimes the projects and ideas needed to solve environmental problems may not be. Sustainable business incubators help by providing seed money and mentorship to entrepreneurs, including blue economy entrepreneurs. If you'd like to explore this area, check out The Centre for Ocean Ventures & Entrepreneurship (COVE)[9], an incubator based in a former Coast Guard facility on Halifax harbor.

The World Bank, and Regional and Central Banks. The World Bank, regional banks (like the Asian Development Bank), and the central banks of many countries employ thousands of people in a variety of careers--as loan and grant officers, in project oversight, in human resources, in sustainability, and so on. Working at one of these pivotal institutions provides the opportunity to help shape (for good or for ill) the development path many countries are following in a variety of sectors--from energy and education, to agriculture, transportation, and climate change. If interested, a good place to start is the World Bank's Young Professionals Program[10].

Resilience Officer. As climate change intensifies, more cities and regions have hired Chief Resilience Officers (CROs) to oversee adaptation to and mitigation of climate change effects, such as intensifying storms, coastal flooding, fires, and increased migration. Following an early effort by the Rockefeller Foundation, many cities are now hiring resilience officers. If this sounds interesting to you, read more about what CROs do here[11].

Green Chemical Engineer: Along with banning plastic, it will be essential to design alternative sustainable materials to replace plastics. This will require chemical engineers. Explore this field[12] and the ways you could make a career[13] in chemistry to help build a greener economy.

---

1 https://oceanconservancy.org/trash-free-seas/international-coastal-cleanup/annual-data-release/
2 https://csp.umn.edu/wp-content/uploads/2019/11/DyeingtoDegrade_HS.pdf
3 http://www.huffingtonpost.com/entry/genius-solid-shampoos-use-less-plastic-packaging-by-leaving-out-water_us_57963f19e4b02d5d5ed24951
4 http://www.marinedebris.engr.uga.edu/
5 https://oceanconservancy.org/trash-free-seas/international-coastal-cleanup/cleanswell/
6 http://seychellessustainable.org/
7 https://www.csmonitor.com/Environment/2021/0107/How-60-000-discarded-flip-flops-ended-up-on-a-remote-island
8 http://seychellessustainable.org/sustainable-travel-tips/
9 https://coveocean.com/about
10 https://www.worldbank.org/en/about/careers/programs-and-internships/young-professionals-program
11 https://www.rockefellerfoundation.org/blog/what-a-chief-resilience-officer-does/
12 https://www.livescience.com/48134-what-is-chemical-engineering.html
13 https://destinationscanner.com/is-chemical-engineering-a-good-career-inyear/

Awareness Campaigns

Iqbal Badruddin, Fridays for Future Pakistan
Pakistan

Call to Action

Create awareness of climate change in your community. Take Action. Support Iqbal's Awareness Campaign @Fridays4FuturePK on FB Fridaysforfuturepk@gmail.com.

Values

- Educator
- Communicator
- Leader
- Visionary
- Activist
- Environmentalist

Lessons Learned

You are never too young to start teaching people about the issues that affect their community; and you are never too old to start learning about the impact humans have on the environment.

There is an important link between ecological disasters and poverty.

It is always possible to find a way to use your skills to fight for a common goal.

Learning needs to come from within the community, through active participation and listening to each other.

Iqbal Badruddin knows how important education is: his family moved from his hometown to the capital of Pakistan when he was a boy so he could get the best education.

The activism that he practices now, as the founder of Fridays For Future Pakistan, is aimed at the roots of his country's main climate-change problems—through educating the people and protecting their water. "Without water we cannot survive," he says. His Awareness Campaigns are focused on reaching 12- 14-year-olds. "They're the ones who will have to live with the consequences of what we do—or don't do—today," he says. The Awareness Campaigns are teaching people about the importance of taking a broad and varied approach to fighting climate change, from minimizing food waste and using public transportation and bicycles, to planting trees. "We all have to pitch in. It's the only way to secure our future," he says.

Language Arts

Create the written content for the website of an imaginary organization that teaches people about the importance of water conservation in your community. You must include an "About Us" page; an "Education Resources" page (this page must contain at least three links to websites that help explain the issue of water conservation around the world, and the challenges many countries face); a "FAQs" page; a "Ways to Get Involved" page; and a "Blog" link (with one blog post).

Write a research paper about how the terrain of a specific geographical area, like Pakistan, can make that place more or less susceptible to problems of accessing clean water. You must use at least two sources, document all the information using MLA formatting, and include a Works Cited page at the end.

What environmental threats can you see in your community and other communities in the US? (Like, for example, Flint, Michigan, and various tribal lands?) What is being done to educate people about this issue? Write a three-minute speech to encourage people in your own community to educate themselves about this problem, and take action.

STEM Activities

One way that Iqbal was able to engage his community was through the use of Awareness Camps. Create an awareness camp for your classroom that includes 2-3 eco-activities, and explain how the activities are teaching people about things that are important for them to understand.

Research the United Nations Sustainability Goals. Select one of them, and create a presentation explaining why you think this is the most important goal for the United States to focus on, and how we can target and reach this goal.

One major component of Iqbal's climate action plan is his desire to build higher and more sustainable buildings so that more space can be used for tree planting, which would reduce greenhouse gases. Create an eco-friendly building and explain the design aspects you would include in order to help to meet your climate change goals.

Sustainability Innovations

Iqbal is not the only innovator who is focused on sustainable design and higher buildings. The Council on Tall Buildings and Urban Habitat[1] is the world leader in developing vertical growth through increased urban density, taller buildings, and sustainable design.

In addition to the standard work of the Council on Tall Buildings and Urban Habitat, they host an annual summit for networking, learning about current innovative design, and collaborating to maximize the effects of this growing industry. This summit is better known as the Tall+Urban Innovation Conference[2].

Iqbal is not alone in focusing on improving education for the future of Pakistan. Through Global Giving, the Fatima Memorial Hospital has started a fund to help educate underprivileged students. Continuing Malala's Dream - Educating Pakistan[3] is one of the many ways organizations are trying to quickly and successfully improve education for Pakistani students.

Organizations and bodies such as the Smart Cities Council[4] are also vital to improving the sustainability of cities from a systematic development stance. Through the success of such endeavors, cities in Pakistan as well as others around the world can begin to reap the benefits.

Sustainability Career Pathways

Sustainable Urban Planner. Iqbal notes that Islamabad is cutting down trees to expand horizontally; he argues that it would be better to grow vertically instead. How a city grows is shaped in large part by urban planners. Urban planners often work for governments (or as consultants) to help identify cities' needs and to develop both short-term and long-term growth plans (or even de-growth plans in the case of shrinking cities). They create plans, reports, and maps; engage with city officials and citizens; and play an important role in the process of shaping urban development. Interested in learning more? Start here[5].

Green Architect. Iqbal argues that building more densely may help save nature; but this will require trained architects. Architects can play a huge role in creating a more sustainable future. For example, designing energy efficient, passive solar, healthy buildings means that less energy will be needed for heating and cooling. Interested in designing buildings? Learn how to become an architect here[6].

Community Environmental Educator. Many communities offer environmental education to their members-- whether through local governments, parks, museums, or even neighborhood associations. Do you love teaching? Working with volunteers? Organizing community events? Then this could be the career for you. Learn more about community environmental education here[7].

Camp Counselor. Summer camps are a really valuable educational tool, and can be used to teach children about sustainability issues. While few can make a career out of camp counseling, it is a great summer job for college students and future educators, and can lead to full-time jobs in directing camps, museums, parks, or other educational programs. Read more here on how to become a camp counselor[8].

1 https://www.ctbuh.org/

2 https://www.tallinnovation.com/

3 https://www.globalgiving.org/projects/continuing-malalas-dream-educating-pakistan/

4 https://www.smartcitiescouncil.com/

5 https://www.thebalancecareers.com/urban-planner-or-regional-planner-526078

6 https://www.environmentalscience.org/career/architect

7 https://naaee.org/eepro/blog/community-environmental-education

8 https://www.zippia.com/camp-counselor-jobs/

Building Community for Climate Refugees

Mohamad Al Jounde, Gharsah
Syria / Sweden

Call to Action

Support the school Mohamed created for Syrian children in Lebanon: donate through Gharsah Sweden. gharsahsweden.org/the-school

Values

- Generosity
- Initiative
- Cooperation
- Persistence
- Community Building

Lessons Learned

Community makes us stronger. Build, develop, and strengthen those around you, and you will change the world.

The Earth nurtures us. If we respect the planet, it will provide everything we need for life.

If you want to build solutions to global problems, support and educate individual communities. A new world can be built one community at a time.

Mohamad Al Jounde grew up in a family of revolutionaries: both of his parents protested in the Syrian revolution.

Mohamad's mother planned protests in the main room of their apartment, and there were always activists coming and going in their home. In 2013, after Mohamad's mother was arrested a second time, they had to flee to Lebanon. But government regulations did not permit Syrian refugees to attend Lebanese schools. One day, when Mohamad volunteered with his mother at a nearby refugee camp, he came up with the idea to build a school. With this project, he discovered a new home, and a new style of activism. In 2017, Mohamad won the International Children's Peace Prize. He started an NGO, Gharsah Sweden, to support the refugee school in Lebanon. Even with global recognition, Mohamad is still working hard to preserve the values most important to him.

Language Arts

How did climate change play a role in Syria's descent into civil war? How did the lack of access to water for farmers affect the political climate in Syria? Write a research essay in which you discuss this issue. Support your position with research from at least two independent sources.

Using only photographs, create a series of posters about Lebanon and the challenges Syrian refugees face there (education, living conditions, health, basic human rights).

Create a presentation about young human rights activists in the Middle East. Choose five of them to profile: who are they, where are they from, what is their cause, and how can people get involved in helping them?

STEM Activities

How much water do you use on an average day (for drinking, bathing, cleaning, etc.)? Where does your water come from, and is it a sustainable source for the next 10 years? If not, how will that affect your daily life?

In this activity[1], identify resources and industries that are vulnerable to climate change in Syria and the Middle East generally, and analyze the relationship between environmental changes and sociopolitical events in the region.

Research the number of Syrian refugees who entered Lebanon the previous five years. Calculate the average rate of growth over the past year. Then, assuming constant growth, calculate the expected average rate of growth in the coming years. Plot the points as a scatter plot and find the regression line, where the independent variable is the month and the dependent variable is the number of refugees in Lebanon. At what rate are Syrian refugees leaving Lebanon? How would this information affect the average increase of Syrian refugees in Lebanon? Source: Refugee population in Lebanon World Bank[2].

Sustainability Innovations

Mohamad began to make an impact on his community by creating a school for climate refugees. Refugees International[3] is one of the world's largest nongovernmental organizations (NGOs): it is helping to bring attention to some of the important refugee, humanitarian, and human rights issues that have resulted from climate change.

Climate refugees have greatly benefited from the work of Mohamad and many others who have prioritized the health and education of children. The global pandemic has created opportunities for organizations like International TEFL Academy[4] to promote teaching English as a foreign language. Virtual education brings layers of safety and has its advantages, but also comes with issues such as access to technology and electricity. Learn about the work of this organization. Is Syria one of the Middle East countries with access to the program? If not, should they be? How could similar programs assist Mohamad's efforts?

In addition to climate refugees and other issues created as a rise in global temperature, Syria has been affected dramatically by its civil war. This article[5] addresses the environmental impact of the ongoing conflict in Syria, including issues of air pollution, deforestation, soil and vegetation degradation, and water depletion. It concludes by suggesting green solutions and potential strategies for post-conflict relief.

Sustainability Career Pathways

Teacher or School Administrator. Providing children with an education, as Mohamad has done, is one of the best ways to create a better future. Teaching is a noble profession and there are never enough passionate teachers, especially ones who have an appreciation of nature and sustainability awareness. Already convinced this is the path for you? Here's a good guide to becoming a teacher[6]. Want to weigh the pros and cons? Start here[7].

Social Entrepreneur. Mohamad, like so many other young heroes, first identified a societal challenge and created a solution--a school for refugee children. Then he created a supporting organization to help sustain it. A social entrepreneur is like a business entrepreneur, but he or she creates something-- a nonprofit, business, or other initiative – in order to solve a societal problem. Interested in becoming a social entrepreneur? Start with this article on "What It Means to be a Social Entrepreneur."[8]

Refugee Aid Worker. Tragically, as climate change triggers more disasters and more conflicts, there will be a growing number of refugees worldwide. Working with refugees, or in international aid operations, can be a difficult, but also a rewarding career. Knowing languages is essential, as is an ability to live in very basic conditions; but the reward is assisting people who are in the greatest need of help. Here is a set of tips for becoming a refugee aid worker[9].

1 https://cmes.uchicago.edu/sites/cmes.uchicago.edu/files/Lesson%20Plan-%20Climate%20Change%20in%20the%20Middle%20East-Revised.pdf

2 https://data.worldbank.org/indicator/SM.POP.REFG?locations=LB

3 https://www.refugeesinternational.org/climate-displacement-program

4 https://www.internationalteflacademy.com/

5 https://www.arab-reform.net/publication/the-environmental-impact-of-syrias-conflict-a-preliminary-survey-of-issues/

6 https://www.teachercertificationdegrees.com/become/

7 https://medium.com/teachers-on-fire/so-youre-thinking-of-becoming-a-teacher-818cb87cceb9

8 https://www.entrepreneur.com/article/281214

9 https://www.humanrightscareers.com/magazine/basic-tips-for-becoming-a-humanitarian-aid-worker/

Digital Toolkits for Inclusive Climate Justice Movements

Jett Zhang, Fridays For Future Digital
Florida

Call to Action

Don't let lockdowns stop you from supporting a cause that's important to you—get out in virtual space and support digital climate protests with Jett at Fridays for Future Digital - fffdigital.carrd.co.

Values

- Creative
- Socially Aware
- Curious
- Communication
- Environmentalism

Lessons Learned

The most important ingredient for change is community. Connect with like-minded people and build solutions from there.

When looking for solutions, communication is crucial. Reach out. Ask questions. Welcome dialogue!

Be creative. Innovate. And most of all: be loud!

While researching an essay on the Paris climate agreement, Jett reached out to Pensacola 350, a local climate action network, for some expertise.

At the meeting, he noticed that very few youth environmentalists were there. So, at 17, he took up the mantle as director of the 350 Pensacola Youth Climate Coalition and began organizing. With his success, he got the attention of Fridays For Future Digital, and began creating far-reaching digital protests to combat climate change. Jett's digital activism quickly expanded all over the globe. Among his many projects, he has helped draft Twitter and email campaigns for Friends of Zoka, a group of northern Ugandans trying to stop illegal logging in the rainforests. And he is helping raise to awareness for the #EscazúAgreement, the first binding treaty in Latin America and the Caribbean that deals with environmental democracy and environmental human rights.

Language Arts

Jett started by reaching out to other like-minded people in social media. What is your favorite sustainability project? What environmental issue do you consider to be the most pressing of our time? Choose three social media platforms, and for each of them, write or design a call to action on the issue of your choice. On a separate piece of paper, write an explanatory essay about why you chose the platforms you chose, and why you created your call to action the way you did.

Working in groups (2-4 students), choose an environmental issue in a place anywhere in the world that you would like to get involved with. Create an awareness campaign to teach people in the U.S. about this issue. Your campaign must include a 5-minute video, a 1-2 page blog article, a series of no less than three digital posters, and a series of no less than 10 tweets.

Write an argumentative essay addressing the following questions: What are the differences between in-person and digital protests? Do you believe that digital protests are as effective as in-person protests? Why or why not? Support your arguments with research on the subject.

One of the reasons Jett has been so successful is because he was lucky enough to be able to attend a school where his entrepreneurial spirit was nurtured. Since then, his success has placed him in a privileged position, which he has chosen to use as a platform for change. Write an essay in which you discuss what privilege is, what it can do for both for individuals and for society in general, and how it can be used to be a catalyst for change.

STEM Activities

Think of a sustainability issue or organization that is important to you and create a digital artifact to raise awareness around it. (Examples of digital artifacts are a website, a video, an infographic, a podcast, etc.)

Use the MIT App Inventor[1] to design and build an app that promotes digital activism. For example, TurnUp[2] is a social network app that helps youth discover and get involved with issues and causes they care about. You can come up with your own idea or research and improve an existing app.

Research 3-5 countries from around the global that have been affected the most by deforestation. Calculate the effect that deforestation will have on the climate if it continues at its current rate for the next 3, 5, and 10 years.

Create a mockup of a digital climate protest. Promote three companies/organizations that donate a portion of their proceeds or time to environmental causes.

Sustainability Innovations

One of Jett's greatest assets is his ability to relate to people and connect with organizations that have less visibility. Here are some projects from the organizations Jett has highlighted.

- **Defend Defenders[3]** This organization highlights the threats and attacks that activists deal with regularly. Their goal is to strengthen the work of human rights defenders and protect them from attacks or unlawful persecution.
- **William Amanzuru[4]** William is the team leader for the Friends of Zoka in Uganda. Friends of Zoka is currently addressing the issue of illegal loggers, timber makers, and coal dealers.

In addition to global climate strikes, it is important to use virtual platforms and tools to combat the climate crisis. The Earthday.org[5] team highlights strategies and ways to host a successful digital climate event.

Greenhouse PR[6] featured 12 top environmental campaigns to shine the light on progress made toward sustainability in 2020. Are you familiar with any of these campaigns? What campaigns do you think should be featured for 2021?

Sustainability Career Pathways

Cybersecurity Specialist. As Jett's story reminds us, a lot of activism has now moved online--not just social media and websites, but the coordination of activism as well. This requires secure communications; having cybersecurity experts is thus a must. Many organizations, universities, and businesses now employ cybersecurity experts to defend them against hackers and ensure secure communications. Is this the path for you? Learn more and take a free online course on cybersecurity here[7].

Social Media Manager. Building a movement online now requires the effective use of social media. Many organizations hire a full-time social media manager to manage their "brand" across a variety of platforms. Good writing, social media, and communication skills are essential. If you're interested in learning more about social media management, check out this introduction[8]. And here are 9 key skills you'll need to thrive in this field[9].

Environmental Investigator. Just as Jett helped stop illegal logging in Uganda, there are NGOs like the Environmental Investigation Agency (EIA) working around the world to stop environmental crimes, from poaching and animal trafficking to illegal dumping. Computer experts, data technicians, and researchers are all needed to help prevent the worst environmental crimes, whether they are working for groups like EIA, government agencies, INTERPOL[10], or local community groups. Learn more at EIA's website[11].

1 https://appinventor.mit.edu/
2 https://www.turnup.us/the-app
3 https://defenddefenders.org/our-work/
4 https://www.frontlinedefenders.org/en/profile/william-amanzuru
5 https://www.earthday.org/actions/plan-a-digital-event/
6 https://www.greenhousepr.co.uk/our-top-12-environmental-campaigns-of-2020/
7 https://www.cisco.com/c/en/us/products/security/what-is-a-cybersecurity-specialist.html#~become-a-cybersecurity-specialist
8 https://www.mediabistro.com/climb-the-ladder/skills-expertise/what-does-a-social-media-manager-do/
9 https://sproutsocial.com/insights/social-media-skills/
10 https://www.interpol.int/en/Crimes/Environmental-crime
11 https://eia-international.org/

Eco-Feminism For Climate Action

Adenike Oladosu, Lead Climate
Nigeria

Call to Action

Join Adenike Oladosu & others around the world in demanding climate action now. You can visit her website womenandcrisis.blogspot.com or follow her on Twitter @the_ecofeminist.

Values

- Solidarity
- Commitment
- Diligence
- Feminism
- Environmentalism

Lessons Learned

Unity brings strength. The only way to defeat climate change is by joining together, regardless of age, race, gender, culture, or nationality.

Education is the most powerful weapon we have.

We share the planet, which means we share our problems. It is time to work together to find and share solutions to the problems.

Traditional knowledge can contribute to climate resilience, and technology can improve people's quality of life. If we can make them work together, we will create a new world.

Adenike Oladosu's journey into the environmental movement began when she witnessed the destruction that climate change was causing in the Lake Chad region in Nigeria.

Climate change is leading to conflict, and conflict is making the effects of climate change worse. When conflict arises, there is more food insecurity, which affects the economy at large. The conflict was so bad that it took Adenike an extra year to finish her studies. That was when she knew she needed to act. She joined Fridays for Future, started by Greta Thunberg to demand climate action in communities across the world. Adenike calls her personal brand of activism "Eco-Feminism." She believes that solutions to climate change must prioritize the safety and wellbeing of women and girls. As Adenike became an international leader in the climate movement, she noticed that there was little focus on or consideration for communities in the Global South. But if international representatives do not recognize the current dangers of climate change in African countries, there will be global repercussions. Adenike's climate activism focuses on engaging the world's youth through education, and on increasing the use of renewable energy. Climate change should be the top priority for everyone, everywhere.

Language Arts

Research the effects of recent droughts in Nigeria and how these have affected the country in the past 30 years. With the information you collect, create a presentation (at least 10 slides) about the effect of drought on Nigeria's farmers, its economy, and its people.

What is the connection between climate change and armed conflict in Nigeria (specifically Boko Haram)? Create a 5-to-10-minute video using secondary sources (for example, news outlets, videos from NGOs, etc.) in which you explain how climate change has created the ideal circumstances for terrorism and war in the country, and how terrorism is affecting Nigeria's youth.

Write a research essay about biodiversity in Africa. What kind of ecosystems exist within the continent? How fragile are they? How are they being affected by climate change, and what can be done to ameliorate the situation?

Write a social media post (or series of posts, depending on the platform you choose), in which you explain how climate change has exacerbated the migration of people from African nations into Europe, and how the situation has become a humanitarian crisis.

Working in groups of 3-4 people, choose any one of the topics you've researched in the previous activities, and design an information campaign to bring awareness about this issue to people your own age. Your campaign must use at least two social media platforms, photographs, and one written article/blog post that explains the issue.

STEM Activities

In this Climate Change Impacts in Nigeria activity[1], students will be introduced to the climate change risk profile for Nigeria, including the impact of climate change on major sectors of the country (agriculture, water resources, human health, ecosystems, energy, infrastructure, and disasters). Students will also analyze data to evaluate the current and future health risks in Nigeria due to climate change.

Using this EarthLabs activity guide[2], develop a working definition of drought, and do a hands-on demonstration to illustrate the role of soil moisture in a drought. Examine precipitation data and streamflow levels, and use them to predict where drought is most severe in the United States. Check your predictions by comparing them to the Palmer Drought Severity Index.

Read the article The Intersection Between Ecofeminism and Agriculture[3] written by Adenike, which you can find on Facebook, Instagram, Twitter, or LinkedIn. Research one way in which Nigerian women are impacted by climate change, and design a technological or scientific solution to help mitigate this.

Sustainability Innovations

When addressing eco-feminism, the topic of intersectional environmentalism is also discussed. Read this article[4] by Leah Thomas. What is the difference between these two terms, and how are they at the forefront of current environmental and social causes?

Assess the UNICEF Chad Appeal[5]. How does it plan to address COVID-19, environmental issues, and conflict-induced displacements? If you and your classmates created a fundraiser to support Lake Chad, which area would you most like to assist in?

Women's Consortium of Nigeria[6] is one of the largest NGOs in Nigeria; it has 10 different focus areas that address opportunities for women and children in Nigeria.

In addition to the focus on women's rights in Nigeria, the presence of business-focused NGOs is growing rapidly. The Association of Nigerian Women Business Network (ANWBN)[7] is a coalition of 52 organizations that are collaborating to enhance the economic status of women in Nigeria.

Sustainability Career Pathways

Eco-feminist. Sometimes having a mission like Adenike's can help to shape one's work, no matter what one's career is. As an eco-feminist, Adenike puts women's well-being and safety first—whether she's working with villagers on education, agricultural issues, or societal reform. While one might think of feminist jobs as being in the realm of activism or academia, applying feminism to the many different environmental career paths can make them richer and more effective. Want to learn more about eco-feminism? Start with Wikipedia's overview[8].

Environmental Security Expert. Just as climate change can cause conflict, conflict can cause ecological damage. There is now a field of environmental security[9] that focuses on reducing environmental conflicts, and preventing environmental damage caused by conflict. Jobs are available in governments, with the United Nations, or institutions like the World Bank, and in "think tanks" like the Woodrow Wilson Center's Environmental Change and Security Program[10], which offers internships[11] in the field.

Ecological Restoration. One of the best ways to limit the local effects of climate change is to heal ecosystems and their functioning whether wetlands, lakes, forests, or others. The field of ecological restoration focuses on this, with restoration ecologists, field technicians, and others working together to "rewild" degraded areas. Learn more about opportunities in this field here[12].

1 https://tropicsu.org/lesson-plan-climate-change-nigeria/
2 https://serc.carleton.edu/eslabs/drought/4.html
3 https://next.blue/articles/the-intersection-between-ecofeminism-and-agriculture
4 https://www.thegoodtrade.com/features/ecofeminism-intersectional-environmentalism-difference
5 https://www.unicef.org/appeals/chad#download
6 https://www.womenconsortiumofnigeria.org/
7 https://www.anwbn.org.ng/
8 https://en.wikipedia.org/wiki/Ecofeminism
9 https://en.wikipedia.org/wiki/Environmental_security
10 https://www.wilsoncenter.org/program/environmental-change-and-security-program
11 https://www.wilsoncenter.org/opportunity/internships-the-environmental-change-and-security-program
12 https://www.ser-rrc.org/what-is-ecological-restoration/

From Invisible to Visible

Michelle Dilhara, Earth Day Network Ambassador
Sri Lanka

Call to Action

The Earth Day Network's global map of climate activists in 17 countries is ever-expanding: www.earthday.org. Follow Michelle on Facebook (@mishdilhara), & Instagram (@michelledilhara).

Values

- Community Service
- Generosity
- Social Justice
- Environmentalism

Lessons Learned

If you bring to light to those who are in the shadows of society, you may change the world.

Everything is connected: the existential threats to those ignored by society will become threats to everyone in the world unless we begin to work for change.

Michelle Dilhara is a well-known television actress in Sri Lanka

But even before she became famous, she was an activist for social rights and the environment. Now she uses both her influence and her income to mobilize others to join the fight for social justice and environmental protection. In 2020 she was named the Earth Day Ambassador for Sri Lanka. "We have a responsibility for the future of the children," she says. "What I always tell everybody is that one small contribution from each of us can make a huge change."

Language Arts

Write a research essay about the link between climate change, poverty, and increased mortality in vulnerable populations. In other words: how and why does climate change affect poor people more harshly?

Choose your own sustainability adventure! For this activity, each student will need to create a Twitter[1] account (they should not use their own accounts, if they have them), and then familiarize themselves with Twitter Polls[2]. After each student has created their own account, the members of the class will follow each other. Using the Twitter accounts created for this purpose, each student creates a narrative about a sustainability adventure of their choice: a young leader who is trying to tackle an environmental problem of their choice. Each student creates their own narrative, which will be published in chunks, as a tweet, and each narrative must have at least three turning points (three "cliffhanger" moments). The narrative will be shared as a serious of tweets with the rest of the class. When a turning point is reached, the student who is creating the narrative will create a Twitter poll in which the rest of the class will vote to decide what happens next. The poll should have at least three scenarios to explore for each turning point. In the end, each student will have their own narrative or short story which will have been developed with the help of the rest of the class (by voting on the Twitter polls on what the hero should do next). After the voting is done, students will share their stories with the rest of the class, and reflect on what did and didn't work about the ideas they shared with each other.

Using FlipGrid[3] (your teacher will set this up beforehand), record a message for people like you, in which you invite them to be agents of change to deal with climate change. Your message should be between one and three minutes long, and it should contain a call to action for a specific cause, and a concrete plan (for example, meeting at a park to clean up trash, collecting electronics for recycling at your school, etc). After you record your message, respond to two of your classmates' videos. Your response must include an explanation as to why you found their submissions interesting, and additional ideas about how to implement their solutions.

STEM Activities

Climate change and extreme weather affects Sri Lanka at large, but farmers and agricultural workers face the worst impacts of it. Research agricultural industries in Sri Lanka and learn how climate change is impacting it. How might the success or failure of these agricultural businesses affect the overall economy?

Identify a project in your area that can help reduce sources of climate change like Michelle did (park/beach/street cleanup, recycling program, etc.), and plan how you would carry it out. Optionally, connect with your school administration or local government to expand the effort.

Sri Lanka is one of the biodiversity hotspots in the world, but its environmental ecosystems are being threatened by climate change. Research a species or type of ecosystem present in Sri Lanka, and learn how climate change is affecting it. Are there any Sri Lankan policies that are helping to mitigate the impact? If not, what are some policies the government could implement to reduce the impact climate change is having on the species or ecosystem?

Sustainability Innovations

Michelle began her career in television, but she has made a greater impact by using her influence for sustainable causes. These actors have also grown their influence over time, and used it to make an impact on the environment:

- **Rosario Dawson:** As an actor and political activist, she has used her influence to develop Voz. Voz[4] helps to mold the concepts of sustainable fashion and indigenous craft/art.
- **Mark Ruffalo:** The Avengers actor is known for his roles on the screen. He supports The Solutions Project, which supports grassroot campaigns with climate changemakers and innovators.

In this 2019 GreenBiz Article[5], companies' use of social media for sustainability marketing is addressed and analyzed. How has social media helped to promote sustainability movements? Are there any sustainability-focused companies that have grown through the use of social media?

In addition to the influence of actors, TikTok and current social media trends are driving sustainability-focused action among Gen Z. This article[6] addresses the trend created via TikTok and explains how social media has changed from promotional to active work within the climate change movement.

☀ Sustainability Career Pathways

Actor. As Michelle notes, along with acting in inspiring movies and TV shows, actors can use their platforms to encourage others to live more sustainably and even -- through programs like Green is Universa[7]l -- help studios to produce movies in ways that are more environmentally responsible. This, of course, is not an easy profession to succeed in, but if you want to become an actor, start here[8].

Teacher. One of the first ways Michelle helped her community was to teach children English. Often people who want to help save the planet think about teaching environmental studies or science. But any subject can incorporate sustainability education--whether instruction in English or other languages, history, social studies, even meditation, like Michelle taught. Teaching is a noble profession, and there are never enough passionate teachers. Already convinced this is the path for you? Here's a good guide on becoming a teacher.[9] Want to weigh the pros and cons? Start here[10].

Extension Agent. Farmers have long been supported by governmental (and nongovernmental) agricultural extension offices (actually for about 2,800 years in China[11]!). Extension agents support farmers in their service area, helping them to improve crop yields and practices--and even helping them adapt to a changing climate. They may also play a role in cultivating the next generation of farmers, for example, through support of youth agriculture groups like 4H. If this sounds like the job for you, learn more here[12].

---

1 https://twitter.com/

2 https://help.twitter.com/en/using-twitter/twitter-polls

3 https://info.flipgrid.com/

4 https://madebyvoz.com/pages/sustainability-people

5 https://www.greenbiz.com/article/here-are-companies-use-social-media-best-sustainability-marketing#:~:text=We%20observed%20that%20most%20companies,platform%20for%20corporate%20sustainability%20teams

6 https://www.refinery29.com/en-us/2020/09/10029101/tiktok-sustainable-fashion-cottagecore-clothes

7 https://www.nbcuniversal.com/article/our-productions

8 https://www.careersinfilm.com/actor/

9 https://www.teachercertificationdegrees.com/become/

10 https://medium.com/teachers-on-fire/so-youre-thinking-of-becoming-a-teacher-818cb87cceb9

11 https://en.wikipedia.org/wiki/Agricultural_extension

12 https://www.thebalancecareers.com/agricultural-extension-agent-125871

Generation Waking Up

Joshua Gorman, Generation Waking Up
California

Call to Action

Connect with Joshua:
www.joshuagorman.com.
Support Generation Waking Up:
www.generationwakingup.com

Values

- Community
- Spirituality
- Sustainability
- Social Justice
- Environmentalism

Lessons Learned

You do have a purpose; and it will reveal itself if you are willing to be still and listen.

Always question your position in the world, and whether you are using it to generate the most positive changes in society.

When in doubt, look to the Earth and to your elders for guidance.

Joshua Gorman is an emerging leader in the field of youth advocacy.
At George Mason University, he created a self-designed major to serve a vital cause that wasn't being served– he called it Global Youth and Social Change. Through this major he began working, volunteering, and mentoring with, and learning from, all types of nonprofits, youth programs, and social justice organizations. Now, as the founder of Generation Waking Up (GenUp), his mission is to ignite young people to bring forth a thriving, just, and sustainable world. GenUp provides a framework for holistically training systemic changemakers and spiritual activists, with a focus on personal and interpersonal leadership. The WakeUp Experience is GenUp's flagship workshop. It's a unique 2–3-hour multimedia experience that asks four specific questions of young leaders: Who are we? Where are we? What has to change? What do we do now? Joshua has been involved with a variety of projects that align environmental activists, youth organizations, and social justice advocates – including election 2020 Gap Year, Thrive East Bay, Youth Passageways, Awakin Call, and more. He is currently writing a book titled Generation Waking Up: The Rise of Global Millennials and a Thriving New World.

Language Arts

After reading the story, participate in a Socratic Seminar about Joshua's work, the need to achieve systemic change in society, and the best ways to go about it.

In the story, Joshua states that "We don't need environmental, political, or economic change. We need systems change -- a complete cultural shift in our values and structure." Write an argumentative essay agreeing or disagreeing with him. Your essay must include a counter argument, and your opinion must be supported by at least two secondary sources.

Who was Joseph Campbell? Write a research essay on his hero's journey and how that work could influence someone who, like Joshua, is trying to bring about significant change in the world.

STEM Activities

In this PBS NewsHour lesson plan[1], students learn about the invention process and design an app to help their community. The components of the project are a one-page business plan; a sketch, model, or prototype of their invention that they will present to key stakeholders (classmates and teacher); a flowchart explaining how the app works; and an app store web page (use this app as a model[2]).

In this lesson plan from Education.com[3], students learn how the brain and prefrontal cortex (PFC) function and change, and how mindfulness can strengthen their brains. Have students use a mindfulness app such as one from this list[4], and record their mood, blood pressure, and other markers before and after doing a mindfulness session.

In this lesson plan from the American Farm Bureau Foundation for Agriculture[5], students learn about the five components of quality agriculture: soil quality and health, water quality and availability, air quality, biodiversity, and animal health and welfare. What is the significance of each in practicing sustainable agriculture? How do farmers care for the environment? Design a small farm management practice to manage resources that align with the five components listed. Construct a model of your solution and calculate the cost of implementing such a solution on your fictional farm.

Sustainability Innovations

Thrive East Bay[6] is a 501(c)(3) based in California that helps to build a community based on arts, social change, and meaning.

Joshua began his path to a more diverse future through Generation Waking Up[7]. In the "WakeUp Experience" workshop, four main questions are asked (Who are we? Where are we? What has to change? and What do we do now?). Which question is most important in terms of your ability to contribute to a diverse and successful community?

The Four Stage Systemic Change Process[8] is one of the main strategies that compares our current reality to a vision for the future. Which of the four stages do you feel is lacking the most in our current society?

Donella Meadows was one of the leaders in systems change and the causes for improvement. Leverage points are places within a complex system where a small shift in one thing produces big changes everywhere. In this article[9], Donella discusses leverage points and their effects on a complex system.

Sustainability Career Pathways

Systems Thinker. Systems thinking can be helpful in any industry: organizational management, science, business, policy. Being a systems leader can help you and the organization you work for leap ahead, identifying both threats and opportunities that opponents may miss. Are you interested in systems thinking? Read this introduction here[10]. And read how to be a "systems leader" on Idealist.org[11].

Business Leadership Trainer and Coach. Many businesses are working hard to transform from Earth-harming to Earth-healing, but they don't know how to go about it. Leadership training and coaching business managers can have profound effects in transforming businesses, and thus society overall. Is this for you? Check out this list of business leadership trainers[12], or explore Presidio Graduate School[13], a sustainable business school, as a starting point for this career track.

Social Entrepreneur. Joshua identified an untapped opportunity—training, supporting, and empowering youth—and created an organization to help achieve this. Social entrepreneurs are like business entrepreneurs, but they are creating something designed to address a societal issue, whether with a nonprofit, business, or other initiative. Interested in becoming a social entrepreneur? Learn more here[14].

Sustainable Farmer. Sometimes tending soil, growing healthy food, weaving into a community, and healing the land is one's calling. Building a sustainable farming business can be a restorative life path. If that sounds right for you, read this introduction to finding jobs in the field of sustainable agriculture[15].

1 https://www.pbs.org/newshour/extra/lessons-plans/lesson-plan-using-gaming-and-technology-to-find-solutions-in-agriculture/
2 https://apps.apple.com/us/app/shazam/id284993459
3 https://www.education.com/lesson-plan/strengthening-our-brains-with-mindfulness/
4 https://www.mindful.org/free-mindfulness-apps-worthy-of-your-attention/
5 https://www.agfoundation.org/sustainability/environmental-stewardship
6 http://www.thriveeastbay.org/
7 http://www.generationwakingup.org/
8 https://www.thenonprofittimes.com/npt_management_tips/change-process-four-easy-steps/
9 https://donellameadows.org/archives/leverage-points-places-to-intervene-in-a-system/
10 https://lindaboothsweeney.net/SOW17_chap12_systems-thinking.pdf
11 https://www.idealist.org/en/careers/how-to-systems-leader
12 https://trainingindustry.com/top-training-companies/leadership/2022-top-leadership-training-companies/
13 http://presidio.edu/
14 https://www.entrepreneur.com/article/281214
15 http://greencollarblog.org/sustainable-agriculture-jobs/

Like Kids Everywhere

Samantha Smith, Cold War Peace Activist
Maine

Call to Action

Pathways to Peace uplifts young people's voices at the United Nations for international peacebuilding, Learn how you can help build peace in our world. pathwaystopeace.org/

Values

- Peacebuilding
- Cooperation
- Understanding
- Internationalism

Lessons Learned

Build bridges. Get to know people. Even if they scare you, make the effort to find what you have in common with them. We have more in common with people from other cultures than we know. Be open to this truth, always.

Do not be afraid to appear vulnerable. Sometimes showing your own vulnerability is a sign of strength.

When Samantha Smith was 10 years old, she became very concerned about the threat of nuclear war between the Soviet Union, and her home country of the United States.

She wrote a letter to the president of the Soviet Union, begging him not to start a war. Several months later she received a letter from him, inviting her to visit the Soviet Union so she could see for herself that his people were very much like people everywhere, and that they wanted peace too. During her visit she made friends with young people her age, and several years later the presidents of the two countries agreed to begin dismantling their weapons. Sadly, Samantha did not live long enough to see the result of her peacemaking efforts: she and her father died in a plane crash shortly before the agreement was signed. However, her words still ring out, loud and true: "God made the world for us to share, and take care of," she said. "Please let's do what he wanted, and have everybody be happy too."

Language Arts

What was the Cold War? What was life like for children during the Cold War? Did your grandparents build a bomb shelter under their house? Create a 5-7 minute video in which you explain what the Cold War was, how it started, which countries were involved, and what life was like—especially for school-aged children—at the time.

How can you follow Samantha's example to help heal division and mistrust in your community, country, and the world? Write a personal essay in which you explain how you will use her example to become an "ambassador of peace" in your community. How could you help heal division and mistrust between the people in your community? Give specific examples, using real-life scenarios.

Create a series of five TikTok videos in which you offer solutions for making your community better and safer: for example, by tackling problems like violence, or political division, or hunger. Use real-life examples from your community or region, and offer concrete ways in which the members of your community can work together to tackle these issues.

Choose two classmates you don't know very well or haven't talked to much in the past. Sit down and have an open, honest, and meaningful conversation with them about what you like, dislike, your interests, etc. Keep the conversation going for at least fifteen minutes. Afterwards, write a short narrative essay in which you explain how this conversation changed your perception of the two people you spoke to: What did you learn about them? What surprised you? What things do you have in common? What can you learn from them? What can they learn from you?

STEM Activities

Use this resource from the Environmental Protection Agency[1] to explore sources of radiation. Calculate your annual exposure to radiation from various sources (the sun, cellphones, food, etc.)

Using this resource on how much the U.S spends on nuclear weapons[2], graph how much money has been dedicated to nuclear weapons each year since 1940. How does it compare to the cost of dismantling nuclear weapons and disposing of nuclear materials/waste?

Research the cost of dealing with the aftermath of the atomic bombings in Hiroshima and Nagasaki (cleaning up radioactive waste, medical costs, etc.). Compare that to the cost of developing the atomic bomb in the U.S. Then calculate the human-to-cost ratio: How much money was spent to develop the bomb per person who died during the attacks?

In this lesson plan from the Health Physics Society[3], students explore cell structure and radioactivity, and learn how radioactivity can cause cell sensitivity and injury.

The Cold War space race gave rise to several technological breakthroughs, including major innovations in computing and rocketry, as well as minor innovations affecting consumer products, like portable vacuum cleaners, wireless headsets, Velcro, scratch-resistant eyeglass lenses, and freeze-dried foods. Select one invention made during this era to research. What led to the invention? What problem was it solving? How much financial and human resources went into it? What was the impact of this invention?

Sustainability Innovations

Samantha's advocacy was the individual effort of a 10-year-old girl; but there have been many other peace and antiwar movements started by students and other youth. Review this Khan Academy article[4]. What do you believe was the end effect of these movements?

Review this Harvard Ed[5] article detailing the advancement of student activism over time. Why is it important? How can students have a special impact on creating change?

In this McKinsey and Company report[6], diversity and inclusion in businesses is assessed. How has this framework helped to shape business and politics? Would Samantha approve of its goals and impacts on the U.S.?

Sustainability Career Pathways

Diplomat. Diplomats help countries to establish and enact agreements (having to do with peace, trade, humanitarian aid, and the environment with other countries. They typically work in embassies, located around the world. Discover more about a career in diplomacy in this introduction[7], or in this step-by-step guide for becoming a diplomat in the U.S[8].

Disarmament Advocate. According to the U.N. Office for Disarmament Affairs (UNODA) disarmament is "vital for sustainable development and global survival." The U.N., governments, and NGOs all have jobs supporting the global reduction of arms. Do you want to help with this essential fight? Learn more, and review job opportunities at UNODA[9].

Interviewer. Between radio, TV, podcasts, and the Internet, there are many opportunities to interview people--just as Samantha did[10]—and help to spread their work to a broader audience. Explore the field here[11]. There are many other careers where interviewing is your job as well, from college admissions to helping people find jobs. Learn more here[12].

---

1 https://www.epa.gov/radiation

2 https://www.brookings.edu/the-hidden-costs-of-our-nuclear-arsenal-overview-of-project-findings/

3 https://hps.org/sciencesupport/documents/radiobiology_lesson_plan.pdf

4 https://www.khanacademy.org/humanities/us-history/postwarera/1960s-america/a/the-student-movement-and-the-antiwar-movement

5 https://www.gse.harvard.edu/news/ed/18/08/student-activism-20

6 https://www.mckinsey.com/featured-insights/diversity-and-inclusion/diversity-wins-how-inclusion-matters

7 https://www.internationalrelationsedu.org/us-diplomat/

8 https://diplomacy.state.gov/diplomacy/how-do-you-become-a-diplomat/

9 https://www.unjobnet.org/organizations/UN%20ODA

10 https://www.youtube.com/watch?v=AoQ_Lji5V70

11 https://superscholar.org/careers/news-media/talk-show-host/

12 https://www.zippia.com/interviewer-jobs/

One Goal At A Time

Lesein Mutunkei, Trees4Goals
Kenya

Call to Action

By planting trees we can fight against the effects of climate change. Are you in a football club? Basketball? Hockey? Plant a tree for every goal or point that you score. Follow Lesein on Instagram and Twitter @Trees4Goals.

Values

- Sportsmanship
- Cooperation
- Commitment
- Creativity
- Leadership
- Environmentalism

Lessons Learned

Do what you can to help others. Every bit of help, no matter how small, makes a difference.

Effective change can happen when we fight for it, one goal at a time.

Always give back more than you take. It's the only way to ensure we are leaving a healthy planet for future generations.

Lesein Mutunkei is passionate about playing football. So when he read about the issues of deforestation and air pollution in his home country of Kenya, he decided to use his passion to do something about it: he started Trees4Goals. He decided that for every goal he scored, he would plant a tree. "No matter how big the problem is, I just needed to make a difference," he says. Soon, people began to notice his activism. His football team joined in the effort, and now Lesein is branching out internationally -- he has started a cooperative relationship with a high school in South Africa.

He also traveled to the Climate Youth Summit, and was even invited to plant a tree together with Kenyan President Uhuru Kenyatta. But Lesein has even bigger plans: he wants FIFA to adopt his strategy. "There'd really be a big number of people that would be talking about it, and I think it will be amazing," he says.

Language Arts

What is the moral of the hummingbird story? How can we relate this story to climate change? Write a personal essay in which you reflect on these questions and explain if you have ever felt "too small to make a difference," and what you would do if you knew that there is no such thing.

Create a 5-7 minute video on the state of Kenya's forests: what they were like fifty years ago, what they are like now, what is being done to preserve them, and how deforestation has affected the people of Kenya (their economy, culture, lifestyle, and health).

Working in groups of 3-5 people, create a social media campaign aimed at sports coaches in which you invite them to join Trees4Goals. Your campaign must include Twitter content (6-10 tweets); 6-10 pictures to post on Instagram; TikTok videos (one by each member of the group); and one Facebook post. Don't limit yourself to football coaches; include the coaches of at least two other sports in your campaign.

STEM Activities

Using this graph that shows the FIFA World Cup goals scored from 1930-2018[1], calculate how many trees would have been planted during that time period if for every goal scored, a tree had been planted. Research how much carbon is stored in an average tree, and calculate the total amount of carbon the planted trees would have removed from our atmosphere. (For an extra challenge, instead of using the average amount of carbon stored in a tree, consider the type of tree and its age when calculating the amount.)

Select one type of ecosystem[2] and research how it is being impacted by deforestation. Create a poster, model, or another type of visual presentation to display the information you have gathered, and present it to your class, parents, and/or the school community.

Explore alternative materials or solutions that can substitute for tree-based paper or wood products (bamboo, hemp paper, etc.).

Sustainability Innovations

Tree Sisters - Kenya[3] focuses on the engagement and value of women working in plant nurseries and planting trees, while also emphasizing the importance of restoring Kenya's watersheds.

Deforestation is one of Kenya's biggest problems, but their water resources and watersheds are at the root of these problems. Kenya Water for Health Organization (KWAHO)[4] is one of the first non-governmental organizations in Kenya to focus on water implementation, sanitation, and hygiene. They have a watershed program that is centered around issues of social accountability.

Review this article[5] highlighting seven different reforestation projects that are revitalizing Africa. Two of these projects are focused in the heart of Kenya. Assess the differences in the projects and how they are affecting the ecosystems of Kenya's communities.

Sustainability Career Pathways

Sustainable Sports. As Lesein notes, football--and sports more broadly--have a great influence over fans, whether by modeling green behavior, or by stars encouraging their fans to take action. There are groups like the Green Sports Alliance, which leverages "the cultural and market influence of sports to promote healthy, sustainable communities." If you love sports, why not join an organization like the Green Sports Alliance[6]? Or contact a specific team's sustainability department, in order to help mobilize fans, franchises, and communities to live more sustainably.

Urban Forester. One of the best places to plant trees is in cities--where they improve air quality, human health, and reduce the urban heat island effect. Most cities, even smaller ones, recognizing the many health and environmental benefits trees (especially native trees) have to offer[7], have an urban forester in their employ. These individuals manage tree plantings and removals, map and manage the canopy (using GIS skills), and so on. Sound like a career for you? Learn more here[8].

Ecological Restoration. One of the best ways to limit the local effects of climate change is to heal the ecosystems and their functioning in your region--whether wetlands, lakes, forests, or others. The field of ecological restoration[9] focuses on this, with restoration ecologists, field technicians, and others working together to "rewild" degraded areas. Learn more about opportunities in this field here[10].

1 https://www.statista.com/statistics/269029/number-of-goals-scored-at-fifa-world-cups-since-1930/
2 https://sciencing.com/types-environmental-ecosystems-8640.html
3 https://treesisters.org/about/our-partners/kenya
4 https://www.kwaho.org/watershed-program/
5 https://www.womenconsortiumofnigeria.org/
6 https://greensportsalliance.org/
7 https://www.americanforests.org/our-work/urban-forestry/
8 https://www.zippia.com/urban-forester-jobs/
9 https://www.ser-rrc.org/what-is-ecological-restoration/
10 https://www.ser-rrc.org/what-is-ecological-restoration/

Planting the Right Kind of Green

Aadya Joshi, The Right Green
India

☀ Call to Action

Plant a garden. Learn about native plants in your community. Keep local biodiversity in mind! Learn more about Aadya's project at www.therightgreen.org.

☀ Values

- Biodiversity
- Sustainability Initiative
- Education
- Environmentalist

☀ Lessons Learned

Good intentions are a wonderful thing, but when you add knowledge, you can literally change the world

It is always possible to rebuild that which is broken, all you need is a strong will and knowledge

On her way to school, Aadya used to walk by a garbage dump.

When she organized a drive to plant an urban garden in its place, she learned about the importance of native plants for local wildlife. She realized that, while there were many trees around, most of them were non-native and therefore didn't support local biodiversity. She started workshops in a local nature park and even built a database of local plant species and the insects and birds they support.

☀ Language Arts

Research which are the ten most common native tree species in your region, and which are the ten most common non-native species of trees in your region. Create a trivia game to educate people about the native and non-native trees in your area and the benefits/risks each one of these species bring to the region

Create a 10-to-15-minute presentation (10-15 slides) about native trees in your region of the world. Focus on which species have disappeared, why, and what have been the consequences to the ecosystem.

Write a research essay on reforestation: What is it? Why is it important? Have there been any reforestation initiatives in your country or region? Were they successful? Why or why not? What were the consequences to the environment?

Create an educational campaign (written text, video, photograph, or a mix of the three) to raise awareness of the problem of improper disposal of trash in your area. In a separate sheet of paper, explain why you made the choices you made.

STEM Activities

Aadya's dream started by acknowledging the collection of trash in her community and wondering why no one had gotten rid of it yet. Complacency and lack of awareness can be two of the main contributing factors in a community's unsustainable practice. Identify a similar issue in your community that is not being addressed and why you believe people don't address it.

- Examples: Lack of recycling, use of excessive plastic or Styrofoam, single-use items, etc.

In addition to the direct effects of trash on the environment, landfills produce greenhouse gases, including methane, that are extremely harmful on the environment. Compare and contrast the effects that landfills, and tree planting have on climate change. Create a chart to display the results of your research.

Identify three types of trees and research what effects they have on the environment around them. Create a presentation to explain the effects that each of the different trees selected can have a positive impact on their environment. This may include:

- Providing food, home and protection to mammals and birds
- Reducing water runoff and reducing erosion, flooding and pollution in waterways
- Moderate temperatures and serve as a windbreak to protect the area

Sustainability Innovations

One Tree Planted[1] is one of the top sustainability nonprofit organizations existing today. They plant trees in North America, Latin America, Asia, Africa, Europe and the Pacific for a donation of $1 per tree. However, in addition to planting trees their T.R.E.E.S school program brings environmental education into grade school, high school and University programs with lesson plans, activities and resources.

In addition to planting trees, recycling and waste reduction is extremely important for reducing greenhouse gases and maintaining a more sustainable planet. National Recycling Coalition[2] and Waste Aid[3] are two great nonprofit organizations that address waste collection and recycling in the communities that need the most assistance.

Polystyrene, commonly known as Styrofoam, is used for insulation, usually in packing material to keep products safe while shipping. This type of packaging is non-biodegradable and difficult to recycle. In order to replace Styrofoam, researchers at the Institute of Natural Products Engineering at TU Dresden[4] developed an insulating material made from recycled paper for shipping temperature-sensitive foods and medicines.

Sustainability Career Pathways

Gardener. While gardening may sound like a hobby, there are increasing numbers of community gardens, city gardens, and school gardens that need managing. You can play a role in caring for, fundraising for these efforts, as well as using these gardens to educate, and often feed, the communities they're located in. Interested in learning more about urban gardening, visit here[5].

Urban Forester. Understanding and managing the trees in a city is a full-time job. Literally. Most cities, even smaller ones, have an urban forester in their employ, recognizing the many health and environmental benefits trees (especially native trees) have to offer[6]. These individuals manage street tree plantings and removals (as older trees die), map and manage the canopy (using GIS skills), and so on. Sound like a career for you? Learn more here[7]. And learn more about the great work of Casy Trees, a leading urban forestry organization, in Washington, DC, here[8].

Park Ranger. Parks are a key place where the public learns about nature--including what's native and non-native to their area. Park rangers are both educators and protectors of the world's parklands. This is a career opportunity for those who want to educate and care for forests and parks. Learn more about being a park ranger here[9].

1 https://onetreeplanted.org/
2 https://urcrecycles.org/
3 https://wasteaid.org/
4 https://www.springwise.com/sustainability-innovation/mobility-transport/cool-packaging-alternative-styrofoam
5 https://bonnieplants.com/gardening/meet-the-urban-gardeners/
6 https://www.americanforests.org/our-work/urban-forestry/
7 https://www.zippia.com/urban-forester-jobs/
8 https://caseytrees.org/about-us/
9 https://www.parkrangeredu.org/

Seeing The Ocean In A New Way

Cruz Erdmann, Young Wildlife Photographer 2019
New Zealand

Call to Action

Natural beauty and life is all around us! Wherever you are, grab a camera and capture natural beauty. Inspire others to protect the environment. You can follow Cruz on Instagram (@cruzerdmann).

Values

- Environmentalism
- Creativity
- Activism
- Compassion

Lessons Learned

Share your perspectives on the world with others. You might have just the right words, or images, to motivate others to start fighting for change.

We are intimately connected to our environment: our interactions with the ecosystems surrounding us affect not only the environment, but ourselves. By caring for the Earth, we are caring for each other too.

Beautiful images of our natural world can inspire change.

True, sustainable change is born from compassion. Be compassionate toward every living creature, and be passionate about your activism.

Cruz Erdmann didn't plan to become a wildlife photographer.

But when he was 10 years old, on one of the many diving trips he took with his dad, his dad gave him his old underwater camera. With that camera, Cruz started documenting the marine wildlife that had fascinated him his entire life. Barely two years later, he won the Young Wildlife Photographer of the Year award, organized by the Natural History Museum of London. He even got to speak at the World Economic Forum, where he presented his photography and his vision: using the power of the visual image to give the creatures living underwater a face for those who do not have the chance to see them any other way. Cruz believes that we have become so disconnected from our oceans that we no longer understand the negative consequences of our consumerism. Overfishing, pollution, and habitat destruction may very well destroy the delicate ecosystems that support marine wildlife. With his photography, Cruz wants to raise global awareness of the importance of these issues.

Language Arts

Find out what endangered species there are in your area. Then create a series of Instagram posts about 3-5 of these species using your own original photographs or drawings (if possible). In your posts, offer information about these species: What makes them unique? What is their importance for the environment? What threats are they facing? How can we help?

Go on a nature walk, or visit a nearby body of water. (Put your electronic devices away while you do this!) Pay close attention to your surroundings. Listen to the sounds around you. Watch the animals, look at the trees, notice the smells. Observe in silence, and take notes. Then write an essay reflecting on what it felt like to pay such close attention to nature. What surprised you about the experience? Why? Do you believe experiencing nature without distractions is beneficial? If so, why, and how is it? Do you believe it would motivate people to become more involved in environmental causes if they had more opportunities to observe nature? How can such opportunities be created?

Create a series of Tik Tok videos in which you discuss the importance of preserving our oceans, rivers, and waterways.

STEM Activities

Optical engineers need to understand how light rays work in order to design and create devices such as cameras, lasers, and fiber optics. In this activity, students will construct their own pinhole cameras to observe the behavior of light. They will learn how light rays travel in straight lines in the processing of images, and use light rays to create a photographic image. Pinhole camera activity[1].

In this lesson, students learn about recent scientific developments by viewing the New York Times slide show "Science in Pictures."[2] They then create their own slide shows documenting the research, discoveries, and ideas they are learning about in science class. Photographing scientific discoveries activity[3].

Cruz uses photography to raise awareness of the negative impacts people are having on our oceans, including through overfishing. For this activity, students will design and conduct research to discover firsthand what type of fish is being sold in their community, where this fish comes from, and whether that fish is an overfished species. They will then choose a method of presenting their findings to their communities to raise awareness of seafood choices available from sustainable fisheries. Know the Fish activity[4].

Sustainability Innovations

In addition to shedding light on sustainable issues through photography, it is important to use sustainable practices in the photographic process. Debris Free Oceans[5] highlights ways to use sustainable photographic processes and techniques, and ways for photographers to reduce waste.

David Attenborough's Great Barrier Reef[6] is one of his most impactful projects. This project explains the importance of Australia's Great Barrier Reef, and gives viewers the opportunity to take a virtual tour and learn about why it is essential to save it. The success of this project has been heavily reliant on individuals like Cruz, who do not necessarily get credit for having taking these images. But they are shaping the views of people who cannot see the reef in person, and helping them to understand why it is important.

Cruz began his photography in Indonesia as a curious young student who realized that this could be his way of sharing the importance of oceans to the rest of the world. The IndoOcean Project[7] is a marine research and ocean conservation project that is aligned with Cruz's goals, by hosting international and local marine conservation projects in Indonesia.

Sustainability Career Pathways

Nature Photographer. It isn't easy to make a career out of a passion for photography, but if you love taking photographs either above or below water, you might be able to make a career as a freelance photographer, perhaps supplemented by teaching, and/or other types of commercial photography. The first step is learning to understand what makes a good photograph[8]; it's also important to learn about how the industry works[9].

Photojournalist. Another way to make a career out of a passion for photography is to become a photojournalist. Especially when combined with strong photo editing and storytelling skills, one can make a career in photojournalism. Here is a direct account from several well-known photojournalists[10] about this career. And here is a list of some resources for budding photojournalists[11].

Oceanographer. An oceanographer is a scientist who studies the ocean, and helps to protect, conserve, and restore marine environments. Oceanographers can study ocean life, chemicals, fluid dynamics and physics, or even the geology of the oceans' floors. Considering that oceans are the true "lungs" of the planet (producing up to 80 percent of the world's oxygen), and the fact that climate change deeply threatens our oceans both through global warming and acidification, the world certainly needs more oceanographers. For more on this field and its vast diversity, visit here[12].

1 https://www.teachengineering.org/activities/view/cub_soundandlight_lesson8_activity1

2 https://www.nytimes.com/section/science

3 https://learning.blogs.nytimes.com/2009/11/25/science-class-in-pictures-photographing-scientific-discoveries/

4 https://www.dropbox.com/s/su7kc6gl61zpap2/Know_the_Fish_WETA.pdf?dl=0

5 https://debrisfreeoceans.org/sustainability-and-photography

6 https://attenboroughsreef.com/understanding_the_reef.php

7 https://indooceanproject.org/

8 https://digital-photography-school.com/9-things-need-know-become-nature-photographer/

9 https://www.masterclass.com/articles/how-to-become-a-nature-photographer#how-to-become-a-nature-photographer

10 https://www.format.com/magazine/resources/photography/how-to-become-a-photojournalist-guide

11 https://www.theartcareerproject.com/become/photojournalist/

12 https://www.environmentalscience.org/career/oceanographer

The Land of Many Waters

Benita Davis, Policy Forum Guyana
Guyana

Call to Action

Clean water is essential to sustaining human life. Learn more about Sandwatch at www.sandwatchfoundation.org

Values

- Humanitarian
- Solidarity
- Creative
- Committed
- Environmentalist

Lessons Learned

We are all part of the ecosystem. By protecting the environment, we protect ourselves.

Education is the one of the most effective weapons when fighting an environmental battle: by educating people we can inspire them to care about and protect our environment.

To understand the urgent need for change, we must first put ourselves in the place of those who are most affected by the problems we have created.

Anyone can become a steward of the Earth, regardless of age, sex, or nationality.

Guyana is called the "land of many waters."

But until she was in college, Benita Davis never truly understood the fundamental importance of water. Then a trip to Guyana's interior opened her eyes to the myriad ways that mining and oil exploration are hurting her country's rivers, lakes, and streams. The time she spent in the Kaieteur National Park—living off the land and the river alongside Indigenous communities—showed her the destructive impact these activities were having on those communities, and inspired her to educate her compatriots about the importance of protecting freshwater resources. Today, as a guardian of those waters, Benita is on the front lines of the battle to protect this precious natural resource.

Language Arts

Benita uses games and cartoons as a way to educate children about the environmental challenges facing the country of Guyana. Choose an environmental issue facing your community and design a game or cartoon to educate young children about the issue. The game should make clear what the problem is; possible solutions to it; and ways for people, even children, to get involved. Share your game or story with your peers.

Conduct research on the country of Guyana: Where is it? How long are its rivers? What percentage of the population is affected by water pollution? What is the major source of water pollution, and how is it affecting the country's economy? Then, with the information you have collected, create a PowerPoint presentation (at least 10 slides) for your classmates.

Using Google Forms, design a digital escape room, using this article[1]. You may choose to create your escape room about your chosen environmental issue (the first activity above), or about the country of Guyana (the second activity above). Then share it with your classmates.

STEM Activities

As in Benita's home country of Guyana, gold and ore mining are a source of water pollution in many small and developing nations. In this activity, students work in groups to learn how various stages of gold extraction and use (mining, production, consumption, disposal) pollute land, air, and water. Then they will discuss how waste products can be managed. Gold mining and impacts activity.[2]

In this activity, break the class into groups of four and ask them to determine the best water solution for each of four different communities. Each student will assume a role as a geologist, climatologist, public health officer, or village elder. Students will each receive a paper with specific information regarding their role in each of the four villages. Using the information from the "Types of Projects" section of The Water Project website, have the groups work together to determine which technology is best for each village. Village Voices Activity Link[3].

More than 800 groups from around the U.S and Canada have signed up to help fund water projects at schools and community centers in Africa. Have your class participate in The Water Project's Water Challenge[4], a fundraiser in which students agree to drink only water for two weeks, and put aside the money they would have spent on other drinks to help provide clean water in Africa. Students will calculate how much money they expect to save by not spending money on sodas, juices, sports drinks, etc. The challenge can be done as a whole class, in teams, or can include students from other classes, and even family members.

Sandwatch is a practical example of how education can be used to further sustainable development. It seeks to empower people of all ages and encourage them to assume responsibility for creating and enjoying a sustainable future. As the Earth faces rising sea levels, changes in storm patterns, and extreme weather events, beaches are among the ecosystems at risk. Start a Sandwatch team and select a beach for the class to monitor. Have the class watch the Sandwatch training videos[5] to learn how to use observation and recording to measure coastal erosion, beach profiles, and analyze water quality, among other things. Students will take the information they have collected and decide how they think action can be taken to address a particular beach-related issue.

Sandwatch in UNESCO[6]: Research and explore Sandwatch projects located in various islands and countries.

Sustainability Innovations

Due to the COVID-19 pandemic, in 2020, much education worldwide shifted to online learning platforms. This has allowed the use of sustainability-focused virtual environmental resources like the Maryland Association for Environmental and Outdoor Education[7]. MAEOE has created home-based environmental education resources to be used by teachers and parents to help teach their children about sustainability issues.

In addition to Benita's efforts, the United Nations Development Programme (UNDP) is focused on addressing sustainability issues in Guyana with their current projects. The three areas of focus for the UNDP - Guyana projects[8] are poverty reduction; democratic governance; and environment, extractive industries, and energy.

South America holds the greatest amount of water resources per capita and per area, but deals with some of the most significant water resource issues regarding availability and pollution. The World Resource Institute[9] highlights organizations and networks in Latin America and the Caribbean that are focusing on solving water issues in these areas.

Sustainability Career Pathways

Game Designer. Like Benita, you can create board games or video games that teach environmental themes: from Spirit Island to Catan: Oil Springs there are now dozens of games that integrate environmental themes and can serve as good educational tools--but only if they're fun to play. Do you love games? Video games, a growing multi-billion-dollar industry, offer a great opportunity to highlight sustainability themes--and make a living too, as this introduction to board game[10] design makes clear. Learn about a career in video game design here[11].

Environmental Scientist. During her stay in the country's interior, Benita discovered the threat that mercury is posing to both Indigenous communities and the waters of Guyana. Environmental scientists test for toxins, and work on programs and policies to prevent pollution and protect communities. This is a growing field, with lots of career opportunities, as this introduction details[12].

Outdoor Educator. Benita's experience with Sandwatch showed her the value of outdoor education. Today, many children are spending more of their time outdoors. Whether as a Scout leader, camp counselor, or forest kindergarten teacher, there are growing numbers of jobs in outdoor education. There are also many jobs that support outdoor education; for example, managers of town recreation departments. Learn more about this career track here[13].

Nutritionist. Benita was initially planning to become a nutritionist. While this is not typically understood as an environmental career, a good diet is a fundamental health and sustainability lifestyle choice. Diets rich in vegetables and low in animal products are better for both the body and the planet; so teaching people how to eat well is definitely a green job! Are you interested in helping people learn how to eat healthier and more sustainably? Learn more here[14].

1 https://www.bespokeclassroom.com/blog/2019/10/4/how-to-build-a-digital-escape-room-using-google-forms

2 https://serc.carleton.edu/integrate/teaching_materials/mineral_resources/activity6-2.html

3 https://thewaterproject.org/resources/lesson-plans/village-voices

4 https://thewaterproject.org/thewaterchallenge

5 https://www.youtube.com/playlist?list=PLKWNXfyQdXKRzc7_VgS9_ZnrW9477xKh2

6 http://www.unesco.org/new/en/natural-sciences/priority-areas/sids/sandwatch/

7 https://maeoe.org/resource-library/home-based-environmental-education-resources

8 https://www.gy.undp.org/content/guyana/en/home/projects.html

9 https://www.wri.org/our-work/project/eutrophication-and-hypoxia/latin-america-caribbean

10 https://mykindofmeeple.com/how-much-do-board-game-designers-earn/

11 https://www.cgspectrum.com/blog/what-is-game-design#:~:text=A%20game%20designer%20is%20the,almost%20every%20platform%20and%20genre.

12 https://www.thebalancecareers.com/what-is-an-environmental-scientist-526015

13 https://www.masterstudies.com/article/5-exciting-careers-for-outdoor-recreation-majors/

14 https://www.naturalhealers.com/nutritionist/

The Peace Corps in Malawi

Jill Bhowmik, Returned Peace Corps Volunteer
California

Call to Action

To get involved with one of the many goodwill Peace Corps Initiatives around the world, please visit www.peacecorps.gov

Values

- Commitment
- Dedication
- Altruism
- Creativity
- Open-Mindedness

Lessons Learned

Innovation and knowledge can be found in ancient traditions, too. Look to people from different cultures, and learn from them.

Our choices affect other people, too. We are citizens of the world, and the consequences of the way we treat our planet affects the global community.

You can always learn from other people, regardless of their age, educational level, or position in life.

As a Peace Corps volunteer, Jill Bhowmik taught English in Malawi; and in the process she inspired countless young people.

"When you decide to go halfway around the world with the Peace Corps, you think you are going to a place like Malawi to teach. And you do. But it didn't take long for me to realize that the amazing people and places involved with the Peace Corps end up teaching you."

As a creative educator, Jill found many novel ways to encourage young people in Malawi, and to accelerate cross-cultural knowledge sharing, which is central to the Peace Corps' overall mission and goals. Today she teaches English and Journalism at Granite Hills High School in San Diego, her alma mater. She also runs the school newspaper and the literary magazine, where the bravery and creativity of her students' writing never ceases to inspire her.

Language Arts

What is the Peace Corps? Write a research essay about the Peace Corps: explain what it is, how it started, what its goals are, and what its mission statement is.

Visit the Peace Corps Website[1]. Choose a country and a project that appeals to you. Create a PowerPoint presentation in which you explain what the Peace Corps is doing in the country you chose, why you think it is important, and how people can help support the cause (aside from donating money).

Malawi is a country with a very small carbon footprint, yet it is suffering from the consequences of climate change brought on by human activity in the industrialized world. Write a compare and contrast essay, in which you compare Malawi's economy and susceptibility to climate change with the situation in the U.S. What conclusions can you reach after making this comparison?

STEM Activities

Investigate the role of soil fertility in improving food security using the The Growing Challenge in Senegal WebQuest activity[2]. Learn from the experiences of two Peace Corps volunteers who worked with Senegalese farmers to use knowledge of the local soil to improve agricultural productivity. After completing the WebQuest, try using a soil-testing kit to determine the nutrient content in soil samples from your community.

Search the UN's website[3] for their estimated and projected total world population, and world population by area (region). What information can you gather from these data and projections? Compare the data with the FAO map of Prevalence of Undernourishment[4] in the Total Population. Given the projected trends, in which regions of the world do you predict the greatest food security challenges in the coming decades? How would a higher or lower rate of population growth change your predictions?

Returned Peace Corps volunteers involved in the Speakers Match[5] program introduce students to the Peace Corps experience and explain how STEM education can be used abroad. Invite a returned volunteer to speak to your students about a specific topic, or area of the world where STEM knowledge is needed.

Sustainability Innovations

Action for Environmental Sustainability[6] is a Malawian organization that was founded in 2007 to address the critical root causes of poverty and environmental degradation. Food security and sanitation are at the source of addressing both of these issues in many of their projects.

Sustainable Rural Growth and Development Initiative[7] is a Malawi-based organization that is focused on economic empowerment, and improving the peoples' lives through better access to clean water and sanitation. They try to address additional cross-cutting areas like HIV & AIDs, gender and women's empowerment, and the response to COVID-19.

Jill was able to use her experience in the Peace Corps as a way to become more globally aware, and to help communities around the world. The Peace Corps is not the only organization that has made it a priority to assist the rest of the world. World Teach[8] is an organization that focuses on similar issues by placing college graduates as volunteer teachers in countries around the globe for one-year teaching commitments at secondary schools.

In addition to volunteers reaching students from around the world and assisting struggling communities, it is important for students to connect with each other too. Collaborative Online International Learning[9] has become an integral way for students to collaborate on global issues. This is vital in order for today's students to develop the ability to grasp world-focused issues and become a part of the solutions to a better future.

Sustainability Career Pathways

Peace Corps or AmeriCorps. While not a lifelong career, Peace Corps and AmeriCorps (or if you're from a developing country, joining a program, like Germany's Weltwärts[10]) offer opportunities to learn new skills and languages, and to discover other cultures--all while helping others by teaching, farming, or other skills. Want to learn more about the Peace Corps? Start here[11].

High School Teacher. Often people who want to help save the planet think about teaching environmental studies or science. But any subject can incorporate sustainability messaging--whether its English literature, history, social studies, even art. Teaching is a noble profession and there are never enough passionate teachers. Already convinced this is the path for you? Here's a good guide on how to become a teacher[12]. Want to weigh the pros and cons? Start here[13].

Journalism Teacher. Today, between local newspapers shutting down and large news outlets becoming more polarized, it's more essential than ever to inspire a new generation of journalists who are passionately committed to discovering and reporting the truth. Jill teaches journalism in order to do just that. Perhaps you'll become a journalist--or, like Jill, maybe you'll teach journalism, to help grow the field. Here's an introduction to getting certified as a journalism teacher.[14] But you don't need to wait. You can start teaching journalism informally right away: get involved with your school paper or magazine; learn all you can about reporting and editing, and help your peers become better writers. Here are six tips[15].

Nonprofit Manager. Many people work for nonprofit organizations. Some even found their own nonprofits. But very few have any formal management training, which is an ongoing problem in this sector. There are programs to train managers for nonprofit organizations specifically. While many of these are masters' level programs (such as these leading programs[16]), there are informal and undergraduate opportunities to learn essential management skills as well. And if you're really serious about this path, here's a 500+ page introduction to the field[17].

1 https://www.peacecorps.gov/
2 https://www.lessonplanet.com/teachers/webquest-the-growing-challenge-in-senegal
3 https://www.un.org/en/
4 http://www.fao.org/economic/ess/ess-fs/en/
5 https://www.peacecorps.gov/educators/speakers-match/
6 https://www.afesmw.org/
7 http://www.srgdi.org/
8 https://www.worldteach.org/
9 https://coil.suny.edu/
10 https://www.weltwaerts.de/en/requirements-volunteers.html
11 https://www.peacecorps.gov/volunteer/is-peace-corps-right-for-me/
12 https://www.teachercertificationdegrees.com/become/
13 https://medium.com/teachers-on-fire/so-youre-thinking-of-becoming-a-teacher-818cb87cceb9
14 https://www.teaching-certification.com/journalism-teacher-certification.html
15 https://secondaryenglishcoffeeshop.blogspot.com/2019/09/six-tips-for-teaching-journalism.html
16 https://www.usnews.com/best-graduate-schools/top-public-affairs-schools/nonprofit-management-rankings
17 https://www.amazon.com/exec/obidos/ASIN/1119585457/stansociinn09-20

Walking Between Worlds

Shilpa Jain, YES!
India/California

Call to Action

Support YES! or sign up for a JAM.
Visit www.yesworld.org.
Follow YES!
FB - yescommunity and
Twitter: yeschangemakers

Values

- Community
- Idealism
- Multiculturalism
- Understanding
- Creativity

Lessons Learned

Living is learning, and learning is living. And unlearning is a vital part of our journeys.

Learn to adapt and see the world through different lenses: "Walk between worlds and build bridges between worlds."

Looking for a way to serve the planet and your community? Follow the paths to truth; live compassionately; and seek connection in everything you do.

Shilpa let go of dominant models of "success" and "achievement" to pursue a life more aligned with nature, spirit, and her values.

She spent 10 years as a "learning activist" at Shikshantar: The Peoples' Institute for Rethinking Education and Development in India. There, she was able to create an integrated life, "where living is learning and learning is living." Later, she learned about YES! Jams: "an ever-expanding network of beloved community; abeautiful cauldron of human potential." Now at YESWorld.org Shilpa collaborates with diverse teams from around the world to offer Jams for artists, activists, educators, lawyers, healers, dreamers, visionaries, and other changemakers. She has seen how Jams transform people's lives and work, and give them even more capacity to build a better world.

Language Arts

What are the three principles that guide Shilpa's activism? Write an explanatory essay about the influence of Jainism in Shilpa's activism, and how you can incorporate these principles into your own life, to be proactive in changing the world.

Shilpa uses creativity in her activism. Working in groups of 3-5 people, create an animated video or a short play in which you educate people about an environmental cause you feel passionate about. Present your play or video to your class.

After watching each group's presentation from the last activity, hold a class discussion in which your class, as a group, chooses the methods they believe are most effective when using creativity to educate young people. Afterwards, write a short, one-page explanatory essay in which you discuss the reasons for your answers.

STEM Activities

How does having diverse educators impact students' literacy rates? Measure the percentage of educators, principals, and/or superintendents of color in communities with a significant minority population, and compare the academic statistics (graduation rates, state assessment scores, etc.) Present your findings in a graph.

Research and compare the percentage of students that graduate from Harvard with a degree in finance, economics, business etc. compared to the percentage that graduate with a degree in sustainability-related studies (environmental science, marine science, sustainability science, conservation, etc.).

Have students examine literacy rates in their own communities and develop strategies for supporting local literacy efforts. Optionally, students can do volunteer work as a service-learning opportunity and a way to develop civic responsibility.

Sustainability Innovations

What is Yes![1]? How do they connect young and intergenerational changemakers around the world?

The North American Leadership Jam[2] is one of the original flagship programs for Yes! Review the staff for the 2021Summit and explain how their backgrounds could add a unique perspective to the Jam. Would you want to participate in this Summit? If so, who would you like to meet?

Review this article[3] about intercultural competence as a key driver for organizational success. How is effective communication highlighted based on a diverse team or organizations? Explain your definition of diversity.

Sustainability Career Pathways

Intercultural Communications Trainer. With society and societal challenges now global, communicating and cooperating across cultures is critical. Today, you can receive training in intercultural communications. Learn more here[4].

Diversity & Inclusion (D&I) Officer. More corporations, organizations, and institutions are recognizing the opportunity and responsibility for maintaining diverse workforces, and ensuring that all workers feel included in the workplace culture. There are now a variety of D&I jobs at larger companies, from VPs of D&I and diversity managers to D&I trainers. This article[5] provides an introduction to this field.

Event Planner for Nonprofits. Shilpa regularly uses the skills of event planning—coordinating guests, logistics, and promotion—when organizing the YES! Jams. From conferences and charitable auctions to concerts, there are abundant opportunities for planning enriching, sustainable events for nonprofits. To learn about the basics of event planning, you can read more here[6].

---

1 https://yesworld.org/about-us/

2 https://oldsite.yesworld.org/najam2019/

3 https://sso.shrm.org/IDBUS/SHRM/PORTAL-EE/JOSSO/SSO/REDIR?josso_cmd=login&josso_partnerapp_id=portal-sp

4 https://en.wikipedia.org/wiki/Intercultural_communication

5 https://www.aihr.com/blog/diversity-and-inclusion-jobs/

6 https://www.thebalancecareers.com/event-planner-525613

We Can Do Better!

Jasper Ralph, Plastic-Free MV
Martha's Vineyard

Call to Action

Adopt sustainable practices in your life: carry your own reusable straws. Bring shopping bags with you to the market. Every little bit helps!
Check out: www.plasticfreemv.com; @plasticfreemv on Instagram and @plasticfreeonmv on Facebook

Values

- Initiative
- Determination
- Commitment
- Community
- Environmentalism

Lessons Learned

Small changes in the usual way we do things can be the beginning of significant change in the world.

You have the power to change what you don't like about the world. People will listen to you, as long as you speak clearly, sincerely, and consistently enough.

The desire for change is contagious. Go spread it!

One day as Jasper Ralph was sitting in a restaurant in Martha's Vineyard enjoying a cool drink, he started to wonder about the plastic straw in his glass.
He hadn't asked for it, and he didn't want it: it seemed like such a waste. So he created a group with other students called Straw Free MV, and together they convinced many businesses on the island to only give out straws to customers when they specifically asked for them. That was just the beginning: Jasper and his friends soon expanded their goal to advocate for a new bylaw that would ban the sale of plastic bottles smaller than 34 ounces on the island. So far they have gotten the bylaw passed in three of the island's six towns. "We really do have the power to change what is happening," Jasper says. "Adults listen to kids: when they see that kids are standing up for something, it makes it look like it's really important."

Language Arts

How would you tackle the issue of plastic pollution created by single-used plastic in your own community? Write down a bullet-point list of possible solutions. Research one of these solutions that you think would be the most viable in your community and write a short pitch which you will then deliver to local business owners. After you do, gather feedback from the people you talked to: were they persuaded by your argument? What was most effective in your pitch?

Working in small groups, write a script for a video or short film about a group of friends who want to help curb plastic waste in the ocean. The story should start on the day they realize there is a problem with plastic waste, and end when they manage to take action.

Working in your groups from the previous activity, create an "escape room" designed to teach people about the danger climate change poses to an island. Make sure your challenges and puzzles test the participants' knowledge about climate change, its consequences, and what can be done about it. Then have the rest of your class participate in the escape room. Once everyone has had a chance to "escape" have a discussion about what everyone learned from the experience.

STEM Activities

We use plastics all the time: so often, in fact, that they're practically invisible to us. In this Earth Day lesson activity guide[1], students will keep a log of their plastic use, take actions to decrease it, and explore systemic approaches (like plastic bag bans, and taxes on bags) to minimize the use of plastics.

Watch this video on the effects of single-use and disposable masks on the environment[2]. Research what disposable masks are made of and how they can affect the environment if disposed of improperly. How can single-use masks be disposed of or recycled in a way that does not harm the environment?

Using this marine science activity[3], explore the threats of plastic waste to our oceans and devise a plan to do a better job of keeping discarded trash from entering our oceans.

Sustainability Innovations

Jasper began his activism within his local community and created permanent and expanding change. Through the global collaboration of businesses and organizations the world is following a similar pattern. The Plastic Pollution Coalition[4] is a global alliance of more than 1200 businesses, organizations, and world leaders who share the mission of a creating a plastic-free world.

Plastic pollution has become a huge world issue because of its long lifespan and because of the number of waterways that can be polluted. The Ocean Cleanup[5] is a technology-focused nonprofit organization that focuses on ridding the ocean and its waterways of plastic: they have developed the first scalable solution to efficiently intercept plastic in rivers before it reaches the ocean.

In addition to dealing with plastic pollution, it is important to protect the world's oceans and value what they contribute to our world. Oceana[6] is the world's largest international advocacy organization that focuses solely on various aspects of ocean conservation.

Sustainability Career Pathways

Materials Engineer: Along with reducing the use of plastic, it is essential that we design sustainable alternative materials to replace plastics. This will take materials engineers. Explore the field of materials engineering[7] to learn about some of the ways you could help grow a greener economy.

Recycling Industry: But Realistically, plastic isn't going to go away anytime soon. So finding better ways to recycle and reutilize plastic and other wasted materials is also essential. Recycling is a huge industry, employing drivers, sorters, mechanics, technicians, and plant managers, to help ensure that materials are made into new products instead of being incinerated. Here's a great overview of the recycling industry[8] if this sounds like the path for you.

Community Environmental Educator. Many communities offer a variety of environmental educational opportunities to their residents- through local governments, parks, museums, and neighborhood associations. Do you love teaching? Working with volunteers? Organizing community events? This could be the career for you. Learn more about community environmental education here[9].

1 https://www.morningsidecenter.org/teachable-moment/lessons/earth-day-lesson-plastics-and-you

2 https://www.youtube.com/watch?v=d0iUCDyrSgE

3 https://worldslargestlesson.globalgoals.org/wp-content/uploads/2020/12/Life-below-water-Marine-Litter-Lesson-Plan-Final.pdf

4 https://www.plasticpollutioncoalition.org/

5 https://theoceancleanup.com/

6 https://oceana.org/

7 https://engineering.purdue.edu/MSE/aboutus/whatsmaterials

8 https://www.bls.gov/green/recycling/

9 https://naaee.org/eepro/blog/community-environmental-education

IV

INNOVATE!

Green Entrepreneurs & Inventors

Young people in this book are the decision makers of tomorrow. As a young student I was inspired to study marine architecture and build cities under the sea. Today my son and daughter, the third Cousteau generation are uniquely motivated toward exploration, discovery and protection of our planet both on land and sea. Our children elevate us all to higher levels of compassion and understanding. We must watch and listen, closely learning from them as they have from us.

JEAN-MICHEL COUSTEAU

Applied Hope: Building Resilient Communities

Ana Sophia Mifsud, RMI
New York

☀ Call to Action

Learn more about green infrastructure, remote electrification, green community education, and RMI: rmi.org.

☀ Values

- Optimistic
- Creative
- Socially
- Mindfulness
- Innovative
- Environmentalist

☀ Lessons Learned

When faced with the opportunity to see the world from a different point of view, embrace it. You will learn about different cultures—and yourself.

Go outside! Enjoy and appreciate the world around you. Learn to appreciate nature, and use your talents to protect it.

When looking for inspiration, focus on what is possible, not what is popular.

Ana Sophia always knew she wanted to work at a mission-driven organization that had an outlook as positive and hopeful as hers is--particularly when it came to developing technical solutions to fight climate change that also lifted up communities economically.

After college, she began working at RMI, where she was introduced to the concept of Applied Hope—a mantra that she had unwittingly been living, and aspiring toward, all her life. According to Amory Lovins, RMI's cofounder, "Applied hope is not about some vague, far-off future, but is expressed and created moment by moment through our choices." In 2017, after Hurricane Maria ravaged Puerto Rico, Ana Sophia helped install microgrids in 10 public schools – giving more than 4,000 students and faculty access to clean, resilient power. "I can't tell you what it was like when the students could see firsthand what is possible. This is what Applied Hope fosters, in its purest form.

☀ Language Arts

What is microgrid technology? Write a research essay on the science of microgrids, their applications, and the environmental benefits they offer.

Ana Sophia talks about how important Applied Hope was in helping the people in Puerto Rico recover from the trauma of Hurricane Maria. Based on Ana Sophia's experiences, how can we apply this concept to facing the climate crisis in the world? Create a series of Tik Tok videos designed to bring positive messages that motivate people to get involved in finding solutions. Your videos should address a wide variety of age groups, from preteens to adults.

Create a presentation on differences in the lifestyle of people in Central America versus South Florida. What environmental, social, and economic challenges do these regions face? Do they share any challenges? Are there ways they could they help each other? Next, write a reflection paper in which you explain the most surprising fact you learned in your research.

STEM Activities

As the world shifts to renewable energy sources, electricity has become one of the main focuses of attention. When assessing the energy powering a home, microgrids and solar panels are two of the innovations that are used. What is the difference between solar microgrids and solar panels? What innovation would you like to include in your house, and why?

In addition to technological innovations, Ana Sophia's goals for youth are to go outside and spend more time in nature. Students today can be overly reliant on technology and lack the interaction with nature like other generations. What are three benefits of being outside in nature, why are they important to our future? Potential options:

- Vitamin D3/Sunlight
- Understanding the factors affecting air quality
- Learning about farming/agriculture

In response to Hurricane Maria's damages to Puerto Rico, Ana Sophia helped install microgrids in schools to keep them operating during rolling blackouts. Schools with resilient energy are invaluable to communities, and can serve as a safe haven in times of crisis. In this activity, students learn about resilient energy systems and explore the impact of loss of power in two different cities, one with a centralized energy system, and the other with decentralized energy systems. Activity link[1] .

Ana Sophia currently works at RMI, where her goal is to get businesses and homes to eliminate combustion in their buildings. Combustion is a reaction where a substance reacts with oxygen gas to produce energy in the form of light and heat. Have students use this online guide[2] to learn about hydrocarbons, the primary component of fossil fuels, and compare the products of combustion of different hydrocarbons. Using the results, students will explain how combustion produces and releases greenhouse gases such as carbon dioxide, contributing to climate change.

Sustainability Innovations

As the world strives to collaborate on addressing global sustainability issues, conferences and conventions continue to expand and develop. The Microgrid Innovation Convention[3] highlights advancements in technologies and real-world case studies of uses and developments.

Collaboration is often required in order to make systemic changes to improve sustainability. Resilient Power Puerto Rico[4] is a 501(c)3 organization that focuses on increasing resources and knowledge to improve the innovation and distribution of renewable energy across the region.

Ana Sophia's work has been amplified by her work as an associate with RMI. RMI[5] has become a leader in transforming the mindset of "Whole of Government" to a "Whole of Society" National Climate Strategy. What are these two different approaches? Why is this transition so important?

Sustainability Career Pathways

Renewable Energy Engineer. Improving the design of batteries, solar panels, and wind turbines will be essential in the transition to a sustainable future; and that will require renewable energy engineers.Want to learn more? Start here[6].

Microgrid Design Engineer. Perhaps like Ana Sophia, you want to help build microgrids, increasing community energy independence and resilience. Start by understanding what a microgrid is[7]. Then, if this is for you, learn more about the industry and job opportunities here[8] .

Renewable Energy Advocate. Renewable energy is a rapidly growing field and will make up an ever-larger percentage of the world's energy mix in decades to come. Becoming part of a renewable energy company[9] --as a manager, salesperson8, or support staff--is a way you can help with this transition. Or, by joining one of the many nonprofit organizations researching, promoting, or lobbying for the transition to renewable energy, you can help draw attention and investments to renewable energy.

1 https://www.cei.washington.edu/drupal/node/81
2 https://tropicsu.org/wp-content/uploads/2018/12/Lesson_Plan_Chem_Env_Sci_Hydrocarbons-and-Climate-Change.pdf
3 http://www.microgridinnovation.com/EMEA/
4 https://resilientpowerpr.org/
5 https://rmi.org/moving-from-a-whole-of-government-to-a-whole-of-society-national-climate-strategy/
6 https://engineeringonline.ucr.edu/blog/career-spotlight-renewable-energy-engineers/
7 https://www.energy.gov/articles/how-microgrids-work
8 https://microgridknowledge.com/distributed-energy-jobs-microgrid-knowledge/
9 https://www.greentechmedia.com/articles/read/cleantech-careers-solar-sales-at-a-residential-installer

A Life of Service: Water.org

Gary White, Water.org
Kansas City, Missouri

Call to Action

To get involved with Gary and Matt's work helping communities gain access to clean water and sanitation, please visit water.org.

Values

- Thoughtfulness
- Empathy
- Innovation
- Entrepreneurship
- Partnership

Lessons Learned

Let the people you admire inspire you to lead a life of service.

The things you take for granted could be seen as a treasure to someone else. Be grateful for what you have, and willing to help those who need it.

Communication with like-minded people is the first step toward fruitful partnerships. If you're looking for the solution to a problem, talking to others in that same field might be exactly what you need.

It is possible to be both an entrepreneur and a humanitarian, and to excel at both.

Gary White was raised for a life of service. "My parents, teachers, and faith really instilled in me a passion for it," he says.

When he was in college he found his calling: to study civil and environmental engineering. That was when he discovered the intersection of his greatest passion and the world's greatest needs. "Engineering answers to the world's problems would be the path that I would take from there on," he says. In 2008, he met Matt Damon at the Clinton Global Initiative. At the time, Gary was running an organization called Water Partners, which helped people living in poverty get access to microloans for clean water and sanitation, and Matt was running an organization called H20 Africa, which was helping to supply people with drinking water in rural Africa. "After talking a while, Matt realized that we had a track record of doing what he was trying to do, and he had the name and brand, and access to new and greater levels of funding that could change the future of water," Gary says. He and Matt merged their organizations to form Water.org. To date, in partnership with its 154 partners around the world, Water.org has mobilized over $2.6 billion in capital to support safe water and sanitation projects around the world.

Language Arts

What is the link between climate change and water scarcity? How does water scarcity affect a community? How does climate change affect flooding? How does flooding affect a community's access to water? What can be done to guarantee that people have access to safe drinking water? Based on your answers, conduct a Round Table discussion with your peers and come up with a list of specific actions your class will take to help tackle this issue, at a global, and at a local scale.

After watching Gary's and Matt's interview with Trevor

Noah[1], write an explanatory essay in which you write about the impact water scarcity has on a country's economic development, the education of its children--especially for young girls--and the quality of life of women in those countries. What is the biggest hurdle for people in regard to gaining access to safe, clean water in countries that suffer from water scarcity? What is Gary's and Matt's organization doing to help fix the problem?

In the interview with Trevor Noah[2], Matt Damon says "It is expensive to be poor." What does he mean by this? Did this fact surprise you? What specific examples does he use to explain this concept? How is water.org helping these people? Record your answers in a short video (no longer than four minutes).

After reading Gary's story, break up into groups of 2-4 people. Your teacher will assign your group one of the following questions to answer: What is the first responsibility society needs to undertake in order to deal with water scarcity, its causes, and its consequences? How can young people rise up to meet the challenges created by climate change and water scarcity? Using the answer you came up with, create a poster which you will then use for a Gallery Walk[3] like the one described in the video. As you complete this exercise, don't forget to ask questions and express your opinions in an informed and respectful manner.

STEM Activities

In this lesson plan on microfinancing[4], students will be introduced to the concepts and practice of microfinance, and will learn how the provision of unsecured loans to low-income, small-scale entrepreneurs in the developing world has improved the business prospects and quality of life for many desperately poor people around the world.

Research the water crisis conditions in a country of your choosing. Formulate a strategy on how to address the problem. Then pretend you are a national, state, or local leader, and present your idea on how to address the concerns about water quality to the class.

Using this Water Remediation Lab[5], measure the effectiveness of water filters in purifying contaminated water by graphing and analyzing test results.

Using this activity from TeachEngineering.org[6], teams practice water quality analysis through turbidity measurement and coliform bacteria counts. Then, they will use information about water treatment processes to design prototype small-scale water treatment systems and test the influent (incoming) and effluent (outgoing) water, to assess how well their prototypes are producing safe water that will prevent water-borne illnesses.

Sustainability Innovations

Water.org[7] has found success by transferring their model to 11 countries in Africa, Asia, and Latin America. Assess their work in two of these countries and compare their models them. How were they able to adapt the model to different challenges in each country?

Gary and Matt have been able to successfully collaborate to address water as one of Africa's major issues. Read this article[8] by the United Nations about the effects that microfinance can have in Africa. Review the section assessing operational efficiency, and discuss ways that this can translate to other sectors or organizations that are not related to water.

One of the main keys to Water.org's success was identifying the issues underlying the availability of water. In this World Economic Forum Article[9], the success of organizations that are working on adaptation to climate change is discussed. What is participatory scenario planning? How has this process allowed organizations to find successful approaches for dealing with future climate conflicts?

Sustainability Career Pathways

Microfinance Industry. As Gary's innovative work reveals, microfinance[10] is a proven tool in helping to create opportunities, and leveraging the resources of the poorest segment of humanity so they can help themselves,. There are many ways into this sector: for example, through finance, policy, or development, as this article[11] details. And databases like UNJobs[12] and DevEx[13] will help you find internships and jobs in microfinance.

Water and Sanitation Engineers and Managers. Water and sanitation engineers help plan and build the water systems and piping needed to deliver fresh water to communities and take away sewage, while managers help to operate existing systems. Learn more about a career as a water engineer here[14] and a career in operating water plants here[15].

Sustainable Beer Industry. Making beer uses a lot of water (not to mention a lot of grain, and a lot of energy). But it can be, and is starting to be, produced more sustainably. Responsible brands can be leveraged to help invest in sustainable development, (as Stella Artois has done with Water.org[16]). With 2.1 million jobs supported by the U.S. beer industry[17], this is a sector filled with opportunities both for jobs and for making a real difference in the way it is made. Read more about sustainable beer industry efforts here[18].

1 https://www.youtube.com/watch?v=Sqeh-ycjiFU
2 https://www.youtube.com/watch?v=Sqeh-ycjiFU
3 https://www.youtube.com/watch?v=pSt5echeRrM
4 https://www.pbs.org/wnet/ascentofmoney/lessons/microfinance-and-entrepreneurship-lesson-overview/32/
5 https://www.teachengineering.org/activities/view/wst_environmental_lesson02_activity2
6 https://www.teachengineering.org/activities/view/cub_waterqtnew_lesson01_activity1
7 https://water.org/our-impact/where-we-work/
8 https://www.un.org/esa/africa/microfinanceinafrica.pdf
9 https://www.weforum.org/agenda/2021/02/climate-change-adaption-resilience-africa/
10 https://www.investopedia.com/articles/07/microfinance.asp
11 https://economics.virginia.edu/career/careers-microfinance
12 https://unjobs.org/
13 https://www.devex.com/
14 https://www.careerexplorer.com/careers/water-engineer/
15 https://www.environmentalscience.org/career/wastewater-treatment-operator
16 https://www.youtube.com/watch?v=kOh3xWT7rsU
17 https://www.foodandwine.com/beer/beer-brewing-industry-jobs-statistics
18 https://daily.sevenfifty.com/how-beer-brewers-are-embracing-sustainability/

A Smart Response to Disaster Relief

Ben Smilowitz, Disaster Accountability Project
Washington D.C

Call to Action

Learn more about the Disaster Accountability Project: disasteraccountability.org or 202-556-3023 or email info@disasteraccountability.org

Values

- Cooperation
- Generosity
- Efficiency
- Community Service
- Social Justice

Lessons Learned

Let your life be of service to others, and take your inspiration from giving back.

To create change, start by meeting and engaging with your neighbors. Change begins with those closest to you.

When fighting for social justice, let your words be clear, and let your voice be loud.

After volunteering to help in the aftermath of Hurricane Katrina, Ben Smilowitz founded the Disaster Accountability Project (DAP), the very first organization of its kind, to provide independent oversight of the agencies and organizations receiving funds to assist with similar national emergency situations.

Among its many notable efforts, DAP filed a successful complaint in New York against the American Red Cross for gross mismanagement of funds after Superstorm Sandy, winning a $4 million release for those who had lost their homes, and much more. Ben then created SmartResponse.org, an interactive data repository where users can sign up, become a part of the disaster relief community, and work together to more efficiently administer local responses to emergency situations. Ben has been an Echoing Green Fellow, and is a graduate of UCONN Law. His work has been covered by the Washington Post, the Wall Street Journal, and CNN.

Language Arts

Hurricane Katrina was one of the most destructive storms to make landfall in the U.S. Since then, we have seen many destructive storms touch land around the world. What is causing this increase in the intensity of storms? Write a research essay that analyzes the causes for the increased number and elevated intensity of these storms.

One of the harshest realities after Hurricane Katrina was the mismanagement of the disaster. Working in groups of 3-5 people, create a presentation in which you analyze what went wrong during the Katrina response; who was responsible; and what could have been done differently to bring relief better, and more quickly, to the people affected by the hurricane. Focus on which sustainable technologies/solutions could have been implemented to ameliorate the effects of the storm.

Write a 2,000-word blog post about the state of government emergency response services in your area. What would happen in the case of a natural disaster? Would people know where to go to get help? What is the importance of having this information available? Have these services kept up with the increased demands caused by climate change? What can be done to improve them?

STEM Activities

In this disaster simulation activity from the Center of Disease Control[1], students act as members of an Emergency Response Council for the City of Calamity. They make decisions about how to proceed in the face of an emergency; how to prepare the community for a potential disaster; and how to keep the citizens of Calamity safe.

In this lesson plan from Health Smart Virginia[2], students create an action plan to prepare for a natural disaster. They learn how to develop an emergency preparedness kit; a family communication plan; a family disaster plan; and a class preparedness plan.

Design a technological solution to make information about your community's emergency response plan easily accessible to members of your community. This can be your school, community organization, church, or town/city. For an added challenge, develop an action plan to implement your solution. Then share it with the leaders of your leaders.

- **Resources:** AdobeExpress[3], piktochart[4], Prezi[5], Canva[6], and Thinglink[7] are all free online tools that can be used to create infographics, posters, cards, pamphlets, or presentations. WeVideo[8] is a free online video editing tool.

This lesson plan from PBS Learning Media[9] introduces students to a variety of natural hazards, emphasizing that when people understand such threats they are better able to avoid or reduce the potential impact of them if/when they occur. Students work in groups to research and discuss specific hazards and learn how and why certain kinds of natural hazards impact specific areas, as well as what people are doing to minimize the threats these hazards pose.

Sustainability Innovations

What can you do when a disaster strikes your home? Review the work of the Disaster Accountability Project[10]. How is DAP working to make organizations like FEMA (the Federal Emergency Management Agency) more effective?

When preparing for a potential disaster, it is important to have both proactive safety strategies and response/relief protocols in place. How does an organization like All Hands and Hearts[11] assist communities in the preparation process?

Ben realized that he needed to find a way to create relief assistance once a disaster strikes. Review this page, www.smartresponse.org[12], and learn how to properly respond if a disaster were to strike your community.

Sustainability Career Pathways

Watchdog Organization. Watchdog organizations—whether governmental, corporate, or nonprofit--are essential in order to sustain democratic practices. Watchdog careers can be in government oversight boards like the GAO[13]; nonprofit organizations like DAP or the Bank Information Center[14]; as well as in journalism[15].

Disaster Management Specialist. The climate crisis has increased the prevalence of flooding, fires, droughts, and other natural disasters. Every community needs a disaster management plan that includes the just and effective allocation and management of limited resources. Learn more here[16].

Data Analyst. Understanding data and turning it into effective findings is essential in order to improve not just disaster relief, but development aid, the transition to clean energy, climate change, and all other fields as well. If you love working with data, finding patterns, and writing reports, check out this career path. Learn more here[17].

1 https://www.cdc.gov/cpr/zombie/00_docs/simulation_lesson.pdf
2 https://healthsmartva.pwnet.org/uploads/rteditor/file/gr9-he-2-disaster-preparedness.pdf
3 https://www.adobe.com/express/
4 https://piktochart.com/
5 https://prezi.com/
6 https://www.canva.com/
7 https://www.thinglink.com/en-us/
8 https://www.wevideo.com/
9 https://mass.pbslearningmedia.org/resource/ess05.sci.ess.earthsys.lp_nathazards/natural-hazards/
10 https://disasteraccountability.org/about-us/our-mission/
11 https://www.allhandsandhearts.org/
12 https://www.smartresponse.org/
13 https://www.gao.gov/
14 https://bankinformationcenter.org/
15 https://en.wikipedia.org/wiki/Watchdog_journalism
16 https://www.environmentalscience.org/career/disaster-management-specialist
17 https://www.rasmussen.edu/degrees/technology/blog/what-does-a-data-analyst-do/

Bali's Huckleberry Finn Cleans Rivers

Gary Bencheghib, Make A Change World
Indonesia

☀ Call to Action

Get involved with Gary and his brother Sam's work of cleaning up our rivers and oceans. Learn how at Make A Change: makeachange.world

☀ Values

- Curiosity
- Concern
- Commitment
- Imagination
- Environmentalism

☀ Lessons Learned

Inaction, just like action, has global consequences. We are all interconnected; if we want change to happen, we need to start acting like we do.

Some problems are more visible than others. Sometimes, in order to solve a problem, you need to be a magician, and find a way to bring the invisible to light.

Finding solutions is about seeking collaboration from all parties, not pointing fingers at each other. A positive attitude will help get people working together to bring solutions to the table.

At 14, Gary Bencheghib formed Make a Change Bali to clean up plastic pollution from the beaches near his home.

Soon he realized that the beaches he cleaned up weren't staying clean. Week after week, plastic kept appearing on the shore. He also realized that it was not possible that the sheer volume of garbage he saw was just from local people littering: this was a much larger problem. A waste management problem. He learned that the problem in Bali was part of a much bigger problem that wasn't local at all – and that rivers were the source of much of the spreading of plastic pollution around the world. To solve this crisis, Gary has created multiple environmental documentaries and businesses that have helped to promote and support river cleanups around the world. His film on the Citarum River even moved Indonesian President Joko Widodo to mobilize the Indonesian Ministry of the Environment to begin working on a nationwide river cleanup project.

☀ Language Arts

Imagine you were tasked with a journey like Gary's: you have to build a plastic bottle raft which you will then use to sail the length of the Mississippi River. Write a short story in which you imagine what this journey would be like, the things you would see, and the challenges you would face (both personal challenges and the challenges presented by river pollution).

Write a research essay on Bali: Where is it? What is its main industry? How dependent is Bali on its waterways? What type of ecosystems are found in this area part of the world? How susceptible to pollution are these ecosystems? What consequences is Bali facing from pollution, and what is being done to restore its waterways?

What is the connection between rivers and the sea? Using secondary sources (videos, animation, images, tables, etc.) create a 5-7 minute video in which you explain how rivers and the sea are connected; what an estuary is; how the ecosystems in rivers and seas are dependent on each other; and how pollution, specifically plastic pollution, is affecting these ecosystems.

Organize a Jigsaw[1] exercise with your class. Assign students the following topics: microplastics (what they are, why they're dangerous, and what can we do to clean them up); chemicals most commonly found in waterways (again, students should focus on what they are, why they're dangerous, and how they can be cleaned up); best methods to clean up ocean waste on a large scale; strategies used to educate people about the hidden dangers of both micro and traditional plastics, and how to improve them; the countries that are the most vulnerable to plastic pollution in rivers and waterways.

STEM Activities

In this lesson plan from Trop ICSU[2], students will examine the climate change risk profile for Indonesia, including the climate impacts on major sectors of the country (agriculture, water resources, human health, ecosystems, energy, infrastructure, and disaster response). They will also analyze the current and future health risks in Indonesia due to climate change.

In this lesson plan from teachengineering.org[3], students will explore ocean currents and how they contribute to plastic migration around the world.

In this lesson plan from teachrock.org[4], students will learn about the chemical makeup of plastics. Then they will develop action plans to curtail plastic waste by learning about the environmental threats posed by plastics, and by assessing existing projects that are seeking to eliminate plastic waste.

Sustainability Innovations

Throughout Gary's youth his home, Bali, had been well-known as a tourist destination, but not as a hub for environmental education. However, today there are schools in Bali that target some of the issues that are threatening their community and their way of life. For example, Green School Bali[5] highlights environmental issues such as renewable energy and waste management within their curriculum. Students learn about issues of sustainability, and help create actionable solutions to accomplish sustainable goals.

In order to fix pollution in Indonesia's rivers, organizations such as Sungai Watch[6] have made it their goal to find innovative solutions to cleaning up the waterways. Not only does Sungai Watch use data and AI to improve their data collection, but they create conversations with corporations, distributors, government, and consumers. Why is it important to target each of these groups when assessing pollution?

In addition to Gary's work, filmmakers and groups around the world have highlighted the shift toward sustainability in their industries. In this article[7], the principles of sustainable filmmaking, green transitions on set, and the Sustainable Production Forum are discussed. What is the impact of using eco-friendly strategies to build a set and film a piece about sustainability?

Sustainability Career Pathways

Documentary Filmmaker. As Gary has demonstrated, film is a very powerful tool in that can be used to draw attention to an issue and spark change. Perhaps you want to become a filmmaker. Here are some tips for becoming a filmmaker by Ken Burns[8]. And here are some tips on how to actually make a living doing it[9].

GIS Specialist. Geographic Information Systems (GIS) is a key technology used in mapping, modelling, and presenting spatial data. Gary employed GIS in tracking his river clean-up progress. Many environmental groups, governments, and businesses use GIS to help with their efforts to make a more sustainable world. Learn more about being a GIS specialist here[10].

Materials Engineer: Along with properly disposing of and reducing the use of plastic, it will be essential to design alternative sustainable materials to replace plastic. This will take materials engineers[11]. Explore the field of materials engineering for possible ways you could help grow a greener economy.

1 https://www.youtube.com/watch?v=euhtXUgBEts
2 https://tropicsu.org/lesson-plan-climate-change-impacts-in-indonesia/
3 https://www.teachengineering.org/lessons/view/uok-2116-plastisphere-microplastics-pollution-wastewater-treatment
4 https://teachrock.org/lesson/cleaning-up-the-plastic-beach/
5 https://www.greenschool.org/bali/support-us/sustainability/
6 https://makeachange.world/sungaiwatch
7 https://sdg.iisd.org/commentary/guest-articles/how-the-film-and-tv-industry-is-working-towards-sustainability/
8 https://www.masterclass.com/articles/ken-burns-shares-tips-for-becoming-a-documentarian#ken-burnss-7-tips-for-becoming-a-documentarian
9 https://www.desktop-documentaries.com/how-to-make-a-full-time-living-as-a-documentary-filmmaker.html
10 https://www.environmentalscience.org/career/geographic-information-systems-specialist
11 https://engineering.purdue.edu/MSE/aboutus/whatsmaterials

Connecting Islands Virtually For Climate Action

James Ellsmoor, Island Innovation
United Kingdom

Call to Action

Visit www.islandinnovation.co/summit/ Support innovative projects to fight climate change & sustain island ecosystems. Follow James on Twitter @jellsmoor

Values

- Innovative
- Creative
- Entrepreneurial
- Environmentalist

Lessons Learned

Technology can be used to solve some of our most challenging environmental problems.

Communication and collaboration among nations around the world is essential in the 21st century.

Communications skills as well as technical skills are needed in order to solve the global problems we are currently facing.

James Ellsmoor is a renewable energy advocate, digital nomad, and serial green entrepreneur.

He is cofounder of Solar Head of State (SHOS), a nonprofit organization whose mission is "To help world leaders become green leaders." SHOS installed solar panels on the White House during Barack Obama's presidency to raise awareness about renewable energy alternatives. They have also completed solar installations for the President of the Maldives, the Office of the Prime Minister of Jamaica, and the Government House in St. Lucia.

James went on to create Island Innovation, a green consultancy and advisory firm focused on small island developing states (SIDS). Out of this, the Virtual Island Summit, a free online event aimed at connecting global island communities on a common digital platform, was created. More than a hundred island communities were involved in the 2019 Summit. In 2017, James was recognized on Forbes Magazine's 30 Under 30 List.

Language Arts

Which environmental cause would you like to fight for and why? Read the article 5 Steps to Write an Inspiring Mission Statement[4], and write your own mission statement for an organization that is dealing with the environmental issue of your choice.

Write two three-minute sales pitches. The first one should be a pitch that you would use to promote your organization to investors. The second should be a recruitment tool for volunteers. Then write a five-paragraph essay comparing and contrasting the two. How are these pitches similar? How are they different?

Create a series of 6-8 digital posters to explain the concept of "Energy Poverty," and what can be done to address this problem.

Choose an island in the Caribbean, and research what day-to-day life is like there for people your age; then create a five-to-eight-minute video to educate people on the problems that your island is facing in terms of energy infrastructure, climate change, and sustainability. Be sure to mention the Paris Agreement, and other possible solutions to these problems.

STEM Activities

In addition to James's experience in and passion for sustainability, he has been able to take advantage of the transition to virtual conferences and platform sharing. What is one topic that you think should be the focus at his next summit? Explain why.

Due to the global pandemic that began in March of 2020, the way we organize conferences and collect information has drastically changed. Choose a topic related to climate change/sustainability and research how the pandemic has affected an organization related to your chosen topic. Then create a presentation describing the pros and cons of the virtual shift, how you could participate (digitally), and how the organization may transition from digital to live participation once the pandemic is over.

Have you ever traveled to an island for vacation? If you have, research the challenges and opportunities that characterize this island community. If you have not, select an island that you would like to travel to, or learn more about, and conduct the same research. Then, in groups or individually, participate in a mock Virtual Island Summit, sharing your research with the class, and comparing and contrasting the findings.

Sustainability Innovations

In addition to the efforts by Island Innovations to connect island communities for the purpose of targeting sustainable issues, organizations like Greenbiz[2] create and enhance the intersection of business, technology, and sustainability. Greenbiz has events, news, and webcasts that educate individuals on the most recent updates in these sectors and how they can collaborate in the future.

Many sustainability organizations plan their projects based on the United Nation Sustainable Development Goals (SDGs). As a part of the UN SDG initiative, the organization has created a sector called Small Island Development States[3]. Small Island Developing States includes 38 countries that are members of the United Nations, as well as 20 nonmembers.

Sustainability Career Pathways

Renewable Energy Advocate. Through his work, James has shown the power of bringing together a diverse set of communities to collaborate with and learn from. Renewable energy is a rapidly growing field and will make up an ever-larger percentage of the world's energy mix in the decades to come. Becoming part of a renewable energy company—as a manager, salesperson[4], or support staff—is one way you can help with this transition. Or, by joining one of the many nonprofit organizations like Solar Head of State[5], you can help draw attention and resources to renewable energy.

Solar PV Installer. Not everyone wants to work in an office all day. Some people would rather help build infrastructure working with their hands. Why not help cover the world's rooftops in solar panels? These jobs pay well, and only require a high school diploma. Learn more here[6].

Solar Electrician. Along with installing photovoltaic cells, trained electricians are needed to wire them properly. This kind of work usually requires a technical degree or apprenticeship. Read more about how to become a solar electrician here[7].

Applied Anthropologist. As James learned through experience, understanding how technologies are used in different countries and cultures is essential for successful adoption of them. Anthropologists study culture, and applied anthropologists use their understanding of culture to help solve environmental or social problems: for example, finding ways to overcome stigmas or misconceptions about using solar energy. Anthropology is a robust field: universities, nonprofits, government agencies, and companies all need them to help achieve their missions. Read more about the field here[8].

1 https://articles.bplans.com/writing-a-mission-statement/
2 https://www.greenbiz.com/
3 https://sustainabledevelopment.un.org/topics/sids
4 https://www.greentechmedia.com/articles/read/cleantech-careers-solar-sales-at-a-residential-installer
5 https://solarheadofstate.org/
6 https://collegegrad.com/careers/solar-photovoltaic-installers
7 https://www.electricianschooledu.org/solar-power-technician/
8 https://www.americananthro.org/AdvanceYourCareer/Content.aspx?ItemNumber=2150

Engineering Solutions to Climate Change Problems

Alex Perkins, Sustainable Manufacturing
Nantucket / Vermont

Call to Action

Identify a problem you feel passionate about, and figure out what skills you need to learn so you can do something about it. Then find others who can work with you to create a solution. Learn more about Alex's work in technological solutions to climate change problems: www.roadpitch.co/pitcher/synticos-llc/

Values

- Caring
- Cooperation
- Imagination
- Determination
- Commitment

Lessons Learned

When you see something, do something! Use the resources you have to solve a problem you feel passionately about?

To solve environmental problems, reach out to others, and get them to work collaboratively toward the same goal.

We need to all work together to find alternatives to plastics that are healthier for people, and for our planet.

Alex Perkins grew up in Nantucket, helping his parents take tourists out on their whale-watching boat.
In high school he spent a semester in the Bahamas, where he learned about sustainability issues, and observed the horrible effects of burning plastic waste. He became fascinated with sustainability issues, and especially with finding technical solutions to these problems. First he joined with others to build a wind turbine at his school. Later he became a mechanical engineer, and even developed a machine that can turn plastic waste into fuel. For Alex, passion, technical skills, and collaborating with others are key to fighting the climate crisis. "We need to find innovative solutions to the problems we're facing," he says. "It's all about collaboration: talking about problems with friends, talking about ideas that you can build together."

Language Arts

Imagine you are part of a group of students tasked with convincing your school to start using energy generated by wind power. In order to do this, you will need the support of other students, teachers, and administrators. Create a promotional piece to educate people in your school about the benefits of wind power. Be creative. You can use video, audio, graphic design, music, anything you like to create your campaign. Then write a reflection paper on the choices you made, and explain why you think this would be the most effective way to create awareness of the issue of your choice.

Create a social media post designed to convince people to join your cause. Address just one specific group of people in your school community (students, teachers, or administrators). You can use still images and/or video. Then write a reflection paper explaining why you made the choices you made: why you chose to address that particular group of people (and how you think they can help your cause); why you addressed them the way you did (the language you used, the tone of the post, etc.); and why you chose the medium you used (video, music, graphics, written word).

Create a PowerPoint presentation about the importance of teaching sustainability in schools. Focus on how including sustainability in the curriculum would add to the quality of kids' educations, and explain why using wind power at your school would contribute to the students' education. Then write a reflection paper explaining why you made the choices you made: why you chose to address that particular group of people (how you think they can help); why you addressed them the way you did (the language you used, the tone of the post, etc.), and why you chose the medium you used (video, music, graphics, written word).

Write a speech to be delivered to the school board on the issue of using wind-generated power for your school district. The speech must address not only the environmental benefits of wind power, but also the practical and financial benefits of this type of electricity. The speech must be no longer than three pages, and it must include facts gathered from research.

STEM Activities

Research areas in and around your community that could be sites for ecotourism. Alex's home in Nantucket is surrounded by the beautiful ocean. But a forested mountain range, a sprawling desert, or a prairie grassland could be equally interesting places to visit. Any places untouched by people are perfect spots to appreciate the beauty of our planet. Remember that it is important to remain respectful of the earth; leave everywhere you go just as it was when you arrived. List three potential ecotourism sites in or near your community, and three global ecotourism sites you may want to visit.

Are there any wind turbines or other sources of renewable energy in your community? If not, do you see any potential sources of renewable energy? For example, if there are large open fields with consistent sunshine upon them, solar panels could be installed to take advantage of the surface area. If you live in a particularly windy area (like Nantucket) a wind turbine could be the perfect answer to providing power to your community! List two renewable energy resources that you think would be a good fit for your community.

Learning is one of the most important steps on any journey; Alex helped his peers by creating a free online library. Check out your local library's selection of online books. Most libraries have books on sustainability and renewable energy; so sign up for a library card online and check out a book on sustainability. The keywords to search for are "sustainability," "renewable energy," "solar power," "geothermal," and "wind power."

Alex used "pyrolysis" to turn plastic waste into fuel. What other waste materials do you think could be recycled into something useful? For example, did you know that scientists have found ways to use corn husks as the base for a biological car fuel? List three items that you do not see being recycled (or that are not recycled efficiently) and think about how they could be turned into something useful.

What is a problem that you struggle with that you think could be aided, or fixed entirely, by technology? Alex says that change can happen even when it's not commercially viable, so don't limit yourselves only to profitable solutions. For example, it costs more money to build elevators in buildings than to simply use the stairs, but we can all agree that 90-story buildings do need elevators!

Sustainability Innovations

SeaAhead[1]: SeaAhead is a blue tech startup platform, based in Boston, that helps build companies and facilitates investments. They are helping to catalyze a blue tech cluster in the Northeast.

AirCarbon[2]: AirCarbon uses natural ocean microorganisms to make PHB from air and greenhouse gases as an alternative to plastic.

ENGIE Impact[3]: ENGIE Impact is a sustainability and energy management company.

Sustainability Career Pathways

Mechanical Engineer. As Alex's story shows, with engineering skills we can redesign our manufacturing processes to make things—from wind turbines to toasters—more efficient and more sustainable! Want to explore the field of engineering? Start here[4].

Renewable Energy Site Design Consultant. A lot goes into identifying an appropriate site for a new renewable energy project, from figuring out whether it will generate enough electricity, to determining what impact it will have on the surrounding environment. As we transition to renewables, there is a great demand for people who are skilled in helping to set up new projects. For example, Geo SubSea[5], a consultancy firm, assesses and maps the design of offshore wind farm sites in the Northeastern United States.

Sustainable Finance. With billions of dollars being invested, where the money goes will shape the future of business. Should we be investing in oil companies, or in renewable energy companies? In downtown real estate or suburban malls? Working with a socially responsible investment firm, or with a university or foundation as an asset manager can be a great way to help develop the sustainable business sector. Here is a brief introduction to the many jobs in the field[6].

Inventor. It's not easy to invent something, and it's even harder to get the world to notice. But a good idea can change the world! Explore these 5 Steps to Inventing Something[7], and these 7 steps to becoming a full-time inventor[8].

---

1 https://sea-ahead.com/
2 https://www.newlight.com/aircarbon
3 https://www.engieimpact.com/
4 https://www.topuniversities.com/courses/engineering/which-type-engineering-should-you-study
5 https://geosubseaconsulting.com/
6 http://finanzasostenibile.it/wp-content/uploads/2017/04/13-04-2017_FBicciato_ProfessioniSRI_SdR.pdf
7 https://www.popularmechanics.com/technology/a5982/how-to-become-an-inventor-in-5-steps/
8 https://www.inc.com/stephen-key/so-you-think-you-want-to-be-a-full-time-inventor.html

Farming the Ocean

Perry Raso, Matunuck Oyster Farm
Rhode Island

Call to Action

Clean up a beach in your area and support organic farm-to-table businesses in your community. To learn about aquaculture, follow Matunuck Oyster on Twitter @MatunuckOyster & Instagram @matunuckoysterbar

Values

- Entrepreneur
- Sustainability
- Initiative
- Education
- Environmentalist

Lessons Learned

Hard work, passion, and creativity lead to innovation. And innovation can make it possible to be both professionally successful and environmentally responsible.

Hard work and a dream are not enough to achieve success. You have to educate yourself, and not be afraid to innovate in your field.

You can build a successful business by working to preserve the environment and using the natural resources available in your community responsibly, instead of depleting them.

Perry Raso started digging for clams when he was just 12 years old.

I knew that the harder I worked, the more money I'd make," he says. "I liked being able to determine how much I made by how hard I worked." When it was time for him to go to college, he knew he wanted to learn how to provide seafood for people. So he studied aquaculture and fisheries technologies at the University of Rhode Island; after that, he was ready to start his own business. He started small, with a one-acre sustainable farm where he grew oysters and sold them at the local farmers' market. His business grew by leaps and bounds: today, in addition to running an oyster bar, Perry devotes a lot of his energy to teaching young people about sustainable aquaculture. "Many people see it as a niche industry," he says. "But I want to change that. It should be viewed in the same way as sustainable agriculture. Then we can really make an impact."

Language Arts

What type of business would you like to be in? Think of ways you might want to open a business, and do it in a sustainable and environmentally friendly way. Write a cover letter introducing yourself to potential investors. Include information about the type of business you plan to start; the skills and experience you have that will be necessary for the business to succeed; and what will make your company better than any other company in the same field. It's important to cover all these points, but the people who will be reading it are probably very busy. So it must also be brief.

After reading this article[1] write your own business proposal. It should include the cover letter you wrote for the previous activity. Then, for this exercise, focus on creating the following: Table of Contents, Executive Summary, and body of the Proposal, as explained in the article.

Create a presentation on aquaculture: what it is, the preferred methods used in aquaculture, and why it is considered a sustainable practice.

STEM Activities

For this activity, students will learn the importance of aquaculture in the sustainable fishing industry by playing Eco Ocean[2]: an overfishing simulation game. They will need to answer the following questions:

- What was your goal during this simulation? How did you attempt to accomplish your goal? How could you change your fishing technique to increase the number of fish you caught?
- There was a surprise factor that you didn't know about before you started fishing. What was this factor? How did this factor impact your fishing success?
- Now that you know about this additional factor, complete the fishing simulation again. How will you change your fishing practices this time?
- How many fish did you catch in your second simulation? How did you place in comparison to the other boats?
- Why do you think it is important to consider both the number of fish that you caught and your sustainability rating when scoring this game?

This resource, from the AQUA Project[3], will give students a hands-on introduction to aquaculture. In this activity, students will design, create, and maintain an aquaculture farm. The activity starts on Section 3, page 11. (Note: This is a long-term project.)

Coastal erosion is the process by which wave action wears away beaches and shorelines; it results in loss of property for landowners, and millions of dollars' worth of damages each year. In this activity, students will develop a cost-effective and environmentally safe engineering solution to show how aquaculture operations can be strategically developed to reduce shoreline damage. Link[4].

Sustainability Innovations

Perry had the perfect storm of drive and determination, along with an ideal geographical location to give him the opportunity to succeed with the Matunuck Oyster Farm. Some individuals are not as lucky; but they can still take advantage of created aquaculture systems to cultivate shrimp, fish, and oysters. There are many challenges with this process, including water organism diseases. Viaqua Therapeutics[5] is one of the leaders in the delivery of oral vaccinations to prevent disease in fish.

Due to lack of area and space for aquaculture and the threat of waste, Better Fish Farming[6] was created as a project of the Recirculating Farms Coalition to emphasize the usage and efficiency of closed-looped fish farming. Atlantic Sapphire[7] is one of the leaders of this project, which has created "blue houses" to farm and cultivate Atlantic salmon.

Perry has a beautiful aquaculture farm because of his ability to use a natural setting, but others have developed the use of technologies to assist them in less conducive conditions. Innovasea[8] is a company that has found success within open ocean aquaculture, land-based aquaculture, and aquaculture intelligence.

Sustainability Career Pathways

Diver. Before he created his shellfish farm, Perry harvested shellfish by scuba diving. Divers are in demand for many other projects as well--from building offshore wind turbines[9], to reseeding coral reefs, to helping to conduct scientific research and archeology. If you love diving, there's potential to make a career out of it! Read about some diving jobs here[10].

Sustainable Aquaculturalist. One of the great ways to heal the ocean is by growing kelp and shellfish to filter and clean the ocean[11]. Farming the seas, or aquaculture[12], is a growth industry, as is working for companies that help seed aquaculture operations. An aquaculturist oversees the breeding and growing of fish, manages staff, and/or operates aquacultural systems. Learn more here[13].

Roboticist. If you love the ocean (and robots), perhaps you should be a roboticist. Roboticists are designing autonomous underwater vehicles that will be the future of ocean exploration, aquaculture, and coral restoration. This is an exciting new sector of the Blue Economy that is growing, and that currently lacks a sufficient number of qualified employees. Even if you don't like oceans, there are dozens of fields in which roboticists are needed. Interested? Learn more about entering the field of robotics here[14].

Sustainable Restauranteur. It's possible that it's never been harder to be a restauranteur than now, due to the COVID pandemic. But for those who love the idea of managing a restaurant, especially one that draws on sustainable ingredients and helps people understand that healthy and sustainable food is delicious, there are many leaders to draw inspiration from. For example, Alice Waters opened her trailbreaking restaurant Chez Panisse in Berkeley, California, in 1971. And in 2021, Ona, a restaurant in a small village in southwestern France, became the first vegan restaurant to receive a Michelin star. Perry's restaurant, Matunuck Oyster Bar[15], has shown how obtaining ingredients from local sources and integrating those sources into the business plan can be successful. Perry now has a Farm-(and Sea)-to-Table enterprise, drawing from his vegetable and oyster farms. Want to learn more about being a restauranteur? Read here[16].

1 https://www.pandadoc.com/blog/how-to-write-a-proposal/
2 http://www.ecoocean.de/play-online/
3 http://www.ctsa.org/files/publications/Aqua_Curriculum.pdf
4 https://extension.umaine.edu/4h/stem-toolkits/innovations-in-aquaculture/activity-5/
5 https://www.viaqua-t.com/
6 https://www.betterfishfarming.org/
7 https://atlanticsapphire.com/
8 https://www.innovasea.com/
9 https://www.maritime-executive.com/article/more-2000-commercial-divers-needed-meet-demands-offshore-wind-sector
10 https://www.tdisdi.com/sdi-diver-news/top-jobs-in-scuba-diving/
11 https://www.fisheries.noaa.gov/feature-story/aquaculture-grower-profiles
12 https://www.fisheries.noaa.gov/topic/aquaculture
13 https://www.discoveryeducation.com/
14 https://www.northeastern.edu/graduate/blog/what-does-a-roboticist-do/
15 https://www.rhodyoysters.com/about/
16 https://www.foodandwine.com/how/how-open-restaurant-restaurateur

Human Nature Projects

Elliot Connor, Human Nature Projects
Australia

Call to Action

Join Elliot's Human Nature Projects: humannatureprojects.org

Values

- Compassion
- Respect
- Collaboration
- Environmentalism

Lessons Learned

We are all guests on this planet. Be gracious, and considerate of other species.

Turn your passion into action!

Success requires a combination of hard work and perseverance.

When Elliot was just 10 years old, he met a leopard in Botswana.

It was a close call, and an experience that he will never forget. However, the encounter only intensified his passion for animals, and when he was 16 years old, he started the charity Human Nature Projects. It connects more than 1,400 volunteers in more than 100 countries around the world, all of them working on conservation issues. Elliot is aiming large: with his organization, he wants to get people to reevaluate their relationship with nature--to rethink what it means for us as humans, to share our planet with other species.

Language Arts

Choose an animal species that is endangered in your area. Create a 5-7 minute video about this species; about why it is endangered, and what can be done to protect it. Finish your video with a Call to Action, to get your peers involved.

Working in groups of 3-5 people, create the content for a website for a fictional conservation project. Your website must be targeted to attract young volunteers. The website must include an About Us section; a section with information about one of the species you want to protect; a FAQs page; a Call to Action page; and two blog posts. Afterwards, create a presentation using the content from your website, and present it to your class.

After watching everyone's presentations, write an essay in which you discuss which presentations were most effective and why. Which of these fictional websites do you think best accomplishes its goal of educating people and getting them engaged in a conservation project? Which websites were more effective, and why?

STEM Activities

The WWF Australia[1] report suggests that as many as 3 billion individual mammals, birds, reptiles, and frogs died or were displaced during the bushfire crisis. Calculate the loss of plant and animal species from the fire. What percentage of Australian species are threatened with extinction as a result of this crisis? How many of those species are unique to Australia? Select one of them and explore what the effect would be if this species were to become extinct.

This lesson plan from the California Academy of Sciences[2] uses the imaginary location of "Conservation Island" to teach students about some of the real-world issues involved in making plans to save endangered species. Students will learn the concepts behind identifying endangered and extinct animals, and develop their own conservation plans for saving three endangered species on the fictional island.

The conservation charity World Wildlife Fund (WWF)[3] has warned that climate change is threatening the existence of the snow leopard in the Himalayas. Research the impacts of climate change on snow leopards and chart their future population trajectory. What human activities are having a significant impact on the sustainability of this species?

Research endangered species that can be found in your community or country, and learn how human activities are contributing to their decreasing population. Then create a website, app, or infographic to raise awareness in your community, by providing information about organizations that are helping to save these species, and how people from the community can support the cause.

Sustainability Innovations

Elliott Connor began his work with Human Nature Projects[4], but he has developed many other projects as well, to assist in the fight to create a more sustainable world. Learn about some of his projects. Which one interests you the most? How can you become engaged in this work?

As the global population collaborates to address our sustainability issues, the need for information expands. Elliot has developed the Human Nature Podcast[5] to share information about animals, and highlight the work of animal experts so we can learn more about the creatures we share the earth with.

Seeing the work of others is great, but it is also important to find ways that you personally can make an impact. Projects Abroad[6] highlights hundreds of different projects that you can participate in, with an emphasis on wildlife and marine conservation.

Sustainability Career Pathways

Conservationist. Conservationists have various roles to play in preserving and protecting wildlife habitats and their inhabitants: they work as animal advocates, liaisons with governments and affected communities, nonprofit managers, and fundraisers, among many other roles. This witty essay looks at the 12 different types of conservationist you could be[7]. And this article introduces you more thoroughly to the field[8].

Wildlife Veterinarian. Caring for sick and injured wild animals can be rewarding as well. Explore how you can become a veterinarian, or check out these many other interesting jobs working with animals here[9].

Volunteer Coordinator. Nonprofits depend on volunteers to get the work done. And the success, management, and training of volunteers depends on good volunteer coordinators. Larger nonprofits hire coordinators to help draw out the energy and passion of volunteers, as well as train them: Learn more about what a volunteer coordinator does here[10].

1 https://www.worldwildlife.org/press-releases/3-billion-animals-impacted-by-australia-s-bushfire-crisis

2 https://www.calacademy.org/educators/lesson-plans/conservation-island

3 https://www.worldwildlife.org/species/snow-leopard

4 https://humannatureprojects.org/what-we-do

5 https://www.elliotconnor.com/podcast

6 https://www.projects-abroad.org/volunteer-abroad/conservation-and-environment/

7 http://www.jamesborrell.com/the-12-types-of-conservation-career-and-how-to-choose-which-one-is-for-you/

8 https://www.thebalancecareers.com/conservationist-526002

9 https://unity.edu/environmental-careers/20-cool-careers-with-animals-that-pay-well/#unusual

10 https://www.indeed.com/hire/job-description/volunteer-coordinator

Invent Something to Help Others!

Gitanjali Rao,
Colorado

Call to Action

Explore STEM learning & project-based opportunities. Invent something to help humanity. Gitanjali has partnered with UNICEF Voices of Youth to educate others on the importance of cyber- safety. Check out her blog www.voice-sofyouth.org/campaign/your-world-reimag-ined

Values

- Imagination
- Compassion
- Confidence
- Commitment
- Determination

Lessons Learned

When you see problems or challenges, follow Gitanjali's example: use your skills and abilities to come up with solutions.

STEM skills can be used to create amazing advancements in society, and young people can help develop them.

STEM skills can be used in many ways to address a variety of problems in society.

The first public health crisis that Gitanjali sought to address scientifically was the water crisis in Flint, Michigan.

"When I saw the broadcast from Flint, I was appalled. I couldn't believe how many kids my age were drinking lead poison every day." So, in 2017, when she was just 13 years old, Gitanjali created Tethys to detect lead contamination in drinking water sources. With this invention, people can tell whether their drinking water has safe levels or not, in real time. For this invention, 3M awarded her a $25,000 prize for winning their Young Scientist Challenge in 2017. She went on to create Epione, an app connected to a testing device that detects how addicted someone is, or isn't, to opioids. And her newest venture, Kindly, is an app that helps parents, educators, and students detect potential bullying situations– and stop them before they happen.

Language Arts

Write a research essay on an environmental issue affecting your community: First explain the problem. What is the source of the problem? How would you raise awareness about it? How would you tackle it?

Write the script for an imaginary conversation between a young inventor trying to obtain funding for his/her invention, and an investor. How would the inventor convince the businessman to invest in their invention? What points would the inventor need to make? What reservations/worries might the investor have? (For this exercise, think of two or three objections, no more). How would the inventor address these concerns?

Working in groups, design a game (it can be a board game, a trivia game, a card game, or even a computer game) that explains why one of Gitanjali's inventions is important, and how it can help people.

STEM Activities

Like many young leaders, Gitanjali found areas of her life that she wanted to improve, and in the process found a way to make a difference for all young people. Find one problem or issue facing young people in your community and create a plan of action to create a solution or gather resources/individuals to help you combat this problem.

In addition to Gitanjali's passion for solving issues of sustainability, she was equally passionate about getting support from adults in her community. Create a "pitch" to teachers, organizations or another group of adults in your community whose help you would need to execute the plan of action created in the previous activity.

As individuals, we go through our daily routines trying to make "sustainable choices." However, we rarely calculate how our activities and our choices directly impact our environment. Create a list of your daily activities (transportation used, food consumed, etc.). Then, with the guidance of an adult, calculate your approximate carbon footprint based on your list (carbon footprint calculator[1]).

When the drinking water in Flint, Michigan became contaminated with lead, causing a major public health crisis, Gitanjali came up with the idea for Tethys, an Arduino-based device that made testing for lead in water cheap and reliable. Visit create.arduino.cc/projecthub[2] and select a project for the students to complete. Alternatively, allow the students, in groups or individually, to select a project themselves. For an added challenge, have students brainstorm ways to improve their project with customized features and functionalities.

Sustainability Innovations

Gitanjali's love for the environment and passion for invention allowed her to carry out her plans and transform her ideas into practical apps that can assist efforts to reduce waste and make them more sustainable. These apps strive to achieve goals similar to Gitanjali's:

- **Ecosia**[3] This browser uses the money it receives from ads to help plant trees.
- **Earthhero**[4] **- Climate Change:** This app allows you to track your personal carbon footprint, set green goals, and compare your emissions reduction with science-based recommendations. After compiling this information, you can share your findings with others.
- **Kora**[5] Like Earthhero, Kora allows users to track their carbon footprint, but has the additional benefit of a system of rewards for changed behaviors. As you reduce your footprint, you can assist current sustainability projects, or purchase items from sustainable companies.

Reducing our carbon footprint is extremely important, but there are many other ways to create a more sustainable planet that need to also be addressed. Identify one other aspect of sustainable living that you would like to address as you design and develop your own app. Create a basic outline and goals for your idea.

Sustainability Career Pathways

Inventor: It's not easy to invent something, and it's even harder to get the world to notice. But a good idea can change the world. Explore these 5 Steps to Inventing Something[6] and these 7 steps to becoming a full-time inventor[7].

Serial Entrepreneur: Gitanjali has created several wildly different, socially beneficial inventions. But to get a product or service into the world takes an integrated network of investors, marketers, and entrepreneurs. An entrepreneur is willing to take on risk in order to create a new business or product and get it into the hands of people. Think you want to be an entrepreneur? Learn more here[8].

App Designer: From lead and addiction-level testing to creating an app to make the internet a kinder place, Gitanjali has explored many different paths. With so much of our time spent on the internet, apps that can improve our lives, and the world, can make a difference. Want to get into app design? Here's a good starting point[9].

STEM Educator: Gitanjali received significant mentoring and support from the adults in her life. Consider a career in education: either as a teacher[10], or in informal education, including museums and science centers, FabLabs, and nature centers.

1 https://www.conservation.org/carbon-footprint-calculator#/
2 https://create.arduino.cc/projecthub
3 https://www.ecosia.org/?c=en
4 https://www.earthhero.org/
5 https://kora.app/
6 https://www.popularmechanics.com/technology/a5982/how-to-become-an-inventor-in-5-steps/
7 https://www.inc.com/stephen-key/so-you-think-you-want-to-be-a-full-time-inventor.html
8 https://hbr.org/2020/07/so-you-want-to-be-an-entrepreneur
9 https://www.appypie.com/how-to-create-an-app
10 https://zety.com/blog/how-to-become-a-teacher

Light and Hope for Puerto Rico

Salvador Gómez-Colón, Light and Hope for Puerto Rico, Puerto Rico

Call to Action

Adopt renewable energy in your home. Learn about solar power. And follow Salvador on Twitter: @sgomezcolon

Values

- Altruistic
- Generous
- Creative
- Dedicated
- Environmentalist
- Philanthropist

Lessons Learned

When bad things happen in your community, figure out a way you can help others.

Young people can become heroes for their communities.

Solving an immediate, local problem can lead to finding solutions for long-term, global problems.

Just one person with a good idea, and the willingness to carry it out, can end up helping thousands of others.

At the age of 15, Salvador Gabriel Gomez Colon lived through the most traumatic night of his life when Hurricane Maria hit his home in Puerto Rico.

The hurricane would change his life forever and set him on an unexpected journey. After the storm, Salvador founded Light and Hope for Puerto Rico, a fundraiser to provide solar lamps and hand-powered washing machines to people who lost power during Maria. He raised more than $160,000—enough to provide 3,500 households in 17 towns across the island with supplies. His activism landed him on stage at the Davos World Economic Forum in Switzerland, where he sounded out a powerful call to world leaders to take action to combat climate change.

Language Arts

Using Salvador's story as an example, write a one-page essay arguing in favor of providing solar-powered lamps, batteries, and chargers to cities and towns.

Imagine there is a natural disaster in your area that causes 90 percent of the people to lose power. You decide to start a petition asking people to donate money in order to buy solar lamps, heaters, chargers, etc. Write a GoFundMe-style pitch to convince people to donate to your cause.

Write a (fake) Twitter exchange with a person who doesn't believe in the importance of giving people access to solar power. The exchange must have a total of ten tweets (five for and five against solar power). You will need to present, build, and defend your thesis to the imaginary person arguing with you.

STEM Activities

Salvador helped raise money to give Puerto Ricans solar lamps and hand-powered washing machines, and researched other sustainable alternatives for appliances we take for granted on a daily basis. List three of the sustainable appliances you've found, and think about how you might integrate them into your life.

The dated power grid supplying Puerto Ricans with their electricity was rendered useless during Hurricane Maria. Think of some ways you would protect powerlines and generators from destruction during a natural disaster. Then, learn how power grids are fortified in real life. How do your ideas compare to what is really used? Do you think your ideas could improve what exists?

Solar power is essentially free unlimited energy. Can you think of some of the reasons people would be hesitant to adopt this technology?

Sustainability Innovations

Team RubiconUSA.org[1] was founded in the wake of the 2010 Haiti earthquake. This organization has worked with military veterans, first responders, medical professionals and trained civilians to assist in 650 disaster relief programs over the past 10 years.

All Hands and Hearts - Disaster relief foundation founded in 2004 after the effects brought on by the Great Indian Ocean Tsunami. They have numerous volunteer opportunities, including in the Bahamas, Louisiana, Florida, Texas, Los Angeles, Mexico, Peru, Nepal, and Australia.

Research disasters that the world has experienced in the last four years.

- Identify 2-3 relief programs that have assisted in these disasters, and explain why you would like to assist with that program in the future.

Sustainability Career Pathways

Community Organizer. Engaging one's community around important environmental and social challenges, as well as in post-disaster situations, is an important career path and opportunity for community service. There are many programs to learn organizing skills, from online courses, to one-year environmental organizing field schools like Green Corps[2].

Fundraiser/Development Officer. Raising money is a skill as well as a viable career path. Every major nonprofit organization has a development officer—from environmental organizations to universities and community aid organizations. For a basic description on what being a development officer entails, visit here[3].

Development and Marketing of Sustainable Technology: Companies like "The Laundry Alternative" can fill a large niche in an economy where electricity is limited. As communities around the world seek to reduce electricity usage in order to limit greenhouse gas emissions, appliances that are human, or even bicycle-powered may be a significant growth market. Inventing, designing, raising capital for, marketing, and distributing are all essential roles (and jobs!) for creating and distributing sustainable technologies.

Social Marketer. In addition to working for a specific company marketing its product(s), marketing brand managers can play a powerful role in drawing attention to sustainable products and services and getting people to use them. From convincing people to put solar panels on their rooftops to getting them to eat sustainable food products, or getting them to use public transportation bicycle, the field of "social marketing" is marketing in service of achieving social goods, rather than just stimulating more consumption of unsustainable products. Learn more about this field here[4].

1 https://teamrubiconusa.org/volunteer/

2 https://greencorps.org/

3 https://www.ziprecruiter.com/Career/Development-Officer/What-Is-How-to-Become#:~:text=Your%20responsibilities%20revolve%20around%20building,finding%20volunteers%20for%20various%20projects

4 https://www.simplilearn.com/what-does-a-social-media-marketer-do-article

Navigating by the Stars: The Polynesian Voyaging Society

Nainoa Thompson, Polynesian Voyaging Society
Hawaii

☀ Call to Action

To learn more about the Polynesian Voyaging Society, please visit www.hokulea.com.

☀ Values

- Courage
- Dedication
- Adventure
- Commitment
- Environmentalism

☀ Lessons Learned

We can find solutions to modern problems by reconnecting with the ancient wisdom included in our heritage.

If you want people to care about nature, you must first help them learn how to connect to it.

Sometimes the best way to secure our future is to learn from the past.

Nainoa Thompson has devoted his life to reviving ancient Hawaiian cultural traditions that were nearly lost to history.

Whether he is working on cultural preservation, environmental advocacy, or championing sustainability education for Hawaiian youth, he credits everything he's achieved to the guidance of generous teachers. "I owe everything I've done to the great teachers I've been fortunate to learn from in my journey of life." In 1976 Nainoa saw the Hōkūle'a—a traditional Polynesian voyaging canoe with no Western implements—set sail from Hawaii en route to Tahiti for the first time in 600 years. Inspired by the Hawaiian cultural renaissance, he became a navigator for the Polynesian Voyage Society. Over a period of 45 years, his voyages have totaled more than 250,000 nautical miles—the equivalent of circumnavigating the earth 20 times!

☀ Language Arts

Working in groups of 3-5 students, create a presentation about the history of Hawaii (starting before it became part of the U.S.). Research the island's culture and traditions. How do Hawaiian culture and traditions differ from Western traditions? How have Western culture, traditions, and economic models affected Hawaii? At the end of the presentation, mention which of the facts that you learned that surprised you and your team members the most, and why.

Climate change and pollution are some of the negative side effects of industrialization and modernization. How have the practices associated with modernization and industrialization affected Hawaii's ecosystems, economy, and culture? Create a 5–10-minute video in which you use secondary sources to answer these questions. Conclude your video by giving concrete suggestions about how more traditional values and practices could be used to create a more sustainable paradigm for the island.

Nainoa says that "our solutions don't evade us because of an absence of technology, but an absence of culture." What do you think he means? Participate in a Socratic Seminar[1] with your peers in which you discuss the meaning of these words in the context of the story, but also in the context of your own community. How would learning, and becoming familiar with our own ancestral culture help us find solutions to problems we perceive as being too technologically advanced?

STEM Activities

What are the differences between Pacific and Western navigation methods? Between Polynesian and Micronesian methods? What natural signs are used by traditional Pacific navigators? When and how do you think these signs were used?

Using this lesson plan (page 19) from UNESCO.org[2], students will learn about the different types of boats and canoes used by Polynesian navigators, and will analyze and explain how certain of their design/structural features contribute to their ability to take such long ocean voyages.

In this lab from the Oregon Museum of Science and Industry[3], students will learn about constellations and how they are used for communication, navigation, and timekeeping. They will then learn how to use a star map, an indispensable tool for touring the night sky.

Sustainability Innovations

As home base of the Polynesian Society, Hawaii has been a centerpiece for the voyages of the Hōkūleʻa. What is the Polynesian Voyaging Society[4]? How can our knowledge of traditional voyages impact our future generations and their view of the Earth?

In addition to the Hōkūleʻa voyages, Hawaiian culture has played an important role in the sustainability and preservation of our Earth. Nonprofits such as The Kohala Center[5] are vital in perpetuating the combination of research, a'ina stewardship, ancestral knowledge, and sustainable systems needed to prepare the islands for a more sustainable future.

One of Nainoa's greatest accomplishments has been serving as a mentor and guide to young students in Hawaii. It is important to perpetuate Indigenous culture in communities that rely on traditional knowledge and history for grounding in their roots. Kupu Hawaii[6] is an organization that helps students identify green careers and connect to the a'ina.

Sustainability Career Pathways

Indigenous Studies Scholar. So much knowledge--of the land, of celestial navigation, of a sustainable way of life, of living through a world-changing societal crisis[7]--exists in the experience and history of Indigenous peoples. Learning from and sharing this knowledge could be a powerful and valuable career path. If this is a path for you, you could start your explorations at the Native American and Indigenous Studies Association[8] or at the Center for World Indigenous Studies[9].

The Shipping Industry. The shipping industry is a key part of the global economy. This field requires captains[10], navigators[11], logistics managers, and crew. Can you imagine yourself working on a ship? How about on a cutting-edge, sustainable ship[12] that uses solar and wind energy to keep its environmental impact minimal? Or perhaps you'd like to design sustainable ships[13]?

Satellite Technology. The modern world runs on satellites, which are used for everything from communications and navigation to sustainability applications like tracking weather and climate patterns in agriculture. Have you ever considered helping to design, launch, and run satellites? Learn more here[14].

1 https://www.youtube.com/watch?v=SW-WQk-UnUg
2 http://www.unesco.org/new/fileadmin/MULTIMEDIA/HQ/SC/pdf/Canoe_teachers_manual_LR.pdf
3 https://omsi.edu/sites/default/files/field/educator-guide/navigating_by_the_stars_teacher_guide.pdf
4 http://www.hokulea.com/moananuiakea/
5 https://kohalacenter.org/
6 https://www.kupuhawaii.org/hysc/
7 http://earthed.info/wp-content/uploads/2017/08/SOW17_chap4_IndigenousEd.pdf
8 https://www.naisa.org/
9 https://www.cwis.org/
10 https://www.yourfreecareertest.com/ship-captain/
11 https://en.wikipedia.org/wiki/Navigator
12 https://solarimpulse.com/sustainable-shipping-solutions
13 https://www.marineinsight.com/green-shipping/13-technologies-to-make-the-ultimate-green-ship/
14 https://www.jyi.org/2013-march/2017/6/25/careers-in-satellite-technology

Never Apologize for Dreaming Big

Daniela Fernandez, Sustainable Ocean Alliance, California

Daniela Fernandez founded the Sustainable Ocean Alliance (SOA) when she was just 19 years old. This organization develops leaders, cultivates ideas, and accelerates solutions in the field of ocean health and sustainability – and is the world's largest network of young environmental leaders, with contributors from more than 150 countries worldwide. SOA leads the way in innovation by offering a leadership program, as well as an Oceans Solutions Accelerator aimed at supporting brilliant startups that can contribute to the health of the ocean.

For her work, Daniela has been recognized by U.S. Secretary John Kerry and former President Bill Clinton among many others. She is also a member of the World Economic Forum's Friends of Ocean Action, and has been nominated by the Forbes 30 Under 30 for her environmental achievements.

Language Arts

Choose a waterway conservation/sustainability project. Write a three-minute pitch designed to recruit young people to help with this project. Then, write a three-minute pitch designed to attract investors to your project. Compare and contrast these two pitches: How are they similar? How are they different?

Which water conservation/sustainability issue needs attention in your area? Imagine that you are deciding to start an organization to tackle this issue. Write a one-page mission statement explaining why this cause is important, what your goals are, and how you plan to achieve them.

Write a script that could be used by a phone operator in a one-minute recruitment call to motivate someone to get involved in the water conservation/sustainability project you have chosen.

Call to Action

Join with the Sustainable Ocean Alliance in finding ways to heal and protect our oceans: www.soalliance.org.

Values

- Imaginative
- Flexible
- Creative
- Committed
- Enthusiastic

Lessons Learned

Daniela changed her career track so she could help encourage entrepreneurs who were doing something to change things.

Communication channels are important so that young people can interact with high-level leaders.

Think about the problems we face. Find ways to propose them to those who can make them happen.

STEM Activities

After her enlightening meeting with the United Nations, Daniela grabbed a pen and paper and turned her realizations into a tangible idea that would become the SOA (Sustainable Oceans Alliance). Many innovative and disruptive ideas start this way, often as a simple idea jotted on a piece of paper. Think about an issue you are passionate about, then grab a pen and paper and brainstorm about three ways you might make an impact. On the first piece of paper, jot down how you could organize people to help you solve your problem. The second page should be about a technological innovation you could create (or use) to solve the problem. On the third page, combine the ideas from the previous two pages, and imagine how this technology could be used in conjunction with your movement to solve the problem you have chosen.

Recent research[1] **found that in 2016, the United States put between 1.1 and 2.2 billion pounds of plastic into the oceans,** through "littering, dumping, and mismanaged exports." Put that number into perspective. What else weighs a billion pounds? Make a comparison.

Since reducing plastic in oceans is of paramount importance (and is specifically addressed in Target #1 of the 14th Sustainable Development Goal (SDG), explore a variety of ways we can reduce plastic production. SDG Indicator 14.1.1 specifically mentions the measuring of "floating plastic debris density." What does this mean? Are these numbers equal around the world? What are the concentrations of plastic in various parts of the world? Explain these concentrations in simple terms to your classmates. What are the effects of this plastic on ocean ecosystems? Consult this report[2] for answers to these questions.

Sustainability Innovations

Daniella has assisted in the development of many ocean-focused projects and hopes to improve current ideas with the Sustainable Ocean Alliance Accelerator Program[3], which is designed to assist solutionists who are focused on improving ocean health. Design an idea for a start-up organization and create an "elevator pitch" to present to Daniela.

Ocean Conservancy.[4] In addition to nonprofit organizations that focus on the development of start-ups, organizations like Ocean Conservancy focus on ocean policy that is based on science-based solutions at both the federal and state government levels.

When assessing the health of our oceans, identify the issue that is currently the greatest risk to its health. Research one organization that is similar to the Sustainable Ocean Alliance that is targeting the issue you have identified.

Sustainability Career Pathways

Oceanographer. An oceanographer is a scientist who studies the ocean, thereby helping to protect, conserve, and restore marine environments. Oceanographers can study the life, chemicals, fluid dynamics and physics, or even the geology of the oceans' floors. Considering that oceans are the true "lungs" of the planet (producing up to 80 percent of the world's oxygen)—and that climate change deeply threatens the ocean, both through warming and acidification—the world certainly needs more oceanographers. For more on this field and its vast diversity, visit here[5].

Aquarist. Do you love marine animals but would rather care for them than study them? Aquarists care for marine life in aquariums and research facilities. This is a niche field and certainly an interesting one to explore[6].

Aquaculturist. One of the great ways to heal the ocean is growing kelp and shellfish to filter and clean it. Farming the seas, or aquaculture[7], is a growth industry, as is working for companies that help seed aquaculture operations. An aquaculturist oversees the breeding and growing of fish, staff management, and the operation of aquacultural systems. Learn more here.[8]

Ocean Activist. If we are to reduce marine pollution, including plastic pollution, and overfishing, we're going to need more activists fighting for the well-being of the world's oceans. Organizing beach cleanups, advocacy efforts, and drawing attention to the 14th Sustainable Development Goal [9]are all ways to get involved right now. As you build your experience in activism, perhaps like Daniela you'll be able to make a career out of this passion as well! One way to get started might be to join the Sustainable Ocean Alliance's Leadership Program.[10]

Blue Entrepreneur. SOA also hosts an Ocean Solutions Accelerator,[11] offering mentoring and micro-grant funding to support new initiatives. Finding strategic ways to heal the ocean and creating a needed product or business service are great ways to make a career, and a difference in our world.

1 https://www.nytimes.com/2020/10/30/climate/plastic-pollution-oceans.html
2 https://onesharedocean.org/public_store/publications/lmes_report_chapters/TWAP_VOLUME_4_TECHNICAL_REPORT_Chapter7.1_1DEC2016.pdf
3 https://www.soalliance.org/ocean-solutions-accelerator/
4 https://oceanconservancy.org/
5 https://www.environmentalscience.org/career/oceanographer
6 https://www.environmentalscience.org/career/aquarist
7 https://www.fisheries.noaa.gov/topic/aquaculture
8 https://www.discoveryeducation.com/
9 https://sdgs.un.org/goals/goal14
10 https://www.soalliance.org/leadership
11 https://www.soalliance.org/ocean-solutions-accelerator/

Rise and Grind: Minimizing Food Waste

Fergus Moore, Revive Eco
Scotland

Call to Action

Turn waste into something useful. Use your imagination to create innovative, positive action. Follow Fergus on Twitter @revive_eco and learn about Revive Eco: revive-eco.com

Values

- Creativity
- Imagination
- Resourcefulness
- Curiosity
- Environmentalism

Lessons Learned

A complex problem is just a compilation of smaller, simpler problems to be solved.

If you feel overwhelmed by the scale of a problem, try breaking it up into smaller parts, and focus on solving them one at a time.

Our culture has created challenges, but also the opportunity to tackle those challenges. Look around you. The solution to the problem might be closer than you think.

Complicated problems can have simple solutions based on logic, common sense—and curiosity!

In Scotland, where every year more than 40,000 tons of used coffee grinds end up in landfills, Fergus Moore and Scott Kennedy—two budding entrepreneurs—set out to find a way to reduce this waste and turn it into something useful.

They founded Revive Eco in 2015 and invented a machine that could convert coffee waste into renewable products. They're now pitching their product to some of the biggest coffee brands in the world, the likes of Starbucks, Lush, and Nestle.

Language Arts

Watch this video on How to Pitch Your Start-Up in 3 Minutes[1]. Then, go to the Shark Tank Scholastic[2] website and download the handouts on how to create a sales pitch. Next, drawing inspiration from Fergus's story, write the script for a business pitch in which your company is offering an innovative piece of technology to deal with waste on a massive scale for a major industry. Your pitch must be three minutes long.

Food waste is a huge problem around the world. Choose one particular product in the food industry that you are interested in, and research the amount and type of waste it produces and the impact this has on the environment, as well as possible ways of mitigating it.

Using the information you gathered in your research, create a presentation for your peers in which you talk about the topic you have chosen. Your presentation must have at least 10 slides, and you must use not only still images, but also video (it can be original video, or video from secondary sources)

STEM Activities

Research what Starbucks is doing to support sustainability. Describe what aspect of their operation is the least sustainable (for example, CO_2 emissions). How do you think this could be improved? How could Revive Eco help to improve sustainability at Starbucks?

Write down all of the actions you take, and products you use, on an average day. Identify one product that you use that is not sustainable, and research alternative products, or companies that are designing ways for the product to be more sustainable.

Fruits and vegetables can do more than just give our bodies energy. In this activity[3], students experiment with different fruits and vegetables to determine how much electrical energy each produces. Then, using the engineering design process, they will design an optimal circuit using a selection of fruits and vegetables that produces enough energy to power a small electronic device.

Many of nature's adaptations result in the conservation of energy and reduction of waste, which are variables of interest to engineers and manufacturers. In this activity[4], students are introduced to the concepts of biomimicry and sustainable design to see how engineers gain inspiration from studying nature and its unique properties to improve human practices, and ultimately protect the environment.

Sustainability Innovations

In addition to Revive Eco, many other companies are finding ways to reuse coffee grounds for other purposes. Kaffee Form[5] is a German-based company that takes coffee grounds and turns them into coffee cups. And Up Circle Beauty[6] uses coffee grounds as a base for their line of skin products.

Many large companies have found innovative ways to transform coffee into a more sustainable product. However, it is not just up to large institutions to reduce waste from coffee. This article[7] tells 15 ways that the average person can practice sustainability by reusing coffee grounds.

The inventors of Revive Eco identified coffee-drinking as a part of their own lives that could be made more sustainable for everyone. There are many other aspects of our daily lives that young entrepreneurs can tackle in order to leave a more sustainable footprint on our world. Young Sustainable Impact Global[8] helps young entrepreneurs find ways to solve sustainability challenges.

Sustainability Career Pathways

Circular Economy Entrepreneur. While people often think about designing products in ways that they can be more easily recycled or reused, another key part of the circular economy is innovating ways to better collect and reuse waste—such as used cups, plastic waste, and coffee grounds, among many other things. As we shift to new ways to consume and do business, there will be lots of opportunities to participate in the circular economy. This article's inspiring circular economy entrepreneur stories can help get your creative juices percolating and thinking about what unique and sustainable niche you might want to be a part of. Read here[9].

Coffee Careers! With so many people loving coffee, there are literally millions of jobs in this industry (1.7 million jobs just in the US!) If you want to make a career in the coffee industry, you could work with sustainable farmers, run a sustainable cafe, or like Revive Eco, find ways to make coffee drinking more sustainable--by addressing the waste created by spent grounds and used cups, or the amount of water and type of energy used in cafes. Want to learn more? Here's an introduction[10] that explores some of the issues to consider in order to make coffee consumption more sustainable (whether you're looking for a particular brand to support, or a good company to work for).

Composter. Your parents might already compost waste in your backyard. But many cities are starting to require food waste of all sorts (including coffee!) to be composted, with some even picking up composted materials, along with garbage and recycling. This means that there are a growing number of jobs in industrial-scale composting, as well as in government management of it. It may not be the "sexiest" career path, but helping to turn food waste into soil is a pretty noble career! If you want to learn more, start with this short essay about the potential growth of the composting industry[11].

---

1 https://www.youtube.com/watch?v=XWRtG_PDRik

2 https://www.youtube.com/watch?v=XWRtG_PDRik

3 https://www.teachengineering.org/activities/view/rut-2497-food-electrical-circuit-device-design

4 https://www.teachengineering.org/lessons/view/van_biomimicry_less4

5 https://www.kaffeeform.com/

6 https://upcirclebeauty.com/

7 https://www.healthline.com/nutrition/uses-for-coffee-grounds

8 https://ysiglobal.com/

9 https://medium.com/age-of-awareness/10-circular-entrepreneurs-in-europe-with-a-passion-for-sustainability-8fb221a37529

10 https://bigcupofcoffee.com/best-sustainable-coffee-brands/

11 https://ilsr.org/composting-sense-tables/

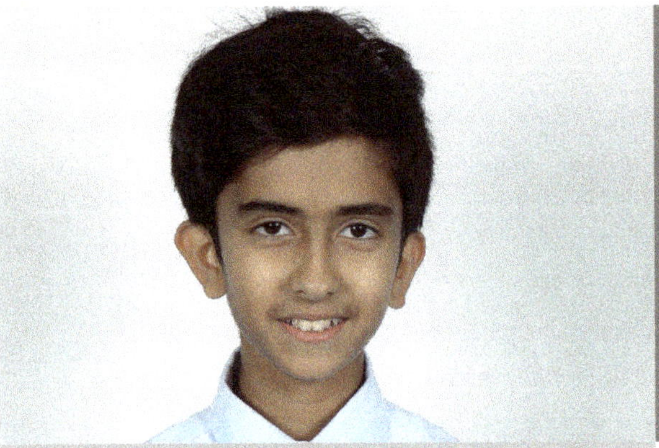

Robots for Fighting Plastic Pollution

Sainath Manikandan
United Arab Emirates

Call to Action

Start from where you are now, & you will have started a wave of change!
Dr. Jane Goodall's Roots & Shoots: www.rootsandshoots.org
JGI UK for Wildlife Research, Education & Conservation: www.janegoodall.org.uk

Values

- Concern
- Imagination
- Patience
- Optimism
- Environmentalism

Lessons Learned

You are already old enough, smart enough, and wise enough to start changing the world; don't wait!

Change has a snowball effect: it may start small, but if you keep at it, it can grow and spread around the world.

Think about what we consider "normal" and the problems it has generated. When you see a problem, think of ways to make it better. Then, tell everyone about it, and get them to help you find a solution.

When faced with a problem, be willing to use your skills in unconventional ways in order to solve it.

Listen to the people around you, learn from their comments, even negative ones, and focus on improving your work.

Sainath Manikandan once read a story about the famous environmentalist, Dr. Jane Goodall.
She'd helped him to see that no matter how small a step might seem, the tiniest effort can eventually make a huge difference. He was just a young boy in school, but he had paid attention when she said that it didn't matter how old someone was; what mattered was the action they took to move the world in the right direction. So Sainath decided to start where he would be able to make a change—in his own school. He'd seen that a lot of his classmates in the United Arab Emirates (UAE) used single-use plastics in their everyday lives. He found this extremely concerning. He'd first noticed the impact of single-use plastics when he had visited his family's hometown in India when he was 8 years old. Sainath was bothered enough by this that when he got home, he did some research. "This is a problem all over the world," he says. "An estimated amount of eight million tons of plastic ends up in the world's oceans every year." If that continues, it is estimated that by 2050 there will be more plastic in the oceans than there is marine wildlife. These shocking numbers made Sainath wonder what he could do about it.

Language Arts

Who is Dr. Jane Goodall, and why is she so important to the environmental movement? Create a 10-minute video about Dr. Goodall, and about her work as an environmentalist/conservationist. Why do you think Sainath was so inspired by her? What parts of her life and career do you (personally) find inspiring?

Write a children's story about Sainath's campaign to collect plastic bags and electronics at his school. Show his journey from the time he learned about Dr. Jane Goodall. Imagine how he connected her story with his own life, his family's trip to India, and how he became more aware of the problem of plastic pollution. Make sure you depict him creating and advancing his project step by step, starting with collecting plastic bags and electronics, and show how this was the seed for greater change.

Choose one environmentalist you admire. What is or was their cause? Create a digital campaign designed to educate people about this cause. What practices are making the problem worse? What can we all do to help mitigate (or even solve!) the problem? Where and how can people get involved in the solution? Your campaign must include written posts (for the digital platform of your choice) as well as video and graphics.

STEM Activities

Watch this video on plastic pollution[1]. Using the information given in the video about how much plastic gets into the ocean every year, create a graph that shows the accumulation of plastic in the ocean over time. Use 1930 as the year of "zero" plastic in the ocean (this was the decade when mass production of plastic began). Then use this graph to predict how much plastic will be in the oceans by the year 2050 if plastic pollution continues at the current rate.

In this activity[2], learn about how ocean currents work, and analyze marine debris data to predict where the debris will end up, based on local currents.

In teams, use Seaperch resources[3] to design and build an underwater remotely-operated vehicle. Use the engineering design process to add additional functionality to the robot, such as the ability to see or grab objects.

Sainath is a member of Dr. Jane Goodall Institute's Roots & Shoots program[4]. Dr. Goodall, known for her work with chimpanzees, is also an advocate for sustainability and climate change action. Find out about one way that Jane Goodall's work has impacted the world (CO_2 emission levels, support for environmental organizations, etc). What would these numbers look like without her contributions?

Sustainability Innovations

In addition to Sainath's innovations to assist with the problem of plastic pollution, many individuals within the industry have created robotic advancements to solve sustainable problems. In this article[5], robotics assistance in six different sectors is highlighted, with strategies to continue to improve sustainability in business.

Plastic pollution has been Sainath's main focus, but sustainable agriculture has also developed extensively with the use of robotics. The Robotics Industry Association[6] highlights innovations and the use of AI in the cultivation of sustainable agriculture.

Sainath's project is one of the many highlights of sustainability innovations in the UAE. Abu Dhabi hosts an annual sustainability week that awarded Eco Wave Power the Global Innovation Award 2021 in the "Life Under Water" category. Learn more about Eco Wave Power's ability to improve wave energy here[7].

Sustainability Career Pathways

Roboticist. If you love the ocean (and robots), perhaps you should be a roboticist. Along with Sainath's M-bot, roboticists are designing autonomous underwater vehicles that will be the future of ocean exploration, aquaculture, and coral restoration--a sector of the Blue Economy that is growing, and that is lacking qualified employees. Even if you don't like oceans, there are dozens of fields in which roboticists are needed. Interested? Learn more about entering the field of robotics here[8].

Recycling Industry. Americans produce more than 290 million tons of waste each year,[9] about a quarter of which is recycled. Recycling is a big business: drivers, sorters, mechanics, technicians, and plant managers are all needed. It's not a "pretty" job, but it's one you can be pretty proud of. After all, one of the best ways to prevent plastic pollution is making sure it is recycled and made into new products. This article gives a great overview of the recycling industry[10].

Conservationist. Like Jane Goodall, you too could be a conservationist, helping to preserve and protect wildlife habitats and their many rare and awe-inspiring wildlife inhabitants. Conservationists play many different roles: as advocates, liaisons with governments and affected communities, managers, fundraisers, and so much more. This witty essay looks at the 12 different types of conservationist[11] you could be. And this article gives a more thorough introduction to the field[12].

Designer in the Circular Economy. Recognizing that waste is a significant cost to companies and to the planet, a whole new generation of designers is creating new things that can be fully dismantled—reusing the long-lived parts, recycling the worn parts, and enabling the services that come from goods without the toxic disposability often designed into our products. For example, while most phones can't be easily recycled or repaired (and are instead designed to have a lifespan of only a few years) Fairphone is designed for long life, and can be completely dismantled and various parts replaced if they break. Why not help design goods that have long lives and that at the end of their lives can be fed, with zero waste, into the next generation of products? Learn more about the circular economy, and get inspired here[13].

1 https://www.calacademy.org/educators/preventing-plastic-pollution
2 https://ocean.si.edu/sites/default/files/2020-11/baydriftlesson.pdf
3 https://seaperch.org/resources/build/
4 https://www.rootsandshoots.org/
5 https://www.allerin.com/blog/how-green-robots-are-helping-with-environmental-sustainability
6 https://www.automate.org/industry-insights/cultivating-robotics-and-ai-for-sustainable-agriculture
7 https://www.ecowavepower.com/
8 https://www.northeastern.edu/graduate/blog/what-does-a-roboticist-do/
9 https://www.epa.gov/facts-and-figures-about-materials-waste-and-recycling/national-overview-facts-and-figures-materials
10 https://www.bls.gov/green/recycling/
11 http://www.jamesborrell.com/the-12-types-of-conservation-career-and-how-to-choose-which-one-is-for-you/
12 https://www.thebalancecareers.com/conservationist-526002
13 https://ellenmacarthurfoundation.org/topics/circular-economy-introduction/overview

Sustainable Farming for Our Future

Vincent Kimura, Smart Yields
Hawaii

Call to Action

Buy local. Get your hands in the dirt. Support small farmers with green businesses. Please visit smartyields.com or www.agrigro.com.

Values

- Environmentalist
- Entrepreneur
- Sustainability
- Creativity
- Collaboration

Lessons Learned

If we respect nature, we will reap more benefits than if we overexploit our resources. Respect leads to sustainable practices; overexploitation leads to the eventual depletion of resources.

You can find inspiration from the past, and knowledge for the future. When you obtain both you will be able to fulfill your dreams.

If we are to build a sustainable economy, economic progress should benefit the people, not exploit them.

Become involved with your community: your neighbors are an important source of knowledge that can help you grow both professionally and personally.

Vincent Kimura is a "serial entrepreneur" in sustainable agriculture and technology.

He strives to center the agricultural conversation as being sustainability-focused, but economically driven. Vincent is the CEO of Smart Yields, a globally recognized agricultural technology company that is revolutionizing the way small and medium-scale farms operate. He is involved in various green enterprises, including AgriGro and Inovi Green.

A main focus of his work is on supporting struggling farmers around the world, and repairing food systems using technology, data, and collaboration between the public, private, and nonprofit sectors.

Vincent is a trusted and inspiring mentor for young people who are seeking to find work and launch sustainable businesses. He runs numerous internship programs, and is a mentor for the Purple Prize, which helps mission-driven companies that use technology to amplify community and regenerate ecosystems. He was also a sponsor of Hawaii's first Agricultural Hackathon in 2018.

Language Arts

What does the term "food security" mean? Create a series of videos (no more than 10 minutes total) in which you explain what this term means; what the consequences are of lacking food security; who is most affected by food insecurity; and what sustainable alternatives are available to tackle this issue.

Vincent believes that "A small farmer struggling is a sign of an unsustainable community." Do you agree or disagree with him? Why? Write an argumentative essay explaining your views. Your essay must include counter arguments to your own point of view, as well as examples from secondary sources that support your opinion.

The years 2020 and 2021 have been a time of unrest for farmers in India. Research both the reasons for their protests and the consequences of them. Then do some research on farmers' protests in the US over the past century, and compare and contrast the two. With the information you collect, create a presentation in which you explain, as well as compare and contrast the protests by farmers in both of these countries.

How can technology help small farmers stay competitive and become more sustainable? Write an essay in which you analyze the role of modern technology in traditional family farms. Start by analyzing Edward Tuft's example from Vincent's story, and find a couple more examples of your own to mention in your essay.

STEM Activities

Over the course of his career, Vincent has focused his efforts on building a number of green businesses. Smart Yields, which gives farmers up-to-date access to their land use, is one of the most impactful. Create a mock-up of a farm with the crops you would hope to grow on a one- acre plot of land. Access the Smart Yields app and track the progress of your farm, or a similar farm in your community.

Family-owned farms are a major focus of Vincent's work, due to their rapid decline in the United States. Design an app that can assist farmers with weather trends, tracking temperature, farmer to farmer collaboration, and/or cattle management, or seeding. Explain to your classmates why you think this is important and how the app design works.

- Bonus: Develop the algorithm or code for your app and explain how this design could be useful to farmers.

Conduct a tour of a farm in your community, or participate in a virtual tour of a farming system. Create a chart highlighting the sustainable practices of the farm you visited, and identifying areas in which the farm could improve. Highlight various farming techniques that could be used, such as Recirculating Aquaculture[1], Environmental Monitoring[2], Crop Covering[3], and other sustainable practices.

Sustainability Innovations

Vincent understands that mentoring is vital for the maintenance and improvement of sustainable farming. The New Entry Sustainable Farming Project[4] is one of many programs that helps new farmers gain experience and get training from mentors, to maximize the success of their farms.

In addition to the standard issues facing farmers, they often spend extremely long hours surveying their crops, or struggle with weather issues. Drones in Agriculture[5] has become one successful use of advanced technologies to identify problems and maximize the use of farmers' time. Drones can help with issues such as mechanical failures in turbines, studying soil variations, fungal and pest problems, and irrigation issues, among many others.

Vincent funded Smart[6] Yields with Republic, a project to get "big data to small farms" in order to help "take the guesswork out of growing."

Farming is often a difficult for students to relate to because they have not been exposed to it. Design a project to teach students about apiary farming, aquaculture, and traditional farming. Assign students to one of these three groups and have them design a basic structure for conducting this farming technique.

- **Apiary farms:** How to Build a Hive[7]

- **Traditional Farming:** Build a Raised Garden [8]
- **Aquaculture**: Simple Backyard Aquaponics[9]

Sustainability Career Pathways

Sustainable Farmer. There is an increase in the number of young people who are being drawn to farming, as groups like The Greenhorns[10] 10 reveal. If you're interested in being a farmer, this 11introduction to the field of sustainable agriculture is a good place to start.[11]

Agricultural Scientist with a specialization in sustainability. If you're interested in making farming more productive, sustainable, and efficient, perhaps you would like to explore the field of agricultural science. Agricultural scientists study plant reproduction, soils, plant genetics, and more to find ways to improve farming techniques and yields while protecting the land. Learn more here[12].

Agricultural Entrepreneur (Agripreneur). Would you like to invent and draw in new technologies to help improve farming? Perhaps you'll be an agripreneur, like Vincent. Learn more about agricultural entrepreneurship here[13] . And you can draw inspiration from the efforts of 16 agripreneurs described here[14].

Extension Agent. Farmers have long been supported by both governmental and nongovernmental agricultural extension offices. (In fact in China, this practice goes back about 2,800 years![15]). Extension agents support farmers in their area, helping them to improve crop yields and practices. They can also play a role in cultivating the next generation of farmers, for example by supporting youth groups like 4H. If this sounds like the job for you, learn more here[16].

1 https://www.innovasea.com/land-based-aquaculture/ras-design/
2 https://www.innovasea.com/aquaculture-intelligence/environmental-monitoring/
3 https://organicgrowersschool.org/gardeners/library/basics-of-cover-cropping/
4 https://nesfp.org/agapprenticeship/mentor-training
5 https://www.grandviewresearch.com/blog/agriculture-drones-the-future-of-farming
6 https://republic.co/smartyields
7 https://www.dadant.com/learn/beehive-components-part-i-building-a-hive-from-the-ground-up/
8 https://www.homedepot.com/c/ah/how-to-build-raised-garden-beds/9ba683603be9fa5395fab90b41bb0da
9 https://inhabitat.com/diy-everything-you-need-to-know-to-build-a-simple-backyard-aquaponics-system/
10 https://greenhorns.org/
11 http://greencollarblog.org/sustainable-agriculture-jobs/
12 https://work.chron.com/food-chemistry-salaries-7195.html
13 https://101entrepreneurship.org/agricultural-entrepreneurship-agripreneur/
14 https://foodtank.com/news/2018/01/young-food-entrepreneurs/
15 https://en.wikipedia.org/wiki/Agricultural_extension
16 https://www.thebalancecareers.com/agricultural-extension-agent-125871

Turning Waste into Fuel

Azza Faiad
Egypt

Call to Action

Ride a bike, or walk to school or work; encourage your community to adapt to solar power. If you have to drive, use electric or hybrid cars. Follow Azza on Twitter: @AzzaFaiad

Values

- Innovative
- Determined
- Persistent
- Diligent
- Imaginative
- Environmentalist

Lessons Learned

Look for innovative solutions to the world's pressing problems, like creating fuel from waste!

Exploring a passion in one discipline can lend itself to many others.

Having one setback doesn't make you a failure.

Azza Faiad is an up-and-coming leader in Egypt's renewable energy space.

In high school she discovered a way to convert plastics into biofuel, while significantly reducing the cost of the manufacturing process with a cheap, abundant catalyst not used before. Her work was supported by the Egyptian Petroleum Research Institute in Cairo, who saw her incredible potential as a scientist and creative thinker. She was awarded the EIRO Forum prize for her work, and was invited to participate in the EU Contest for Young Scientists (EUCYS). She studied engineering at Alexandria University, and is currently a researcher in the Electrical and Control Engineering Department with the Arab Academy for Science, Technology and Maritime Transport.

Language Arts

Design a social media campaign of at least five posts, using images and words designed to make people more aware of the need to substitute more sustainable sources of fuel than fossil fuels. What other options would you promote? Why?

Write a cause-and-effect essay explaining why an increase in the price of oil causes an increase in everything we consume.

Write a research essay focusing on which cultural changes need to happen in our society in order to embrace the changes we need to make in order to build a more sustainable world.

Azza Faiad is a woman in the engineering field. Research the situation of women in STEM in the Middle East. Based on this research, what challenges do you think Azza had to overcome in order to become successful in her field? Based on what you know about the U.S., what challenges do you think a woman trying to achieve success would face in the U.S.? What challenges would they share? Which would be different?

STEM Activities

Biofuel feedstocks that contain a lot of water, for example, food waste, cannot be burned; but they can be reused to produce biogas. Biogas can be burned to produce heat for cooking, warming homes, and producing electricity. Have students evaluate the pros and cons of biogas feedstocks, research the features of a biogas generator, and design a biogas generator using common household materials. If materials are provided for the students to build the generator, this activity can be done in an hour-long session; or it could be a long-term project that students can come back to, to collect the biogas produced. Students can compare the amount of biogas produced by different biofuel feedstocks, or the same feedstock can be used and the effect of different climates can be simulated by placing the generator in different locations (for example, near a window, outside, or in a dark closet).

Our society's dependence on oil has caused a plethora of problems, including but not limited to the long petrol lines Azza was experiencing when she was inspired to research and develop an innovative alternative source of fuel. The best way to reduce pollution from oil is to simply stop using it in the first place. Research alternative energy sources at Project Drawdown (https://www.drawdown.org/sectors/electricity[1]) and list three that you think could directly replace oil in specific contexts.

Azza talks about minimizing the "carbon footprint" of many industries, but corporations aren't the only ones with carbon footprints (though theirs is the largest and most harmful). Find out what the carbon footprint for your household is, using the U.S. Environmental Protection Agency's Carbon Footprint Calculator: https://www3.epa.gov/carbon-footprint-calculator/[2]. What is the main activity through which you are adding to your house's carbon footprint? How do you think you could help to reduce this number?

Sustainability Innovations

Throughout Azza's life, she has targeted many different problems of sustainability. Here is a list of organizations and entities that have made it their mission to find biofuel alternatives, and reduce their carbon footprint.

- **Brightmark -** This company focuses on converting not easily recyclable plastic waste into wax and eco-friendly fuels. https://www.brightmark.com[3]

Countries across the world are making efforts to reduce emissions and find alternatives to our current emission issues.

- Paris, Mexico City, Madrid, and Athens have implemented a ban of diesel vehicles by 2025.
- The City of Portland, Oregon is proposing a healthy climate fee and a clean air protection fee to apply to the city's largest polluters. Fees would range from $15,000-$2.6 million.
- The Portland Bureau of Transportation has closed off more than 100 miles of streets to through traffic to promote safety, the use of bicycles, and walking during the pandemic.

The growing need for sustainability has never been more imperative that it is today. Identify one sustainable policy, organization, or initiative in your community, and one worldwide that has a positive impact on reducing our carbon footprint on the Earth.

Sustainability Career Pathways

Chemical Engineer. Azza worked to help develop a new catalyst to break down plastic waste and turn it into a new source of fuel. Chemistry is at the heart of modern economies: from fuels and fungicides, to flavorings and fertilizers (and that's just one letter of the alphabet!). Explore this field[4] and learn about ways you could make a career in chemistry[5] to help build a greener economy.

Renewable Energy Scientist. Great leaps are being made in renewable energy every year: from higher-efficiency wind turbines to transparent solar energy-generating glass. Do you want to help advance the field? Learn more about being a renewable energy scientist here[6].

Renewable Energy Technician. Are you interested in expanding our use of renewable energy, rather than developing the science and technology behind it? Would you like to be involved in installing solar panels and wind turbines? Explore the career of Renewable Energy Technician[7].

Welder. Building wind turbines and other advanced technology requires the skill of welding. This is not often considered as a green job, but when using it to build green technologies, it certainly is. Learn more here[8].

Waste Manager. Waste, unfortunately, is a major side effect of the industrial economy--a reality Azza saw to her dismay as she drove past the seemingly endless landfill between Alexandria and Cairo. Determining strategies to reduce waste, and manage the waste produced in safe and sustainable ways is an essential green career. [9]

Bicycle Mechanic. Ultimately, in order to reduce our dependence on fossil fuels, it'll take more than electrifying cars or moving to mass transit. We'll need to also live more local lives, where walking and cycling are primary ways of moving ourselves around. This will mean a boon in the bicycle industry: manufacturing, marketing, sales, and keeping bicycles up and running. Are you good with your hands? Consider learning the trade of bicycle mechanics. Here's a great introduction[10].

1 https://www.drawdown.org/sectors/electricity
2 https://www3.epa.gov/carbon-footprint-calculator/
3 https://www.brightmark.com/
4 https://www.livescience.com/48134-what-is-chemical-engineering.html
5 https://destinationscanner.com/is-chemical-engineering-a-good-career-inyear/
6 https://climatekids.nasa.gov/career-wind-energy/
7 https://work.chron.com/job-description-renewable-energy-technician-17008.html
8 https://www.yourfreecareertest.com/welder/
9 https://www.onlinecollege.org/jobs/energy-environment/waste-manager/
10 https://www.bikerandbicycle.com/how-to-become-a-bicycle-mechanic-a-guide/

V

DOING WELL BY DOING GOOD FOR THE PLANET!

Sustainable Business

I'm grateful to all these extraordinary young people featured in this book who are demanding that their voices be heard. May we be inspired by their radical bravery and ingenuity as they lead the charge for a healthier and more sustainable future.

Laura Dern

A Future Forged in Radical Inclusion

Jonah Wittkamper, NEXUS
New York

Call to Action

Engage with the growing community of youth philanthropists and social entrepreneurs Jonah is leading with NEXUS. Find out how you can get involved at nexusglobal.org.

Values

- Compassion.
- Tolerance
- Imagination
- Social Inclusion
- Environmentalism

Lessons Learned

Open your heart and your mind to those you don't understand. You might find you have more in common with them than you think.

Find common humanity in inclusion. We are all children of the earth, so let's start acting like it!

Practicing philanthropy is a good way to find people who share your interests, and a sense of belonging.

At 15, Jonah enrolled at Camp Rising Sun in New York, where he was accepted by an international community of youth leaders, and began practicing a personal philosophy of "Radical Inclusion" – and he hasn't looked back since.

Influenced by this formative experience, Jonah went on to found NEXUS around a framework and culture of celebrating differences, while amplifying the voice of the global youth he credits for setting him on this path. NEXUS is a global youth network of influential philanthropists and social entrepreneurs that are tackling a wide array of socially responsible causes and issues, and they are at the forefront of innovations in a variety of environmental spaces. Through the NEXUS Impact Accelerator program, Jonah is striving to get resources directly to those social entrepreneurs who are working on the most critical global environmental challenges. In 2018, he founded the Healthy Democracy Coalition (HDC) to help mend the political divide in the United States, by bringing Republican and Democratic donors together to address societal problems that have been ignored, and even exacerbated, as a result of the increasing divisiveness. Jonah strongly believes that getting youth involved in decision making along with adults is very important, especially at a time when people are so divided. He sees investing in young people as a crucial, and positive investment in our future.

Language Arts

What is Radical Inclusion? Create a presentation in which you explain the concept, the benefits of the practice, and how people your age can practice it in their community. (Give specific examples).

After watching Jonah's discussion on the Rights of Nature[1], write a summary of the main points discussed in

the video. Afterwards, have a class discussion in which you go over the main points of the video. Discuss your point of view with your peers, and listen to theirs.

Visit the NEXUS website[2]. Choose three of their initiatives (under the "Initiatives" tab), and answer the following questions: What is this initiative about? Why do you think it's important? What, exactly, is the problem they are trying to solve? How can you get involved? Use your answers to create a series of Tik Tok videos to educate people on these issues.

A Call to Action (CTA for short) is a type of statement used in marketing to get people interested in a product or an organization. After reading this article on CTAs[3], write a 500-word CTA in which you invite people your own age to get involved with one of the philanthropic causes you mentioned in your videos from the previous activity.

STEM Activities

Research the process of micro-fragmentation being used by scientists at Coral Vita, and find out how it is helping to rebuild coral reefs.

In groups, or individually, identify and research one current social and/or environmental problem, and design a business-oriented solution to it.

Hurricane Dorian caused $3.5 billion dollars of damage to the Bahamas. Calculate the annual GDP of the Bahamas and compare these numbers. What long-term effects did this storm have on the main industries in the Bahamas?

Research has found that every $1 invested in prevention could save $6 in disaster mitigation[4]. Now you do the math. What if the $2 million in aid donated by businesses to the Bahamas after Hurricane Dorian had been given beforehand, instead, in disaster prevention? What could businesses have done to reduce the effects of Hurricane Dorian before it happened? What could they do now to mitigate the effects of future hurricanes?

Sustainability Innovations

One of Nexus Global's[5] most impactful projects includes 10 different working groups that are centered around member-led initiatives addressing problems that they are passionate about. Research the working group that you would like to know more about, and create an "11th" working group that could address an issue that is has not been previously discussed.

Jonah's passion for change is one of the key reasons why he has become successful in his pursuit of building Nexus Global. This article[6] highlights other young entrepreneurs whose passion for environmental and social justice led to the development and expansion of their businesses to make the world a better place. philanthropynewyork.org/diversity-philanthropy[7]

Sustainability Career Pathways

Social Entrepreneur. Jonah identified an untapped opportunity—connecting, supporting, and empowering youth—and created an organization to help achieve this. A social entrepreneur is like a business entrepreneur, but is creating something to address a societal issue, whether with a nonprofit, business, or other initiative. Interested in becoming a social entrepreneur? Learn more here[8].

Fundraiser/Development Officer. Raising money is a skill as well as a viable career path. Not only do collaborative networks like NEXUS cultivate philanthropic giving, but every major nonprofit organization has a development officer—from environmental organizations to universities and community aid organizations. For a basic description of what being a development officer entails, visit here[9].

Organizational Leader. Many great leaders are "conveners," or individuals who, like Jonah, "bring people together to address a problem, solution, or opportunity[10]," even across a diversity of political views, values, sectors, and institutions Today, there are many college and masters' degree programs focused specifically on organizational leadership, rather than on teaching more traditional management techniques. Learn more here[11].

Camp Counselor. Summer camps are a really valuable educational tool. Some of them teach children about collaborative leadership, like Camp Rising Sun[12] does. While few make a career out of camp counseling, it is a great summer job for college students and future educators, and can lead to full-time jobs in directing camps, museums, parks, or other educational programs. Read more here on how to become a camp counselor[13].

1 https://www.youtube.com/watch?v=_ezjfhpDHT0
2 https://nexusglobal.org/about/team/
3 https://www.thebalancesmb.com/call-to-action-1794380
4 https://www.pewtrusts.org/en/research-and-analysis/articles/2018/01/11/every-$1-invested-in-disaster-mitigation-saves-$6
5 https://nexusglobal.org/initiatives/working-groups/
6 https://www.euronews.com/green/2020/09/05/the-millennial-entrepreneurs-creating-a-more-sustainable-world
7 https://philanthropynewyork.org/diversity-philanthropy
8 https://www.entrepreneur.com/article/281214
9 https://bestaccreditedcolleges.org/articles/development-officer-job-description-and-education-requirements.html
10 https://collaborativeleadersnetwork.org/leaders/the-role-of-the-convenor/
11 https://www.snhu.edu/about-us/newsroom/business/what-is-organizational-leadership
12 https://www.lajf.org/
13 https://www.zippia.com/camp-counselor-jobs/

Blue Planet Foundation: A Sustainable Legacy of Blue Innovation

Henk Rogers, Blue Planet Foundation
Hawaii

Call to Action

To get involved with the Blue Planet Foundation and its innovative projects, which are helping to shape Hawaii's blue future, please visit blueplanetfoundation.org.

Values

- Innovation
- Creativity
- Community Service
- Environmentalism

Lessons Learned

You can listen to the conventional wisdom – but it's ok to challenge it too.

Use your creativity, your resources, and your passion to achieve your goals.

Learn how to delegate, and ask for help from those older—and younger—than you. Everyone can contribute, and we need everyone working together to solve our problems.

When presented with a problem, look for solutions from different perspectives. Unconventional approaches are sometimes the key to solving a puzzle.

Your dreams can help shape the future. Make your dreams your goals!

One day Henk Rogers found himself in the back of an ambulance, with a 100 percent blockage of the largest artery to his heart.

Later, in the recovery room, as he was flipping through a newspaper, he saw a tiny snippet that alerted him that all of the coral in the world would be dead by the end of the century. "I realized that there are all of these things going on with climate change that people are just not aware of. And if we don't do something about them, they will happen. That was when I understood what my mission in life was." Henk founded the Blue Planet Foundation to drive change, empower youth, and inspire action that will help power the transition to 100 percent clean energy in Hawaii and beyond. And with his help, Hawaii became the first state to mandate this goal.

Language Arts

What would happen to the Earth if coral reefs disappeared? Write a research essay about coral reefs: what they are, their importance to the environment, to our food supply, and what the consequences of their disappearance would be.

Using the information from your research paper, create a series of TikTok videos in which you advocate for the preservation of marine ecosystems in general, and coral reefs in particular. Use the videos to educate people about the importance of coral reefs, and to appeal to your followers to take action to help restore them.

Choose one of the templates from the Discovery Education website[1], and create a puzzle to educate people on the importance of transitioning to clean energy. (You may use Hawaii as your case study, or you can use your own community). On a separate sheet of paper, explain why you chose to ask those particular questions.

STEM Activities

Identify the various renewable energy sources in Hawaii, and compare them to renewable energy projects in your local community.

Download the carbon footprint and CO2 tracker app. Track your carbon footprint based on your vehicle, your home, and your daily lifestyle. Compare your emissions to the Island Pulse[2] clean energy tracker. Are you more or less eco-friendly than the tracker in Hawaii? How could you adjust your lifestyle to become more eco-friendly?

The Blue Planet Foundation hosts a student energy summit annually that motivates students to find clean energy solutions within their communities. Design a project that you would like to send to Henk along with your application to the student energy summit.

In this activity students will learn the role of carbon dioxide (CO2) in photosynthesis and cellular respiration; and learn about carbonic acid's impact on the calcification and dissolution of coral skeletons, and its ability to influence pH.

- Background information[3]
- Link to activity[4]

The fictitious town of Solutionville has decided to replace coal, their current source for electricity, with more sustainable energy sources. Students are tasked with designing Solutionville's sustainable energy future. (A basic understanding of fossil fuels and their impacts on the environment is recommended before doing this activity.)

- Fossil Fuels Video[5]
- Fossil Fuels Cause & Effect[6]
- Link to Solutionville activity[7]

Sustainability Innovations

In Hawaii's search to become more sustainable, the global coronavirus pandemic has brought about both questions and answers. Hawaii's economy is heavily reliant on the tourism industry, and has been decimated by the lack of tourism in 2020. However, its coral reefs have flourished due to the lack of human destruction during that year. The Kohala Center[8] is currently focused on growing Hawaii's coral reefs and using native plants to reduce the nitrogen that is affecting coral reefs.

Hawaii is the first state to establish a ban of sunscreen that omits toxins that are detrimental to marine life. This study[9] addresses the sunscreen ban, how these toxins affect marine ecology (in particular coral reefs), and how they can also contribute to skin cancer among humans.

The Blue Planet Foundation[10] uses Island Pulse to give real-time estimates of energy uses on the way to transitioning to 100% clean energy. This tool[11] displays energy watt usage, clean energy vs. fossil fuels, and the current energy mix of oil, wind, waste, coal, solar, and biofuel.

Henk began his involvement with technology by founding Tetris, and it has been at the center of his focus for a shift toward blue technology. Video games began as a means of entertainment for both children and adults, but they have recently undergone a shift. Virtual games are now being created to increase the knowledge and application of sustainability issues. Eco[12] is a virtual game in which players must collaborate to build a society where all of their actions affect the environment.

EPA's Clean Energy Programs[13] are important to utilize as a point of collaboration with organizations like the Blue Planet Foundation to help us work our way toward being a carbon-neutral country.

Sustainability Career Pathways

Renewable Energy Engineer. Henk started as a video game designer, morphed into a philanthropist and renewable energy advocate, and now is working to improve battery storage systems. Improving the design of batteries, solar panels, and wind turbines will be essential in our Want to learn more? Start here[14].

Solar PV and Battery Installer. Not everyone wants to work in an office all day. Some people would rather help build the infrastructure with their own hands. Why not help cover the world's rooftops in solar panels and, like Blue Planet Energy, help take people off-grid? These jobs pay well and only require a high school diploma. Learn more here[15].

Renewable Energy Advocate. Renewable energy is a rapidly growing field that will make up an ever-larger percentage of the world's energy mix in the decades to come. Becoming part of a renewable energy company--as a manager, salesperson, or support staff--is a way you can help with this transition. Or, by joining one of the many nonprofit organizations promoting and/or lobbying for the transition to renewable energy, you can help draw attention and investments to renewable energy.

Renewable Energy Project Permitting. With most renewable energy projects, getting permission is key, as is convincing the community and state that the project is beneficial. There are many jobs connected to this process: from government jobs reviewing and approving permits, to consulting firms that design and apply for the permits, to lawyers who review the agreements. It may not be the most exciting aspect of the transition to renewable energy, but it is an essential one. Studying law and policy are good starting points for this career track, as is understanding the permitting process. Here is a list some of the many government agencies and organizations involved in renewable energy permitting.

---

1 https://puzzlemaker.discoveryeducation.com/
2 https://www.islandpulse.org/
3 https://www.coral.noaa.gov/images/resources/cleo/Carbon_Dioxide_background.pdf
4 https://www.coral.noaa.gov/images/resources/cleo/CO2Activity.pdf
5 https://www.calacademy.org/educators/whats-the-deal-with-fossil-fuels
6 https://www.calacademy.org/educators/lesson-plans/the-heat-is-on-cause-and-effect-and-climate
7 https://www.calacademy.org/educators/lesson-plans/optimal-and-sustainable-renewable-energy-revamp
8 https://kohalacenter.org/
9 https://onlinelibrary.wiley.com/doi/pdf/10.1111/jcpt.12778
10 https://blueplanetfoundation.org/island-pulse/
11 https://www.islandpulse.org/
12 https://play.eco/
13 https://www.epa.gov/energy/clean-energy-programs
14 https://engineeringonline.ucr.edu/blog/career-spotlight-renewable-energy-engineers/
15 https://collegegrad.com/careers/solar-photovoltaic-installers

Building a Sustainable Business Ecosystem

Elliot Hoffman, REV Sustainability
California

Call to Action

To get your business involved in the Sustainability Circles Program, check out REV Sustainability at www.revsustainability.com

Values

- Sustainability
- Cooperation
- Leadership
- Environmentalism

Lessons Learned

Community, cooperation, and kindness are the real riches we should all strive for.

Being environmentally friendly helps the Earth, but it will also help us all transition into a better economic future.

Be an example: if you want large-scale change, you have to start by changing your own behavior.

Cooperation Equals Power.

That was the message Elliot saw scrawled on the wall of the electric power plant he saw each day on his way to school, when he was growing up in the Amalgamated housing cooperative in the Bronx. "Being a cooperative human being is just built into my DNA," he says. "So when I went into business, I did it with sustainability and social responsibility in mind." He cofounded his company, Just Desserts, with his wife in 1974, and led it into a sustainable future, establishing himself as one of the pioneers of the sustainable business movement at a time when few were thinking within this framework.

In 2013, he founded REV, an enterprise that helps small and midsize companies transition to a more just and sustainable way of operating. "We want to destroy the myth that sustainability is a cost. If I can show companies that they can do good for the environment and keep money in their pockets through the process, we can have them picking up the slack they should have picked up decades ago, on a large scale."

Language Arts

In your opinion, what does the motto "Cooperation Equals Power" mean? Write an essay in which you explain how you would use this philosophy to fight for sustainability and conservation.

Choose a business you are interested in (for example, clothing manufacturing, or food). Imagine you can create an environmentally conscious company to operate in the business of your choice. Write a Mission Statement[1] for your imaginary company that focuses not only on what you will produce, but how you will use sustainable business practices to improve the industry as a whole, increase profits, and enhance the quality of your own products.

What is the REV[2] program? Create a combination of TikTok videos (no less than four) and SnapChat posts (no less than three) in which you explain what the REV program is; how it has benefited businesses at the local level; and how it could benefit businesses at a global scale.

STEM Activities

By adopting sustainable practices in his business, Elliot didn't just reduce the negative impact on the environment; he also saved money! Calculate the average amount of water, electricity, or waste your household uses, and their associated costs. Then research sustainable alternatives (techniques or technology) to conserve or reduce this amount. How much money would your household save over a period of time if you were to adopt these alternatives? Graph your findings.

Think of a type of business or service you'd be interested in starting (clothing, restaurant, health store, spa, etc.). How would you design your business or service so that it could help improve environmental problems in the community? Consider all of the aspects of your products or services, including the costs, the impacts on the environment, and the people in the community. Then, present your design in the form of advertisements to the class. Activity guide[3].

Fossil fuels are a key component in powering businesses. Burning fossil fuels for energy, however, produces a number of pollutants, including carbon dioxide (CO2). Calculate the carbon footprint of a business, and learn how it directly or indirectly produces CO2. Then, find out how that business could decrease their carbon footprint. If possible, select a local business and present your findings to them. Be sure to present it in a positive way!

Sustainability Innovations

One of Elliot's greatest success stories includes the work of REV Sustainability. Rev Sustainability[4] focuses on integrating sustainability and behavior changes within a company to see positive business impact. Review one of the four stories featured as a part of REV's success.

Some traditional businesses have struggled to evolve into using more sustainable practices while others have flourished in the transition. It is important to have the requisite individuals consulting businesses and engaging in sustainable transformation. Green Biz[5] has developed a professional certificate program that addresses consulting/leading businesses in sustainable transformation. Could this certification help you be a part of positive change for the future?

In addition to the work of REV, there are many organizations and companies in California that are focused on improving the transition to sustainability. Environmental Innovations[6] is a certified B-Corp that provides innovative sustainability solutions to government, individuals, businesses, and education.

The transition to a more sustainable future often requires collaboration from everyone, as Elliot proved with The Garden Project. Transformative Climate Communities[7] is an important government-funded project that highlights community-led transformation in Californian communities that are most affected by pollution.

Sustainability Career Pathways

Green Business Manager. Business can be a force for good, as Elliot's story reveals. Today there are sustainability-focused MBA programs, like Presidio's Sustainable MBA program[8] and many others[9]. Many MBA programs offer sustainability-focused courses, in order to provide their students with a strong training in sustainable and responsible business. And as more businesses put sustainability first, or even incorporate as B (Benefit) Corporations[10], the opportunities for sustainability-trained business leaders will surely grow.

Corporate Sustainability Officer. Companies too often prioritize growth, even at the expense of the environment—and therefore, their own and society's long-term well-being as well. Corporate cultures are slow to change, but change has started. Many companies now hire consultants like Elliot or even host sustainability officers within the company to help drive change from within. This is an opportunity to improve the environmental effects of the world's most influential entities. Want to learn how? Read here[11] or this personal account here[12].

Prison Sustainability Educator. Did you know nearly 2.3 million people[13] are incarcerated in the United States? Too few of them have educational or rehabilitation opportunities. Compare that to prisons like Bastoy high-security prison in Norway[14], an island prison where prisoners farm, do forestry, and live in dorms instead of cells. Fortunately, there are programs like the Sustainability in Prisons project[15] that are providing prisoners with cutting-edge skills and helping them become future green leaders in their communities. Prison education is an important career path, to help break this unjust prison cycle. Want to learn more? Read this article[16] and this essay[17].

---

1 https://www.thebalancesmb.com/how-to-write-a-mission-statement-2948001
2 http://www.revsustainability.com/
3 https://www.teachengineering.org/activities/view/wst_environmental_lesson01_activity1
4 https://revsustainability.com/success-stories/
5 https://www.wholeworks-lst.com/greenbiz
6 https://environmentalin.com/
7 https://sgc.ca.gov/programs/tcc/
8 https://www.presidio.edu/academics/mba-in-sustainability/
9 https://www.bestcollegereviews.org/top/masters-degrees-sustainability/
10 https://benefitcorp.net/
11 https://www.careerexplorer.com/careers/sustainability-officer/
12 https://impakter.com/choosing-the-harder-path-the-journey-towards-a-job-in-corporate-sustainability/
13 https://www.prisonpolicy.org/reports/pie2020.html
14 https://en.wikipedia.org/wiki/Bast%C3%B8y_Prison
15 http://sustainabilityinprisons.org/
16 http://earthed.info/wp-content/uploads/2017/08/SOW17_chap19_sustainability-ed-prisons.pdf
17 https://teach.com/blog/teaching-in-prison-system/

Creating Mission-Driven Companies

David Dietz, SUpR
New York City

☀ Call to Action

Encourage your sports teams to take the SUPR's Plastic Free Pledge to reduce plastic pollution. Spread the word bluestandard.com/programs/sports-program/

☀ Values

- Compassion
- Innovation
- Imagination
- Environmentalism

☀ Lessons Learned

Be a witness. When you observe history unfolding around you, make sure to record what you see, so future generations can learn from it.

Dig deeper into stories that may seem irrelevant to you. Truth is often hidden from plain view. Ask questions. Explore!

Raising awareness about injustice is good. Doing something about injustice is what changes the world.

Share your story and live with passion, and people will follow you.

As a young reporter, David Dietz embarked on a dangerous journey to the Middle East, to cover the political situation that came to be known as the Arab Spring.

He saw revolution in six countries, and was on the ground for critical developments in political movements as they were happening across the region. David covered many stories as the Arab Spring unfolded. But it was through one feature story he wrote about the Egyptian cotton industry that he learned about harmful industrial and agricultural practices that were having a devastating toll on the health of farmers; and the direction of his career changed almost immediately. He has gone on to found multiple mission-driven companies, from Modavanti, an ethical boutique fashion business, to his current project, SUpR, which is working with professional sports teams to reduce single-use plastic waste. "We are at a tipping point," he says. "Saving the planet will be part and parcel of successful businesses of the future."

☀ Language Arts

Conduct research into the cotton industry in Egypt: What are the common practices (both in cultivation and in processing)? Why are these practices dangerous to humans, and the environment? How can they be improved? Then, compare the practices used in Egypt to the ones used in the US. What similarities do you see? What differences? With the information you gather, create a short video (no longer than 5 minutes) in which you explain the health risks associated with the cotton industry for those who work in it.

How do you start a new company in a field you know nothing about? Choose an industry you're unfamiliar with but that could benefit from a more environmentally-friendly approach.

Working in groups of 3-5 people, create a presentation in which you detail the steps necessary to learn all you can about this industry and the traditional practices associated with it. How can these traditional practices be replaced by environmentally-friendly and sustainable practices? How would you market and handle the day-to-day operations of this company? What would be the main challenges?

After reading David's story, participate in a Socratic Seminar[1] with your whole class, in which you discuss David's story as well as his motivations, achievements, and impact on the world.

STEM Activities

In groups, research one of three aspects of sustainable cotton farming practices: you can choose to focus on water[2], biotech[3], or land[4]. How do sustainable farming practices help the environment and improve human health in relation to the aspect you have chosen to study?

Select an article of clothing you own made from cotton. Research the origin of the cotton used to make it and the production process used by the company behind it. Do they use sustainable processes? If not, what companies and brands are known to use sustainable farming and production techniques? Create a poster presentation of your research: include figures on the resources and byproducts used to create your clothing item.

Attend a school-sponsored event such as a sports game, dance, or a play and take note of any waste, particularly plastic waste, that you see there. Does your school provide/sell products made or packaged with plastic during these events? If so, devise a solution to reduce the amount of plastic waste used at school events. Present your idea to the class and/or a school administrator, including any data you have collected to support your idea.

Sustainability Innovations

David's passion for sustainability began when he learned that cotton was the second-most destructive industry in the world, after oil and gas. Today, U.S. Cotton[5] and the U.S. Cotton Trust Protocols are serving as a barrier against non-sustainable cotton practices. U.S. Cotton is complying with UN Sustainability standards in order to align the demand for sustainable cotton with the growing UN Sustainable Development Goals.

One of David's current success stories is centered around SUpR. SUpR has three different levels of certification for their partners (Bronze, Silver, Gold). What are the requirements for each certification level, and which sports teams are involved? If one of your favorite teams is not SUpR certified, write them a letter explaining why they should participate in a SUpR certification.

In this article[6], the 10 worst single-use plastics and their eco-alternatives are highlighted. Do you regularly use any of these single-use plastics? If so, track your plastic usage for a month and find eco-friendly substitutes to your normal daily choices.

In the fight to reduce plastic usage, bioplastics[7] have been developed. Read this description of bioplastics and the potential substances that can be used to create them. Create a list of pros and cons of bioplastic usage and identify the areas in which they can be most effective.

Sustainability Career Pathways

Sustainable Fashion Industry. New clothes will continue to be made, of course, but they can be made sustainably. Materials like organic cotton or recycled plastics can be utilized, and designed in such a way that the clothing at the end of its (ideally long) lifespan can be recycled or composted (for example by not mixing natural and synthetic fibers). Here is a great introduction to the field[8]. And an article on the many ways sustainability is shaping the future of the fashion industry[9].

Environmental Journalist. Many people who love to write make their careers as full-time journalists. Some dedicate their writing to chronicling the many environmental problems we face, as well as exploring the many innovative solutions to our sustainability challenges that are being developed. Some are freelancers, pitching stories to a variety of outlets. Others work full time for a news outlet, or with nonprofits, or even government offices. To learn more about this career, read here[10]. And here's a valuable resource: the Society of Environmental Journalists[11], which offers job boards, mentoring, annual conferences, and listservs for environmental journalists.

Permaculturist. Cotton farming as it is currently practiced, like other forms of modern agriculture, is toxic to humans, animals, and the soil. Sustainable farming, or permaculture[12], can produce higher yields, heal the land, and not harm people or animals. Today there are hundreds of permaculture training opportunities, and this skill can be applied on large farms, farmsteads, backyards, urban or school gardens, or anywhere you might grow plants. Learn more at freepermaculture.com[13], which includes an online introduction to permaculture and a database of permaculture jobs and volunteer opportunities.

---

1 https://www.readwritethink.org/professional-development/strategy-guides/socratic-seminars#:~:text=The%20Socratic%20seminar%20is%20a,to%20the%20thoughts%20of%20others.
2 https://cottontoday.cottoninc.com/cotton-production/water/
3 https://cottontoday.cottoninc.com/cotton-production/biotech/
4 https://cottontoday.cottoninc.com/cotton-production/land/
5 https://cottonusa.org/sustainability
6 https://www.wwf.org.au/news/blogs/10-worst-single-use-plastics-and-eco-friendly-alternatives#gs.1iypkk
7 https://www.plasticsindustry.org/supply-chain/recycling-sustainability/bioplastics
8 https://en.wikipedia.org/wiki/Sustainable_fashion
9 https://www.thegoodtrade.com/features/sustainable-fashion-jobs
10 https://www.openschoolofjournalism.com/specializations/environmental-journalism
11 https://www.sej.org/
12 https://en.wikipedia.org/wiki/Permaculture
13 https://www.freepermaculture.com/

Creating a New Social Contract

Sam Jacobs, Resource Generation
New York City

Call to Action

Join Sam in using philanthropy to fight systemic inequalities. Visit resourcegeneration.org
Follow them on Twitter: @resourcegen

Values

- Altruistic
- Generous
- Curious
- Idealistic
- Courageous
- Humble

Lessons Learned

Sam searches for the root causes of poverty and works with others to find ways to fight income inequality and promote social justice.

In order to galvanize others into action, it's important to set a good example yourself first.

It's important to create social safety nets, ensuring people's basic needs for food and housing are met—and that everyone is given an equal chance to succeed.

James Ellsmoor is a renewable energy advocate, digital nomad, and serial green entrepreneur.
He is cofounder of Solar Head of State (SHOS), a nonprofit organization whose mission is "To help world leaders become green leaders." SHOS installed solar panels on the White House during Barack Obama's presidency to raise awareness about renewable energy alternatives. They have also completed solar installations for the President of the Maldives, the Office of the Prime Minister of Jamaica, and the Government House in St. Lucia.
James went on to create Island Innovation, a green consultancy and advisory firm focused on small island developing states (SIDS). Out of this, the Virtual Island Summit, a free online event aimed at connecting global island communities on a common digital platform, was created. More than a hundred island communities were involved in the 2019 Summit. In 2017, James was recognized on Forbes Magazine's 30 Under 30 List.

Language Arts

Drawing inspiration from Sam's story, write a mission statement for a charity that is dedicated to a cause close to your own heart.

Now imagine someone gave you a million dollars to invest in that cause. How would you spend it?

Write five questions you would ask Sam in an interview. Then explain why you chose to ask him those questions. How would his answers help people better understand his work?

Write an essay explaining what gentrification means and how it impacts communities. If you have personal experiences with gentrification, housing scarcity, or housing rights, you can incorporate them into your essay.

Explore how the COVID-19 pandemic has affected the housing crisis in large cities like New York. Then research how climate change has affected the housing crisis (for example, through fires in California, and/or coastal areas affected by hurricanes). How do these two challenges compare to each other? How are they similar—or different—in developing countries than they are in industrial countries?

STEM Activities

The United Nations Sustainable Development Goals (SDGs) include one focused on making "cities and human settlements inclusive, safe, resilient, and sustainable[1]." Among the goals are ensuring access for all to adequate, safe, and affordable housing and basic services, and upgrading slums by 2030; and providing universal access to safe, inclusive, and accessible, green and public spaces, in particular for women and children, older persons, and persons with disabilities.

- **Investigate the number of "slums" there are in the U.S. and worldwide.** Is the world on track with "upgrading slums"? What factors are helping to achieve this? What factors are inhibiting it? Think of up to three policies that might help improve the situation of slum dwellers, and write a few paragraphs on the most promising ones.
- **Using available data, research the amount of green space available per person in various cities with various types of climate and other geographical factors, in both developing and industrial countries.** Compare this data to per capita income, health indicators, and education. What effects does access to green space have on people's physical and mental health?
- **Sam has partnered with the NBA and law enforcement to help hold police officers accountable for their actions.** Today, police officers are often required to wear body cameras that record their actions in the event of a conflict. What are some other technologies that could be used to make communities safer for everyone? List three of them and then write a five-sentence paragraph about how one of these technologies could be successfully implemented.

Sustainability Innovations

Philanthropy is an important component that contributes to our democracy even as it addresses inequalities in racial, societal, economic, and environmental conditions. Sam's grandfather was wise to educate his family to become strategic philanthropists. Private family foundations represent 85 percent of all U.S. philanthropy. Find out about one that provides support in your community. What are their priorities? Who is involved with this foundation?

Resource Generation and the Tides Foundation are good examples of sustainability innovations. Do you know of others?

Sustainability Career Pathways

Housing Reformer and Organizer. Housing and urban activism to prevent gentrification and make housing affordable for all is an essential realm to engage in—especially in the time of COVID, when many are threatened with eviction and foreclosure. For those who want to learn more about this area, read this introduction[2]. If you are really inspired, here is a journal introduction to the field of Housing Activism[3].

Manager in a Nonprofit Organization. Many people work for nonprofits, but very few have any formal management training. There are programs to train managers specifically for nonprofit organizations. While many of these are masters' level programs (such as these leading programs[4]), there are informal and undergraduate opportunities to learn essential management skills as well.

Foundation Officer. Sam's experience shows the importance of not just having access to resources to distribute, but the importance of sharing those funds justly and wisely. There are more than 119,000 foundations in the United States distributing funding to organizations working toward social change. Many of these rely on program officers to vet organizations, and then to engage with and mentor them. These jobs offer an important career path and lever for social change.

1 https://unstats.un.org/sdgs/report/2016/goal-11

2 https://www.thenation.com/article/archive/the-way-home/

3 https://www.tandfonline.com/doi/full/10.1080/02673037.2019.1658721

4 https://www.collegechoice.net/business/non-profit-management/best-masters-degrees/

For Tomorrow's Child: An Environmental Epiphany

John Lanier, Ray C. Anderson Foundation
Atlanta, Georgia

Call to Action

To learn more about the Ray C. Anderson Foundation, visit: www.raycandersonfoundation.org/nextgen/

Values

- Philanthropy
- Commitment
- Innovation
- Environmentalism
- Sustainability

Lessons Learned

It is important for older generations to pass their legacy on to the younger ones.

Are you facing a challenge? Educate yourself. Become an expert. Learn with passion, and then take action.

In business, it's important to explore innovative and novel ways of thinking in order to stay competitive and profitable. Successful businesspeople embrace challenges.

Introducing sustainable practices into a business can make the business more profitable, not less.

It took Ray C. Anderson, founder and CEO of Interface Inc., 60 years to have his environmental epiphany.
While reading The Ecology of Commerce by Paul Hawken, Anderson realized that this book basically convicted him of being a plunderer of the earth. This "spear to the chest moment " defined the remaining 17 years of Anderson's life, as he worked desperately to drive the necessary innovations that would allow his company to take a pledge of sustainability and set the stage for a new way forward in the realm of sustainable business.
For the man who became known as "The Greenest CEO in America," the work was never about establishing a personal legacy. He believed wholeheartedly that future generations must benefit from business leaders addressing and solving the environmental challenges of the day. "I'm doing this for the generation to come, for tomorrow's child." he said. And with his grandson John Lanier leading the way, his grandchildren are carrying on that legacy.

Language Arts

What is "Sustainability in Manufacturing"? Choose one industry (it can be food, building materials, clothing, or something else). Create a presentation (at least 10 slides) in which you explain to your peers what Sustainability in Manufacturing means for the industry you chose.

What is the meaning of the poem "Tomorrow's Child"? Write an explanation of the poem in which you analyze the images and symbols used and the effect these have on the reader. How is this poem relevant to John's story?

Ray Anderson evokes the principle of nonviolence in his philosophy of "Do no harm." Write a 5-paragraph opinion essay in which you defend this philosophy as beneficial not only for the planet, but also for workers, customers, and businesses in general.

STEM Activities

During Ray Anderson's tenure as the founder and chairman of Interface, the company was able to reduce greenhouse gas emissions by 82 percent. Compare the carbon emissions of Interface and three other flooring and carpeting companies. Describe the differences and what some of the contributing factors for each company are.

Research the approximate cost of a sustainable house including the costs of water use, waste, greenhouse gas emissions, and any other factors that are important to you. Make a plan for building your own home using Interface[1] materials, and an alternate plan using materials from other sustainably focused housing brands. Compare the ecofootprint and the sustainability value for both homes.

- Eco-friendly housing materials you could use include:
    - Renewed Materials Inc[2]
    - Liveroof[3]
    - Icestone[4]
    - Kirei[5]

Electric power in the United States is primarily generated through the combustion of fossil fuels. In this module[6], students will explore electricity generation and use, and the resulting greenhouse gas emissions.

Solar panels generate the most electricity when the incoming light is perpendicular to the panel. A solar tracker rotates the panel along one or two axes so that it is always facing the sun directly, which can add up to 25 percent more energy than a fixed panel. In this engineering activity[7], students will use the Arduino kit to combine sensors and logic to build a solar tracker.

Sustainability Innovations

In addition to the shift toward more sustainable materials in companies such as Interface, people have become more cognizant of the CO2 emissions that can result from having a large home. Tiny Homes[8] have been found to produce only approximately 2,000 pounds of CO2 emissions, compared to the 28,000 of CO2 emissions that an average home in America (2,598 square feet) produces.

Drawdown Georgia[9] was founded in October 2020 with the target of creating a low carbon and more diverse future. This nonprofit has identified 20 high impact solutions that target five main sectors: transportation, electricity, food and agriculture, land sinks, and energy.

When addressing carbon neutrality, it is important to address all sectors of the economy: however, the transportation sector has become one of the major focuses of 2021. In January 2021, President Joe Biden announced that he plans to replace the entire government fleet with electric vehicles. Here are some of the companies that are helping to lead this shift:

- **EVgo[10]** is the nation's largest electric vehicle fast-charging network, with over 800 fast-charging stations.
- **Wallbox's[11]** quasar is the world's first bidirectional charger for home use: it allows you to charge and discharge your vehicle so that it can assist in powering your home.
- **Ocean Power Technologies[12]** is a pioneer in transforming wave-energy technology into electricity.

Sustainability Career Pathways

Green Business Manager. As John's grandfather, Ray Anderson, demonstrated, when sustainability is prioritized, business can be a force for good. Today there are sustainability-focused MBA programs--like Presidio's Sustainable MBA program[13] and many others[14]. Plus, many MBA programs offer sustainability-focused courses, in order to provide a strong training in sustainable and responsible business. And as more businesses put sustainability first, or even incorporate as B (Benefit) Corporations[15], opportunities for sustainability-trained business leaders will surely grow.

Foundation Officer: As director of the Ray Anderson Foundation, John has leveraged resources to help make Georgia and the world a more sustainable place. There are more than 119,000 foundations[16] in the United States, and they distribute funding to millions of organizations working toward social change. Many of these rely on program officers to vet organizations, and to engage with, and mentor them. These jobs[17] offer an important career path, and lever for social change.

Carbon Mitigation Specialist. Collectively humanity will need to create a carbon-restorative economy by 2050 (which means actually pulling more CO2 out of the air than we are putting in) if we are to slow down and reverse the adverse effects of climate change. That'll mean a whole new sector of carbon mitigation will crop up in the years to come through afforestation and forest management, effective landscaping, restorative agriculture, energy efficiency, renewables, even painting roofs white to reflect sunlight into space. (These are all sectors that will be offering an abundance of jobs themselves). As Drawdown Georgia[18] demonstrates, to be most effective, these actions will need to be coordinated. Perhaps that's a job for you? One group, The Carbon Trust[19], demonstrates the integrated approach that specialists can provide.

1 https://www.interface.com/US/en-US/homepage?r=1
2 http://www.renewedmaterials.com/
3 https://liveroof.com/
4 https://icestoneusa.com/
5 https://www.kireiusa.com/
6 https://www.clarkson.edu/stem/project-based-climate-modules/power-profiler
7 https://create.arduino.cc/projecthub/igorF2/solar-charged-battery-powered-arduino-uno-645d89
8 https://www.aia.org/articles/141631-sustainable-and-small-the-tiny-house-moveme:36
9 https://www.drawdownga.org/beyond-carbon/environment/
10 https://www.evgo.com/
11 https://wallbox.com/en_us
12 https://oceanpowertechnologies.com/
13 https://www.presidio.edu/academics/mba-in-sustainability/
14 https://www.bestcollegereviews.org/top/masters-degrees-sustainability/
15 https://benefitcorp.net/
16 https://www.issuelab.org/resources/36381/36381.pdf
17 https://www.foundationlist.org/top-10-employment-websites-for-finding-foundation-jobs/
18 https://www.drawdownga.org/
19 https://www.carbontrust.com/who-we-are/our-mission

Healthier Skin with True Botanicals

Hillary Peterson, True Botanicals
California

Call to Action

Help Hillary inspire more businesses in the personal care industry to pursue sustainability by visiting truebotanicals.com.

Values

- Imagination
- Enterpreneurism
- Health
- Environmentalism

Lessons Learned

Our quality of life is linked to the quality of the air we breathe. If you want to improve the quality of your life, you must improve the quality of your environment.

Educate yourself, research, and be critical about conventional wisdom. Knowledge will protect you.

Lead with the truth and people will be drawn to your cause. If you want to change the world, start by telling the truth about why it needs to be changed.

Growing up just outside of Los Angeles, Hillary Peterson was aware of the role toxic environments could have on one's health.

She remembers the smog that always lingered over the city. "It was so bad we couldn't play sports outside after school. I'd go home and have to stay inside." When she was 32, Hillary was diagnosed with cancer. And when she learned that the toxic chemicals found in women's personal care products were being found in their babies' blood, she was furious. "How could the beauty industry be selling products with these toxins in them to the people they were claiming to want to help look and feel better?" she says. Her response was to start True Botanicals—a sustainable organic cosmetics enterprise. With its rigorous dedication to using organic ingredients and processes, True Botanicals has become a guidepost for the cosmetics industry, leading toward a more sustainable future. Laura Dern has used her platform as an actress to champion important environmental issues, including organic cosmetics. She has helped guide True Botanicals "with all the dynamism I could have expected, and more," says Hillary.

Language Arts

What is air quality? Working in groups (between 3 and 5 people), choose a region of the United States, and research the concept of air quality. How it is measured? What is the air quality like for the part of the U.S. you have chosen? How is it affecting the local population? Present your findings to your class, and draw three conclusions from the data you researched.

What is the link between our environment and our health? Create a series of 6-8 digital posters in which you explain the effects of air pollution, plastic pollution, and lifestyle on things like types of cancer, percentage of cancer diagnoses per year in areas with higher pollution, and preventative measures people can take to minimize the effects of the toxic substances they come into contact with every day (like cosmetics).

This is a partial list of harmful chemicals found in cosmetics: Formaldehyde, Paraformaldehyde, Methylene Glycol, Quaternium 15, Mercury, Dibutyl Phthalates, and Diethylhexyl Phthalates. Choose three of these compounds and research their toxicity (that is, the negative effects they have on the human body). What conclusions can you make from the data you found? Record a 3-5 minute video in which you share your findings and your conclusions with the public.

Hillary draws inspiration from other pioneers in sustainability and clean living, like Zach Bush of Farmer's Footprint. Write a personal essay in which you explain the impact Hillary's story has had on your personal view of the world, the cosmetics industry, our health, and the quest for a sustainable future. How has she inspired you?

STEM Activities

Select a hygiene product you use regularly (such as shampoo, lotion, makeup, deodorant, etc.) and research the ingredients used. Why is that ingredient included (what is its function)? Are any of them toxic to the human body or the environment? What are some nontoxic alternatives to these chemicals?

Using this lesson plan on the endocrine system[1], learn about 3 types of endocrine disruptors (bisphenol A (BPA), triclosan, and phthalates), and the impact they have on the human body. Then evaluate whether or not parabens, a preservative commonly used in cosmetic products, are endocrine disruptors by analyzing their molecular structure.

In this activity from PBS Learning Media[2], students will learn why cell growth is limited and why it requires cell division. They will explore the different phases of mitosis and learn about uncontrolled cell division - cancer, the oncogenes that cause it, and possible treatments for it.

Sustainability Innovations

As the fashion industry continues to grow, innovations are being developed at rapid rates. This article[3] by Green Matters highlights 5 sustainability innovations from 2021 that have changed their industries. Assess the products in the article and identify a beauty product in your daily regimen that should become more sustainable.

Hillary's battle with cancer was the event that started the journey of True Botanicals. Her realization that the toxic products that go on your skin affect your body initiated the development True Botanicals. Assess the Clinical Trial Results[4] of three True Botanical products and compare them to their competitors. As a user, would you feel more comfortable using True Botanicals products, based on the results?

In this article[5] by the David Suzuki Foundation, the "dirty dozen" cosmetic chemicals found in beauty products are highlighted. Research two of your favorite products, one sustainably-conscious brand, and one every-day use brand. Do any of these products contain any of the listed chemicals?

Sustainability Career Pathways

Sustainable Cosmetics Industry. Designers, chemists, marketers, managers, shopkeepers, production associates, salespersons, and other personnel are all part of the cosmetics industry, which was worth $380 billion in 2019[6] and is projected to grow to $464 billion by 2027. As consumers increasingly seek to avoid toxins, the subsector of sustainable cosmetics is growing even faster. This Teen Vogue article[7] explores the growing field of "Sustainable Beauty," its challenges, and the opportunities within this field.

Eco-entrepreneur. With toxic chemicals and unsustainable materials hidden in so many products, there are countless opportunities to reinvent products in healthy and sustainable ways--from cosmetics to cookware, from clothes to cars. If this is a career path you'd like to consider, learn more about becoming an eco-entrepreneur here[8].

Green Chemist: Designing sustainable cosmetics requires experts in chemistry. Explore the field of green chemistry[9] and ways you could make a career in chemistry[10] to help build a greener economy.

1 https://www.lifescitrc.org/resource.cfm?submissionID=9844

2 https://mass.pbslearningmedia.org/resource/tdc02.sci.life.cell.lp_divide/cell-replication-and-cancerous-cells/

3 https://www.greenmatters.com/p/sustainable-beauty-products

4 https://truebotanicals.com/pages/clinical-trial-results-independent-scientific-clinical-studies-randomized-comparative-double-blind-trials

5 https://davidsuzuki.org/queen-of-green/dirty-dozen-cosmetic-chemicals-avoid/

6 https://www.alliedmarketresearch.com/cosmetics-market

7 https://www.teenvogue.com/story/a-deep-dive-sustainable-beauty

8 https://ecoally.co/becoming-an-eco-entrepreneur/

9 https://www.epa.gov/greenchemistry/basics-green-chemistry

10 https://destinationscanner.com/is-chemical-engineering-a-good-career-inyear/

Ice Cream and Climate Action!

Ben Cohen, Ben & Jerry's Foundation
Vermont

Call to Action

Follow Ben & Jerry's on Twitter: @benandjerrys

Values

- Entrepreneurship
- Social Justice
- Sustainability
- Environmentalism
- Community

Lessons Learned

A truly successful business exists in harmony with the environment and with the principles of social justice.

Start small; find people who support you; grow; and stay true to your noble goals.

To be successful you must be willing to be unique and take a stand for your beliefs.

Social justice is built by building community.

Ben Cohen founded Ben & Jerry's with his best friend, Jerry Greenfield.

They invented the yummy ice cream with the extra-large chunks. As their company grew - from their garage, to a single homemade ice cream shop in Vermont, to a global operation - they did everything they could to minimize their carbon footprint, run a socially responsible company, and support environmental and social justice initiatives around the United States. "So many times, people don't start something because they feel like they don't have enough experience, or they don't know enough," Ben says. "I think it's important to just start really small: if what you're doing resonates with people, it will grow."

Language Arts

What does Ben mean when he says "He who is silent consents"? In what context is he using these words? Do you agree or disagree with him? Write an argumentative essay in which you explain your position on this issue. Your essay must include a counter-argument, and secondary sources to support your opinion.

What is the connection between making ice cream and climate change? Create a video in which you explain how the ice cream industry contributes to climate change, and how Ben & Jerry's has managed to offset the negative consequences of their large-scale manufacturing, while also building an extremely successful business.

How is Ben & Jerry's engaged in achieving change? Working in groups of 3-5 people, create a presentation in which you explain three of the last campaigns Ben and Jerry's has been involved in. For each campaign, make sure you cover the following: What was the campaign about? Why was it important? How did Ben & Jerry's participate? What did they achieve?

STEM Activities

Select an ice cream brand or shop, and research the ingredients used in that ice cream, and find out what the company's sources are. Calculate the carbon footprint of producing your favorite ice cream from the brand or shop you have chosen.

Read the post Flavors We Could Lose to Climate Change[1] on Ben & Jerry's blog. Select one of the flavors listed and research the impact climate change has on its production. What kind of environment is needed to produce the source of this flavor? Create a presentation on the effects of climate change on the crop's production using graphs, and include projections of future production.

Research the number of carbon emissions being caused by palm oil-related deforestation. Compare this to the effect of palm oil that is sustainably produced, or the use of palm oil alternatives. Resource: Palm Oil: The Carbon Cost of Deforestation[2].

Sustainability Innovations

Ben and Jerry's provides a model for integrating the principles of sustainability into businesses. Review this article[3], which details their corporate sustainability concept, and the strategies they have used to combine concern for the public interest and sustainable, successful business practices.

Ben and Jerry's website hosts this page[4], which highlights their goals, and their impact on creating a sustainable future. Research one of your favorite companies and review their website. Does this company have similar sustainability-focused goals or missions? Why would this be important to you as a consumer?

In addition to climate-focused goals, Ben and Jerry's has taken a strong stance on prison reform and improvements in the justice system. Review their stance[5] and explore how you, as a student, can get involved in making a difference!

Sustainability Career Pathways

Eco-Entrepreneur. Ben is a champion for green companies and entrepreneurs. Think about a green company that you'd like to start or join. Learn more about becoming an eco-entrepreneur here.[6]

Foundation Officer. Ben & Jerry's Foundation is one of 119,000 foundations[7] in the United States that give funding to millions of organizations working toward social change. They rely on program officers to research and vet organizations, to decide who is aligned with their mission and will use their precious funds effectively. These jobs[8] offer an important career path and lever for social change.

Sustainable Product Development Manager. Companies are constantly launching new products. They need managers to research, develop, and assess the market. Learn more about product management here[9], and learn about a career in product development here[10].

Ice Cream Maker. There are dozens of sustainable ice cream brands, brands that use better ingredients and packaging, give back to their communities, and through their choices are helping to improve farming methods. Learn about the most sustainable ice cream brands[11]; or sample jobs at Ben & Jerry's here[12].

1 https://www.benjerry.com/home/whats-new/2016/endangered-pints

2 https://www.sciencedaily.com/releases/2018/06/180619123018.htm

3 https://www.performancemagazine.org/ben-jerrys-sustainability-business/

4 https://www.benjerry.com/about-us/media-center/sustainable-agriculture-vision

5 https://www.benjerry.com/values/issues-we-care-about/justice-remixd

6 https://ecoally.co/becoming-an-eco-entrepreneur/

7 https://www.issuelab.org/resources/36381/36381.pdf

8 https://www.foundationlist.org/top-10-employment-websites-for-finding-foundation-jobs/

9 https://online.stanford.edu/what-you-need-know-build-career-product-management

10 https://www.marketing-schools.org/careers/product-development-manager/

11 https://www.greenmatters.com/food/2017/06/30/23mw7w/ice-cream-recs

12 https://www.benjerry.com/about-us/jobs

Learning as Leadership: Humanizing Business

Lara & Claire Nuer, Learning As Leadership
San Francisco & Paris

Call to Action

Go beyond ego to create a context for humanity working together.
Learning as Leadership: www.learnaslead.com
Nuer Foundation: www.nuerfoundation.org

Values

- Sharing
- Cooperation
- Humanism
- Resilience
- Compassion

Lessons Learned

Find strength within yourself and face every challenge you encounter with hope and compassion. Even the worst tragedies can bring about positive change.

The power of hope is infinite. Even at the darkest moments, hope will get you through; you just have to let it.

Human-centered organizations become more successful organizations.

Lara Nuer was 14 years old when her mother, Claire, was diagnosed with cancer and told that she had just three months to live.

Although Lara had been harboring a great deal of teenage resentment of her mother before this, when she realized she might lose her mother, she immediately became determined to do what she could to save her life. Claire too was determined not to die; she became a whirlwind of powerful, positive, healing energy that served not only to beat her own disease into remission but to serve as a model and an inspiration for many others. Eventually Claire founded an organization aimed at humanizing business and helping people "bring their best selves" to their families, their coworkers, and their world. She lived 17 years after her diagnosis; after she died Lara and her brother took over the reins of the company she had started. Today the leadership training they offer is chosen by many Fortune 500 companies as an effective way to make businesses more humane—and the people who work in them healthier, happier people as well.

Language Arts

What is humanism? What does it mean to say that a business has a "humanist approach"? Create a 10-minute PowerPoint presentation in which you explain this concept, why it is important, and how it can be applied in business.

When Lara's family started their journey toward emotional healing, they began by exploring the idea of always "showing up as your best self." How can this principle be applied to motivating people to work toward a more sustainable future? Create a video between 5 and 10 minutes long, in which you discuss concrete ways people can be the best version of themselves, and can help to enact change in their families, communities, societies, and ultimately, the world.

Can tragedy help us find purpose? Can loss help us find strength and goodness within ourselves? How can we use difficult circumstances as a motivator to better ourselves and the world? Using Claire's example, write a personal essay in which you explore these issues. If you need more information (or inspiration) about Claire, watch this video[1]. This essay is about your opinion and your experiences (if you choose to share them), so you won't need to do any research unless you want to. You may use personal experience (your own, or that of a family member or a friend) as your examples, or any person/events you know about from history. Make sure you write what you truly and honestly believe.

STEM Activities

This Forbes article[2] highlights three strategies for building a strong company culture. Imagine that you work for a large company: describe 3-5 personality traits that you believe are the most important to company culture, and explain how you think these traits could help move the company toward greater sustainability.

Imagine working as a sustainability advisor at a nonprofit organization, and at a medium-to-large business. What tactics and strategies would you use to improve the leadership and the organization's sustainability goals in each of them? How would these strategies help in each environment?

When Lara was 14 years old, her mom was diagnosed with cancer and was told that she had just 3 months to live. Regular checkups and early detection can greatly improve someone's chance of surviving cancer, but there are many people who skip the tests because they worry about pain or discomfort. Using this guide[3], learn about how cancer is detected, and design a way to detect tumors that would be less painful but still reliable. (Note: This activity[4] is designed for students in an AP or advanced physics course; it will teach the concepts of stress, strain, and Hooke's law, which students will apply to solve the design challenge.)

Lara's mom was told she had only 3 months to live, but she went on to live for 17 more years! Studies have been done to explore the effect of mood on cancer patients, and see if there is a psychological component to how tumors grow. Find one such study and evaluate the quality of the experiment. How would you design a study to evaluate the connection between mood and cancer growth/survival? Include a research question, test subjects, control group, and methods of data collection. Present your design to the class.

Sustainability Innovations

Learning as Leadership (LAL)[5] highlights Lara's skills as a cultural change leader who helps companies transform their business environments. LAL focuses on the transformation from an "ego system" to an "ecosystem" that brings out the best in all of a company's team members.

In addition to leadership training, cultural and diversity training has become an important way to grow success within a company. In this article by CCI Consulting[6], the strategic advantage of proper diversity and inclusion training is highlighted through case studies that show the positive effects on businesses.

The Nuer Foundation was founded on Claire's hard work and dreams for a better future. Claire's Teachings[7] are highlighted in "her story" and through "her voice." How are the sentiments she expressed even more important today?

Do sustainability and leadership go hand in hand? How can we emphasize the importance of both in the success of a company? Russell Reynolds Associates[8] highlights sustainable leadership and what it can mean to the success of companies.

Sustainability Career Pathways

Corporate Leadership Trainer and Coach. Many businesses are working hard to transform from being Earth-harming to Earth-healing, but they don't know how to go about it. Providing humanistic leadership training and coaching to corporate managers, like Claire and Lara have done, could have profound effects in transforming business culture and thus society. Is this the path for you? As a starting point for this career track, learn more about this model at Learning as Leadership[9], or explore the many transformative business schools that offer sustainable business experience, like Presidio Graduate School.[10]

Environmental Health Advocate or Practitioner. Many cancers are caused by exposure to toxins in the air, water, soil, or in one's diet (that is, exposure to elements in the environment). Preventing exposure to toxins can play a key role in reducing health burdens. You can become an advocate for environmental health[11]; or by becoming a doctor, nurse, or medical professional, you can draw attention to the links between environmental and human well-being. Here is an introduction to the field of environmental health[12].

Environmental Historian. Sometimes the best way to prevent future tragedies is to better understand the past. From the Holocaust to the Dust Bowl, the destruction of the Aral Sea, the collapse of the Atlantic northwest cod fishery[13], the end of ancient civilizations; many of the challenges we are facing today are not really new. We can learn much by studying the mistakes made by people throughout history, and choosing to go in a different direction. Want to become an environmental historian? The American Society for Environmental History[14] is a good place to start. So is this overview on becoming an Environmental Historian[15].

1 https://www.youtube.com/watch?v=PunXR6kp-OM
2 https://www.forbes.com/sites/nazbeheshti/2018/09/17/3-strategies-to-build-a-strong-company-culture/?sh=34ab87232732
3 https://www.teachengineering.org/curricularunits/view/van_cancer_curricularunit
4 https://www.teachengineering.org/curricularunits/view/van_cancer_curricularunit
5 http://learnaslead.com/
6 https://www.cciconsulting.com/services/engage-grow/culture-diversity-inclusion/
7 https://www.nuerfoundation.org/claires-teachings
8 https://www.russellreynolds.com/en/insights/articles/sustainability-as-a-leadership-imperative
9 http://learnaslead.com/
10 http://presidio.edu/
11 https://www.healthypeople.gov/2020/topics-objectives/topic/environmental-health
12 https://www.apha.org/topics-and-issues/environmental-health
13 https://en.wikipedia.org/wiki/Collapse_of_the_Atlantic_northwest_cod_fishery
14 https://aseh.org/
15 https://www.environmentalscience.org/career/historian

Sea2See Eyewear: Sustainable Products with a Conscience Conscience

François van den Abeele, Sea2See Eyewear
Spain

Call to Action

Learn how you can turn a problem into a new business: check out the Sea2See's sustainable products: www.sea2see.org.

Values

- Innovative
- Creative
- Entrepreneurial
- Environmentalist

Lessons Learned

Technology can be used to solve some of our most challenging environmental problems.

Communication and collaboration among nations around the world is essential in the 21st century.

Communications skills as well as technical skills are needed in order to solve the global problems we are currently facing.

"You don't just get out of bed one day and say 'I want to manufacture eyeglasses out of plastic waste'," says François van den Abeele.

His vision for cleaning up the plastic in the oceans was ambitious, but it was not unrealistic. He'd worked with impact businesses before. And as a journalist and documentarian, he had covered social and environmental issues in roughly 130 countries - including in many of the world's most vulnerable regions, in the Middle East and Sub-Saharan Africa. The crisis of plastic pollution in waterways was always at the top of the list.

François created Sea2See, an innovative sustainable business that is addressing the planet's most universal and most pressing environmental issue. Sea2See gathers plastic waste from the ocean and transforms it into affordable consumer goods - including eyeglasses and wristwatches. As of March 2021, Sea2See has collected 443 tons of plastic from oceans and waterways in Spain, France, and Africa.

Language Arts

Sea2See uses a process called depolymerization with the trash they collect. Read this article[1] and this article[2] about depolymerization. Create a school-friendly graphic summary of both articles.

Watch Javier Bardem's video[3] about his experience with Sea2See. Then create a five-minute video (it can be a live video or an animated one) about what your venture would look like if you were to find a way to tackle plastic pollution in the ocean.

Write a short (one-act) play, or a short story in which you tell the story of François and the African fishermen he works with; tell it from the point of view of one of the fishermen.

What other uses can you come up with for plastic waste? Choose a business you are interested in (it can involve fashion, building materials, automotive parts, or something else). Imagine how you would use plastic waste as part of the manufacturing process. Then create a three-minute pitch[4] to convince imaginary investors to invest in your idea.

STEM Activities

Using page 42 of this Plastic Pollution Curriculum guide[5], explore the properties of different types of plastics. Then, examine some common plastics and perform tests to identify them.

Select a product that contains plastic in its packaging, and develop a new or alternative type of packaging for the product.

Think about how François found a way to reuse plastic waste to make eyeglasses; then think of another product that could be created from plastic waste. Next, gather some plastic waste from your home and build a prototype of your idea. Keep in mind which types of plastics could be used to make the product, and what their properties are.

Sustainability Innovations

Sea2See is an example of a business that has addressed one of the world's largest issues and created a product that appeals to the younger generation from a fashion and social activist standpoint. Plastic for Change[6] helps businesses address plastic neutrality and plastic offsets within their business model.

Like Sea2See, there are many U.S.-based businesses that have identified the eyeglass industry as a focus for environmental and social improvements. Proof Eyewear[7], based in Boise, Idaho, creates glasses from repurposed skateboard and FSC-certified wood. (FSC-certified is the "gold standard" to describe wood that has been responsibly managed and that offers social, economic, and environmental benefits.) In addition to their products, Proof Eyewear plants five trees for every pair of glasses they sell, assists in health screening in underprivileged communities, and participates in many other positive initiatives.

Visit the Sea2See website[8] and learn about their WAVES approach to sustainability. What does each letter in the WAVES acronym stand for? Which is the most important to you?

What are bioplastics? Review this article[9], which addresses the difference between bioplastics and plastics and explains how bioplastics can shift the future of the plastics industry.

Sustainability Career Pathways

Circular Economy Entrepreneur. As we change the ways we consume and do business, there will many opportunities to help create a fully circular economy, one in which products are designed to last, and waste products become the material for future products. Do you want to be part of that revolution? Would you like to design fully circular sunglasses, phones, sneakers, furniture, and other products? Want to learn about more inspiring circular economy entrepreneur stories to get your creative juices percolating and help you discover your niche? Read here[10].

Sustainable Fashion Industry. New clothes and apparel will continue to be made, of course, but they can be made sustainably. Materials like organic cotton or recycled plastics can be utilized, and designed in a way that the apparel at the end of its (ideally long) lifespans can be recycled or composted (by not mixing natural and synthetic fibers). Here is a great introduction to the field[11]. And an article on the many ways sustainability is shaping the future of the fashion industry[12].

Environmental Journalist. Many people who love to write make a career as a full-time journalist. Some dedicate their writing to chronicling the many environmental problems we face, as well as exploring the many innovative solutions to our sustainability challenges that are being developed. Some are freelancers, pitching stories to a variety of outlets. Others work full time for a news outlet, or with nonprofits, or even government offices. To learn more about this career, read here[13]. And here's a valuable resource: the Society of Environmental Journalists[14], which offers job boards, mentoring, annual conferences, and listservs for environmental journalists.

1 https://energydigital.com/smart-energy/itronic-successfully-tests-manganese-recovery-process

2 https://academickids.com/encyclopedia/index.php/Thermal_depolymerization

3 https://www.youtube.com/watch?v=gWNgtblRIvU

4 https://www.marcstoiber.com/compelling-three-minute-pitch/

5 https://seagrant.psu.edu/sites/default/files/Lessons%20for%20NIE%202%20and%203%205GyresALLACTIVITIESPlasticPollutionCurriculum.pdf

6 https://www.plasticsforchange.org/blog/category/plastics-for-change-is-now-an-ocean-bound-plastic-certified-collector#:~:text=Introduced%20in%202020%20by%20Zero,adhere%20to%20fair%20trade%20guidelines

7 https://www.iwantproof.com/pages/do-good-program

8 https://www.sea2see.org/pages/our-aproach

9 https://www.biopak.com/sg/resources/bioplastic-vs-regular-plastic#:~:text=Conventional%20plastics%2C%20such%20as%20fossil,%2C%20recycled%20food%20waste%2C%20etc

10 https://medium.com/age-of-awareness/10-circular-entrepreneurs-in-europe-with-a-passion-for-sustainability-8fb221a37529

11 https://en.wikipedia.org/wiki/Sustainable_fashion

12 https://www.thegoodtrade.com/features/sustainable-fashion-jobs

13 https://therevelator.org/environmental-journalism/

14 https://www.sej.org/

Service Is Just What You Do

Gary Hirshberg, Stonyfield Farm
New Hampshire

Call to Action

Find the local farmer's market nearest to your home--it's fresh food, locally produced, and 100 percent good for the environment. Or find a CSA (community supported agriculture) to support: they'll deliver fresh organic food right to your home.

Values

- Determination
- Persistence
- Community
- Enterpreneurism
- Environmentalism

Lessons Learned

It is up to all of us to give back to the world.

If you want to succeed in your endeavors, be determined. Don't give up when things get hard!

Inspire, and be inspired: Follow the example of those who came before you, and make sure you are a good example for those who will come after you.

As a child Gary Hirshberg had learned from his mother about the importance of serving others; a lesson that was reinforced through his family's friendship with the family of Dr. Martin Luther King, Jr.

So when he had turned a tiny farm with just a couple of cows into Stonyfield Farm, the leading producer of organic yogurt worldwide, Gary and his business partner made sure that they would give back. They decided that 10 percent of their profits would be spent on initiatives to help fight the effects of climate change. Through the years they have taken many measures to minimize the carbon footprint of their company, and to support environmental causes. They have also built up a network of organic farmers by teaching them about sustainable agricultural practices. "Determination is the most important and underappreciated characteristic needed to be an entrepreneur," Gary says. "Nothing takes the place of hard work and passion."

Language Arts

Businesses can be the engine that propels our economy. Working in groups of 3-5 people, create a business plan for an environmentally friendly and sustainable business in the food industry of your choice. Your business plan must consist of an Executive Summary describing your objectives, products and services, and target markets); your products and services (product summary, including pricing); and an external analysis describing relevant economic indicators, market research, and current trends.

Based on the business plan you and your team have created, write a three-minute pitch[1] aimed at a theoretical investor, to seek funding for your business.

Write a research paper about the impact the food industry has on the environment. Choose one type of food for example, fresh produce, ice cream) or any other food product. Then write a research essay about the impact the practices associated with this industry have on the environment, and how they can be improved.

STEM Activities

Research the process of how conventionally produced vs. organic yogurt is made, and the source of its ingredients. Identify the parts of the process—or the ingredients--that contribute to climate change, environmental destruction, or health problems.

Using the claim, evidence, and reasoning model, in this lesson plan from National Agriculture in the Classroom[2], students compare and contrast organic vs. conventionally produced foods to discover the differences and similarities of each style of farm production.

Have students explore some of their favorite fruits and vegetables using the interactive Pesticide Residue Calculator.[3] Following the prompts on the website, students can read about pesticide residues found on produce, and click on various fruits and vegetables to discover how many servings of that particular fruit or vegetable must be consumed in one day to experience a negative reaction to the pesticides.

Assign student groups to create a multimedia presentation (stop-motion video, video, Prezi, etc.) about a specific crop. Students should show the growth of the plant from start to finish, and highlight the differences between conventional and organic production of their crop.

Sustainability Innovations

Review the Stonyfield Farms[4] page. What foods do they get from organic sources, and why do they partner with specific farms for blueberries, pomegranates, and other fruits?

In addition to organic and traditional farming approaches, many farmers are discovering innovations to improve year-round crop production, reduce emissions, and maintain freshness. What is Vertical Farming[5]? This agricultural technique allows the use of urban farming practices to create sustainable foods and conserve space.

Review the on-farm research and regenerative agriculture techniques of Wolfe's Neck Center for Agriculture and the Environment[6]. How has their partnership with Stonyfield and other companies improved the process of training farmers and preserving the environment?

Sustainability Career Pathways

Sustainable Business Manager. Check out these sustainability-focused MBA programs--like Presidio's Sustainable MBA program[7] and others[8]. Opportunities for sustainability-trained business leaders are growing as businesses put sustainability first, and incorporate as B (Benefit) Corporations[9].

Green Marketer. Stonyfield has developed innovative ways to promote their business--from charitable giving to their Adopt-a-Cow program[10]. Green marketing finds ways to cultivate brand loyalty for more cost-intensive sustainable brands. Learn more here[11].

Sustainable Rancher. Innovative ranchers are working to make raising cows a more sustainable endeavor -- consuming fewer resources and producing fewer greenhouse gases. Innovators like Joel Salatin[12], companies like Niman Ranch[13], and NGOs like WWF[14] are all working to make ranching sustainable. Interested? Here are 7 ways to become a sustainable rancher[15].

1 https://www.youtube.com/watch?v=XWRtG_PDRik
2 https://agclassroom.org/matrix/lesson/667/
3 https://www.safefruitsandveggies.com/pesticide-residue-calculator/
4 https://www.stonyfield.com/organic/environment/sustainability
5 https://babylonmicrofarms.com/the-future-of-environmental-sustainability-in-agriculture/
6 https://www.wolfesneck.org/
7 https://www.presidio.edu/academics/mba-in-sustainability/
8 https://www.bestcollegereviews.org/top/masters-degrees-sustainability/
9 https://benefitcorp.net/
10 https://www.youtube.com/watch?v=ZuNSeucUMOM
11 https://www.thebalancesmb.com/green-marketing-2948347
12 https://www.polyfacefarms.com/
13 https://www.nimanranch.com/raised-with-care/sustainable-agriculture/
14 https://www.worldwildlife.org/projects/sustainable-ranching-initiative
15 https://www.beefmagazine.com/pasture-range/so-you-want-be-sustainable-rancher-7-steps-make-it-happen

Speaking Truth to Power

Maria Ressa, Rappler!
The Philippines

Call to Action

Be awake, aware, and use social media responsibly. To join or support Maria's Rappler Plus: www.rappler.com/plus.

Values

- Compassionate
- Imaginative
- Courageous
- Dedicated
- Environmentalist

Lessons Learned

It is important to understand your roots. Maria achieved success in her career by connecting with her identity and returning to her roots.

It is crucial to always engage in dialogue. Listen to each other. Try to understand someone else's point of view.

Use your voice, no matter what the critics say. Speak the truth, and don't be afraid to challenge stereotypes.

Journalism plays a crucial role in a healthy democracy.

Maria Ressa, who is originally from the Philippines, wants to bring some of the tactics of climate change and human rights activists to journalism.

For Maria, journalism shouldn't just inform; it must also make change. Maria founded Rappler, a site that creates change through both rap (talking) and ripple (making waves). This journalism start-up made a big difference in the lives of everyday people when a typhoon hit the Philippines in 2013. The little truck that brought Rappler journalists through the storm to cover the news also served as a lifeline for the local residents who were directly affected by it.

Language Arts

Choose an important recent news story in your area. Learn as much as you can about the issue. As you go through the information you've gathered, be aware of the point of view from which the news is being covered. How is this issue being covered? Are all possible points of view represented in the story or stories you've read? Write an article of your own about the issue in which you cover the most underrepresented points of view.

Write a series of at least six tweets aimed at educating people about a particular issue that interests you but isn't getting much coverage in the news, or that very few people know about. Your tweets must cover both sides of the issue: the side you agree with, and the side you disagree with. Then, write a reflection paper explaining what you learned by researching and understanding a point of view contrary to your own.

Maria says that it is essential to "Speak truth to power," and she certainly has done that in her career. What does this mean for journalists? Create a series of posters or Instagram posts (at least six) in which you show examples of people who have spoken truth to power about climate change issues. On a separate sheet of paper, explain why you chose the people you chose, and how you can draw inspiration from their activism.

Sign up to receive Rappler notifications. Gather at least three articles that report on climate change issues in Asia. Write a one-page summary for each article.

STEM Activities

Imagine being the founder of Rappler and dealing with government backlash while trying to post news about sustainability issues. How would you deal with this kind of challenge?

Create a chart that compares the sustainability goals and government policies of the United States and the Philippines. What is the most difficult issue that the Philippines is facing that the U.S. is not?

Research news articles focused on sustainability in the U.S. and in the Philippines. Explain the difference in the points of view expressed, as well as the actual issues described in these articles, and the pros and cons of current media outlets in terms of covering sustainability issues.

Sustainability Innovations

In addition to small news outlets like Rappler, large media outlets like The Guardian[1] do a great job of featuring more environmental articles than other news outlets.

The global shift toward sustainability is more prominent today than it has ever been before. Earthsight[2] is one of the strongest UK-based news outlets that almost solely focuses on the environment.

Maria realized that social media has the ability to get people around the world working together to achieve sustainability and environmental change. Greta Thunberg and Fridays for Future[3] have used similar methods to engage individuals globally to reach people around the world.

Sustainability Career Pathways

Investigative Journalist. As Maria's story demonstrates, a good investigative news story can play a powerful role in making governments and corporations accountable for their actions, and can help push them to improve their environmental and social records. This is not an easy job, and it may even hold risks, but it can be a very rewarding career, especially if you love researching, interviewing, writing, and making a difference. Here's an introduction to the field[4].

Sustainability Data Analyst. To become a good investigative journalist, you have to be good at analyzing data--whether it is information about financial matters, toxic releases, or other types of data. Data analysis is its own career specialty; data analysts help identify and understand trends in sales, logistics, audience engagement, or costs[5]. (For example, in transportation, data analysts could help reduce a company's fuel usage by figuring out how to make delivery routes more efficient.) If you love analyzing data and looking for patterns, this may be a career path for you. Learn more here[6].

Media Entrepreneur. Maria's creation of Rappler shows the power of thinking big and doing things differently. The media is constantly being reinvented, especially as consumers move from print media to audio and digital channels--and even AR (augmented reality) or VR (virtual reality) news. There's lots of opportunity to become a media entrepreneur, from being a freelancer, to starting your own blog or podcast, to helping create a media start-up company. This article provides an introduction to media entrepreneurship[7]; and this one is about how to become a media entrepreneur[8].

1 https://www.theguardian.com/us/environment

2 https://www.earthsight.org.uk/

3 https://fridaysforfuture.org/

4 https://online.maryville.edu/online-bachelors-degrees/english/careers/how-to-become-an-investigative-journalist/

5 https://www.careerexplorer.com/careers/data-analyst/

6 https://www.rasmussen.edu/degrees/technology/blog/what-does-a-data-analyst-do/

7 http://mediashift.org/2016/06/teaching-media-entrepreneurship-mean/

8 http://teemingmedia.com/2009/01/how-to-be-a-media-entrepreneur/

Sustainable Business, Sustainable Living

Ed Begley Jr., Actor, Begley's Best, California

Call to Action

To keep up with the sustainable business ventures that Ed Begley is building and supporting, visit www.begleyliving.com.

Values

- Sustainability
- Committed
- Generous
- Ingenious
- Environmentalist

Lessons Learned

Environmental activism changes your life. It can become a lifestyle. Commit to it!

Environmentalism is about survival; it is not a political affiliation. It's time to put ideologies aside and work together towards saving our home: the Earth.

When tackling a problem, allow your ideas to grow; nurture them, and you too can become a part of the solution.

After the first Earth Day in 1970, Ed Begley Jr. began pondering what the future could look like if the momentum from this event was leveraged to make an even broader impact.

So, he went to some of the leaders who had put Earth Day together, including Senator Gaylord Nelson, and posed a question: "It's fine to have this one day," he said. "But as a movement, and a community, what are we going to do the other 364 days of the year?" For his part, Ed has championed sustainable living for more than 50 years, making it a part of his legacy from his days as a struggling actor to today, when he is a celebrated actor who has starred in hundreds of film and TV shows.

Aside from acting, he runs a sustainable business that features a line of green indoor cleaning products called Begley's Best. And through his family foundation, he gives tens of thousands of dollars of his profits each year to support green initiatives he believes in.

Language Arts

Ed's inspiration to get involved in the sustainability movement was inspired when the first Earth Day in 1970 caused him to wonder "What would happen if...?" Write a short story in which you explore the idea of a world in which Earth Day had a paradigm-changing effect in the world. What could our society, planet, and economy look like if world governments and businesses put the well-being of our planet first?

What is smog? What is it made of? Create a presentation in which you explain what smog is; the dangers it presents to human beings when they are exposed to it for extended periods of time; and what can be done to mitigate its effects on those who are more vulnerable.

How long have electric cars been around? How hard is it to convert a regular car to electric? Using Google Forms, create a digital escape room designed to teach people about the history, mechanics, and benefits of electric cars.

In your opinion, what is the most pressing environmental challenge your generation will face? Create a series of digital posters designed to educate others about the issue you chose: What it is? What risks does it pose to the planet and to humanity? What are some possible options to fix the situation? and what is currently being done about it?

Ed created a sustainable line of household cleaners. Why is this an important part of his activism? Write a research paper in which you discuss the damage that conventional household cleaners cause to the environment, and what alternative chemicals we should be using instead.

STEM Activities

Ed embodied sustainable practices in his life as his way of contributing to a healthier Earth. How would you contribute your time and finances to the world?

- **In a mock scenario, you have $50,000 to contribute to sustainable organizations.** Which organizations or programs would you support, and why?
- **Bonus:** Imagine being an activist for a day and you can participate in any project or program you like. What project would you choose, and how would you spend your day promoting this program?

Create a list of appliances, vehicles, and electrical devices that your family owns.

- **Assess** the carbon footprint of your vehicles based on average annual miles.
- **Does your home have solar panels?** Compare the sustainable impact of your home based on average electric usage with solar panels vs. traditional energy sources.

Some cities, like Los Angeles, where Ed lives, have a visible air pollution problem, and personal vehicles are one of the main sources of the problem. As part of his commitment to living sustainably, Ed drives electric vehicles and has sometimes even tinkered with conventional gas vehicles, converting them to electric. In teams, have students design an eco-friendly car[1] using the engineering design process[2], and make a presentation to showcase their presentation. Designs must satisfy the following constraints:

- Must have at least 5 features;
- 3 features to decrease pollution/increase efficiency;
- 2 features to improve appearance.

Sustainability Innovations

Vehicles and transportation are one of the focus areas of the green transition. The EPA[3] has created a guide that assesses vehicles and their impact on the environment. Identify the sustainable traits that Ed Begley's vehicles have possessed, and try to figure out some of the reasons he may have chosen these vehicles.

Ed has made it part of his mission to inform and engage others on how to live sustainably. Begley Living[4] features the inspiring sustainable life Ed and his family are living. This website features 13 different blog topics and the Begley family podcast, Begleyesque.

- Read one of the blog posts about the sustainable topic that you would most like to learn about.

Habitat for Humanity Michigan[5] is one of many organizations that have emphasized sustainability in their company's mission. Habitat Home Construction Technologies[6] highlights sustainable buildings and the criteria that homes need to meet in order to participate in these projects.

Sustainability Career Pathways

Actor. Over the course of his career, Ed Begley Jr. has starred in well over a hundred films and TV shows, and even a reality show about his efforts to live a green lifestyle[7]. Actors can use their platforms to encourage others to live more sustainably and even—through programs like Green is Universal[8] —can help studios produce movies in a way that is more environmentally 9 responsible. Want to become an actor? Start here[9].

Green Home Builder. Ed's home is a work of sustainability-art. Most homes today only minimally factor in green design, but this is a growing niche--as is retrofitting existing houses to be more sustainable. Maybe you want to build green homes. If so, the Shelter Institute's website[10] which offers information and introductory courses, is a good place to start.

Sustainable Real Estate Developer. Maybe you don't want to just build houses; maybe you'd like to create entire developments of sustainable homes in neighborhoods that are designed to be walkable, and that conserve natural lands as well. This profession, too, could focus on retrofitting. Malls, which were overbuilt in the past 50 years, are increasingly failing[11]. What will be done with these buildings? Could they become new eco-villages? University campuses? Business incubators? Homeless shelters[12]? Perhaps you can help figure out what to do with them. Learn more about development here[13].

1 https://www.teachengineering.org/activities/view/cub_intro_lesson02_activity1
2 https://www.teachengineering.org/design/designprocess
3 https://www.epa.gov/greenvehicles
4 https://begleyliving.com/
5 https://www.habitatmichigan.org/what-we-do/sustainable-housing-innovations
6 https://www.habitat.org/impact/our-work/home-construction/technologies
7 https://en.wikipedia.org/wiki/Living_with_Ed
8 https://www.nbcuniversal.com/article/our-productions
9 https://www.careersinfilm.com/actor/
10 https://www.shelterinstitute.com/home
11 https://en.wikipedia.org/wiki/Retail_apocalypse
12 https://www.washingtonpost.com/news/inspired-life/wp/2018/07/06/americas-malls-are-emptying-so-this-vacant-macys-became-a-homeless-shelter/
13 https://study.com/articles/How_to_Become_a_Real_Estate_Developer_Education_and_Career_Roadmap.html

VI

PASSING THE TORCH

Intergenerational Legacy

Young people in the 21st century have the superpower of knowing what no one could know when I was a child. Individually and together, we can use the mighty power of knowing to restore what we can as if our lives depend on it, because they do. I'm grateful to these young people in this book who are carrying on our legacy.

DR. SYLVIA EARLE

A Citizen of the World

Leila Ndabirabe, Maison Shalom
Burundi

Call to Action

Follow Leila on Instagram: @leila.nda
Support the Maison Shalom & help refugee children in Burundi and Rwanda live their dreams of a brighter future: www.maisonshalom.org

Values

- Altruistic
- Generous
- Compassionate
- Curious
- Leadership

Lessons Learned

Your own unique experiences, whatever they are, are important. They can teach people to look at the world from a different point of view.

Curiosity is a wonderful asset. It helps you to learn, and to see things in a new way. Be curious! Ask questions. Learn from as many people as you can.

You can become an inspiration to others if you follow your passion and are not afraid to tell your story.

Model, activist, citizen of the world.

Leila Ndabirabe, who grew up in Burundi and Belgium, likes to think of herself as being all three in one. In 2000, Leila and her family fled a violent civil war in their home country of Burundi. At first, arriving in Belgium, Leila struggled to fit in in her new country, and reconcile her previous dreams of what Europe would be like with her new reality. But as she grew, both in age and in confidence, she learned to make the most of her opportunities; and now, as a successful model, she has endeavored to give back as much as she can to help future generations of young Burundian women. She has partnered with Marguerite Barankitse of the Maison Shalom to support Burundian refugees in Rwanda, helping them to achieve their dreams of education and a brighter future.

Language Arts

Create a presentation in which you explain the impact of inhabitants of rural areas migrating to cities. Discuss how migration affects the environment, the food supply chain, and the quality of life for people both in cities, and in rural towns.

Compare and contrast the way migration of the people of Burundi is similar to or different from the migration of Central American people to the United States.

Create a 3–5-minute video (you may use animation software, pictures, videos from the internet, etc.) that explains how the increasing lack of food in Burundi contributed to the civil war.

Write a personal essay about how you would use your own professional success to bring attention to, and help solve an important global problem you feel passionate about, or one that affects you personally.

STEM Activities

In the United States, fame is something that is often admired and desired. However, the trend of celebrities using their fame for positive change and reform is relatively new. Imagine an alternate reality in 10 years: write a letter to your future self explaining how life felt in 2021, and how you would like to contribute to creating an alternate reality by 2031—and a sustainable future for the world.

One of the most important moments in Leila's life was the one where she took a chance and committed herself to trying to become a model. Often the greatest ideas present the most risk—but also the chance of the greatest rewards. Design a mock company with a focus on sustainability. Include a timeline, budget, core values and team member goals. Then compare this project to an existing organization or company that has sustainability as a core value, and explain why the potential rewards of your project are worth taking the risk.

- **Example:** Tesla is one of the greatest examples of a sustainable, risk vs. reward company. They went "all in" on their ability to enhance and expand electric vehicles, and are now one of the most successful companies in the world.

Leila is one great example of an influential individual using her fame to create positive change in the world. Research some of your favorite celebrities and identify 2-3 projects they are working on that are helping to create a more sustainable world. Would you like to participate in any of these projects? If so, why?

Sustainability Innovations

Leila is not the only model making waves in the world of sustainability and giving back to her home country. Miranda Kerr is one of the world's most famous supermodels: she has shifted her attention to Kora Organics[1], a certified organic skincare product that is known to support women-based organizations.

In addition to supermodels like Leila and Miranda serving as advocates for sustainable products, many fashion companies are following suit by improving their sustainable footprint. Sustainable Apparel Coalition[2] is composed of companies such as Target, Patagonia, Brooks, and many others to collaborate on targeting both environmental and societal factors that need attention.

In addition to large retailers, companies like Econic Apparel[3] allow you to self-design clothing that is sustainable and ethical. They have supplied the David Suzuki Foundation, LUSH, and the Canadian National Swim Team, among their partners.

Sustainability Career Pathways

Refugee Aid Worker. (Health, Community Well-being and Culture; Policy and Governance) Tragically, as climate change triggers more and more disasters, and increasing sea level rise, in the future there will be a growing number of refugees worldwide. Working with refugees, or in international aid operations can be a difficult but also very rewarding career. Learning other languages is an essential skill, as is the ability to live in very basic conditions, but the reward is being able to assist people who are in great need of help. Here is a set of tips for becoming a refugee aid worker[4].

Translator. Leila's knowledge of seven languages certainly helped her adapt to her new home in Belgium, and to develop new educational and career opportunities for herself. Language skills increase a person's career potential significantly--and open up the field of translation, which can be used in international governance, conferences, publishing, medicine, refugee centers, and many other contexts. If you love languages and want to learn about how to become a translator, read this seven-step guide[5].

Model with a Cause. It's definitely not a job for everyone, but as Leila has shown, any position of fame, from artist or novelist to actor or model to entrepreneur in a variety of areas, can be used as a platform to encourage social change and environmental sustainability. Here's an introduction on how to become a model[6].

1 https://us.koraorganics.com/

2 https://apparelcoalition.org/

3 https://www.econicapparel.com/

4 https://www.humanrightscareers.com/magazine/basic-tips-for-becoming-a-humanitarian-aid-worker/

5 https://www.fluentu.com/blog/how-to-become-a-translator/

6 https://www.indeed.com/career-advice/career-development/how-to-become-a-model

An Opportunity to Give Back--via Zoom!!

Demi Weitz, RW Quarantunes
California

Call to Action

Find ways to care for those less fortunate. Create a GoFundMe campaign to support local social services in your community. Learn more about Demi's project at quarantunes.unitedwayla.org.

Values

- Creative
- Imagination
- Compassion
- Altruistic
- Enthusiastic

Lessons Learned

When Demi's birthday party was cancelled she was disappointed, but she (and her father) found a way to turn things around to benefit not only Demi, but thousands of other people. Talk about "turning lemons into lemonade!"

Good things can come out of bad situations if we are flexible and creative, and always look for creative ways to turn things around, or make the best of a bad situation.

Demi saw almost instantly that there was a way to help those less fortunate than herself by using Zoom.

Demi had imagined that her 17th birthday would be quite different from what it turned out to be.
The COVID-19 pandemic got in the way of her party plans, so instead her father organized a Zoom party for her, with some recording artists he was friends with. This gave Demi an idea: why not organize Zoom concerts to benefit charities? This was the start of Quarantunes, and the beginning of an amazing success story. With her fundraising work, in a very short period of time Demi has raised almost $3 million for pandemic relief efforts, to benefit low-income populations particularly affected by the pandemic and by climate change. "It has been really great to connect to people, to have the chance to shed light on crucial issues and raise awareness this way," she says. "When you strip everything else away, the whole purpose of this is just to help."

Language Arts

Create three images that you would use for an Instagram campaign to promote Zoom events dedicated to uniting communities during the quarantine. Explain your choices of images and words. How do these choices help to convey your message?

Write the lyrics to a song you would use to promote an event similar to Demi's concert series. You can write it based on any genre of music. How will your song get the message of unity and community across to your audience?

Write a three-minute sales pitch designed to convince corporate donors to match the donations people make during your event to help various charities during the pandemic. What can you say that might make them willing to do this?

STEM Activities

To organize her concerts, Demi had to become proficient with a number of digital tools - namely, the popular video chat program Zoom. Find and list three digital tools that you could use to raise money for a cause of your choice.

Create goals for a GoFundMe Campaign, and map out the potential growth (perhaps using a mathematical function) for each goal you wish to reach. It might help you to imagine how many people might donate at first, and how much they would donate. Then map out an exponential growth chart that predicts how much the donations might rise over time.

Estimate the energy costs that Demi may have saved by running her events online. You can use the following (fictional) sample data:

- An in-person concert uses 2,000 MW of energy per hour.
- 1 MW of energy costs an average of $10 to produce through traditional (average) means.
- Demi has run 20 online concerts, with an average of 3 hours per concert.

Sustainability Innovations

MeetGreen: This women-owned ISO 20121 organization works with progressive global organizations to increase financial and ecological awareness. Their services include conference and event management, sustainable consulting, and virtual sustainable event development.

Island Innovation: Founded by James Ellsmoor, this social enterprise and digital media company assists island communities in forming connections with similar island communities in order to help them address the kinds of similar economic, social, and ecological sustainability problems they are facing. They connect public, private, NGO, and academic stakeholders and help them discover how their collaboration can help to solve larger issues in island communities.

Although Quarantunes is a very unique endeavor, the global pandemic we have experienced in 2020 has caused a major shift to virtual platforms and advancements in technology. The organizations listed above are some of the front-runners in maximizing the benefits of virtual platforms to find successful pathways for targeting sustainability issues. Brainstorm: Determine one social, ecological, or economically-driven sustainability topic that you would like to address. Create a model for using a virtual platform to help to gain awareness of this issue, or to combat it.

Sustainability Career Pathways

Artist: Visual and performing artists can use their talents to draw attention to social and environmental challenges through their works of art and their songs, and/or through the platform their fame offers. If you are driven to be an artist, don't forget about the opportunity it may give you to draw attention and resources to the causes you care about. Here is an article about many musicians[1]—from Paul McCartney and Sheryl Crowe to Grimes and Lil Dickey—who are using their celebrity to draw attention to climate change.

Fundraiser/Development Officer: Raising money is a valuable skill as well as a viable career path. Every major nonprofit organization has a development officer—from environmental organizations to universities and community aid organizations. For a basic description of what being a development officer entails, visit here[2]. Demi's experience shows that a person can raise money for good causes independently with the use of crowdfunding tools, but having some formal or informal fundraising training can help drive even greater success.

Event Planner: Demi needed to use a number of event-planning skills—coordinating performers, guests, venues, fees, and promotion—in order to plan her Zoom concerts. Organizing events sustainably, and drawing attention to and raising money for good causes is an important part of the green economy. From conferences and charitable auctions to concerts and even green weddings, there is abundant opportunity for planning enriching, sustainable events. For basics on event planning, you can read more here[3].

1 https://www.newscientist.com/article/2206461-the-musicians-helping-make-climate-change-a-cultural-movement/

2 https://www.greatsampleresume.com/job-responsibilities/administrative/development-officer

3 https://www.thebalancesmb.com/event-planning-basics-4161510

A Voice for The Voiceless

Betsabe Reyna, Pathways to Peace
New Jersey

Call to Action

The refugee crisis is real, and it is worldwide. Learn how you can help by visiting Pathways to Peace: pathwaystopeace.org

Values

- Dedication
- Commitment
- Creativity
- Communication
- Environmentalism

Lessons Learned

Real change starts when we decide to listen—really listen—to each other's stories.

The wisdom of your elders is one of the greatest treasures you can have. Embrace it!

Every human being wants the same thing: to feel safe, and to live in peace. Make a habit of asking yourself how you can help those seeking these basic human needs.

At the age of 16, Betsabe Reyna was offered the opportunity to travel to Mexico with a few other kids her age. During this trip, she discovered her role as a changemaker. From then on, she has found ways to immerse herself in other cultures and work with people from diverse backgrounds. During the Syrian refugee crisis, Betsabe worked on the frontlines at a refugee camp in Turkey near the Syrian border. Regardless of their religion and culture, Betsabe saw the people staying in the refugee camp as her brothers and sisters. Today, she is a delegate for the United Nations Program, Pathways to Peace, where she is carrying out the legacy of Avon Mattison, who inspires her to continue her work, helping to design peaceful solutions in chaotic circumstances. By preserving Avon's legacy, Betsabe is continuing to fight for vulnerable populations across the world.

Language Arts

Conduct a Round Table discussion[1] with your class and talk about the refugee crisis in Europe. What prompted this crisis? How has climate change contributed to it? Which countries are the most supportive of refugees? What are they doing to help them? What kinds of policies are global leaders recommending?

Research and write a paper about the refugee situation in Greece: where do the refugees come from, and why did they leave their homeland? What is being done to help them begin new lives? How can people get involved to help better their conditions?

Write a compare and contrast essay in which you juxtapose the refugee crisis in Europe and the humanitarian crisis at the Mexican border in the U.S. How are they similar? How are they different?

STEM Activities

In this activity from TropICSU[2], students use a climate migration tool to learn about regions and communities affected by climate change. They explore the science behind erosion, drought, and desertification, and use what they learn to explain how climate change has contributed to the mass migration of Syrian refugees to Turkey. http://storymaps.esri.com/stories/2017/climate-migrants/index.html[3]

Given the average number of Syrian refugees who have entered Turkey each month for the past five years, how many refugees can Turkey expect to be supporting five years from now?

Given the Syrian community's disproportionately young population, the birth rate is expected to increase. Meanwhile, Turkey's fertility rate has been falling for years, and is now at the replacement-level rate of 2.1 children per woman. Assuming a constant rate of growth, estimate how many years it will take for the Syrian population to become the majority in Turkey. This resource[4], with information on the population of Turkey, will help you.

Sustainability Innovations

Betsabe gained experience and perspective when she traveled overseas, but action is the only way to help people in need. Learn about YerYuzu Doktalari[5]. How are they assisting in the crises in Gaza, Yemen, Syria, and Myanmar? Why is it important for the U.S. to be engaged in these global issues?

Avon Mattison[6], the cofounder of Pathways to Peace[7], has served as a role model for Betsabe and others who have identified collaboration between countries as the way to solve some of our sustainability issues. Learn about Pathways to Peace and the eight pathways they have identified to engage people as peacebuilders. Which of the pathways do you think needs the most improvement in order to accomplish the goal of peace?

Review the impact of the International Rescue Committee[8] on the Syrian crisis. How has a decade of war affected the lives of children in Syria? Read this article[9], featuring the perspective of 10-year-olds who have known nothing but war.

Sustainability Career Pathways

Refugee Aid Worker. Working with refugees, or in international aid operations can be a difficult but rewarding career. Knowing other languages is essential, as is the ability to live in very basic conditions. Here is a set of tips for becoming a refugee aid worker[10]. You can also explore job opportunities with groups like International Rescue Committee, or closer to home, as a refugee case manager[11] in whatever city you live in.

Human Rights Advocate. There are many ways to fight for human rights. Within this sector, there are educators, lawyers, social media experts, programmers, campaigners, and fundraisers. Here is an introduction to all the ways you can help advance human rights[12], and a list of five exciting human rights careers to explore[13].

Medical Personnel. One way to help refugees is as a doctor, psychologist, or nurse. Needs are great in refugee camps and conflict zones. Learn more on how you can help through organizations like Doctors without Borders[14].

1 https://www.youtube.com/watch?v=KvhPDg6EH7U&t=134s

2 https://tropicsu.org/wp-content/uploads/2018/06/LessonPlan_SocialSciences_ClimateRefugees_PDF.pdf

3 https://storymaps.arcgis.com/collections/af3858d32f84488f92dfaeef068ff52

4 https://www.americanprogress.org/issues/security/reports/2019/03/13/467183/turkeys-refugee-dilemma/

5 https://www.yyd.org.tr/en/who-we-are

6 https://pathwaystopeace.org/team/avon-mattison/

7 https://pathwaystopeace.org/

8 https://www.rescue.org/country/syria

9 https://www.rescue.org/article/syrian-10-year-olds-whove-known-nothing-war

10 https://www.humanrightscareers.com/magazine/basic-tips-for-becoming-a-humanitarian-aid-worker/

11 https://www.indeed.com/q-Refugee-case-manager-jobs.html

12 https://www.humanrightscareers.com/careers/

13 https://www.humanrightscareers.com/magazine/5-exciting-human-rights-career-paths/

14 https://www.doctorswithoutborders.org/careers

Carrying on His Grandfather's Legacy

Cesar Chavez, Cesar Chavez Foundation
California

Call to Action

Find ways to use technology to educate and bring hope to oppressed people. Tune in to Radio Campesino: campesina.com. Support the Cesar E. Chavez Foundation: www.chavezfoundation.org.

Values

- Solidarity
- Community
- Service
- Tolerance
- Leadership
- Environmentalism

Lessons Learned

When faced with adversity, remember: Sí, se puede!

Always stand up for human rights.

In the fight for climate change, communication is key. Ask yourself: how can your message reach the most people?

"When you bring people together who believe in something very strongly, good things can happen," Cesar Chavez's grandfather had taught him. Cesar saw how hard his grandfather worked; how he brought people together; and how never gave up trying to create a better world for the migrant farmworkers who brought grapes and other food to the tables of their fellow Americans. Cesar also saw how his grandfather never let the negativity of others affect his ability to spread peace and goodwill. "There is enough love in our movement to give us energy, and still have plenty left over to change the climate of hate and fear around us," he said. As a teenager, Cesar helped his father set up a radio station to inform migrant workers of their rights, and let them know about services that were available to them. Today he shares his grandfather's message in communities across California. "My grandfather inspired me to dedicate my life to helping others in any way I can," he says. "He was our pine tree, and we are his forest."

Language Arts

Cesar describes his grandfather by using a Mexican saying: "Cesar was our pine tree, and we are his forest." Think about what a tree symbolizes, and what the forest symbolizes. What is Cesar saying about his grandfather and the impact he had in people's lives? Write an explanatory essay in which you explain what this metaphor means.

Watch this interview of Cesar Chavez from 1992[1]. Write a summary of the interview, and then do some research on Cesar Chavez (the grandson). Identify ten ways in which he has continued building on his grandfather's legacy. Design a poster sharing your findings.

Based on the summary you wrote, pick one main cause Cesar Chavez worked for. Write a short script or short story in which you detail how you would help his grandson, Cesar, keep fighting for that cause: what new ideas do you have for him? What new ways of protest would you propose?

STEM Activities

In this lesson plan from BrainPop Educators[2], use BrainPOP resources to connect the life and achievements of Cesar Chavez to current events. Students will develop an understanding of the effectiveness of non-violent strikes, boycotts, and protest marches in making changes. They will also learn about the typical working conditions of migrant farm workers, and explore how unions are effective by creating their own "union."

This lesson plan from the National Park Service[3] introduces students to the United Farm Workers. They explore how the impact of one person can be magnified through coalition-building and collective action through a simulation.

In this lesson plan from Calacademy.org[4], students practice distinguishing between correlation and causation within the context of global climate change. They analyze various datasets related to what might be causing increasing temperatures in a fictitious town called Solutionville, as well as around the globe. The temperature and carbon dioxide data they will be analyzing are real, and will enable them to see relationships between global temperatures and atmospheric carbon dioxide levels.

Sustainability Innovations

What is the Cesar Chavez Foundation[5]? How is it perpetuating the legacy of Cesar Chavez, and helping to address the needs of working families?

Using radio as a vehicle for communication is one of the greatest gifts Cesar Chavez gave to the world. In this 2021 article, "Radio Resistance,"[6] an 11-episode podcast addressing the role artists, activists, and scholars play in activism in St. Louis, is addressed. Why is this vehicle, and broadening the framework of change, important?

What is Farmworker Justice[7]? How do they help support farmers, and why is it important to provide them with legal advice and assistance?

Sustainability Career Pathways

Union Organizer. Unions play an important role in protecting and expanding the rights of workers. Organizers play a role both in strengthening those rights and in expanding unions to unprotected industries. Do you have what it takes to be a union organizer? Learn more here[8], and get a free three-day virtual training here[9].

Radio Broadcaster. Radio is a powerful means for informing and influencing people--from what music is played, to news stories, interviews, and talk shows. There are many career opportunities in radio: there are jobs for broadcasters, managers, technicians, digital designers, and administrators. If you love radio, this may be the path for you. Learn more in this comprehensive introduction here[10].

Sustainable Farmer. Shifting industrial farming practices is important to our health, our planet, and to farm workers. Building sustainable farming enterprises that value workers and the planet is another. This introduction to finding jobs in the field of sustainable agriculture is a good place to start[11].

1 https://www.youtube.com/watch?v=HWOFShsD_pU

2 https://educators.brainpop.com/lesson-plan/chavez-day-lesson-plan/?bp-topic=cesar-chavez

3 https://www.nps.gov/teachers/classrooms/the-power-of-one-lessonplan.htm

4 https://www.calacademy.org/educators/lesson-plans/the-heat-is-on-cause-and-effect-and-climate

5 https://chavezfoundation.org/

6 https://news.stlpublicradio.org/show/st-louis-on-the-air/2021-03-15/wednesday-radio-resistance-explores-connection-between-activism-in-st-louis-and-the-world

7 https://www.farmworkerjustice.org/

8 https://en.wikipedia.org/wiki/Union_organizer

9 https://aflcio.org/about-us/programs/organizing-institute

10 https://www.broadcastcareerlink.com/documents/NABRadioCareers.pdf

11 http://greencollarblog.org/sustainable-agriculture-jobs/

Captain Planet: A Philanthropic Environmental Leader

John R. Seydel, Turner Foundation, Mayor's Office of Resilience, Atlanta

Call to Action

Looking to become a Planeteer? Check out Captain Planet and the Turner Foundation on Instagram, Twitter, LinkedIn, & Facebook. Reach out to John R. on Twitter & let him know you read about his story here: @JohnRSeydel

Values

- Philanthropy
- Leadership
- Public Service
- Environmentalism

Lessons Learned

Remember the Planeteers' words: The power is yours!

Strive to preserve the legacy of those who worked to improve the world before you.

We are all citizens of the Earth. We must work together for a common goal: preserving our home.

Growing up, John R. Seydel loved the cartoon series Captain Planet, which was co-created by his grandfather, media mogul and environmental philanthropist Ted Turner.

At the end of every episode, there would be a Planeteer Alert, where the diverse team of global heroes would talk directly to the audience about ways to find solutions to the environmental problems in their communities. "It taught us how to be part of the solution, not part of the problem—and to inspire others along the way," he says. John R. is carrying on this legacy through serving on the boards of a variety of Turner family foundations, including the Captain Planet Foundation. He is also currently serving as the City of Atlanta's Director of Sustainability; in that role he is proudly working to make Atlanta a top-tier sustainable city, and to help them reach their goal of 100 percent renewable energy by 2035.

Language Arts

John R. was inspired and empowered by Captain Planet and his Planeteers. Using these characters, create your own original story about Captain Planet tackling one of the issues facing your generation when it comes to climate change. You may write your response as a short story, or if you are more artistically inclined, as a graphic novel (with original artwork).

In this video[1], John R. lays out several reasons (environmental, economic, and business) why sustainability is crucial. Choose one of the reasons he mentions and expand on it, by creating your own 3-minute video explaining (from the perspective you have chosen) why we should all become involved in sustainability.

What does the term "endangered" mean? Conduct research

about endangered species in your area of the country and choose one to learn about. Write an argumentative essay about the importance of saving that one particular species, and the impact its disappearance would have for the region.

STEM Activities

Select an endangered animal and research why it is considered an endangered species. Do human choices play a role in the sustainability of animal species? What are some of the things we can do to save the species you chose? Present the animal you have chosen to the class.

In this set of activities from PBS[2], learn about sustainability in an urban context. Then describe your vision of a sustainable city; identify the challenges facing cities; and discover the ecosystem services nature can provide cities.

Using this PBS lesson plan on renewable energy[3], explore various sources of energy (both renewable and nonrenewable). Then, in groups or individually, design, model, or build a prototype of an invention that uses renewable energy in the community or region where you live.

Sustainability Innovations

Assess the Captain Planet Foundation Programs[4]. Which of these programs would be effective for the students at your school? Write a letter to your principal detailing why this program could be an important addition to your school's extracurricular activities.

As the Director of Sustainability in Atlanta, John R. is one of the key leaders of the city in implementing their Resilience Initiatives[5]. Which of the resilience initiatives can be used as an example for other cities and communities to emulate?

In addition to John R.'s work, there are many other funds and organizations that are creating sustainable solutions for a brighter future. The Kendeda Fund[6] divides their work into seven program areas to assist in building leaders and advancing ideas for a more sustainable community.

Sustainability Career Pathways

Urban Sustainability. Through his commitment to making Atlanta more sustainable, John R.'s story reveals several different career paths: sustainable urban planning; urban farming; lobbying for 100 percent renewable energy; and working with the mayor to make the city more resilient to climate change. Many big cities have sustainability and resilience departments now, and urban planners are needed everywhere. Here's a great introduction to opportunities in the field of urban sustainability[7].

Working with Endangered Species. Are you as passionate about saving endangered species as John R. is? There are many ways to work to protect and help endangered species and their habitats: from wildlife veterinarians and biologists, to wildlife forensic scientists and conservation officers. Want to learn more? Here is an article about eight careers that help protect endangered species[8].

Storyteller. Telling stories is a powerful way to mobilize people, as Captain Planet's influence on John R. so clearly demonstrates. Stories can inspire, inform, and encourage others to take action. Becoming a journalist (including for your school paper), or a blogger, novelist, filmmaker, cartoonist, or other type of communicator can channel your storytelling skills to make a difference in the world. Learn more about effective storytelling for leaders in this Forbes article[9], and receive training in climate communications at the Climate Reality Project[10].

1 https://www.youtube.com/watch?app=desktop&v=5lAaWdFuKV4

2 https://mass.pbslearningmedia.org/resource/nature-works-everywhere-sustainable-cities-lp/nature-works-everywhere-sustainable-cities-lp/

3 https://www.pbs.org/newshour/extra/lessons-plans/lesson-plan-how-to-turn-a-lake-into-an-electric-battery/

4 https://captainplanetfoundation.org/programs/

5 https://www.atlantaga.gov/government/mayor-s-office/executive-offices/office-of-resilience/sustainability-initiatives

6 https://kendedafund.org/

7 https://www.trade-schools.net/articles/wildlife-jobs

8 https://www.trade-schools.net/articles/wildlife-jobs

9 https://www.forbes.com/sites/forbescoachescouncil/2020/09/30/leaders-seven-tips-for-becoming-a-better-storyteller/?sh=1be3e1d94606

10 https://www.climaterealityproject.org/training

Empowering Women to Lead

Hafsat Abiola-Costello, Kudirat Initiative for Democracy (KIND), Nigeria

Call to Action

Support female leadership and empowerment; support Women in Africa: wia-initiative.com/en/ Follow Hafsat on Twitter: @Hafsat-KIND.

Values

- Altruistic
- Brave
- Dedicated
- Community Oriented
- Feminist

Lessons Learned

From both of her parents, Hafsat learned the value of giving back to one's community.

Even when a heroic person who has stood up for the rights of his or her people is killed, the message does not die; in fact, it often becomes stronger.

When bad things happen to people, they can surmount the pain and turn tragedy into positive action.

Growing up in Nigeria, Hafsat Abiola spent her days playing hide and seek, climbing trees, and playing spy games.

But it wasn't all play: from an early age, Hafsat's mother and father had taught her how to live. Her father, Moshood Kashimawo Olawale Abiola, was a political activist and philanthropist who was imprisoned by the Nigerian junta after his presidential bid. His imprisonment triggered a wave of demonstrations led by Hafsat's mother, Kudirat: in 1996, she was assassinated. After her mother's death, Hafsat vowed to continue the work that she had sacrificed her life for. Two years later, her father died in prison. Hafsat channeled her immense loss into activism. Her mother had taught her to take care of others and fight for equal rights. Her father had shown her how economic equality can transform individuals' lives and generate systematic change. Today, she continues carrying out the legacy of her parents by working to bring women into local, national, and global economic systems. She is the president of Women in Africa, an organization that supports female entrepreneurs in all 54 African nations.

Language Arts

Write an argumentative essay answering this question: How can the US apply some of the ideas from KIND to help low-income families who have little or no access to prenatal care? Are there any organizations or government programs based in the U.S. with a similar mission? If there are, identify them and explain their role in their communities.

Create a presentation on the importance of giving women affordable access to prenatal care. Focus on KIND's mission, and how it is helping Nigerian women.

Write an essay about the place women occupy in Nigerian

society, specifically in the country's economy. Describe how their role in Nigerian society impacts their ability to sustain themselves and their families, and explain how Hafsat's work is helping to improve their situation.

STEM Activities

Hafsat represents a cultural shift that is bringing more females into positions of importance in the world today. Learn about five different influential jobs within the American economy that are primarily held by males. Calculate the discrepancy in the percentage of these jobs that are held by men and by women, and explain why it is imperative that more females are hired to fill these positions.

Identify three famous historical STEM figures who were women, and explain why they stand as models for change in the history of the world. Explain how their accomplishments have made the world, or the United States, a better place.

- **Male students:** If you were selected to work with a partner on a project, choose one female classmate or female member of your family, and explain how some of her strengths could help you in areas that you aren't as strong in.
- **Female students:** Imagine being paired with a male student (teacher's choice) in your class on a science project. Explain how you and your partner would benefit from this partnership, and the unique skills that you can bring to it.

Sustainability Innovations

In addition to Hafsat's work with KIND, there are many women in Africa who are striving to improve life for other African women. Lola Omolola is one such woman who took it upon herself to connect like-minded individuals via a Facebook group. She has used social media to her advantage by creating a private group where 1.7 million females explain their lives, and share their experiences: Female in Nigeria Facebook Group[1].

UN Women[2] is one of the largest female-focused groups in the world; it highlights the positions and work that women do as a part of the United Nations.

In addition to their international presence, U.S. based organizations such as Vote Run Lead[3] are focused on training women to run for office—and win! Helping female leaders gain a greater presence in politics worldwide is essential in order to create a better world for our future.

Sustainability Career Pathways

Election Worker. Free and fair elections are at the heart of all democracies. Ensuring that they are free and fair requires many people: from poll workers, to voter outreach coordinators, to translators to help get out the vote in diverse communities, to election technology specialists. If you want to support free and fair elections, check out this short article that describes five election jobs to consider[4].

Midwife or Doula. Many women around the world face a lack of access to hospitals when giving birth. Even where hospitals are affordable, many doctors regard surgical birth as more efficient, and the percentage of these births (called caesareans) is skyrocketing[5] (in the US it is now 1 out of 3 births). Midwives help mothers deliver their babies naturally; this is both more affordable and generally healthier for mothers, children, and the planet; and it is an increasingly available option for mothers to choose, both in and out of hospitals. Doulas also play an important role in supporting women during the delivery of their babies (and the training doesn't require intensive schooling). Both of these are important career paths. You can learn about midwifery here[6] and here[7], and doulas here[8].

Public Health Worker. Prevention, above all else, is the best way to ensure that a population is healthy. Public health workers play an important role in prevention--from educating people about healthy living, to organizing vaccination programs, to helping to create policies that improve health outcomes (such as policies regarding seatbelt use, or smoking). Public health workers can work directly with individuals, organize community programs, or work in government. To learn more, visit here[9].

1 https://www.npr.org/sections/alltechconsidered/2018/06/04/613460142/one-womans-facebook-success-story-a-support-group-for-1-7-million

2 https://www.unwomen.org/en/what-we-do/leadership-and-political-participation/facts-and-figures

3 https://www.voterunlead.org/

4 https://www.monster.com/career-advice/article/election-jobs

5 https://www.npr.org/sections/goatsandsoda/2018/10/12/656198429/rate-of-c-sections-is-rising-at-an-alarming-rate

6 https://fairygodboss.com/career-topics/how-to-become-a-midwife

7 https://mana.org/resources/become-a-midwife

8 https://www.dona.org/become-a-doula/

9 https://www.goodwin.edu/enews/what-do-public-health-workers-do/

Planting the Seeds for Peace

Sami Awad, The Holy Land Trust
Palestine

Call to Action

Support Sami and the Holy Land Trust in building resilient communities through nonviolent resistance in Palestine: holylandtrust.org. Follow Sami on Twitter: @Sami_Awad

Values

- Imagination
- Dedication
- Leadership
- Commitment
- Tolerance
- Compassion

Lessons Learned

People need to be engaged in the peace process, and need to find ways to achieve peace together through nonviolent means.

The past continues to affect us, and all the decisions we make, in the present.

Conflict resolution is about communication, and communication can only truly begin when we are ready to listen to each other. It's important to listen to others, including those with whom you do not agree.

As the nephew of Mubarak Awad—known to many as the "Gandhi of Palestine" for his nonviolent resistance to Israeli occupation—Sami Awad grew up with big shoes to fill.

Since being inspired by his uncle at the age of 12, Sami has dedicated his life to the study and practice of nonviolence. He founded the Holy Land Trust to unite Palestinians and Israelis in an effort to promote peaceful dialogue and conflict resolution. He now works with young people on a number of environmental projects in the Middle East.

Language Arts

Write an essay about nonviolence, and the role Mohandas Gandhi played in it.

Sami's uncle has been called "The Gandhi of Palestine." What does this mean? Create a five-minute video explaining who Gandhi was; what nonviolence meant to him; why it is important; how it can be used to bring about social change (give several examples from history); and how you could use it in your own day-to-day interactions with people.

Based on your research, is there a link between sustainability and nonviolence? How does climate change contribute to regional political tensions and conflicts, and how can sustainability help ease these tensions? (Use Sami's story as an example.)

Create a series of at least six posters, or one short animated film in which you explain how the climate crisis is worsening the Israel-Palestinian conflict, and how a nonviolent approach to problem solving can help.

Create an information campaign using video, words, and

images, to encourage people your age to understand and practice the principles of nonviolence. How would you encourage them to adopt a nonviolent lifestyle?

Compare activism in the 1980s or 90s to activism and peaceful protesting today. How are the approaches similar? How are they different? Do you think we have learned anything from the history of activism? If so, explain what we have learned.

STEM Activities

Create a timeline either from your own experience, or the story of someone you admire who had to deal with immigration and adjusting to life in a new country. Explain how you think such an experience can help to expand a person's view of the world, and why understanding other cultures is important.

Research the concept of sustainability, and explain how Sami's story embodies the principles of sustainability. Why is sustainability important as it pertains to culture, activism, and human rights?

Follow this math activity[1] to analyze and interpret hate crime data and put it into graphs using statistical analysis. What do hate crimes have to do with climate change, or other sustainability issues?

Sustainability Innovations

Sami's work has begun to transform Palestine in its fight for human rights and sustainability. The Palestine Wildlife Society[2] has assisted in this process by prioritizing ecological sustainability in Palestine.

Seeds of Peace[3] is a nonpolitical nonprofit organization that helps teenagers learn peacemaking skills. They bring young people together at a traditional summer camp setting in the woods of Maine, where they offer a safe and supportive environment in which participants can share opposing views with each other and learn listening, communication, and other conflict resolution skills that can help them develop empathy for one another.

Kids for Peace[4] is a California-based global nonprofit that is making our world a better place through love and action. Inspired by Gandhi's quote, "If we are to achieve lasting peace, we must begin with the children," Kids for Peace was founded in 2006 by a mom and a high school student. From its start as a small club of caring kids, Kids for Peace has grown to become a global children's movement that promotes peace, compassion, and kindness. It now includes 350 chapters in 121 countries, with boys and girls of all ages and socioeconomic backgrounds.

The United Nations Youth 2030 Strategy[5] recognizes that young people can make positive contributions as agents of change. It seeks to empower youth to stand up for their rights, and aims to ensure youth engagement and participation in the 2030 Agenda for Sustainable Development[6], as well as other relevant global agendas and frameworks.

Neve Shalom[7], established in 1970, is a village of Palestinian and Jewish citizens of Israel ded¬icated to building justice, peace and equality in the country and challenging the racism and discrimination that is prevalent in the country.

Sustainability Career Pathways

Conflict Mediator. There are a growing number of career opportunities in the field of conflict resolution as mediators, arbitrators, and consensus-builders, among others. Mediators help parties resolve conflicts--whether they involve just two individuals, or whole organizations or communities--and whether the conflicts involve financial issues, territorial disputes, and even environmental concerns.

Want to learn more about this field? Visit here[8]. And if you are interested in a career in conflict resolution read this step-by-step guide[9].

Nonviolence Trainer. Nonviolence is not only recognized as an effective protest strategy, but is increasingly sought after as a more effective means of crisis prevention. Hospitals, nursing homes, prisons, and schools are all starting to recognize the value in proactive, nonviolent de-escalation of conflicts. Want to become an expert in nonviolent approaches to conflict, and train others to use these skills as well? Here's one example of nonviolent crisis intervention training to explore: The Crisis Prevention Institute[10].

Orchardist. At one point, Sami's uncle planted olive trees to prevent the confiscation of land. Trees that provide fruit and nuts are a central source of food, and when done correctly can also be a way to heal the land. Interested in being an orchardist? Start here[11].

1 https://advancingjustice-la.org/what-we-do/leadership-development/untold-civil-rights-stories/unit-plan-math-alg-1-statistics-hate-0
2 http://www.wildlife-pal.org/
3 https://www.seedsofpeace.org/
4 https://kidsforpeaceglobal.org/
5 https://www.un.org/youthenvoy/youth-un/
6 https://sustainabledevelopment.un.org/post2015/transformingourworld
7 https://wasns.org/
8 https://careersinpsychology.org/conflict-resolution-careers/
9 https://www.indeed.com/career-advice/finding-a-job/how-to-become-a-mediator
10 https://www.crisisprevention.com/
11 https://www.acsgarden.com/learning/careers/orchardist.aspx

Ripples of Hope

Kerry Kennedy, Robert F. Kennedy Foundation
Washington D.C

Call to Action

Learn more about Kerry's work, & explore the extensive humanitarian network supporting equal rights for everyone around the world at Robert F. Kennedy Human Rights: rfkhumanrights.org/people/kerry-kennedy.

Values

- Community Service
- Justice
- Compassion
- Generosity
- Commitment

Lessons Learned

If you are looking for personal fulfillment, remember: helping others gives meaning to life.

It is both our duty and our honor to bring hope to those who need it. Defending human rights is defending our shared humanity.

If you want to change the world, start by using your position in your community to help those who are less fortunate. Make ripples. Be seen helping, and others will follow.

Kerry Kennedy learned from her father early on that public service was "just really what you wanted to do because that was what made life meaningful."
So it wasn't so much a sense of obligation or a burden, or a demand to serve others that she heard coming from him: it was just something you did because it was right, and it made you feel better to be helping. But one day, after experiencing extreme poverty in the Mississippi Delta, she remembers her father saying to a roomful of people, "You have to be involved." That moment, as much as any other, Kerry says, set her on her lifelong journey in advocacy – a journey aimed at "exposing the many abuses that go on around this world, in all of its forms." She has always kept her father's words before her as a beacon, to keep striving toward a better world. "Each time a man stands up for an ideal, or acts to improve the lot of others, or strikes out against injustice, he sends forth a tiny ripple of hope…and those ripples build a current which can sweep down the mightiest walls of oppression and resistance."

Language Arts

Kerry's father, Robert F. Kennedy, taught her that our actions should create "a ripple of hope." Create a series of Tik Tok videos or tweets in which you offer concrete ways in which people can generate a "tiny ripple of hope" in their communities.

What is Robert F. Kennedy Human Rights? Create a five-minute video in which you explain the organization's mission, the relevance of its work, the causes it supports, and how people can support it.

What is the current state of poverty and hunger in the United States, specifically in the region of Appalachia? Write a research essay in which you describe the poverty rate and the number of people who experience hunger in Appalachia today;

and how this population is being disproportionately affected by environmental threats.

STEM Activities

Climate change negatively affects people's health and quality of life. Those who are already disadvantaged because of their race or income are usually the most affected by environmental hazards and disasters. Use the EPA's environmental justice screening and mapping tool[1] to identify and analyze an area near you with increased environmental burdens and vulnerable populations. Activity link[2].

Research and describe the impacts of changing climate conditions on human health with an emphasis on vulnerable populations; then apply systems thinking to create a visual model of the various health implications arising from climate change. Finally, use local, state, or regional data and the US Climate Resilience Toolkit to evaluate climate adaptation and mitigation strategies that protect human health. Activity link[3].

Using your research from the activity above, plan a project to address a human health impact that is related to climate change and is relevant in your community.

In this activity[4], students will analyze the income distribution of the three most populous racial/ethnic groups in the United States to evaluate whether or not these distributions have become more equitable over time. Using data from the 2013 U.S. Census, students will compare the percentages of total income earned by different subgroups, and decide whether or not the "American Dream" is equally achievable by all Americans.

Sustainability Innovations

As a part of her leadership role in Robert F. Kennedy Human Rights, Kerry participated in #breakbreadnotfamilies[5] by fasting for 24 days to protest the 2,400 students that have been separated from their families.

As a leader in Robert F. Kennedy Human Rights, Kerry engages in the organization's work of teaching and protecting human rights, inspiring young leaders, and engaging the business community. Go to the teaching human rights resource[6] and complete the virtual field trip. What did you learn by watching these videos? Did you expand your knowledge of activism?

In addition to RFK Human Rights personal projects, they have partnerships with Discovery Education, Civic Works, and many other organizations, to promote and expand Speaking Truth to Power!

Sustainability Career Pathways

Public Servant. There are countless ways to become a public servant: working for a government agency like the EPA[7], running for office[8], or being an organizer[9], whether for the climate, environmental justice, or agricultural reform, like Cesar Chavez, who was one of Kerry's heroes. The only limit on where to put your energy is your own imagination.

Sustainable Development. There is a vast field of people working in sustainable development--from rural Appalachia to Africa, from Indianapolis to India. Here is a large database of international development jobs[10]. Or explore working with The Peace Corps[11] or AmeriCorps[12], in which you help with development projects either internationally or within the U.S.

Human Rights Advocate. As Kerry has demonstrated, there are many ways to fight for human rights. Within this sector, there are educators, lawyers, social media experts, programmers, campaigners, and fundraisers. Here is an introduction to all the ways you can help advance human rights[13] and a list of five exciting human rights careers to explore[14].

1 https://www.epa.gov/ejscreen

2 https://grist.org/climate/lesson-plan-environmental-justice-climate-change/

3 https://www.niehs.nih.gov/health/assets/docs_a_e/climate_change_and_human_health_lesson_plan_a_508.pdf

4 https://www.citizenmath.com/lessons

5 https://www.breakbreadnotfamilies.org/

6 https://rfkhumanrights.org/our-programs/speak-truth-to-power

7 https://www.epa.gov/careers/why-work-epa

8 https://www.npr.org/2019/10/15/770332855/how-to-run-for-office

9 https://www.idealist.org/en/careers/a-career-as-a-community-organizer

10 https://www.devnetjobs.org/

11 https://www.peacecorps.gov/

12 https://americorps.gov/

13 https://www.humanrightscareers.com/careers/

14 https://www.humanrightscareers.com/magazine/5-exciting-human-rights-career-paths/

Tackling The Root Causes Of Hunger

Anna Lappé, Small Planet Fund, Real Food Media
California

Call to Action

Make a difference by being conscientious about where your food comes from, and choosing products from farms that take care of both their workers and the planet.

- realfoodmedia.org

- smallplanet.org

- smallplanetfund.org

Values

- Commitment
- Healthy Living
- Collaboration
- Sustainability
- Environmentalism

Lessons Learned

Pay attention to what you eat - it affects your body's health, and your mind's ability to make good decisions. A healthy planet begins with healthy people.

Fighting for a healthy environment, food security, and quality jobs begins with being aware of the food you eat.

The fight for social and environmental change needs everyone to participate, regardless of age, social class, race, or place of origin.

Everything changed for Anna Lappé in middle school, when she took a trip with her mother to rural Ohio. There, for the first time, she met some of the farmworkers who had grown the food she had been eating her whole life. Anna's parents are both passionate activists who share a common goal: to make the world a healthier, safer, more equitable place. Anna's mother, Frances Moore Lappé, is a food-systems activist. In 1971, she published Diet For a Small Planet, a book that encourages people to have plant-based, environmentally friendly diets. Her mother's activism inspired Anna to do the same. Working with her mother, Anna realized the importance of generations working together for change. After all everyone, from the very young to the very old, is affected by environmental policies and practices, because everyone needs to eat.

Today Anna is an advocate for better food systems that will protect the environment, promote health, and provide people with quality jobs with dignity. Anna is continuing to carry out her mother's legacy by helping to ensure that people everywhere have access to nutritious food that is produced both ethically and sustainably.

Language Arts

Make a list of the main issues Anna is passionate about. Then, working in groups of 3-5, choose one of them, and create a presentation in which you explain the problem; some possible solutions; what is being done to deal with this issue; and how people can be part of the solution.

In her book, *Diet for a Hot Planet*, Anna explores the link between diet and global warming. Write an argumentative essay agreeing or disagreeing with her position. Support your position with research that cites at least three secondary sources.

Anna was involved in her mother's second book, *Hope's Edge, The Next Diet for a Small Planet* in which they continue to explore the ideas in the original *Diet for a Small Planet* and go even further, researching who is doing what to help solve these problems. What is the thesis of Frances Moore Lappé's first book? What is the second book about? Do you agree or disagree with the premise for the first book? Discuss your answer with the rest of your class.

STEM Activities

The following STEM activities are from FoodSpan.org[1]:

Students explore how crops are grown in industrial agriculture, and how those practices are impacting human health and ecosystems. This lesson[2] covers the importance of soil, freshwater, and biodiversity in agriculture, and describes some ecological alternatives to industrial crop production.

This lesson[3] **allows students to "zoom out" and see how the food system is linked to the global issue of climate change.** Students will learn about how climate change occurs; analyze the connections between climate change and agricultural practices; and consider ways to reduce the greenhouse gas emissions generated by food systems.

In this lesson[4], **students explore alternatives to the agricultural industrial model, and consider what it means for agriculture to be "sustainable."** They will examine agroecology as an approach to food production that nourishes, rather than depletes natural ecosystems and human communities, and will imagine what a different agricultural paradigm could look like, and share that vision with others.

At least one in six members of the U.S. workforce are employed in the food chain, from farmers' fields to food service. In this lesson[5], students will learn about a variety of these jobs, examine their working conditions, and consider how to improve the health and quality of life of workers.

Sustainability Innovations

Learn about Real Food Media[6]. How is this organization able to provide critical analysis and strategies for one of the most corporate-dominant industries in the world?

In addition to innovations in growing food, it is important to have advancements in the technology for storing and keeping food fresh.

- **Apeel Sciences[7]** is a California-based company that extracts lipids from food waste and transforms it into an edible coating that helps to keep food fresh.
- **Cold Hubs[8]** is a Nigerian-based company that has created solar-powered refrigerators to help local farmers keep their produce fresh.

Review the projects that Food System Innovations [9]has been involved in. Select one project, and create an in-depth review; then share what you have learned with your class.

- Example: What are the most important animal products to replace, from the perspective of lives saved.

Review this article[10], which details how food system innovations can affect the ability of countries to meet their sustainable development goals (SDGs). What types of innovations are having the most success? Which areas need the most work?

Sustainability Career Pathways

Food Policy Advocate. Many organizations are working for a more just and sustainable food system—from large organizations like Food and Water Watch, to local food policy councils. Is there a career path for you in food policy? Read about six ways to get involved.[11]

Nutritionist. One way to reform the food system is to help one individual at a time. Nutritionists help people make dietary choices that are better for themselves and the planet, for example by consuming less soda, sugar, and meat, and more vegetables. Learn more about this career here.[12]

Sustainable Food Company Employee. Food companies -- grocery chains, agricultural commodities, and well-known brands need help to make the transition to sustainable practices. For example, they need sustainability-minded employees, from web designers and marketers to lawyers and lobbyists, to food manufacturers and supply chain managers. Explore some of the leading sustainable food companies here.[13]

---

1 https://www.foodspan.org/lesson-plans/
2 https://www.foodspan.org/_pdf/lesson-plan/unit2/lesson1-crops-lessonplan.pdf
3 https://www.foodspan.org/_pdf/lesson-plan/unit2/lesson5-climate-lessonplan.pdf
4 https://www.foodspan.org/_pdf/lesson-plan/unit2/lesson6-sustainability-lessonplan.pdf
5 https://www.foodspan.org/_pdf/lesson-plan/unit2/lesson4-hands-that-feed-us-lessonplan.pdf
6 https://realfoodmedia.org/
7 https://www.springwise.com/food-waste-repurposed-as-edible-coating-to-keep-farm-produce-fresh/
8 https://www.springwise.com/sustainability-innovation/food-drink/coldhubs-solar-powered-refrigerators
9 https://www.foodsysteminnovations.com/projects
10 https://www.thelancet.com/journals/lanplh/article/PIIS2542-5196(20)30277-1/fulltext
11 https://foodprint.org/blog/6-ways-to-get-involved-with-food-policy/
12 https://universityhq.org/how-to-become/nutritionist-careers/
13 https://www.motherearthliving.com/food-for-health/sustainable-food-companies-zmoz12jazmel

The Children Will Lead the Way

Valentina Ossaa, Student Climate Action
New York

☀ Call to Action

Speak up for what you believe in. Find a way to get involved--join a protest or a climate change organization; or start your own project. Find a way to do something! Follow Valentina on Twitter @valentinaossa11 & Bethany on Instagram: @bethanyyarrowmusic

☀ Values

- Activism
- Dissent
- Commitment
- Dedication
- Environmentalism

☀ Lessons Learned

Be brave and follow the example of those who came before you.

Be fearless and lead the way!

Youth can be an asset. When confronted with a problem no one knows how to solve, sometimes young eyes can see what others have been trained to ignore.

Valentina went to her first protest when she was only five years old, and she has been involved as an activist in a number of issues ever since.

When she was in middle school, she organized a collective school walk-out on the day of the global school strike (March 15, 2019). But she didn't stop there: since then she has spoken at a number of climate protests, and even at a demonstration in front of the White House in Washington.

☀ Language Arts

After reading Valentina's story, go over it a second time and underline the main ideas. Then, on a separate sheet of paper, choose one of those ideas and write a speech asking people to express their support in a concrete way (that is, take action!) on an issue related to that particular idea.

Create a presentation about the pros and cons of the fracking industry. What are the risks of fracking? What benefits do the fracking companies claim there are? Do the risks outweigh the benefits? Why or why not?

Write a letter to the governor of your state, asking him or her to take action on one specific environmental issue that is affecting your community. Read your letter in front of your class. After everyone has read their letters, have a class discussion to come up with the five most effective persuasive strategies people used in their letters, and explain why they were the most effective.

STEM Activities

What is hydraulic fracturing? Why is it so controversial? In this lesson plan from The New York Times Learning Network[1], students will define hydrofracking; identify how the demand for natural gas is changing; then research and map how natural gas development can impact a community.

In this lesson plan from PBS Learning Media[2], students learn about health concerns related to exposure to the chemicals used in natural gas drilling. They will explore the challenges of investigating the link between these chemicals and illnesses -- since the gas industry is not required to disclose which chemicals they use in fracking fluids.

Source your energy. With this lesson plan,[3] funded by the American Petroleum Institute, students investigate what turns on their lights. What are the sources of energy in your community? What percentage comes from natural gas power? What actions might help increase the use of renewable energy?

Sustainability Innovations

New York is one of the most developed cities in the U.S., in a state that ranks in the top 10 in CO2 emissions produced. Urban Future Lab[4] is a sustainability company that helps to develop market-solutions to reduce climate change. As a part of UFL, the Carbon to Value Initiative is helping to drive an innovative ecosystem focused on the commercialization of carbon tech to reduce emissions. How could this help New York deal with its high level of CO2 emissions?

In January 2020, Governor Cuomo banned fracking in the state of New York. In this article[5], fracking, its impact on New York, and findings demonstrating the health and environmental risks are addressed. How can this affect plans for the future of New York State, and finding alternatives to fracking?

As innovations develop, many U.S. cities are evolving into "smart cities" and developing sustainability policies. Review the New York Smart Cities Innovation Partnership[6]. What are some of the priorities within the supply chain, cyber security, and real-time utility monitoring?

Sustainability Career Pathways

Environmental Organizer. Engaging one's community in dealing with environmental and social challenges is an important career path. Explore programs that teach community organizing, from online courses (such as this one[7]), to one-year environmental organizing field schools like Green Corps[8].

Environmental Mental Health Counselor. As environmental conditions worsen, more people are suffering mental health challenges due to the effects of climate change and fears about the looming sustainability crisis[9]. Maybe you would like to consider the field of psychology, mental health counseling, or even ecotherapy[10] (which draws on nature to heal psychological trauma). Here[11] is an introduction to the field.

Renewable Energy Advocate. Developing sources of renewable energy is key to replacing fracked gas and oil in order to achieve the world's energy needs. As an employee of a renewable energy company--as a manager, salesperson[12], or support staff—you can help with this transition. Or join a nonprofit organization to promote and lobby for the transition to renewable energy.

Green Investor. With billions of dollars being invested, where that money goes will shape the future of business. Do we want to invest in oil companies, or renewable energy companies? In downtown real estate or suburban malls? Working with a socially responsible investment firm, or with a university, city, or foundation as an asset manager can be a great way to help develop the sustainable business sector. Here is a brief introduction[13] to the many jobs in the field.

1 https://learning.blogs.nytimes.com/2012/09/12/fuel-for-debate-examining-the-natural-gas-fracking-controversy/
2 https://mass.pbslearningmedia.org/resource/envh10.sci.phys.energy.fracking/fracking/
3 http://sciencenetlinks.com/lessons/energy-for-you/
4 http://ufl.nyc/
5 https://newyork.psr.org/issues/fracking/
6 https://esd.ny.gov/new-york-smart-cities-innovation-partnership
7 https://www.coursera.org/learn/community-organizing
8 https://greencorps.org/
9 https://www.latimes.com/politics/story/2020-12-27/for-young-californians-climate-change-is-a-mental-health-crisis-too
10 https://www.goodtherapy.org/learn-about-therapy/types/econature-therapy
11 https://onlinecounselingprograms.com/become-a-counselor/counseling-careers/mental-health-counselor/
12 https://www.greentechmedia.com/articles/read/cleantech-careers-solar-sales-at-a-residential-installer
13 http://finanzasostenibile.it/wp-content/uploads/2017/04/13-04-2017_FBicciato_ProfessioniSRI_SdR.pdf

The Girl Who Silenced the World For Five Minutes

Severn Suzuki, David Suzuki Foundation
Canada

Call to Action

Learn more, get involved, & show your support for any number of environmental causes at David Suzuki Foundation: davidsuzuki.org.

Values

- Courage
- Clarity
- Commitment
- Dedication
- Environmentalism

Lessons Learned

If you want to learn about sustainability, you need look no further than Indigenous people. They have been living sustainably for centuries.

Change begins small and grows as we realize the truth: the problems of the underrepresented are our problems too, and we need to unite to solve them.

The economy should serve all the people of the country. If we sacrifice the needs of the people by allowing the economy to dictate our decision making, we will end up destroying the planet.

At age 12, Severn Suzuki traveled with the Environmental Children's Organization (ECO) to the UN Earth Summit in Rio de Janeiro, Brazil – the very country that had inspired her activism on a trip to the Amazon some years prior.

When one of the speakers at the summit dropped out, Severn realized she had the perfect opportunity to get the youth perspective on these issues out to the world. "We were watching as all of these old people were sitting around discussing the future; but we would be the ones to suffer the consequences of their decisions," she says. "And who was speaking for us?" So, she stepped up, and showed great strength as she gave a powerful speech in front of many of the leading figures in the environmental movement. Years later, her speech became a viral internet sensation, called "The Girl Who Silenced the World For 5 Minutes." It has reached more than 32 million people.

Language Arts

What is the importance of the Amazon rainforest to our planet? What are the consequences of its destruction? What are the biggest threats threatening the Amazon nowadays? Create your own Kahoot[1]! game designed to teach people about the Amazon, its importance, the threats it is under, and the dangers of its destruction. You must create at least 12 questions--and answers!

Create a presentation in which you explain the pros and cons of hydroelectric power. In your presentation make sure to answer the following questions: Why is hydroelectric power considered a better alternative than other, more traditional methods of power generation, like coal? Is hydroelectric power always harmful to the environment, or are there ways to build plants that don't threaten the environment? Are there any alternatives other that are more environmentally friendly than hydroelectric generated power?

The line between economic development and protecting the environment can be a delicate one, especially for underdeveloped countries. Write a three-minute speech in which you try to convince the leadership of a developing country (you can choose the country) to, in Severn's words, build "an architecture for a different way of being, and it should be intergenerational."

Imagine you could convince world leaders to start building the world in an environmentally responsible way: a way in which the economy works for the people and respects the environment, and where no one needs to choose between clean air and economic activity. Write a short story in which you describe this world, how we got there, and what it took to get there in terms of financial investment, creativity, and political will.

STEM Activities

Severn's family has worked with Indigenous peoples for many years, fighting the impact deforestation has on their lands. In this activity[2], students will use videos and satellite images to investigate the impact of deforestation on forest cover and changes in the carbon cycle by using an interactive time series developed by NASA to analyze forest cover changes in the Amazon rainforest. Students then use the Global Forest Watch tool from the World Resources Institute to develop their own original research question on changes in forest cover using real-time data, images, and other information from the tool to use in a presentation.

One major impact of climate change is water pollution, which is an important resource for Indigenous cultures. In teams, students will practice analyzing water quality, and will use information about water treatment processes to design a prototype for a small-scale water treatment system. Then they will test it to assess how well their prototype produces safe water to prevent water-borne illnesses. Activity link[3].

Severn and her parents have always been interested in Indigenous groups and have been working to help solve the problems they face. Find a group of Indigenous people in your area or region, and research the issues that are affecting their community (deforestation, pollution, water quality, etc.). Explore ways this community is working to address these issues. What is affecting their success? Are there ways they could be more successful?

Sustainability Innovations

Severn's work in the Amazon began when she was just a young girl, and she was catapulted into focusing on the impact of sustainability in her life. Today there are many organizations and companies working to save the rainforest. Amazon Conservation[4] is one of the main organizations that highlights the threats to the Amazon, while actively combining manpower and technology to find solutions to the problems.

Severn is famous for "stopping the world" for 5 minutes in 1992 at the United Nations Earth Summit; but she knows that the voices of kids today are just as important as her voice was then. Visit her website[5] to listen to her original speech, and the anniversary of it, which highlights students today who feel like "I'm only a child but…"

Deforestation has become a growing issue globally, not just in the Amazon. This article[6] highlights 8 different ways that you can contribute to the reduction of deforestation. How can you get involved in stopping deforestation?

As a society we are constantly looking for ways to improve our Earth; some organizations have found success and withstood the test of time. Since 1996, Amazon Watch[7] has evolved and found successful ways to assist in the fight against deforestation, and utilize advanced Indigenous solutions to addressing these issues.

Sustainability Career Pathways

Science Communicator. Severn's father, David Suzuki, was a famous scientist and science communicator. Too few scientists are able to take the time to translate their complex understandings into language that the public can understand and be moved by. This field requires a lot of studying--of both science and communications--so is an intense one. But it can be very rewarding as well. Read more about the field of science communications[8] and this Nature article[9] about one academic who made the switch to science communications.

Environmental Lawyer. Severn is supporting youth as they sue Canada in order to protect the climate. Lawyers are central in this fight. Perhaps this is the path for you? Here is a brief overview of what an environmental lawyer is[10], how to become one[11], and a guide to careers in Environmental Law[12].

Nonprofit Director. Many people work for nonprofit organizations; some, like Severn, even direct nonprofits. If this is your ambition, keep in mind that you may benefit from getting management training. There are programs to train managers for nonprofit organizations specifically. While many of these are masters' levels programs (such as these leading programs)[13], there are also informal and undergraduate opportunities to learn essential management skills as well. If you're really serious about this path, here's a 500+ page introduction to the field![14]

1 https://kahoot.com/
2 https://serc.carleton.edu/earthlabs/carbon/lab_4.html
3 https://www.teachengineering.org/activities/view/cub_waterqtnew_lesson01_activity1
4 https://www.amazonconservation.org/
5 https://severncullissuzuki.com/bio/
6 https://innovate-eco.com/8-innovative-solutions-to-deforestation/
7 https://amazonwatch.org/work
8 https://en.wikipedia.org/wiki/Science_communication
9 https://www.nature.com/articles/d41586-019-02387-w
10 https://www.environmentalscience.org/career/environmental-lawyer
11 https://www.sierraclub.org/sierra/cool-schools-2017/how-be-environmental-lawyer
12 https://hls.harvard.edu/content/uploads/2008/07/full-working-draft.pdf
13 https://www.usnews.com/best-graduate-schools/top-public-affairs-schools/nonprofit-management-rankings
14 https://www.amazon.com/exec/obidos/ASIN/1119585457/stansociinn09-20

We Must Be the Change We Want to See in The World

Arun Gandhi, Total Nonviolence
New York / South Africa

Call to Action

Become involved with Arun's work to create a better, safer, more humane world by visiting The M.K. Gandhi Institute for Nonviolence at gandhiinstitute.org

Values

- Compassion
- Thoughtfulness
- Peace
- Nonviolence
- Respect

Lessons Learned

Remember to live by Gandhi's words: "We must live what we want others to learn." This means always striving for your actions to be a good example.

The seeds of anger only bring pain and suffering. Instead, you can choose to be a "peace farmer."

Real solutions to the world's problems are born from compassion.

Born and brought up in South Africa, Arun Gandhi faced a lot of prejudice because of the color of his skin "It filled me with a lot of anger. I wanted an eye for an eye." Thankfully, his parents brought him to India, to study the ways of ahimsa under his beloved grandfather, Mahatma Gandhi. Ahimsa is the principle of nonviolence toward all living things. As a self-described "peace farmer," Arun has taught countless numbers of people over the years how to properly abide by ahimsa through his lectures, reporting, and his work at the M.K. Gandhi Institute for Nonviolence. Arun has seen a lot of destruction of the environment, in both South Africa and India. To address the climate crisis we are in, he urges our leaders to listen to the wise words of his grandfather: We must live what we want others to learn.

Language Arts

Imagine that you were the 12-year-old grandson of Mahatma Gandhi. What would it be like to be his grandson? Write a 1,000 word narrative essay in which you describe what you imagine a day in the life of Gandhi's grandson would be like. Finish your essay by answering this question: Why is Mahatma Gandhi's legacy still important in our world today?

What is ahimsa? Create a five-minute video to explain the concept, its origins, how it has been used throughout history, and how it can be applied today. Give three concrete examples of what ahimsa is, and why it should be taught in schools as part of the curriculum.

Based on Arun Gandhi's definition of violence, and the various kinds of violence society exposes us to, create a series of six TikTok videos in which you explain what violence is; give concrete examples of it (based on Arun's definition); and offer ways to deal with violence in a way that promotes ahimsa.

Working in small groups (2-4 people), create a presentation in which you propose concrete ways that ahimsa can be used to fight climate change. Offer concrete examples of several climate change issues, and explain how practicing ahimsa can help find practical solutions to these problems.

STEM Activities

In this activity from the California Academy of Sciences[1], students "mine" chocolate chips out of cookies to demonstrate the effects mining can have on habitats. Students will summarize the environmental impacts of obtaining and using fossil fuels, and explore solutions for reducing the use of them.

In this lesson plan from TropICSU[2], students explore issues of poverty, in particular how it is exacerbated by climate change, and the measures needed to manage it, using the guidelines provided by the United Nations Development Programme (UNDP) for the sustainable development goals (SDGs).

This lesson plan from TropICSU[3] provides an introduction to climate change. Students analyze the climate change risk profile for South Africa, including climate impacts on major sectors of the country: agriculture, water resources, human health, ecosystems, energy, infrastructure, and disasters.

Sustainability Innovations

The M.K. Gandhi Institute for Nonviolence[4] is working to extend the legacy of Mahatma Gandhi. Two of the main projects of the Institute are the School Climate Transformation, and Nonviolence in Prisons. How can these projects impact students such as yourselves?

Arun has used the Gandhi Worldwide Education Institute[5] to address poverty worldwide through the Institute's three founding principles. These principles are centered around proper education, family and community involvement, and equality for all people, regardless of their socioeconomic status. Visit the Institute[6] to view the three principles.

Review this article[7], which highlights diversity and inclusion within higher education in the U.S. After assessing the disparities shown among students in the U.S., how do you think this compares to other countries? Why is it important to have a society that is rooted in fundamental humanitarian values, independent of socioeconomic status?

Sustainability Career Pathways

Nonviolence Trainer. Nonviolence is not only recognized as an effective protest strategy; it is also increasingly being sought after as a more effective means of crisis prevention. Hospitals, nursing homes, prisons, and schools are all starting to recognize the value of nonviolent de-escalation in potentially violent situations. Want to become an expert in nonviolence, and train others to use these skills? Learn more about nonviolence, along with career and internship opportunities at the M.K. Gandhi Institute for Nonviolence.[8]

Microfinance Loan Officer. Microfinance is a proven tool for helping to create opportunities, and leveraging the resources of the poorest segment of humanity to help themselves. Read this article[9] to learn how to be a microfinance loan officer, or to help with policy or field development. Check out these databases: UNJobs[10] and DevEx[11] to find jobs and internships.

Earth's Rights Advocate. True harmony with the Earth means that like all humans, the Earth also has its rights recognized and protected. There is a growing field in expanding rights to the planet, through the use of law and advocacy. Learn more about this budding new field here.[12]

---

1 https://www.calacademy.org/educators/lesson-plans/fossil-fuels-chocolate-chip-mining

2 https://tropicsu.org/lesson-plan-poverty/

3 https://tropicsu.org/lesson-plan-climate-change-impacts-south-africa/

4 https://gandhiinstitute.org/

5 https://www.gandhiforchildren.org/about/

6 https://www.gandhiforchildren.org/about/

7 https://www2.ed.gov/rschstat/research/pubs/advancing-diversity-inclusion.pdf

8 https://gandhiinstitute.org/

9 https://www.investopedia.com/articles/07/microfinance.asp

10 https://unjobs.org/

11 https://www.devex.com/jobs/

12 https://earthrights.org/about/

YouthForce Carries on His Legacy

Dr. A.T. Ariyaratne, Tiara and Niven Ganegama , Youth Force / Sarvodaya, Sri Lanka

Call to Action

Support Sarvodaya's work of building and sustaining healthy communities in Sri Lanka: www.sarvodaya.org

Values

- Compassion
- Commitment
- Shramadama
- Community Service
- Environmentalism

Lessons Learned

Helping one person see the truth can lead to the whole world opening their eyes to the truth.

Real change is born out of inspiration. Be an example. Inspire people to be better!

When faced with war, take a stand for peace.

Niven and Tiara Ganegama were born in the United States, where their father was working.

Although Sri Lanka was in a state of war, their parents decided to move the family back there so that the children could be near their grandparents. Niven and Tiara's grandfather, Dr. Ari Ariyaratne, led peace marches that eventually led to an end to the country's civil war. Now in their teens, Niven and Tiara are carrying on their grandfather's legacy in a variety of ways, from collecting books and school supplies for children in a remote village, to helping village children learn English, to sponsoring tree planting programs through YouthForce, an organization they founded to help improve the lives of the people in Sri Lanka. Dr. Ari's message has always been the same: by awakening one person, it could lead to awakening a whole family; then an entire community; and one day, even the world. "I'll never forget my grandfather's message," Niven says. "Awakening, caring for others, sharing our gifts. That is his legacy."

Language Arts

What is the importance of service? Conduct research on the importance of getting young children involved in helping others. Then create a 5-7 minute video in which you share your findings and encourage others to get involved with charitable work. (Hints: look up the concept of empathy; but also look at the practical skills people who work at nonprofits need to develop).

Working in groups of 3-5 people, create a 10–15-minute presentation about the effects of climate change in Sri Lanka, especially the 2004 tsunami. Research the economic, social, and environmental consequences of the tsunami, and the recovery process. (How long it has taken? How much money has it cost? What role have nonprofits played in the recovery of the country?) Dr. Ari's organization, Sarvodaya, won an award for their involvement in the recovery efforts after the tsunami. What was their role during the recovery? Why did they win this award?

How do people learn a new language? Write a research paper in which you explore how a new language is learned, and why Youth Force's involvement in teaching English while engaging children in environmentally friendly practices is a great approach to learning a new academic skill while also learning how to take environmental action in their community.

STEM Activities

Sri Lanka is one of the biodiversity hotspots in the world, but its environmental ecosystems are being threatened by climate change. Research one species or type of ecosystem present in Sri Lanka and learn about how climate change is affecting it. Are there any Sri Lankan policies that are helping to reduce the impact of climate change on this species or ecosystem? If not, what are some policies the government could implement to reduce the impact?

Climate change and extreme weather affect Sri Lanka at large, but farmers and agricultural workers face the worst consequences. Research agricultural industries in Sri Lanka and learn how climate change is impacting it. How might the success or failure of these agricultural businesses affect the country's economy?

Identify a problem in your community like Niven and Tiara did, and then create a project to address it. Maybe you would like to organize a tree planting effort, or a reading program to help improve literacy rates. How would you carry out your plan? As an option, you might want to connect with your school administration or local government to help you expand the effort.

Read this article[1] about a cargo ship carrying dangerous chemicals that sank off the coast of Sri Lanka, causing an environmental disaster. What was the impact of the cargo sinking? How many pounds of microplastics leaked into the ocean? One study[2] estimated that Sri Lankans release 3 kilograms of plastic waste per capita each year. How many Sri Lankans would it take to produce the amount of plastic waste spilled from the cargo ship in a single day?

Sustainability Innovations

Review the Youth Force Website[3]. Does it accurately present the work that Niven and Tiara have accomplished? Why is it important to get funding and support for small nonprofits, and spread awareness of their success?

In addition to the voices of youth, it is important to have support from businesses and organizations. The National Cleaner Production Centre Sri Lanka[4] is a leader in addressing sustainability goals through improved resource productivity.

Sarvodaya[5] is one of the largest and most unique organizations in Sri Lanka. Their practices are based on the concept of *Shramadama* (sharing of one's time, thoughts, labor, and energy). Review the organization and compare its core principles with U.S.-based charitable organizations.

Sustainability Career Pathways

English Teacher. English teachers are in high demand all around the world. And English opens up many doors, making this a good subject to teach. Any subject can incorporate sustainability education-- English, history, social studies, and other subjects too. Here's a good guide [6] on how to become a teacher.

International Sustainable Development Officer. Sarvodaya is a leader in sustainable development in Sri Lanka. Many international organizations are increasingly important in helping with community and regional development around the globe. Read this primer to learn more[7].

Hydrologist. Hydrologists play a role in finding and researching water availability and quality. Sustaining the availability of clean, fresh water--especially with increasing climate change--is a challenge. Learn how you can help here[8].

1 https://www.npr.org/2021/06/05/1003445739/the-ship-sinking-off-sri-lanka-looks-like-a-lasting-environmental-disaster

2 https://onlinelibrary.wiley.com/action/doSearch?ContribAuthorStored=Samarasinghe%2C+Keshan

3 https://youth-force-sri-lanka.business.site/#testimonials

4 https://www.ncpcsrilanka.org/

5 https://www.sarvodaya.org/

6 https://www.teachercertificationdegrees.com/become/

7 https://www.netimpact.org/careers/international-development/big-picture

8 https://www.thebalancecareers.com/hydrologist-525671

VII

EACH ONE TEACH ONE

Emerging Island Leaders

These dedicated young people are a shining example of how we can imagine a more sustainable world. Let's get to work! It's going to take all of us working together. The planet is counting on us, and so are our children.

TED DANSON

A Multicultural Dreamer

Taynara Goncalves, MV Youth Leadership Initiative
Martha's Vineyard / Brazil

Call to Action

Learn how multicultural youth are becoming leaders of a sustainable world: www.MVYLI.org

Values

- Persistence
- Determination
- Generosity
- Resilience
- Compassion

Lessons Learned

Cultural diversity enriches a community. Instead of fearing those we don't know, we should make an effort to get to know them and embrace what they have to offer.

Dreams are built on hard work, persistence, and resilience. Every day ask yourself: What am I working toward today?

Challenges are opportunities to learn and grow. When you face a challenge, ask yourself: What can I learn from this? How will this help me grow?

Taynara Goncalves has always dreamed of being a doctor -- ever since she was a very young girl living in a little village in Brazil.

It was hard to earn a living there, so when she was three years old, her family moved to Martha's Vineyard, an island off the coast of Massachusetts, because her father thought he could find work there and create a better life for his family. It wasn't always easy for Taynara—some of the local people resented new immigrants and feared that their presence might limit their own economic opportunities. But others offered support. Learning about the Martha's Vineyard Youth Leadership Initiative was a turning point for Taynara. There she found friends, mentors, and guidance toward her unwavering goal. Today she works as a medical assistant in the Island Health Care Center, and is preparing to fulfill her dream by applying to medical school and becoming a doctor.

Language Arts

What is multiculturalism? Create a presentation in which you explain the concept, and the benefits of being multicultural, not only to the economy and to society, but also to a person's brain. Finish your presentation with a reflection on how we can use multiculturalism as a tool to create a more sustainable world.

One of the shocks Taynara suffered when she went back to her village in Brazil for a visit was to see not only the poverty, but the ravages climate change was wreaking in the community. Write a research paper on the types of climate found in Brazil, and how climate change has affected them. Don't forget to look into how these environmental changes have affected the economy, the people living in the region, and what can be done to mitigate some of the damage.

Taynara went from a warm, sometimes dry climate to Martha's Vineyard, which has extreme winters and very warm summers. Despite these geographical differences, both areas are facing threats because of climate change. Write a compare and contrast essay about Martha's Vineyard and Mantenópolis, Brazil, where Taynara was born: How has climate change affected each of these places? What challenges are the people who live there facing? What is being done to mitigate the damage? What else can be done?

Write an essay about the effects that being multicultural has on brain development and brain activity. Use the information from your paper to create a short oral presentation summarizing your findings.

STEM Activities

Multicultural youth have been at the forefront of the development of greater opportunities in many different fields.

- **Research the percentage of individuals in the following professions** who had multicultural backgrounds between 2000-2010; then research the figures from 2010-2020, and compare them.
    - Doctors:
    - Physician Assistants:
    - Sustainability Consulting:
- **Interpret the percentages** and the underlying factors that may be influencing this disparity.

Ever since she was a little girl, Taynara knew she wanted to become a medical professional. In this activity[1], students will simulate a doctor's office, playing the roles of physician, nurse, patients, and timekeeper, with the objective of improving the waiting time for patients. Students will use engineering principles and engineering design approaches to suggest how the process could be improved by collecting, graphing, and analyzing data.

It is no secret that climate change can have an impact on our health. Research and describe the impacts of changing climate conditions on human health, with an emphasis on the effects on vulnerable populations. Create a visual model of the various health implications arising from climate change. The activity can be found here[2].

Due to the origin and spread of Covid-19, there has been an increase in racism and xenophobia directed toward people of Asian descent. In March 2021 a new spike of the Covid-19 P.1 variant appeared, which has been largely traced back to Brazil. In this activity[3], students will create and prioritize questions about Covid-19, and will evaluate scientific and/or technical information from multiple authoritative sources, assessing the evidence and the usefulness of each source for answering their questions. Because there have been documented cases of unfounded and harmful racially-driven responses to the outbreak, students will also discuss appropriate and inappropriate responses to this new development.

Sustainability Innovations

Different fields of work are not necessarily mutually exclusive. The University of Washington Sustainability[4] has created two new initiatives that connect health care academics and operations with sustainability opportunities and challenges. How can similar initiatives be used to assist other institutional programs?

Should it be a requirement for physicians to lead environmental sustainability efforts? This 2017 article[5] in the AMA Journal of Ethics addresses this issue and targets sustainable business models.

In addition to the need for collaboration within the fields of medicine and sustainability, delivery of healthcare can be a major contributor to fossil fuels in the UK. This article[6] discusses this issue and the ability to address environmental, social, and financial constraints. Should healthcare facilities be required to follow sustainability-focused policy and codes.

Sustainability Career Pathways

Doctor. Being a doctor, and helping to heal the sick is an honorable path, especially when the doctor recognizes the value of preventive medicine and has a holistic awareness of how the environment plays a key role in one's health and well-being. This includes broader issues such as the adverse effects of air, water, and soil pollution as well as elements in an individual's immediate environment--diet, toxins in the home, and access to green space. Unfortunately, too few doctors have a clear understanding of the importance of environmental health. Are you interested in becoming a doctor? Here's[7] how to do it step-by-step. And here[8] is an article exploring how medical schools are starting to better incorporate the principles of sustainability and environmental health into their curricula.

Environmental Health Advocate. If you're interested in health, but not in practicing medicine, another path is to become an advocate for environmental health[9]. There are many organizations working to reduce toxic exposure, defend and clean up toxified cities, improve nutrition, expand access to green spaces, and so on. Is this the field for you? Here[10] is an introduction to the field of environmental health.

High School Guidance Counselor. Taynara's dream was almost crushed before it began, due to some bad advice she was given by her high school guidance counselor. But good guidance counselors serve as mentors and guides for young people, and can play a pivotal role in shaping their ambitions and dreams--including a dream for a sustainable future. If you like mentoring young people, this may be the path for you. Here[11] is an introduction to becoming a school counselor.

1 https://www.teachengineering.org/activities/view/usf_healthcare_lesson01_activity1
2 https://www.niehs.nih.gov/health/assets/docs_a_e/a_student_exploration_of_the_impacts_of_climate_change_on_human_health_in_the_united_states_lesson_plan_508.pdf
3 https://www.nsta.org/novel-coronavirus-whats-real-story
4 https://green.uw.edu/sam#:~:text=Sustainability%20and%20Medicine%20(SAM)%20is,efficiency%2C%20and%20strengthen%20stakeholder%20relationships
5 https://journalofethics.ama-assn.org/article/are-physicians-obliged-lead-environmental-sustainability-efforts-health-care-organizations/2017-12
6 https://www.rcpjournals.org/content/futurehosp/7/2/102
7 https://www.learnhowtobecome.org/doctor/
8 http://earthed.info/wp-content/uploads/2021/04/SOW17_chap24_medical-ed.pdf
9 https://www.healthypeople.gov/2020/topics-objectives/topic/environmental-health
10 https://www.apha.org/topics-and-issues/environmental-health
11 https://www.teachercertificationdegrees.com/careers/school-counselor/

Be the Change

Chris Aring, MV Youth Leadership Initiative
Martha's Vineyard

Call to Action

Learn about how Chris's idea is changing lives: check out the Institute's SustainabilityisFun.com

Values

- Creative
- Generous
- Leadership
- Environmentalist

Lessons Learned

Innovation and technology can help better lives not only by providing high-paying careers, but as tools for positive social change.

Challenge those in your community to use their skills to help you change the world: they may surprise you!

When you're looking for a great idea, often the best thing to do is what comes naturally. *Overthinking sometimes kills creativity.*

When it comes to the need for change, time is of the essence: the sooner you act, the more lives you will be able to impact in a positive way.

Chris Aring had always known that he wanted to find a way to use technology to serve humanity.

When he heard that Gandhi's grandson, Arun, was going to speak at a Youth Leadership Summit on Martha's Vineyard, he was inspired: and when Arun Gandhi asked the Stone Soup Leadership Institute to find a way to share their innovative educational tools with students in India, Chris knew he wanted to be involved. That was the first step in his journey toward working with others to create digital tools that could be used to not only teach students about the importance of sustainability, but also to create ways to use technology to help youth get jobs in this emerging field.

Language Arts

What is leadership? What are the traits of an effective leader? Write a personal essay in which you explore the meaning of the word and what it means to you in your own life. How can you become a leader and inspire those around you to work to better the world?

Imagine you had the opportunity to create a website to educate people on sustainability and climate change issues. What would you call it? What type of content would you put in it? Choose a topic related to sustainability or climate change that interests you, and create the content for an imaginary website. You must include the following: an "About Us" page, a "FAQs" page (for this one, focus on questions about the issue you have chosen), a "How to Get Involved" page, and a "News" page, in which you will post real updates on the cause you are interested in.

Chris was inspired by Mahatma Gandhi's words to his grandson: "Be the change you want to see in the world." Create a 3–5-minute video in which you explain how you plan to "be the change." Finish your video with a call to action to inspire others to become the change they think the world needs.

STEM Activities

As an extension of the second Language Arts activity above, use the content you created to build a real website. You can use website builders such as Wix.com[1], Squarespace.com[2], or build it from scratch using HTML and CSS[3].

Chris aspires to use technology to help humanity. What is one problem facing the world today that technology can help solve? Research and design a type of technology (app, device, technological process, etc.) that can be used to help solve this problem. Present your ideas to the class. You can also set up a way to pitch your idea to potential funders.

Chris began his innovative processes by participating in Hack-a-thons that were focused strictly on design. Could your classroom benefit from participating in a Hack-a-thon? This article[4] details the steps necessary to host a Hack-a-thon, and offers tips for how to make the event a success.

Sustainability Innovations

Technological innovations in sustainability have gained increasing attention with the climate crisis. This 2019 article[5] highlights sustainability innovations that could become important in our future. Which of these innovations has advanced the most since 2021, and is best positioned to help us build a sustainable future?

Chris began thinking about the intersection of technology and sustainability as a youth at his first Sustainability Summit. This intersection is at the forefront of sustainable innovations and conferences. The two main forums for such innovation are tech trade shows like CES[6], or sustainable tech conferences such as The International Conference on Sustainable Technology and Development[7]. Identify a successful sustainable innovation from each of these events, and explain how each of them can contribute to a more sustainable future.

Sustainability Career Pathways

Environmental Engineer. As an engineering student, Chris can choose from one of many paths for helping make the world more sustainable. One is as an environmental engineer, which is an engineer that uses his or her training to help ensure that industrial activities do not cause pollution, and to help find solutions to environmental problems. If this sounds like a path for you, this introduction[8] to environmental engineering is very informative.

Website Designer and Manager. The internet is now a primary educational tool and means of communication. At the heart of every organization or movement there is a website. Website designers and managers find ways to make them easy to navigate and engaging for visitors. This is a field that offers boundless employment opportunities. Interested in designing or maintaining websites? Read more about the specifics here[9], and a day in the life of a web manager here[10].

App Designer. Increasingly, people aren't just exploring the world through the internet, but also through numerous smartphone apps. This is another potential way to use technology to help educate and encourage more sustainable living, from designing anything from a carbon calculator to apps that help you borrow or buy used instead of buying new stuff[11]. Want to get into App Design? Here's a good starting point.[12]

1 https://www.wix.com/

2 https://www.squarespace.com/

3 https://www.khanacademy.org/computing/computer-programming/html-css

4 https://medium.com/innovation-machine/hacking-the-hackathon-40c109c1a6ea

5 https://www.mckinsey.com/business-functions/sustainability/our-insights/sustainability-blog/these-9-technological-innovations-will-shape-the-sustainability-agenda-in-2019

6 https://www.ces.tech/Topics/5G-and-Internet-of-Things-(IoT)/Sustainability.aspx

7 https://www.elsevier.com/events/conferences/international-conference-on-sustainable-technology-and-development

8 https://www.livescience.com/48390-environmental-engineering.html

9 https://www.zippia.com/web-manager-jobs/

10 https://www.careerprofiles.com/blog/one-day-in-the-life-of-a-web-content-manager/

11 https://www.cnet.com/news/10-apps-that-help-you-be-more-sustainable-in-every-area-of-life/

12 https://learnappmaking.com/how-to-make-an-app/

From Recycling to Resale: Rebag

Kassandra Castillo Cruz, Kavani Handmade
Puerto Rico/New York

Call to Action

Invest in young people to help them realize their dreams.
Visit the Vieques Youth Leadership Initiative: www.vyli.org.
Check out Kassandra's company on Instagram: kavani_handmade.

Values

- Vision
- Determination
- Persistence
- Generosity
- Environmentalism

Lessons Learned

Dreams can come true through effort, hard work, and creativity.

Building - or rebuilding - a home is a community effort that will benefit the whole community. The same is true for a country and for the world.

You can find treasures everywhere, if you are willing to look in places others may regard as being worthless.

When Kassandra Castillo Cruz was 14 years old, a friend invited her to join a new youth leadership program, the Vieques Youth Leadership Initiative (VYLI). When she was asked, "What is your dream for your life, your island, and your community?" Kassandra declared that she wanted to become a top model -- a dream that due to her persistence and hard work eventually came true. But that wasn't her main goal: her main goal was to get a good education and then return to her island so she could help others find ways to realize their dreams too.

Today she is head of operations for Rebag Infinity, a $50 million worldwide resale retailer that gives consumers the chance to buy and sell back their luxury handbags, giving them a much longer life, and keeping them out of the trash.

Language Arts

What is the impact of the fashion industry on the environment? Choose one branch of this industry -- make-up, clothing, handbags, shoes, accessories, etc. -- and write a research essay about the manufacturing and distribution practices in the industry, and their cost to the environment.

Create a series of Tik Tok videos in which you explain how to keep up with fashion in an environmentally responsible way. Offer advice and resources, from websites where you can exchange or repurpose merchandise, to practices that can extend the life of a purse, shoes, or clothing.

Hurricane Maria was a devastating event for the island of Puerto Rico. Create a presentation in which you explain the ecological damage caused by the hurricane and how it affected the economy, culture, and social fabric of the island. Finish your presentation by suggesting ways in which people can help in the ongoing reconstruction efforts.

Create a presentation on the effects the U.S. military base has had on the island of Vieques: How did the base affect the island's environment, its economy, and the people who lived there? What efforts were necessary to end the use of the island as a military base? What is being done to restore the island, its economy, and its people?

STEM Activities

Even if you aren't interested in fashion or shopping, you are part of the fashion industry because you wear clothing every day, and will buy and wear a large number of clothes throughout your lifetime. Many natural resources are used to produce our clothes. Watch this video on the lifecycle of a basic t-shirt[1]. How can the industry be regulated to be more sustainable?

Collect data about your clothing at home, then use the data you collected to calculate approximately how many resources went into making the clothes (water, land, and carbon). How much of the world's resources have gone into creating the clothes you don't wear? What could you do with them to keep them in use and to minimize their environmental impact?

In September 2017, Hurricane Maria became regarded as the worst natural disaster to ever hit Puerto Rico, causing billions of dollars' worth of damages and leaving many of its people without power. In this activity, students will investigate the connection between climate change and extreme weather events. What are some ways that the fashion industry and consumer habits are contributing to climate change, and ultimately the formation of some of these natural disasters?

Sustainability Innovations

These companies have followed paths similar to Kassandra's, by developing sustainable advancements in the fashion industry:

- **Mango Materials**[2] produces bio-polyester that can be used as an alternative to the polyester currently being used in the fashion industry.
- **Orange Fiber**[3] is an Italian-based company that created the first sustainable fabric by reusing citrus-based by-products.
- **Paptic**[4] uses sustainably sourced wood fibers to create a sustainable alternative to the plastic used in packaging.
- **BioGlitz**[5] is a company that has created the world's first biodegradable glitter.

In addition to sustainable products, some companies have also pledged to take action in their communities and help the environment. Patagonia[6] is one of the global leaders among businesses who prioritize the materials they use, and environmental and social responsibility programs.

The world of fashion needs more companies to promote reuse and sustainability within the industry. This article by The Good Trade[7] highlights 10 impactful ways to recycle and repurpose clothing.

Sustainability Career Pathways

Reused Retail. Did you know there are more than 25,000 resale stores in the United States[8], and that selling used stuff is an $18 billion industry? Reselling is not only a useful business, but a sustainable one too--helping to keep good clothing, furniture, books, and other items out of the garbage and in people's hands and homes. Working for a company like ReBag or ThredUp, setting up a consignment store, or managing a thrift shop are all good ways to help your community and the planet. Curious to learn more? Here's an article about what it's like to work at a thrift store[9].

Resilience Officer. As climate change intensifies, more cities, regions, and islands have hired chief resilience officers (CROs) to oversee adaptation to and mitigation of the effects of climate change, such as hurricanes, coastal flooding, fires, and increased migration. If this sounds interesting to you, read more about what CROs do here[10].

Sustainable Fashion Industry. New clothes will continue to be made, of course, but they can be made sustainably. Materials like organic cotton or recycled plastics can be used, and designed in a way that the clothing at the end of its (ideally long) lifespan can be recycled or composted (for example, by not mixing natural and synthetic fibers). Here is a great introduction to the field[11]. And an article[12] on the many ways sustainability is shaping the future of the fashion industry.

1 https://www.youtube.com/watch?v=BiSYoeqb_VY
2 https://www.mangomaterials.com/
3 http://orangefiber.it/en/
4 https://paptic.com/
5 https://www.bioglitz.co/
6 https://www.patagonia.com/our-footprint/
7 https://www.thegoodtrade.com/features/how-to-recycle-and-repurpose-clothing
8 https://www.census.gov/newsroom/stories/thrift-store-day.html
9 https://www.mentalfloss.com/article/625945/thermacell-mosquito-repellent-lantern?utm_content=infinitescroll1
10 https://www.rockefellerfoundation.org/blog/what-a-chief-resilience-officer-does/
11 https://en.wikipedia.org/wiki/Sustainable_fashion
12 https://www.thegoodtrade.com/features/sustainable-fashion-jobs

How Can I Help?

Josue A. Cruz, J.D. , Vieques Youth Leadership Initiative, Vieques, Puerto Rico

Call to Action

Urge your congresspeople to vote for urgent funds to rebuild Puerto Rico after Hurricane Maria.
Support Josue's social justice & legal practice: Facebook: @abogadojcruz; abogadojosuecruz@gmail.com

Values

- Justice
- Compassion
- Solidarity
- Determination
- Cooperation

Lessons Learned

Be empathetic of the plight of others, and offer to help.

When making a decision always ask yourself: What is the legacy I want to leave behind? Then act accordingly.

The four most powerful words you can say are "How can I help?"

When Josue Cruz was 14, he was invited to serve as a youth delegate to a Youth Leadership Summit being held in his home of Vieques, Puerto Rico.

When he arrived there, his first question was, "How can I help?" Then he saw a poster that said "What is your dream for your life, for your island, and for the world?" and he realized that for the first time in his life, he was being encouraged to dream big. "My dream for my life is to become a lawyer," he said to himself. That was the beginning of a challenging journey--and an illustrious career--for Josue. After working very hard, he became a lawyer, and his first clients were the people in Vieques, whose land had been confiscated by the U.S. Navy. Josue helped them to reclaim their land: it was a long, arduous process and he spent many days pleading their cases. Today Josue lives in Texas, where he is defending the rights of border wall refugees from Central America. Now 30 years old, Josue loves seeing all the young people he has mentored at the Institute's Sustainability Summits who are pursuing their dreams. The work he started goes on! To Josue, this is life's greatest reward.

Language Arts

How has climate change affected Caribbean islands, particularly Puerto Rico? Create a timeline showing how the weather in the region has changed in the past 50 years, and how those changes have affected the economy, health, and quality of life of the people in this region. Make a digital poster presenting your findings and share it with your class.

Write a personal narrative in which you explore the concept of empathy and how you could help those less fortunate in your community. Choose a particular issue that has resulted in people being treated unfairly, and using specific examples to explain how you would fight the injustice.

Vieques was home to a military base for three generations. Working in groups of 3-5 people, create a poster on one of the following topics: 1. Sonic pollution, heavy metal pollution, economic restrictions imposed by the military base, and their consequences; 2. The importance of learning a second language in school; and 3. What is a nonviolent protest? Using your posters, create a Gallery Walk[1] with the rest of your class.

Write an essay comparing the treatment of the people of Vieques by the U.S Navy with the treatment of refugees at the southern U.S. border wall by U.S immigration officials.

☀ STEM Activities

Research the rates for various diseases (cancer, cardiovascular, diabetes) in Vieques, Puerto Rico, and the Caribbean as a whole. Create a graph highlighting the distribution between regions. Do you see any trends in the data? Are the rates for some illnesses higher in Vieques than the average rates for Puerto Rico overall, or the Caribbean? Why do you think that is?

Research how the effects of the U.S. Navy testing still affect the people of Vieques to this day. What can the Navy, or the U.S. government, do to mitigate these impacts? What would the cost be of implementing such a solution? Where might that fit into the annual U.S. budget?

Research the economy of the island since the departure of the U.S Navy from Vieques in 2003. What are the main industries present on the island today? What are the sources of income for the residents? Graph the income distribution among demographics - local vs. mainland U.S. What percentage of the population falls below the federal income poverty line? Use the U.S Census report for Puerto Rico[2] as a guide.

How much land was sold to the U.S Navy? How much did the Navy pay the locals for their land? What is the land being used for today, and how much is it worth? What percentage of the land was returned to the people of Vieques?

☀ Sustainability Innovations

Earth Justice[3] is one of the premier nonprofit public interest environmental law organizations in the world. Review some of their recent victories and learn how they are contributing to creating a more sustainable world.

Earth Justice is one of the 20 environmentally-focused organizations specializing in law and policy that are highlighted in this article[4]. Why is it important to understand the scope of law as it pertains to environmental and social justice?

In addition to addressing issues of environmental law, it is important to protect organizations that specialize in solving sustainability issues. The Environmental Defense Center[5] specializes in providing legal counsel to sustainability-focused organizations.

After Hurricane Maria, Vieques became a hotspot for organizations focused on disaster preparation and community empowerment. Vieques Lov[6]e is one of the major organizations focused on preparing communities for disasters.

☀ Sustainability Career Pathways

Environmental Lawyer. Lawyers are central in the fight for a sustainable future, whether addressing local, national, or global challenges. Perhaps this is the path for you? Here is a brief overview of what an environmental lawyer is[7], how to become one[8], and a guide to careers in environmental law[9].

Disarmament Advocate. According to the U.N. Office for Disarmament Affairs (UN ODA), disarmament is "vital for sustainable development and global survival." The U.N., national governments, and NGOs all have jobs supporting the global reduction of arms. Do you want to help with this essential fight? Learn more at UN ODA, and review job opportunities[10].

Immigration Services Officer. Climate change will increase cross-border movement and immigration. Helping people adjust to life in a new country and navigate the difficult legal challenges involved is a noble career path. Investigate immigration services here[11].

---

1 https://www.youtube.com/watch?v=pSt5echeRrM
2 https://www.census.gov/quickfacts/PR
3 https://earthjustice.org/our_work/victories
4 https://www.humanrightscareers.com/magazine/20-international-ngos-defending-environmental-rights/
5 https://www.environmentaldefensecenter.org/mission/
6 https://viequeslove.org/
7 https://www.environmentalscience.org/career/environmental-lawyer
8 https://www.sierraclub.org/sierra/cool-schools-2017/how-be-environmental-lawyer
9 https://hls.harvard.edu/content/uploads/2008/07/full-working-draft.pdf
10 https://www.unjobnet.org/organizations/UN ODA
11 https://study.com/articles/Careers_in_Immigration_Services_Education_Requirements_and_Job_Options.html

Nature's Little Secrets

Feliza Fenty, VG Youth Leadership Initiative
Virgin Gorda, BVI

Call to Action

Learn more about the Virgin Gorda Youth Leadership Initiative: www.vgyli.org and Feliza's project: www.preetbird.com

Values

- Empathy
- Leadership
- Community Service
- Environmentalism

Lessons Learned

Only by conquering your fears can you build a better world for yourself. Have the courage, and then jump!

Knowledge is power. Knowledge allows you to truly see. Once you see the truth, you can go almost anywhere, and do almost anything you set your mind to.

Learn from those who came before you, your neighbors, and your peers. Everyone has a valuable lesson to teach you if you are willing to listen.

True strength comes from the ability to adapt to ever-changing circumstances. Learn to be resilient, and you will become stronger than you ever thought possible.

Growing up on the tiny island of Virgin Gorda in the British Virgin Islands, Feliza Fenty saw income inequality close up from an early age.

Her parents both had a good education and were able to provide her with a comfortable middle-class lifestyle: but many of her friends in school were not as lucky. When she was 16 years old and she learned about work being done by the Vieques Youth Leadership Initiative in nearby Puerto Rico, she was inspired and energized. "If they can do it, we can do it too!" she said to herself, and she soon convinced some of her friends that she was right. That was the moment that led eventually to her career in public service. Today she uses her organizing and communication skills to work with women on Virgin Gorda to teach them how to create better, healthier lives for themselves and their families.

Language Arts

Write a personal essay in which you answer Feliza's question: "What is your dream for your community and the world?" Then go a little further: What do you plan to do to make it happen?

How has climate change affected the Caribbean Islands? Their people? Their economy? Create a series of short videos explaining this issue, and finish with a call to action. Ask people to do something ,and offer suggestions as to how they can begin to get involved.

A big problem in the Caribbean is the destruction of the ecosystem by the tourism industry. For example, coral reefs are decimated every year by uneducated motor boaters who anchor their boats on the reefs, destroying the very coral they came to "admire." Write a research essay on the threat that tourism poses to these ecosystems.

Is there a way to avoid the destruction that uneducated tourists cause to an ecosystem? Working in groups of 3-4 people, create an information campaign (2 videos, 3 posters, and 2 posts in social media platforms of your choice) about sustainable tourism: what it is, why it is important, and where to find information about environmentally friendly tourism companies.

How serious is the issue of inequality in the Caribbean islands? Why is the distribution of wealth in this area of the world so unfair? Who is responsible? More important: How does inequality affect the residents of the island? How about the environment in the region? Create a series of short videos (a total of five) in which you answer these questions. Plan one video for question, and make each video no longer than three minutes.

STEM Activities

Coral reefs are one of the most diverse ecosystems on the planet, yet nearly two-thirds of the reefs in the Caribbean are threatened by human activities. In this module[1], students will use real data to investigate the consequences of rising sea temperature on coral reefs. They will also consider the importance of coral reefs in their own lives.

Sargassum is a seaweed that provides a home for a variety of marine species, but is also known to cover local beaches with a foul-smelling, unsightly organic waste that threatens not only the environment but the tourism industry throughout the Caribbean. Conduct research on sargassum, both its economic importance and its impact on the environment. Based on your findings, do you think sargassum is an invasive species, or a vital component of an ecosystem? What are some ways we can reduce its impact on the environment but maintain its benefits?

Growing up in the British Virgin Islands, Feliza saw the effects of income inequality on the people around her. Research and find income data for households in British Virgin Islands and separate it evenly into quintiles[2]. Then watch this tutorial video[3] to help you graph a Lorenz curve and calculate the gini coefficient based on the data.

Sustainability Innovations

Green VI[4] is a nonprofit organization that is currently focused on improving net sustainable impact, and developing innovations to help combat the sustainable issues that the BVI and the U.S. Virgin Islands face. Green VI includes innovations such as organic photovoltaics, farm pods, upcycling, among many other sustainable innovations.

In addition to the battle against climate change, the British Virgin Islands is host to a community that thrives through collaboration. The Unite BVI Foundation[5] focuses on community enrichment, environmental conservation, and the empowerment of entrepreneurs. Driven by their slogan, "Unite by name, unite by nature" the Unite BVI Foundation helps to find short-term fixes and long-term solutions for the people of the British Virgin Islands.

In addition to environmentally-focused issues, the people of the British Virgin Islands have to deal with an increased risk of disease. Bugout BVI[6] is a nonprofit organization that helps to protect the Virgin Gorda community from diseases spread by Aedes Aegypti mosquitoes, such as Zika, Dengue, Chikunguya, and the West Nile Virus.

Sustainability Career Pathways

Sustainable Tourism. Tourism can be unsustainable if it includes global travel, but it can also help to inspire deeper connection to the Earth and other cultures. Today there is a growing sustainable tourism sector, one that embeds environmental knowledge in tours, makes hotels greener, encourages more local experiences, and so on. There are many ways to be part of this industry, from tour operator, to travel guide, from hotelier, to turning part of your home into an Airbnb and offering green tours of your town. If this is a path for you, read these 10 tips on how to make a career in sustainable tourism[7].

Community Organizer. As Feliza discovered, engaging one's community around important environmental and social challenges is an important career path and type of community service. There are many programs to learn organizing, from online courses (such as this one[8]), to one-year environmental organizing field schools like Green Corps.[9]

Environmental Journalist. Many people who love to write make a career as a full-time journalist. Some dedicate their writing to chronicling the many environmental problems we face, as well as exploring the many innovative solutions to our sustainability challenges that are being developed. Some are freelancers, pitching stories to a variety of outlets. Others work full time for a news outlet, or with nonprofits, or even government offices. To learn more about this career, read here.[10] And here's a valuable resource: the Society of Environmental Journalists[11], which offers job boards, mentoring, annual conferences, and listservs for environmental journalists.

1 https://dataintheclassroom.noaa.gov/content/coral-bleaching
2 https://www.statisticshowto.com/quintile-definition/
3 https://www.khanacademy.org/economics-finance-domain/ap-microeconomics/ap-consumer-producer-surplus/inequality/v/gini-coefficient-and-lorenz-curve
4 https://greenvi.org/innovation/
5 https://www.unitebvi.com/our-work
6 https://www.bugoutbvi.org/about/about-bugout/
7 https://sustainability-leaders.com/ten-tips-sustainable-tourism-career/
8 https://www.coursera.org/learn/community-organizing
9 https://greencorps.org/
10 https://www.openschoolofjournalism.com/specializations/environmental-journalism
11 https://www.sej.org/

What Does Sustainability Mean to You?

Trevor Tanaka, Sustainable Hawaii Youth Leadership Initiative, Hawaii

Call to Action

To learn more about opportunities to learn and build a sustainable world visit:

- **sustainablehawaiitoolkit.com**
- **SustainWDN.com**
- **SustainabilityisFun.com**

Values

- Passionate
- Determined
- Persistent
- Resourceful
- Risktaker

Lessons Learned

Many ideas can be great ideas, but acting on them requires consistent effort and persistence.

Everyone's voice matters, regardless of their age, stature, or background.

Young people have the right to demand a good education.

It's important to address people who hold positions of power with both respect and confidence.

Trevor Tanaka grew up on the Big Island of Hawaii, and from an early age he was taught by his family to honor the land.

In middle school, he attempted to enter an essay writing competition that asked the question "What does sustainability mean to you?" When he realized that he didn't have an answer to that question, he figured out that it was because he hadn't been taught about sustainability in school. Knowing that other students needed to be taught about something so important, he worked with legislators to implement a law requiring all schools to teach Hawaiians how to live sustainably. But that wasn't enough for Trevor: he also went on to create an online toolkit making it possible for Hawaiians, and people in a number of other states, to find the best sustainability resources, listings for green jobs, and other useful information.

Now studying to achieve his MBA, he is also working with other members of the Stone Soup team to create a Sustainable Workforce Development Network --an online ecosystem to connect youth, educators, and companies who are dedicated to building a sustainable economy.

Language Arts

Write a resolution on a topic related to sustainability or climate that is important to you, and create a five-minute presentation to support your resolution. Practice your presentation in front of family and friends.

Invite your friends and family to participate in a brainstorming session in which you will come up with three ideas for implementing sustainability practices in your community. Then, as a group, start a letter-writing campaign to your elected officials, asking them to implement these practices.

Create an information campaign to educate other students in your community about sustainability: what it means, what efforts are being made in your community to make sustainability more feasible, and what kinds of sustainability projects would benefit your community.

STEM Activities

Research and rank 10 colleges based on the STEM, sustainability, and climate change courses offered.

Ask teachers or administrators at your school to offer STEM, sustainability, and climate change courses.

Research organizations that need volunteers and would be willing to partner with your school to start a sustainability initiative for the community (for example, a club or an internship program, or a community clean-up project).

Use SurveyMonkey to collect data about issues that are affecting your school or local community. Create a website to share that data, and use social media to educate your community on the most prevalent issues and to suggest some possible solutions.

Sustainability Innovations

Research to learn about resolutions that have been created by youth in your state, country, or in the world. Write a paper or create a presentation on your findings to your class.

Learn about the young people of Our Children's Trust who filed a lawsuit against the U.S. government, and Greta Thunberg's lawsuit concerning the UN Convention on the Rights of the Child. Based on what you learned through your research as well as your opinion, explain the importance of these lawsuits.

Have two students, or a group of students build an effective argument about a specific sustainability issue through research. Then hold a debate, with one student or group for and the other against the issue. Have the audience reflect on and discuss which argument was the most convincing, and why.

Hold a Model United Nations where students represent different countries at a climate change council. This online guide[1] may help in structuring the activity.

Sustainability Career Pathways

Environmental Educator. A surprising number of schools lack educators who are versed in sustainability and environmental issues. Educators who either indirectly incorporate sustainability, or directly introduce sustainability into the curriculum by teaching environmental studies, whether in schools or in other forums, are essential in helping future generations understand the environmental challenges we face--and their possible solutions. Learn more about this field here[2].

Environmental Lawyers. Environmental lawyers are also an essential part of the blue/green economy, and law is a great career path for protecting and restoring nature. Here are three resources for exploring this field:

- What is an Environmental Lawyer? [3]
- How To Be an Environmental Lawyer (Sierra Club) [4]
- A Trail Guide to Careers in Environmental Law (Harvard guide)[5]

Government Employee. The government plays an essential role in regulating and enforcing environmentally sustainable behavior. Working for a national or state government agency or local government can be a rewarding and useful career path: for example, working with the Environmental Protection Agency. The EPA employs 15,000 people around the United States and needs people with a variety of skills, from communications to computer programming. Want to learn more? Visit here.[6]

Legislative Staffer. Another important path is working for a senator or representative as part of their legislative staff. Representatives and senators drive new policies and start new bills. Working with them as a "staffer" can be fun and rewarding, and as you go up the ranks you could help in writing and driving a new piece of legislation. Does this sound like the path for you? Explore this introduction[7].

Elected Official. Finally, if you'd rather run for office than work for an elected official, that's a possible path too, though typically one starts by running for local office or working for an elected official to learn the ropes. Curious? Listen to this NPR story[8] to get a better sense of the process.

---

1 https://www.startthechange.eu/2019/11/07/caras-un/?lang=en

2 https://www.environmentalscience.org/career/environmental-educator

3 https://www.environmentalscience.org/career/environmental-lawyer

4 https://www.sierraclub.org/sierra/cool-schools-2017/how-be-environmental-lawyer

5 https://hls.harvard.edu/content/uploads/2008/07/full-working-draft.pdf

6 https://www.epa.gov/careers/why-work-epa

7 https://www.thebalancecareers.com/government-job-profile-congressional-staffer-1669626

8 https://www.npr.org/2019/10/15/770332855/how-to-run-for-office

STONE SOUP

LEADERSHIP INSTITUTE

Background

The Stone Soup Leadership Institute is a 501c3 nonprofit organization founded in 1997 on Martha's Vineyard. For over 25 years, the Institute has been a leader in developing dynamic educational tools, trainings, and initiatives that empower young people to become leaders of a more just, equitable and sustainable world.

The Stone Soup Model integrates Design Thinking, Systems Change, and Healthy Communities to build partnerships with business, education, government and civic leaders to maximizes public-private partnerships to train the next generation of youth to create a sustainable economy. We use the Stone Soup fable to invite everyone to share of their time, talents, and resources to support young people. We've received celebrity support to maximize the impact of our social media campaigns and have a positive impact on those who are on the frontlines, doing the work to fight climate change. We are leveraging our collective resources to nurture and support the brave young people around the world who are working so hard to make a safe, healthy, and sustainable future for life on this planet.

The Stone Soup Ed-Tech Platform scales up our 25 years of real-world experience, using our rich bilingual content and methodologies to train young people to become leaders in their communities. This values-based, video-enhanced, content-driven, blended experiential learning environment features resources that educate, engage, and connect people with sustainable solutions to empower the next generation of changemakers. Working directly with community-based programs, we've synthesized lessons we've learned along the way, and developed a grassroots model to train local leaders, exchange innovative solutions with others, and build resilient communities.

Stone Soup for a Sustainable World: Life Changing Stories of Young Heroes features the stories of 100 climate change trailblazers, environmental justice changemakers, educator champions, sustainable business leaders, intergenerational legacy figures, green inventors and entrepreneurs, and emerging island leaders from 38 countries, and 31 cities in the U.S. who are building a more just, equitable, and sustainable world.

The Stone Soup Climate Education Curriculum is a comprehensive library of dynamic educational tools for teachers to use in teaching their students using our books, videos and curricular material for Stone Soup for a Sustainable World: Life-Changing Stories of Young Heroes. It brings their stories to life with lesson plans that highlight values and the basic academic disciplines of Language Arts and STEM activities, as well as guidance toward sustainable career pathways. We incorporate best practices and sustainability innovations from 38 countries. This platform is aligned with the UN Sustainable Development Goals; NGIS (Next Gen STEM Standards); and state standards that fulfill state mandates.

Multifaceted Social Media Campaign. Each week we showcase one of the 200 stories featured in our books with a week-long series of posts that bring them to life. An Honor Roll and Call to Action invites people to support these efforts. These posts are featured on Facebook, Instagram, Twitter, and LinkedIn. Videos are featured on YouTube Safe for Kids.

SustainWDN™ Sustainable Workforce Development is a cutting-edge online platform that connects green companies with educators and guidance counselors in order to guide students toward sustainable career pathways. The SustainWDN™ Surveys collect data on green job projections to help local communities plan to build a sustainable regional economy. This proprietary program pairs our climate and sustainability-oriented curriculum with educational materials on present and future sustainable career pathways, while connecting these communities with businesses and mentors, in order to create a full-cycle professional development program. This community-based workforce development pipeline actively builds and strengthens public private partnerships to help communities keep up with the burgeoning blue-green economy and the estimated 10 million jobs that are going to be created in the next decade.

Professional Development Modules is a train-the-trainer program for teachers that has been developed in our sites. Our SustainWDN™ training program for guidance counselors is designed to help them help their students in navigating sustainable career pathways during the transition to a sustainable economy.

» ***Sustainable Career Mentor Initiative*** is a disruptive model designed to fast-track this emerging sustainability economy. We are seeking sustainability practitioners to serve as mentors to help inspire and guide the next generation in creating a greener, healthier, more productive world for all of us.

Stone Soup for the World: Life-Changing Stories of Everyday Heroes honors 100 people, organizations, and companies from 65 communities and 29 countries around the world. Walter Cronkite, who served as The Institute's chairperson for over a decade called it a "handbook for humanitarians" and "a road map for building a better world."

Pan Y Vino Para el Camino: Spanish Book and Curriculum: Actor/activist Edward James Olmos asked us to translate Stone Soup for the World into Spanish. We did so, and we launched this book at the first Latino Book Festival in Los Angeles, where we presented Olmos with the Institute's first Cesar Chavez Award.

Diversity & SEL (Social Emotional Learning) Education Curriculum: Piloted by the YMCA in eight states, this curriculum offers lesson plans for developing multicultural literacy, critical thinking and leadership development skills, and character education through social studies, service learning, and citizenship activities. The curriculum, which includes audio and video elements, is a structured two-year program used by educators, after-school programs, corporate mentors, volunteers, and churches. It has been used in more than 120 communities to prepare our next generation of leaders to address the economic, environmental, and social challenges of the 21st century.

Proceeds from our books support the Stone Soup Leadership Institute's mission. Over the last 25 years, the Institute has invested in training young people around the world to become leaders in their communities and the world. The Institute's ***Young Heroes Fund*** provides mentors, training, and financial support to assist these youth leaders in expanding their important work.

Youth & Community Leadership Initiatives: For over 25 years, the Institute has worked alongside ocean communities from Puerto Rico to Martha's Vineyard, from Hawaii to Rhode Island, from the British Virgin Islands to the Philippines. Our year-round youth community leadership initiatives have helped young people develop the skills they need to develop their personal, professional, and planetary goals through our Career Mentor & Job Shadow Day, and College Prep & Community Service programs, as well as our Sustainability Summits. Youth leaders from these communities created a 2020 Report for Sustainable Development that challenged their leaders to develop policies that balance protecting their communities' fragile ecosystems, providing for their families, creating opportunities for their children, and building a just, equitable, and sustainable future. Through this work we've inspired hundreds of underserved multicultural youth around the world to become effective leaders.

Measurable, Actionable Results Along with the Institute's educational programs, training, and career pipeline network in each of our partner sites, we offer carefully crafted surveys at various stages of our process to produce actionable metrics that allow community leaders to track progress, identify gaps and career tracks, and more (youth surveys, organizational surveys, business surveys, performance metrics). The Institute's ***Performance Metrics*** measure the program's impact on skills essential to the 21st century job market: communication, teamwork, conflict resolution, problem solving, adaptability, critical thinking, and project management skills.

Building Sustainable Communities: Case Studies Report

The Stone Soup Leadership Institute's 25 Year Journey

For over 25 years, the Institute has worked with leaders -- governors, senators, mayors and commissioners -- to develop strategic initiatives that support their vision of a sustainable world —from New England to Hawaii; Puerto Rico, the British Virgin Islands and the Philippines.

Massachusetts: From Climate Education to a Sustainable Workforce Development In Support of the Green New Deal & the Transition to a Sustainable Economy For over 20 years, the Institute has worked with communities on the Southeast Coast of Massachusetts and Rhode Island to prepare students for sustainable career pathways in the Blue Economy Corridor.

Martha's Vineyard: The Martha's Vineyard Commission conducted an extensive five-year community-wide planning process to determine the Island's needs and develop a vision for its future. Unfortunately, the comprehensive Island Plan didn't include young people. To ensure that young people's voices were heard, The Institute trained Martha's Vineyard youth with Vieques youth leaders to develop their ***2020 Sustainable Vision Reports: Challenging Leaders to Create Sustainable Policies.***

» Martha's Vineyard Commission: 2010-2018[1]

» MVYLI 5 Year Report[2]

» VIDEO Martha's Vineyard: Ocean Sustainability[3]

MVYLI youth leaders worked for a full year to research and understand the Island's Plan and then worked with the MV Commission's top cartographer to create a Sustainable Vineyard Map as a visible way to share their vision for how to create a sustainable Martha's Vineyard for future generations. During the Institute's Sustainability Summits and year-round youth-community leadership initiatives, these young people developed the skills, training, and experience they need to speak truth to power, and to challenge their leaders to create policies for adapting to climate change realities. They have represented their island communities at state, national, and global events like U.S. Secretary Kerry's Ocean Summit, along with leaders like Dr. Sylvia Earle, Leonardo DiCaprio, and Monaco's Prince Albert. In 2014, Martha's Vineyard youth leaders presented the report to the Island's seasonal residents at The Institute's Walter Cronkite Awards.

Southeast Coast of Massachusetts: For the last five years, The Institute developed partnerships with education, government, and community leaders to develop customized leadership

1 https://mvyli.org/

2 https://mvyli.org/5-year-report

3 https://mvyli.org/ocean-sustainability

programs as hybrid interactive learning experiences from students across Massachusetts. In 2019, students from Global Learning Public Charter School in New Bedford, MA, participated in the Institute's first virtual program. Following its success, in 2021, The Institute created the first ever hybrid leadership program in partnership with Durfee High School in Fall River, MA. This program culminated with a Sustainability Tour of companies, educational institutions, and organizations in the region. The Institute's 2022-2023 program connects students from Bristol County Agricultural High School with students from Terceira, Portugal for the 2023 Youth Leadership Summit.

» State Senator Marc Pacheco: 2022-[4]

» Fall River Mayor Coogan: 2021-2022[5]

» New Bedford Mayor Mitchell: 2018-2020[6]

» Cape Cod Academy: 2020[7]

» Boston Commissioner Morales Youth & Families: 2018[8]

» Holyoke Mayor Morse: 2017-2019[9]

Rhode Island: The Institute's Rhode Island Youth Leadership Initiative was formed by emerging leaders from Martha's Vineyard and Vieques, Puerto Rico. Rhode Island youth were nominated by educators to serve as youth delegates to the Institute's Sustainability Summits. They participated in the Institute's year-round program with College Field trips and developed sustainability in-action projects to support their community. In 2018 and 2019, The Institute's youth leaders were honored to be the only young people at Senator Whitehouse's Annual Energy, Environmental and Ocean Leader's Day. They were fascinated to hear about the efforts occurring in grassroots-based, multicultural, color-led climate movements.

» U.S. Senator Whitehouse: 2018+2019[10]

» Newport Mayor Bova[11]

Hawaii: Support Governor Ige's Vision of 100% Renewable Energy by 2045: When he was just16 years old, Trevor Tanaka secured champions in Hawaii's House of Representatives and Senate, made presentations, solicited testimonials from community leaders—and just six months later got his Sustainability Resolution passed in both houses of government. For the following nine years, he's been working on getting it implemented. Through this process, he—and all of our youth leaders—have learned a lot. We call this Policy-In- Action. It started with President Obama's speech at the 2011 APEC Summit in Honolulu, and led to the Institute's Sustainability Forums with youth, business, community, and government leaders and the Hawaii Department of Education. There, Trevor proudly presented a report on strategic recommendations from the Hawaii Governor's Report on Climate Preparedness Resiliency to President Obama. He then secured a grant from Hawaii's Department of Tourism, Business, and Economic Development to create an online system, the Sustainable Hawaii Toolkit. All of this effort was to ensure that all of Hawaii's

---

4 https://stonesoupleadership.org/pdf/sen-pacheco-presentation.pdf
5 https://sustainwdn.com/durfee-high-school/
6 http://sustainwdn.com/wp-content/uploads/2020/10/beta-2019.pdf
7 https://sustainwdn.com/beta-2020/
8 http://www.riyli.org/wp-content/uploads/2019/03/JSD-Newsletter-2018-c.pdf
9 http://shyli.co/
10 http://www.riyli.org/wp-content/uploads/2020/07/Whitehouse-Newsletter-2019.pdf
11 http://www.riyli.org/

young people would learn about the importance of climate education and sustainability in schools. Trevor achieved this by standing on the shoulders of youth leaders from Puerto Rico and Martha's Vineyard, who had championed their own successful Policy-In- Action projects.

» Hawaii Governor Ige: 2014-2018[12]

» Hawaii Island Mayor Billy Kenoi: 2011-2016[13]

2020 Sustainable Vision Reports: Challenging Our Leaders to Create Sustainable Policies: As part of The Institute's youth leadership initiatives, we invite youth leaders to envision a sustainable future for their communities. Youth leaders from these communities from Vieques, Puerto Rico and Martha's Vineyard created a 2020 Report for Sustainable Development, in which they challenged their leaders to develop policies that will protect their communities' fragile ecosystems, provide for their families, create opportunities for their children, and build a just, equitable, and sustainable future. Through our annual Sustainability Summits, Career Mentor & Job Shadow Day Program, College Prep & Community Service Programs and year-round youth community leadership initiatives we've inspired multicultural young people to become effective leaders of a more just, equitable and sustainable world. Through an intensive four-year visioning and community engagement process, participating youth prepared well-researched, well- documented presentations. They attracted like-minded people to join them in preserving their communities by attracting philanthropists, socially responsible investors, and venture capitalists to help them develop green projects. The report was presented to the Governor of Puerto Rico and the Mayor of Vieques, who gifted 300 acres to build a green community for landless families.

Puerto Rico: Support Governor Calderón to Assist with Implementing Healthy Communities Model: Puerto Rico's Governor Sila Calderón was an ardent supporter of the Healthy Communities movement. She was pleased to learn that Marianne Larned, The Institute's founding director was one of its co- founders in the early 90's. She was intrigued that the book and curriculum, Stone Soup for the World: Life-Changing Stories of Everyday Heroes (Pan Y Vino Para El Camino in Spanish) integrates the principles of healthy communities. She was impressed that there were ten Latin heroes in the book to showcase how people from Latin countries were rebuilding their communities. She invited The Institute to use the Spanish curriculum to realize her goal of empowering local communities to work together to address social, economic inequities in Puerto Rico. The Institute developed the Vieques Youth Leadership Initiative as a showcase for the Healthy Communities model.

» Puerto Rico Demonstration Project: 2004-2007[14]

» Puerto Rico Governor Acaveda: 2005-2007[15]

» Puerto Rico Tourism Authority: 2007[16]

» Mayor Damaso Economic Development Exchange: 2006 [17]

British Virgin Islands: Sustainable Economic Development Mission: 2008-2010. The Institute organized an Economic Development Mission with the Mayor of Vieques, Puerto Rico

12 http://sustainablehawaiitoolkit.com/
13 https://shyli.org/
14 https://vyli.com/programs/
15 http://vyli.com/building/
16 http://vyli.com/2020-report/
17 http://vgyli.org/pdf/VGYLI%20historical%20overview.pdf

and his Economic Development Council to the British Virgin Islands (BVI) to study sustainable island economic models. There Vieques youth presented their 2020 Sustainable Vision Report. BVI Prime Minister Orlando Smith was so impressed with their presentation that he asked the Institute to develop what later became the Virgin Gorda Youth Leadership Initiative.

» Premier Orlando Smith, British Virgin Islands[18]

» Ministry of Education & Culture[19]

» Caribbean Media Exchange [20]

California: 2022 In 2022, The Institute partnered with Redwood High School in Redwood City, CA to test the Stone Soup Climate Education Curriculum. This teacher-led model allowed our site to utilize the stories in the book, Stone Soup for a Sustainable World and lesson plans to supplemental the traditional education practices in her classroom. Students were inspired by the customized videos featuring people in the book who worked in sustainability-based fields or advocating for sustainably-based causes.

» Redwood High School, Environmental Science Program, Redwood City, CA[21]

» West Valley College Regenerative Agriculture Program, Saratoga, CA

The Philippines: Soon after the People Power movement in the Philippines in 1986, Marianne Larned, The Institute's founding director began a 30-year relationship with the Philippines. For her first assignment, she worked with President Cory Aquino's Ministry of Trade & Economic Development to develop a multi-national campaign to engage companies and individuals in supporting the new government. The theme of *Bayanihan* built on their cultural tradition of inspiring people to work together for the good of their country.

The inspiring story of People Power is included in the book, *Stone Soup for the World: Life-Changing Stories of Everyday Heroes.* The story spotlights the pioneering work of Marietta Primicias Goco who was a champion for women's rights and economic development. In 2003 Mrs. Goco traveled from the Philippines to New York City to receive The Institute's Eleanor Roosevelt Award at a prestigious event attended by Walter Cronkite, Dr. Muhammad Yunus, and other dignitaries. That same year, the Franklin & Eleanor Roosevelt Institute sponsored a fact-finding mission to study how Mrs. Goco was following the role model model of embodied Eleanor Roosevelt as a champion for women's rights with her microcredit/microfinance programs. She spearheaded the Social Reform Act, the first legislation of its kind in the country, and then served as head of the President's Commission to Fight Poverty, the first such commission in the world.

Thanks to the global press she received, Mrs. Goco experienced celebrity status, which she used to champion the arduous process of changing the Constitution of the Philippines. One of the significant outcomes of this historic initiative was that previously marginalized indigenous fisherfolk could now have equal representation, and her country could begin to develop a more equitable economy. The resulting programs for indigenous fisherfolk have had a far-reaching effect on this vulnerable island nation, leading to a reduction in the exploitative and destructive practices of detonating the seas to catch endangered fish. The story of 22-year-old Mitzi Jonelle Tan, who

18 http://vgyli.org/
19 http://vgyli.org/pdf/VGYLI Overview.pdf
20 http://vgyli.org/pdf/CMEx-2007-2008.pdf
21 https://sustainwdn.com/redwood-high-school-beta/

stands with and amplifies the voices of Filipino indigenous fisherfolk, is featured in the new book, *Stone Soup for a Sustainable World: Life-Changing Stories of Young Heroes.*

The Institute's Sustainability Journey

The transition to a sustainable economy is the most challenging issue of the 21st century.

Young people want to get involved with sustainability - and are eager to learn what they can do. They are especially eager to get jobs and careers that will help rebuild the planet. The stories in this book have been thoughtfully chosen to showcase solutions to the most pressing issues of our time. Our companion curriculum makes it easy for educators to bring these stories to life in their classrooms. We are committed to bringing these educational tools to our schools. We hope you will join with us!

What We've Learned

For 25 years, we've worked alongside young people who are on the front lines of climate change, social justice, and economic equity issues. Island people are now "the canaries in the coal mine." Every day they see their coastlines eroding, their fish supplies depleted, plastics littering their beaches, and toxic waste and environmental hazards dumped into their pristine waters.

The Stone Soup Climate Education Curriculum

Over the years, we have become a leader in developing educational tools by listening to and learning from young people and their community's leaders. Our multicultural youth are leading the way toward a reimagined future, where sustainability and environmental justice are at the forefront. Our books, lesson plans, career mentoring, and sustainable workforce development programs we offer are custom designed to prepare the next generation of youth leaders to build a more just, equitable, and sustainable world. Our programs align with the Green New Deal and President Biden's Plan for Climate Change and Environmental Justice.

The Institute is partnering with forward-thinking allies across a variety of industries, working with educators, and with universities, businesses, environmental organizations, educational institutions, technical and vocational programs, and most importantly ***young people*** who are eager to build a sustainable future. We are eager to scale this platform to reach more schools and businesses nationwide, so that together we can begin to really make a difference.

SustainWDN™ our online workforce development ecosystem--is building bridges between young people, educators, and blue and green companies, to develop a 21st century workforce development pipeline. It offers educators and career counselors tools to guide students toward sustainable career pathways and serves as an economic planning tool to help communities transition to a sustainable economy. It also helps companies realize a triple bottom line by preparing young people to contribute to a sustainable workforce, and a resilient community.

The Professional Development Modules: gives educators and career counselors tools to use in preparing their students for the green/blue economy of the 21st century. This engaging resource is building bridges between employers, educational institutions, community organizations, and young people who are seeking ways to rebuild their communities and the planet.

The Institute's Educational Tools

Sustainability Is Fun connects young people with engaging, fun, and interactive educational activities like virtual sustainability tours; games; videos; and an educational curriculum. It can be customized by region or state to provide targeted resources.

Virtual Sustainability Tours Our YouTube channel features inspiring videos that give students a firsthand view of the fragility of our ecosystems and teach them how they can help preserve and protect the planet for future generations.

Sustainability-In-Action Projects. Students learn critical thinking and decision-making skills; how to troubleshoot challenges; make engaging presentations; and develop strategies for recruiting youth and convincing local decision makers to take action.

The ***Sustainable Hawaii Toolkit*** provides free resources, learning tools, videos, and information about jobs in the sustainable workforce. It is contributing to Hawaii's goal of having 100% Renewable Energy by 2045. Based on the UN's Sustainable Development Goals, this toolkit serves as a global model.

The ***Sustainable Virtual Field Station*** on Martha's Vineyard is a student-designed, web-based educational and research tool with maps, tools, and websites. It is an invaluable resource for connecting young people with real-life science applications – leading to collaboration and sharing of data with nonprofits, as well as increased youth success with local and state Science Fairs.

The ***Sustainability Summits*** are the cornerstone of our work with the hundreds of multicultural youth around the world who have been trained to become leaders by taking initiative in their lives, their communities, and their world. To date we've hosted 19 Sustainability Summits in four communities, in two countries. ***Sustainability Summit Speakers*** inspire young people to deepen their understanding and appreciation of science, and to pursue sustainable career pathways with blue and green companies.

Praise For the Stone Soup Leadership Institute

The Stone Soup Leadership Institute is continuing the legacy of past environmentalists by fostering youth leadership throughout the world. Launching the "Green Revolution" from a grassroots base will be integral to future policymaking; it is up to these youth delegates to lead this movement. With a focus on sustainable building, sustainable economies, cultural sustainability, and sustainable agriculture, this year's Sustainability Summit will continue to tackle the most difficult problems our world community faces. Use this Summit as a tool to help hone your already-budding leadership qualities into a strength that can help you connect with people from all walks of life.

John Kerry
U.S. Special Presidential Envoy for Climate

Your dedication, compassion, and care for the island communities you work with is greatly appreciated and your efforts have not gone unnoticed. The work you have done for sustainable development across the globe is a valuable contribution to the future of our environment.

U.S. Senator Elizabeth Warren, Massachusetts

The Stone Soup Leadership Institute's work of inspiring, educating, and empowering young people to take initiative in their communities is a critical step in ensuring the success and longevity of our oceans, island sustainability and our planet.

Joe Kennedy, The Groundwork Project

I've had the privilege of working with some of the Institute's young people who are featured in the book, Stone Soup for a Sustainable World. I've seen the uplifting power they have on their communities and our world. If you like inspirational stories, pick up this book… if you want to be an inspirational story, pick a cause, and follow these trailblazing youth leaders into a greener future.

Nancy Slonim Aronie, Author, NPR Commentator,
Martha's Vineyard

The young people in Stone Soup for a Sustainable World are on the front lines of climate change. In times like these, their courage, bravery and perseverance in the face of overwhelming odds give us hope. They deserve our support.

Rose Styron, Author, Martha's Vineyard

The Stone Soup Leadership Institute's Virtual Education Toolkit and courses based on the book, Stone Soup for the World: Life-Changing Stories of Everyday Heroes is a treasure. It gives educators a powerful way to engage students through real-life stories with meaningful lessons that address the importance of SEL (social-emotional learning) values of caring for ourselves, others, and for the community. The Institute's noble work with students, teachers, and schools reminds me of how we created one of the nation's first SEL curriculum and founded two schools with SEL as a central pillar. We worked alongside educators, political and business leaders, and a group of Nobel Laureates to reflect on the educational needs of our society. We decided that the central foundation of a school is beyond students' knowledge. We must give them an opportunity to think, act, and lay the foundation for life-long learning. The Institute's curriculum and online courses gives teachers the tools they need to bring SEL into their classrooms. I encourage everyone who cares about our children, their future, and ours to bring these tools into our schools.

Karen Stone McCown, Founder The Nueva Learning Center, The Synapse School

I have had the privilege of working with Marianne Larned on a number of projects in Martha's Vineyard. She epitomizes what dedication and leadership really means to a cause, which in itself is leadership. She has nurtured so many young people to be strong role models in their communities and beyond. All the best for her continued success.

Gerri Laurino, Martha's Vineyard/Florida

The Stone Soup Leadership Institute has been a leader in sustainability education and youth leadership development for over two decades–it's time the Institute is recognized for its novel contributions to the cause.

The Rev. Dr. Carol C. Saysette, California

I was present when the real celebrity/dignitaries, Walter Cronkite and Marianne Larned, gave life to a concept that was to become Stone Soup for the World … and led us here today. Having had the great honor to witness the beginning, I am thrilled to be part of this event to celebrate all of the 100 impressive heroes featured in Stone Soup for a Sustainable World: Life Changing Stories of Young Heroes, who are the manifestation of that dream. I applaud you all for your brilliance, ingenuity, and commitment to helping our planet and its inhabitants. The iconic Walter Cronkite was a man of unimpeachable integrity, and great foresight and imagination. He also was an environmentalist. When Marianne shared her dream of challenging people to find their passion and use it for the betterment of mankind, he challenged her to light the way. I have no doubt that he envisioned what would follow–and is smiling down on you now, from his nearby perch, reveling in the life-changing effect you all are having on our world. Walter and Marianne both understood that it would be up to your generation to alter our course. My deepest gratitude for the enduring impact your contributions are making today, and for lighting the way for the heroes of tomorrow.

Marlene Adler, Former Chief of Staff to Walter Cronkite

CPSIA information can be obtained
at www.ICGtesting.com
Printed in the USA
JSHW060549200523
41971JS00009BA/58

9 798218 078522